Utilizing AI in Network and Mobile Security for Threat Detection and Prevention

Mohammed Amin Almaiah
University of Jordan, Jordan

IGI Global
Scientific Publishing
Publishing Tomorrow's Research Today

Vice President of Editorial | Melissa Wagner
Director of Acquisitions | Mikaela Felty
Director of Book Development | Jocelynn Hessler
Production Manager | Mike Brehm
Cover Design | Phillip Shickler

Published in the United States of America by
IGI Global Scientific Publishing
701 East Chocolate Avenue
Hershey, PA, 17033, USA
Tel: 717-533-8845
Fax: 717-533-7115
Website: https://www.igi-global.com E-mail: cust@igi-global.com

Library of Congress Cataloging-in-Publication Data

LCCN: 2024054418 (CIP Data Pending)
ISBN13: 9798369399194
Isbn13Softcover: 9798369399200
EISBN13: 9798369399217

British Cataloguing in Publication Data
A Cataloguing in Publication record for this book is available from the British Library.

Table of Contents

Preface xiii

Chapter 1
Fortifying the Digital World and Shielding Smart Infrastructures: Artificial Intelligence (AI)-Enabled Malware and Threat 1
Bhupinder Singh, Sharda University, India
Christian Kaunert, Dublin City University, Ireland & University of South Wales, UK

Chapter 2
Proactively Approaching Cybersecurity With AI-Powered Malware Detection Is Essential 23
Spandan Agrawal, VIT Bhopal University, India
Lakshya Pandey, VIT Bhopal University, India
D. Lakshmi, VIT Bhopal University, India

Chapter 3
Art of Network Monitoring and Security Enhancement Using AI-Driven Tools 43
G. Pradeep Kumar, Velammal Educational Trust, India
B. Sridevi, Velammal Educational Trust, India
P. Suveetha Dhanaselvam, Velammal Educational Trust, India
K. Kavitha, Velammal Educational Trust, India
P. Karthikeyan, Velammal Educational Trust, India
B. Karthikeyan, Velammal Educational Trust, India

Chapter 4
Autoencoder-Based Anomaly Detection for Cyber Threat Monitoring 59
Abinaya Devi, Mepco Schlenk Engineering College, India
Manoj Kumar Prabhakaran, Mepco Schlenk Engineering College, India
J. S. Prasanna Kumar, Mepco Schlenk Engineering College, India
J. Nithish Kumar, Mepco Schlenk Engineering College, India

Chapter 5
Malicious Anomaly Detection and Prediction Using Prophet Luminol and RNN 81
R. Suganya, New Horizon College of Engineering, India
Sashikanth Reddy Avula, Nitte Meenakshi Institute of Technology, India
Balasubramanian Prabhu Kavin, SRM University, India
Priyan Malarvizhi Kumar, University of North Texas, USA
Jeeva Selvaraj, Jain University, India
Gan Hong Seng, Xi'an Jiaotong-Liverpool University, China

Chapter 6
A Framework for Insider Threat Detection Using Role-Based Profile Assessment and Threshold 97
Qais Al-Na'amneh, Applied Science Private University, Jordan
Mahmoud Aljawarneh, Applied Science Private University, Jordan
Rahaf Hazaymih, Jordan University of Science and Technology, Jordan

Chapter 7
Attacks Detection and Mitigation of IoT Using Machine Learning Model 115
Qais Al-Na'amneh, Applied Science Private University, Jordan
Mohammed Almaiah, University of Jordan, Jordan
Saja Smadi, Yarmouk University, Jordan
Rahaf Hazaymih, Jordan University of Science and Technology, Jordan
Laheeb Alabadi, Applied Science Private University, Jordan

Chapter 8
Analysis for Detection and Mitigation of Version Number Modification Attack in the Internet of Things 133
Qais Al-Na'amneh, Applied Science Private University, Jordan
Walid Dhifallah, University of Gabes, Tunisia
Rahaf Hazaymih, Jordan University of Science and Technology, Jordan
Laith Alzboon, Applied Science Private University, Jordan
Ayoub Alsarhan, Hashemite University, Jordan
Mohammed Alshinwan, Applied Science Private University, Jordan
Rabia Emhamed Al Mamlook, Trine University, Libya

Chapter 9
Semantic Search for IoT-Based Object Recognition Using Clustering and Classification 151
R. Prasath, RMK College of Engineering and Technology, India
V. Vasantha Kumar, KCG College of Technology, India
V. Jaisankari, AMET University, India
R. Sivasubramani, RMK College of Engineering and Technology, India

Chapter 10
Ethical Issues in Cyber-Security for Autonomous Vehicles (AV) and Automated Driving: A Comprehensive Review... 173
Qais Al-Na'amneh, Applied Science Private University, Jordan
Mahmoud Aljawarneh, Applied Science Private University, Jordan
Rahaf Hazaymih, Jordan University of Science and Technology, Jordan
Rabia Emhamed Al Mamlook, Trine University, Libya

Chapter 11
Post-Quantum Cryptography in the Age of Quantum Computing 197
Silvio Andrae, Independent Researcher, Germany

Chapter 12
Data Security With Replication for Cloud Computing 217
Cigdem Bakir, Dumlupinar University, Turkey
Mecit Yüzkat, Presidency of Turkish Health Institutes, Turkey

Chapter 13
Trust Evaluation Enhancing Security in the Cloud Market Based on Trust Framework Using Metric Parameter Selection 233
Qais Al-Na'amneh, Applied Science Private University, Jordan
Mahmoud Aljawarneh, Applied Science Private University, Jordan
Rahaf Hazaymih, Jordan University of Science and Technology, Jordan
Laith Alzboon, Applied Science Private University, Jordan
Dena Abu Laila, Zarqa University, Jordan
Sahel Albawaneh, Yarmouk University, Jordan

Chapter 14
Secure Cloud-Marketplaces: A Trust Framework for Evaluating Security for Client Service Providers 255
Qais Al-Na'amneh, Applied Science Private University, Jordan
Rahaf Hazaymih, Jordan University of Science and Technology, Jordan
Mohammed Almaiah, University of Jordan, Jordan
Laith Alzboon, Applied Science Private University, Jordan

Chapter 15
Evolution of Data Security in E-Commerce 281
Deepak Varadam, M.S. Ramaiah University of Applied Sciences, India
Sahana P. Shankar, M.S. Ramaiah University of Applied Sciences, India
J. Priyanka, M.S. Ramaiah University of Applied Sciences, India
Mummadi Shyam Kumar Reddy, M.S. Ramaiah University of Applied Sciences, India
R. Mohan, M.S. Ramaiah University of Applied Sciences, India
Aditya Katare, M.S. Ramaiah University of Applied Sciences, India

Compilation of References 305

About the Contributors 339

Index 343

Detailed Table of Contents

Preface.. xiii

Chapter 1
Fortifying the Digital World and Shielding Smart Infrastructures: Artificial Intelligence (AI)-Enabled Malware and Threat 1
Bhupinder Singh, Sharda University, India
Christian Kaunert, Dublin City University, Ireland & University of South Wales, UK

The basic principle of utilizing Artificial Intelligence (AI) in network and mobile security has effectively changed the way threats are exposed and shut down. AI-powered solutions increase the capability of identifying and alerting in case of cyberattack at real-time, thereby reducing the risks to escalate. Through a subset of AI known as machine learning (ML) algorithms, ML algorithms can further evaluate network traffic data and determine what is considered abnormal behavior in the system that may indicate signs of malware, phishing or intrusion attempts into your security perimeter. These models evolve meaning always learning and improving in new training on attack vectors without the need for a human to retrain frequently. AI helps in reinforcing the security of the device against advanced levels of ransomware, data breaches and unauthorized access as part of challenges encountered in mobile security. This chapter comprehensively explore the fortifying the digital world and shielding smart infrastructures with artificial intelligence (AI) enabled malware and threat detection.

Chapter 2
Proactively Approaching Cybersecurity With AI-Powered Malware Detection Is Essential 23
Spandan Agrawal, VIT Bhopal University, India
Lakshya Pandey, VIT Bhopal University, India
D. Lakshmi, VIT Bhopal University, India

The rapid increase in ransomware attacks has created a need for new cybersecurity methods. This research introduces a multi-faceted approach using Artificial Intelligence (AI), Machine Learning (ML), Deep Learning (DL), and Natural Language Processing (NLP) to improve the detection and prevention of ransomware attacks. It uses various AI and ML techniques to detect ransomware signatures, analyze system activities, and understand the evolving threat landscape. It can detect phishing attacks by analyzing email content and user behavior. It can also identify insider threats and assess the security posture of third-party vendors. By using these AI-powered solutions, organizations can strengthen their cybersecurity capabilities, detect threats at an earlier stage, and respond more effectively to cyber attacks. In the future, AI and ML will become more advanced in identifying and addressing complex cyber threats, such as Advanced Persistent Threats (APTs) and zero-day attacks.

Chapter 3
Art of Network Monitoring and Security Enhancement Using AI-Driven Tools 43
G. Pradeep Kumar, Velammal Educational Trust, India
B. Sridevi, Velammal Educational Trust, India
P. Suveetha Dhanaselvam, Velammal Educational Trust, India
K. Kavitha, Velammal Educational Trust, India
P. Karthikeyan, Velammal Educational Trust, India
B. Karthikeyan, Velammal Educational Trust, India

This paper explores the "Art of Network Monitoring and Security Enhancement Using AI-Driven Tools," examining how artificial intelligence (AI) is revolutionizing network security by enhancing threat detection, incident response, and overall network resilience. Traditional security measures often struggle to keep pace with the dynamic nature of modern threats, leading to increased vulnerability and potential for significant disruption. AI, with its ability to analyse vast amounts of data, identify patterns, and make predictions, offers a powerful solution to these challenges. This paper delves into various AI/ML techniques, such as machine learning, deep learning, and natural language processing, and their applications in network security, including threat detection, intrusion prevention, incident response, and network traffic analysis. By embracing AI-driven solutions, organizations can effectively address the challenges of the evolving threat landscape and protect their critical assets in the digital age.

Chapter 4
Autoencoder-Based Anomaly Detection for Cyber Threat Monitoring 59
Abinaya Devi, Mepco Schlenk Engineering College, India
Manoj Kumar Prabhakaran, Mepco Schlenk Engineering College, India
J. S. Prasanna Kumar, Mepco Schlenk Engineering College, India
J. Nithish Kumar, Mepco Schlenk Engineering College, India

To identify and defend networks against attacks such as Distributed Denial of Service (DDoS), Probe assaults, Remote-to-Local (R2L), and User-to-Root (U2R), the Intrusion Detection System (IDS), we used autoencoders and machine learning algorithms. We applied label encoding on the NSL KDD-99 dataset. To address class imbalances, many autoencoder models are used along with the generation of synthetic data via a Conditional Tabular Generative Adversarial Network (CTGAN). To extract ensemble features, autoencoder models like SNDAE, SAE, and SSDAE are coupled. Prior to training, dimensionality reduction is implemented. The collected characteristics are concatenated and utilized to train various classifiers (Random Forest, KNN, and SVM-OVO). A testing dataset is used to evaluate the trained model. A comparison is made between the classifiers and the ensemble model output.

Chapter 5
Malicious Anomaly Detection and Prediction Using Prophet Luminol and RNN 81
R. Suganya, New Horizon College of Engineering, India
Sashikanth Reddy Avula, Nitte Meenakshi Institute of Technology, India
Balasubramanian Prabhu Kavin, SRM University, India
Priyan Malarvizhi Kumar, University of North Texas, USA
Jeeva Selvaraj, Jain University, India
Gan Hong Seng, Xi'an Jiaotong-Liverpool University, China

Machine learning (ML) has brought about many advancements in today's world which is benefiting humans and machines. Because of the growth of digital services, malicious anomalies have increased on the transmission media. This has compromised crucial and important data of several organizations and companies. Vulnerabilities in network have increased in recent years and problems such as loss of data have increased. The process of detecting anomalies in network traffic becomes very important activity. An effective system for detection of these anomalies should be utilized to stop such attacks. Machine learning mechanisms for anomaly detection can prove to be the most accurate and best form of detecting malware or botnets on network so that we can prevent further threats. In this work one can understand the new implementation methods for anomaly detection. By importing python libraries and building ML models, one can learn certain outliers and different anomalies presence.

Chapter 6
A Framework for Insider Threat Detection Using Role-Based Profile Assessment and Threshold 97
Qais Al-Na'amneh, Applied Science Private University, Jordan
Mahmoud Aljawarneh, Applied Science Private University, Jordan
Rahaf Hazaymih, Jordan University of Science and Technology, Jordan

Insider threats are a major worry for organizations and governments. Insiders often have significant knowledge of an organization's architecture, making traditional intrusion detection systems ineffective. Sophisticated measures are needed to analyze internal behaviors and assess potential threats. The insider threat has started to represent a significant growing challenge for organizations and companies This chapter dives into the nature of insider threats in general, with a special focus on the malicious insider psychological factors exploring their causes and impacts, and how that can help predict and prevent such incidents. In comparison, providing and examining real-world cases and providing suggestions on how to deal with them .Furthermore, this chapter proposes a framework approach for detecting insider threats. The model is built on a layered method that connects the real world, measurements, and parameters to assess the likelihood of an insider threat.

Chapter 7
Attacks Detection and Mitigation of IoT Using Machine Learning Model 115
Qais Al-Na'amneh, Applied Science Private University, Jordan
Mohammed Almaiah, University of Jordan, Jordan
Saja Smadi, Yarmouk University, Jordan
Rahaf Hazaymih, Jordan University of Science and Technology, Jordan
Laheeb Alabadi, Applied Science Private University, Jordan

The RPL protocol has been increasingly used in low-loss networks and Internet of Things networks in recent years. The RPL protocol is exposed to many attacks that affect the network performance and disrupt the connection. In this study, a machine learning-based intrusion detection system (IDS) was developed to distinguish between benign and malicious attacks. Ensemble learning was applied by stacking three models: Random Forest, Gradient Boosting, and Linear SVC with hyperparameter optimization using Random search CV. The proposed approach was applied to version number, Decreased rank, and Hello Flooding database. The results obtained indicate that this approach provides a reliable and effective solution to protect networks from attacks, and it also sought to achieve a balance between detection accuracy and computational efficiency. The proposed model achieved an accuracy of 98% for HF database, 97% for VN database, and 95% for DR database.

Chapter 8
Analysis for Detection and Mitigation of Version Number Modification Attack in the Internet of Things 133
Qais Al-Na'amneh, Applied Science Private University, Jordan
Walid Dhifallah, University of Gabes, Tunisia
Rahaf Hazaymih, Jordan University of Science and Technology, Jordan
Laith Alzboon, Applied Science Private University, Jordan
Ayoub Alsarhan, Hashemite University, Jordan
Mohammed Alshinwan, Applied Science Private University, Jordan
Rabia Emhamed Al Mamlook, Trine University, Libya

The connectivity of devices and the ability to collect massive amounts of data, the Internet of Things (IoT) has radically changed networking. However, security and privacy issues still exist, especially in networks with limited resources. In IoT applications, the RPL routing protocol is frequently used for routing; However, version number attacks represent a security issue. Considering sensor node mobility IoT has evolved into IoET (internet of Everything), which encompasses all electronic devices, including body sensor networks, VANETs, and smart grid stations. This paper studies the effects of version number attacks on RPL networks. To detect rogue nodes, save overhead, and improve security in lossy and low-power networks, a version number modification approach is proposed as well as to demonstrate how to create and test these attacks using COOJA and Contiki-NG.

Chapter 9
Semantic Search for IoT-Based Object Recognition Using Clustering and Classification 151
R. Prasath, RMK College of Engineering and Technology, India
V. Vasantha Kumar, KCG College of Technology, India
V. Jaisankari, AMET University, India
R. Sivasubramani, RMK College of Engineering and Technology, India

A search engine helps retrieve information from large datasets using data retrieval techniques. Enterprise search engines analyze diverse organizational data, while open-source engines focus on customization. For code acquisition, data (code, docstrings) is processed into pairs for training models. Optimizations like B-tree-based P2P indexing and syntax-aware tokenization improve efficiency. Real-time object recognition requires at least 10 fps, which may be achievable with newer Intel NCS versions. The system also scales well for IoT applications, achieving 80% accuracy.

Chapter 10
Ethical Issues in Cyber-Security for Autonomous Vehicles (AV) and Automated Driving: A Comprehensive Review 173
Qais Al-Na'amneh, Applied Science Private University, Jordan
Mahmoud Aljawarneh, Applied Science Private University, Jordan
Rahaf Hazaymih, Jordan University of Science and Technology, Jordan
Rabia Emhamed Al Mamlook, Trine University, Libya

Autonomous Vehicles (AVs) revolutionize the transportation landscape, they also introduce a profound set of ethical dilemmas. The convergence of complex networks, sensors, software, and AI creates an unprecedented cybersecurity risk, imperiling not only user privacy and data security but also safety. This study shines a light on the critical ethical concerns surrounding liability, responsibility, and decision-making algorithms, posing fundamental questions about how we allocate blame in the event of cyber breaches and ensure fairness in AV decision-making during life-or-death scenarios. In this groundbreaking research, we delve into the depths of these ethical challenges, offering comprehensive solutions and expert recommendations for fortifying cybersecurity in AVs. By exploring the intricate interplay between ethics, technology, and society, we can create a safer, more trustworthy, and equitable future for autonomous vehicles.

Chapter 11
Post-Quantum Cryptography in the Age of Quantum Computing 197
Silvio Andrae, Independent Researcher, Germany

The ongoing development of powerful quantum computers poses a significant threat to the security of conventional encryption methods such as Rivest Shamir Adleman (RSA) and Elliptic Curve Cryptography (ECC). With algorithms such as Shor's Algorithm, quantum computers can solve the mathematical problems on which these methods are based and thus break them within a few hours. This work highlights this development's challenges and examines post-quantum cryptography (PQC) as a solution. PQC offers quantum-safe encryption based on mathematical problems that are difficult to solve, even for quantum computers. The text analyzes lattice, hash, and isogeny-based approaches and introduces the new NIST standards, including Kyber, Dilithium, and Sphinx+. It also discusses practical challenges in implementing quantum-safe systems, including performance degradation and cryptographic agility. It concludes with recommendations for migrating to PQC to ensure long-term security in an era increasingly characterized by quantum computing.

Chapter 12
Data Security With Replication for Cloud Computing 217
Cigdem Bakir, Dumlupinar University, Turkey
Mecit Yüzkat, Presidency of Turkish Health Institutes, Turkey

Cloud computing is an advanced technology that provides access to different services via the internet. These services include applications such as servers, networking, data storage, databases, and software. Instead of storing files on local storage device, cloud-based storage makes it possible to store files in a secure database. As long as an electronic device has access to the web, it has access to data and the software programs to run it. For this reason, this technology is very popular for institutions and individuals for many reasons such as cost, production, efficiency and speed. However, with the advantages of cloud computing, some security risks also arise. At the beginning of these security risks are data breaches and data losses caused by malicious software applications. In this study, data replication is discussed in order to solve security breaches in cloud computing technologies.

Chapter 13
Trust Evaluation Enhancing Security in the Cloud Market Based on Trust Framework Using Metric Parameter Selection 233
Qais Al-Na'amneh, Applied Science Private University, Jordan
Mahmoud Aljawarneh, Applied Science Private University, Jordan
Rahaf Hazaymih, Jordan University of Science and Technology, Jordan
Laith Alzboon, Applied Science Private University, Jordan
Dena Abu Laila, Zarqa University, Jordan
Sahel Albawaneh, Yarmouk University, Jordan

Cloud services have become popular in global technology because they let users rent computers, networks, and storage infrastructure resources that are specific to their needs., trust in the cloud relationship is essential before interaction takes place between cloud providers and consumers. The concept of trust encompasses multiple elements. The usability, security, scalability, and availability characteristics of IaaS, PaaS, SaaS, and DaaS are among these dimensions. Fuzzy characteristics and linguistic terminology characterize each of these dimensions. This chapter applies fuzzy-set theory to create models for each dimension of IaaS services. The Mamdani fuzzy-inference approach is used to assess the trustworthiness of cloud providers generally. Evaluating cloud metrics across multiple domains can be challenging. In this work, we propose a trust framework. We consider level trust; the node's level trust Score uses a fuzzy model to evaluate trust in cloud computing. The proposed model is evaluated for its efficacy and resilience through tests and findings.

Chapter 14
Secure Cloud-Marketplaces: A Trust Framework for Evaluating Security for Client Service Providers 255
Qais Al-Na'amneh, Applied Science Private University, Jordan
Rahaf Hazaymih, Jordan University of Science and Technology, Jordan
Mohammed Almaiah, University of Jordan, Jordan
Laith Alzboon, Applied Science Private University, Jordan

Trustworthy cloud service selection is a major concern in growing marketplaces. The Cloud Security Alliance (CSA) has developed a framework for cloud providers to self-assess their security policies and capabilities. This framework allows users to choose a cloud service based on the capabilities and controls published by providers. Cloud services improve efficiency in managing IT resources and operations. Cloud services are gaining popularity in on-demand and information and communication technology industries, leading to significant market expansion both locally and globally. In this paper, the trust-based framework is proposed to determine trustworthiness in Intercloud computing environments using many scenarios based on different parameters and contextual parameters (e.g., privacy, security, reliability, reputation, support, transparency, and compliance) which are important means to evaluate the Client Service Providers in cloud Marketplaces

Chapter 15
Evolution of Data Security in E-Commerce 281
Deepak Varadam, M.S. Ramaiah University of Applied Sciences, India
Sahana P. Shankar, M.S. Ramaiah University of Applied Sciences, India
J. Priyanka, M.S. Ramaiah University of Applied Sciences, India
Mummadi Shyam Kumar Reddy, M.S. Ramaiah University of Applied Sciences, India
R. Mohan, M.S. Ramaiah University of Applied Sciences, India
Aditya Katare, M.S. Ramaiah University of Applied Sciences, India

The rise of consumerism and technology has accelerated the demands of the general public. With the growth of ecommerce platforms there has been an exponential growth in the rate of trade that takes place which was previously unimaginable. The need for data security and preventing fraudulent activities has now been at the highest level of scrutiny than ever and the need for more advanced systems that can handle increasing number of challenges has been discussed in our chapter. The debate on whether traditional methods of data security and detecting such vulnerabilities have been talked about for a while now. The need for today is a system that is robust, adaptive to new fraudulent trends and also be proactive in detecting and mitigating threats. Artificial Intelligence and Machine Learning are now pivotal technologies that help shape better robust systems. Their ability of identifying patterns and thus outliers that go hand in hand with what an anomaly or a fraudulent event is has been automating security services without the need of any human intervention.

Compilation of References 305

About the Contributors 339

Index 343

Preface

INTRODUCTION

The evolving landscape of cybersecurity is increasingly shaped by artificial intelligence (AI), revolutionizing the way threats are detected, analyzed, and prevented. Traditional security methods, particularly signature-based malware detection, have long struggled to keep pace with the ever-expanding range of cyber threats. These methods rely on predefined signatures to recognize known malware, leaving systems vulnerable to emerging and previously unknown attacks. AI addresses this challenge by leveraging advanced machine learning algorithms to analyze vast datasets, detect anomalies, and identify malicious behavior in real time.

Utilizing AI in Network and Mobile Security for Threat Detection and Prevention provides an in-depth exploration of AI's transformative role in cybersecurity. This book highlights the fundamental AI techniques—such as anomaly detection, deep learning, and neural networks—that empower security systems to monitor network traffic, detect unusual patterns, and proactively mitigate risks. AI-driven cybersecurity solutions offer adaptability to novel attack vectors, enhancing resilience against sophisticated cyber threats, including zero-day attacks. The integration of predictive analytics further strengthens security postures by allowing organizations to anticipate and counteract potential breaches before they occur.

This book aims to bridge the gap between theoretical knowledge and practical implementation in AI-driven cybersecurity. It serves as an invaluable resource for academia, researchers, university staff, postgraduate students, policymakers, developers, and cybersecurity professionals. Readers will gain insight into:

- The role of AI in enhancing cybersecurity measures and detecting cyber threats.
- Techniques for anomaly and intrusion detection using AI models.
- Practical approaches to developing AI-driven threat detection systems.
- Machine learning applications in malware analysis and detection.
- The application of predictive analytics in cybersecurity scenarios.
- Ethical considerations and real-world applications of AI in cybersecurity.

By combining academic research with industry expertise, this book provides a comprehensive overview of the latest developments in AI-powered cybersecurity solutions. We hope this work inspires further innovation and equips cybersecurity professionals with the necessary tools to navigate the ever-changing digital security landscape.

ORGANIZATION OF THE BOOK

Chapter 1: Fortifying the Digital World and Shielding Smart Infrastructures: Artificial Intelligence (AI) Enabled Malware and Threat Detection

The integration of Artificial Intelligence (AI) in network and mobile security has fundamentally transformed the detection and mitigation of cyber threats. This chapter explores how AI-powered solutions enhance real-time threat identification and response, reducing the risk of cyberattacks. With the application of Machine Learning (ML) algorithms, AI systems continuously analyze network traffic, detect anomalies, and identify signs of malware, phishing, and unauthorized intrusions. These evolving models autonomously learn and adapt to new attack vectors, eliminating the need for frequent human intervention. AI plays a crucial role in safeguarding devices against sophisticated cyber threats, including ransomware and data breaches. This chapter delves into the role of AI-enabled malware and threat detection in fortifying digital infrastructures and strengthening cybersecurity resilience.

Chapter 2: Proactively Approaching Cybersecurity With AI-Powered Malware Detection

As ransomware attacks continue to escalate, traditional cybersecurity measures have proven insufficient in combating evolving threats. This chapter introduces an AI-driven, multi-faceted approach that leverages Machine Learning (ML), Deep Learning (DL), and Natural Language Processing (NLP) to enhance threat detection and prevention. AI-powered systems analyze ransomware signatures, monitor system activities, and detect phishing attempts by evaluating email content and user behavior. Furthermore, AI is instrumental in identifying insider threats and assessing third-party vendor security risks. The chapter also highlights the future potential of AI and ML in addressing complex cyber threats, including Advanced Persistent Threats (APTs) and zero-day vulnerabilities. By embracing AI-powered malware detection, organizations can significantly enhance their cybersecurity posture, enabling early threat detection and effective mitigation strategies.

Chapter 3: The Art of Network Monitoring and Security Enhancement Using AI-Driven Tools

The dynamic nature of modern cyber threats has rendered traditional security measures inadequate, necessitating the adoption of AI-driven solutions for network monitoring and security enhancement. This chapter examines how AI-powered tools revolutionize cybersecurity by improving threat detection, intrusion prevention, and incident response. AI's capability to process vast amounts of data and identify malicious patterns enables organizations to bolster network resilience. The discussion covers key AI/ML techniques, including machine learning, deep learning, and natural language processing, and their applications in securing network infrastructures. By leveraging AI-driven network security, organizations can proactively counter cyber threats, mitigate disruptions, and safeguard critical digital assets.

Chapter 4: Autoencoder-Based Anomaly Detection for Cyber Threat Monitoring

Anomaly detection is a critical component of modern cybersecurity, particularly in identifying and mitigating sophisticated cyber threats. This chapter explores the use of autoencoder-based models and machine learning algorithms in detecting Distributed Denial of Service (DDoS), Remote-to-Local (R2L), User-to-Root (U2R), and probe attacks. Utilizing the NSL-KDD dataset, this study employs label encoding and addresses class imbalances through synthetic data generation via a Conditional Tabular Generative Adversarial Network (CTGAN). Various autoencoder models, including SNDAE, SAE, and SSDAE, are integrated for feature extraction, followed by dimensionality reduction techniques. The effectiveness of different classifiers—Random Forest, KNN, and SVM-OVO—is assessed using a test dataset. This chapter provides a comparative analysis of classifiers and ensemble models, offering insights into optimizing anomaly detection for robust cyber threat monitoring.

Chapter 5: Malicious Anomaly Detection and Prediction Using Prophet Luminol and RNN

With the rapid expansion of digital services, network vulnerabilities have increased, leading to a rise in malicious anomalies that threaten organizational data security. This chapter focuses on leveraging machine learning (ML) techniques, particularly Prophet Luminol and recurrent neural networks (RNN), to detect and predict malicious anomalies in network traffic. An effective anomaly detection system is essential for identifying malware, botnets, and other cyber threats before they escalate. By implementing Python-based ML models, organizations can recognize network outliers and anomalies in real-time. This chapter provides an in-depth analysis of advanced ML techniques for anomaly detection, emphasizing their practical applications in mitigating cyber threats and securing digital infrastructure.

Chapter 6: A Framework for Insider Threat Detection Using Role-Based Profile Assessment and Thresholds

Insider threats pose a significant challenge to organizations due to the privileged access and deep knowledge insiders possess about internal systems. This chapter examines the growing concern of insider threats, focusing on their psychological factors, causes, and consequences. It proposes a structured framework for insider threat detection, utilizing role-based profile assessments and threshold-based monitoring. By analyzing behavioral patterns and assessing real-world case studies, the framework enhances the ability to predict and mitigate insider threats. The chapter highlights the importance of integrating sophisticated detection measures into security policies to proactively address insider risks and prevent data breaches.

Chapter 7: Attack Detection and Mitigation of IoT Using Machine Learning Models

The rapid proliferation of Internet of Things (IoT) devices has introduced new security vulnerabilities, particularly in networks utilizing the Routing Protocol for Low-Power and Lossy Networks (RPL). This chapter presents a machine learning-based intrusion detection system (IDS) designed to identify and mitigate attacks targeting IoT networks. The study employs ensemble learning techniques, combining

Random Forest, Gradient Boosting, and Linear SVC models optimized through Random Search CV. The effectiveness of the proposed system is demonstrated through its application to various IoT attack datasets, achieving high detection accuracy. This chapter provides valuable insights into securing IoT infrastructures against evolving cyber threats.

Chapter 8: Analysis for Detection and Mitigation of Version Number Modification Attack in the Internet of Things

Security concerns in IoT networks remain a critical issue, particularly with the emergence of version number modification attacks in RPL-based networks. This chapter explores the impact of such attacks and proposes a novel approach for detecting rogue nodes and improving security in low-power, lossy networks. Using simulation tools such as COOJA and Contiki-NG, the study demonstrates how version number attacks disrupt IoT network performance. The proposed mitigation strategy enhances security by minimizing overhead and ensuring robust protection for IoT applications, including body sensor networks, vehicular ad hoc networks (VANETs), and smart grids.

Chapter 9: Semantic Search for IoT-Based Object Recognition Using Clustering and Classification

Efficient information retrieval is essential for large-scale IoT applications, particularly in object recognition tasks. This chapter explores the implementation of semantic search mechanisms using clustering and classification techniques. It examines enterprise search engines and open-source alternatives, emphasizing their role in processing organizational data. Advanced indexing methods, such as B-tree-based peer-to-peer (P2P) indexing and syntax-aware tokenization, enhance search efficiency. The chapter also discusses real-time object recognition performance, highlighting the feasibility of achieving high frame rates with modern computing hardware. By integrating these methodologies, IoT-based object recognition systems can achieve improved accuracy and scalability.

Chapter 10: Ethical Issues in Cybersecurity for Autonomous Vehicles (AV) and Automated Driving

As autonomous vehicles (AVs) become increasingly integrated into modern transportation, they raise profound ethical and cybersecurity concerns. This chapter explores the intersection of ethics, AI, and cybersecurity in AV systems, addressing critical issues such as liability, data privacy, and decision-making algorithms. The potential for cyberattacks on AVs poses significant risks to public safety, necessitating robust security measures and ethical frameworks. By analyzing real-world case studies and proposing regulatory solutions, this chapter offers comprehensive insights into securing AVs while ensuring fairness and transparency in their decision-making processes.

Chapter 11: Post-Quantum Cryptography in the Age of Quantum Computing

Quantum computing presents a significant threat to traditional cryptographic methods, as algorithms like Shor's Algorithm can efficiently break RSA and ECC encryption. This chapter examines the emergence of post-quantum cryptography (PQC) as a viable solution for securing digital communications.

Various PQC techniques, including lattice-based, hash-based, and isogeny-based cryptography, are analyzed in the context of evolving NIST standards such as Kyber, Dilithium, and Sphinx+. The chapter also discusses challenges in PQC implementation, including performance trade-offs and cryptographic agility, and provides strategic recommendations for transitioning to quantum-safe encryption.

Chapter 12: Data Security with Replication for Cloud Computing

Cloud computing has revolutionized the way individuals and organizations store, manage, and access data. Offering significant benefits such as cost reduction, operational efficiency, and scalability, cloud services have become an essential component of modern digital infrastructure. However, the widespread adoption of cloud technology also brings critical security risks, including data breaches and losses caused by malicious software. This chapter explores data replication as a robust solution to mitigate security vulnerabilities in cloud computing environments. By ensuring that copies of data are stored across multiple locations, replication enhances resilience against potential cyber threats and system failures. The discussion provides insights into how data replication strategies can be effectively implemented to secure cloud-based infrastructures, thereby improving data integrity, availability, and overall security in cloud computing systems.

Chapter 13: Trust Evaluation Enhancing Security in the Cloud Market Based on Trust Framework Using Metric Parameter Selection

As cloud services continue to evolve, trust remains a fundamental element in the relationship between providers and consumers. The reliability of cloud-based infrastructure, including IaaS, PaaS, SaaS, and DaaS, depends on multiple factors such as usability, security, scalability, and availability. This chapter introduces a trust evaluation framework based on metric parameter selection, incorporating fuzzy-set theory to model and assess trust in cloud computing. Using the Mamdani fuzzy-inference approach, the study proposes a structured methodology to evaluate the trustworthiness of cloud service providers. The model provides a comprehensive mechanism to assess cloud metrics across different domains, addressing challenges in establishing secure and reliable cloud interactions. Through rigorous testing, the framework demonstrates its effectiveness in enhancing security and trust in cloud marketplaces, ultimately enabling users to make informed decisions when selecting cloud services.

Chapter 14: Secure Cloud-Marketplaces: A Trust Framework for Evaluating Security for Client Service Providers

With the rapid expansion of cloud services, ensuring trust and security in cloud marketplaces has become a growing concern. The Cloud Security Alliance (CSA) has introduced a self-assessment framework to help cloud providers communicate their security policies and capabilities to consumers. Building on this foundation, this chapter presents a trust-based framework for evaluating security in intercloud computing environments. The proposed model assesses trustworthiness based on key parameters such as privacy, security, reliability, reputation, support, transparency, and compliance. By applying this trust evaluation system, organizations can systematically assess cloud service providers, ensuring that security and reliability standards are met. The chapter provides a comprehensive analysis of how contextual parameters influence trust in cloud marketplaces, offering valuable insights for businesses and IT professionals navigating the complexities of cloud adoption.

Chapter 15: Evolution of Data Security in E-Commerce

The exponential growth of e-commerce has transformed global trade, facilitating transactions on an unprecedented scale. However, this rapid expansion has also heightened concerns surrounding data security and fraud prevention. Traditional security methods are no longer sufficient to combat evolving cyber threats, necessitating the adoption of more sophisticated security frameworks. This chapter examines the evolution of data security in e-commerce, emphasizing the critical role of Artificial Intelligence (AI) and Machine Learning (ML) in fraud detection and prevention. By identifying patterns and anomalies indicative of fraudulent activities, AI-driven systems offer proactive and adaptive security measures without requiring human intervention. The chapter explores the limitations of conventional security approaches and highlights the necessity for AI-powered solutions that enhance resilience against emerging cyber threats. Through this discussion, readers gain a deeper understanding of how technological advancements are shaping the future of secure e-commerce transactions.

CONCLUSION

In conclusion, the chapters compiled within this reference book offer a comprehensive exploration of the intersection between cloud computing, data security, and trust frameworks, highlighting the evolving challenges and innovative solutions that shape the future of digital infrastructure. As the digital landscape continues to expand, organizations and individuals must be equipped with the tools and knowledge to navigate the complexities of cloud-based environments and secure data management. The contributions presented here not only address the technological advancements driving this change but also emphasize the importance of building trust and ensuring security across cloud platforms.

From data replication strategies to the integration of AI and machine learning in fraud detection, the insights provided throughout the book offer invaluable perspectives for researchers, practitioners, and policymakers working to strengthen digital ecosystems. The frameworks and methodologies discussed serve as critical resources for enhancing the resilience of cloud computing systems, ensuring that they can meet the demands of both today and tomorrow's challenges.

We trust that the collective wisdom shared within these pages will inspire further research, development, and application of innovative solutions, ultimately contributing to a safer, more efficient digital future. As the realm of cloud computing and data security continues to evolve, we hope that this book serves as a vital reference for those working at the forefront of this dynamic field.

Chapter 1
Fortifying the Digital World and Shielding Smart Infrastructures:
Artificial Intelligence (AI)-Enabled Malware and Threat

Bhupinder Singh
https://orcid.org/0009-0006-4779-2553
Sharda University, India

Christian Kaunert
https://orcid.org/0000-0002-4493-2235
Dublin City University, Ireland & University of South Wales, UK

ABSTRACT

The basic principle of utilizing Artificial Intelligence (AI) in network and mobile security has effectively changed the way threats are exposed and shut down. AI-powered solutions increase the capability of identifying and alerting in case of cyberattack at real-time, thereby reducing the risks to escalate. Through a subset of AI known as machine learning (ML) algorithms, ML algorithms can further evaluate network traffic data and determine what is considered abnormal behavior in the system that may indicate signs of malware, phishing or intrusion attempts into your security perimeter. These models evolve meaning always learning and improving in new training on attack vectors without the need for a human to retrain frequently. AI helps in reinforcing the security of the device against advanced levels of ransomware, data breaches and unauthorized access as part of challenges encountered in mobile security. This chapter comprehensively explore the fortifying the digital world and shielding smart infrastructures with artificial intelligence (AI) enabled malware and threat detection.

1. INTRODUCTION

Using AI to analyze user behavior and app usage patterns allows for the detection of anomalies that can signal a breach, resulting in an immediate response to thwart a potential threat. AI leads to automation which translates into better accuracy, quicker resolution times and reduced response time. The predictive functionality of AI further helps in letting organizations anticipate vulnerabilities and address

DOI: 10.4018/979-8-3693-9919-4.ch001

them upfront. AI has transformed the culture of network and mobile security by providing more flexible, scalable, and evolving ways to detect threats now. With latest evolution in cyber threats, companies are supposed to have an AI powered security system which can protect both network infrastructure and mobile environments.

The growth of smart infrastructures worldwide, driven by digital transformation brings security threats at an alarming frequency. Turned out, smart cities and IoT systems are rapidly globalizing & intermingling into large digital ecosystems (Ali et al., 2024). They are not only critcal in urban planning and public services but also pervasive from transportation to healthcare & energy mgmt. At the same time, this rapid connectivity leads to an increased attack surface that exposes smart infrastructure systems to a wide range of cyber threats like malware and ransomware as well as advanced persistent threats (APTs) and phishing attacks. Standard cybersecurity tools, while essential, often do not have the flexibility necessary to defend an enterprise against dynamic and manifold attacks.

The digital security world has learned to harness the benefit from AI- a tremendous boon in combating and tackling advanced cyber threats with an ensemble cast for detection prevention, response. AI to its malware and threat detection systems, the teams silently improve their speed and accuracy that is just as necessary for recognizing dangers at any moment in seconds or minutes, rather than waiting hours before harm takes place. AI typically employs machine learning and deep learning models to uncover abnormal patterns in large data stores, differentiating between normal operations from potentially harmful activity. AI also improves network and mobile security, the most basic safety measures required for safeguarding personal devices and protecting networks that keep smart infrastructures in place. AI enables security frameworks to automatically detect, adjust and learn from new threats taking a proactive defense as the threat landscape evolves.

This chapter aims to study the use of AI in strengthening smart infrastructures by providing efficient malware detection and threat prevention. It analyzes AI usage for network and mobile security use cases, illustrating capabilities within the realms of AI driven solutions that can help to solve today's for now unsolvable cybersecurity issues in the specific context of smart ecosystems. As those roads, bridges and utilities rapidly become digital infrastructure in their own right AI becomes an essential technology to protect this data and maintain a system that allows us always-on access to critical services like emergency response or medical care (East & Smith, 2024). This article is an overview on the security of digital & smart infrastructures and how AI has grown over time in trying to protect them, becoming a keystone behind next-gen cybersecurity.

Figure 1. Dimensions of introduction section (Original)

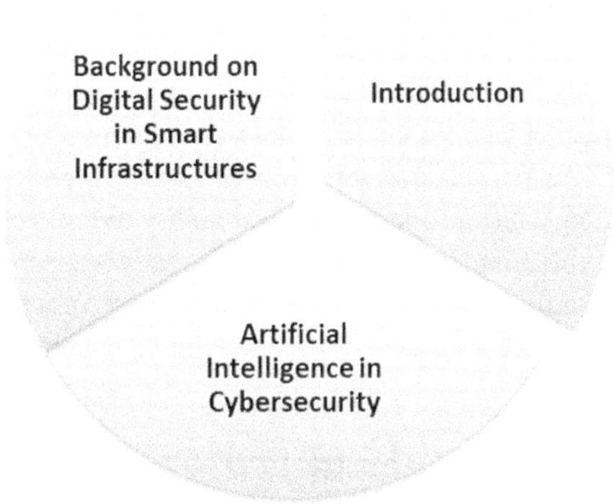

1.1 Background on Digital Security in Smart Infrastructures

With integrating networks, sensors and data analytics on a large-scale smart infrastructure are changing cities, healthcare system transportation management and energy consumption. These systems enable greater resource utilization, more immediate monitoring and delivery of services which results in the amount revitalized systems that enhances quality of life. This means that vulnerabilities are present in layers of these infrastructures such as IoT devices, data storage systems to communication networks and there can be unauthorized access or data breach or disrupt an attack (Preston, 2024).

Due to the criticality of smart infrastructures, cyber threats that target such systems could lead not only to loss or compromise data integrity and operational downtime but also may result in public safety risks. Some threats include ransomware, distributed denial of service (DDoS) attacks and advanced persistent threat (APT), all capable in taking down essential services or stealing intrinsic data. While traditional cyber security approaches are key, they do not have the scale and agility needed to respond immediately against these fast moving threats. This makes it incumbent on organizations to deploy a more responsive security solution that can both adapt quickly and dynamically choose how the IoT devices need to be secured or sterilized against malware attacks in real-time. Solving this requirement is growingly an integral part in the digital security to host a smart grid infrastructure by Artificial Intelligence (AI).

1.2 Artificial Intelligence in Cybersecurity

AI (Artificial Intelligence) is changing the game of cybersecurity with its superior detection, analysis and response capability to cyber-threats more effectively than ever before. Today's advanced threat landscape is highly complex, rapidly changing and traditional security models often suffer from rule-based / signature-based detections too (Camacho, 2024). AI on the other hand uses machine learning and deep learning algorithms able to detect patterns, abnormalities as well as potential attacks through historical data. These are the algorithms that enable a security system to eventually understand what is bad or good in an environment, as they learn from having seen many malicious incidents, and thus improve their ability to detect novel threats.

AI is used to deconstruct every individual process associated with software, which helps in real-time behavioral analysis for malware detection: deviations are spotted and potential security issues detected before they spread. In a way, the same goes for network and mobile security systems with AI capabilities that offer automatic threat detection features to secure devices and networks in automated infrastructures. AI-enabled cybersecurity frameworks are now more proactive and resilient, equipping organizations with a crucial imperative in protecting data and operational availability. What is clear today, though, is that AI will play a significant part in cybersecurity with its predictive analysis capabilities threat intelligence and the use of stealing or scripts call for all add up to making this group cornerstone technology for venture against increasingly sophisticated cyberattacks across smart digital bunches (Kasowaki & Ahmet, 2024).

2. UNDERSTANDING SMART INFRASTRUCTURE AND CYBER THREAT LANDSCAPE

The city Infrastructures in modern cities, industry 4.0 and critical sectors are becoming smart the built environment is getting intelligence embedded into it, to become more efficient in terms of energy/water/ etc., connected/ connectable with IoT devices & work streams securely across networked domains etc. These infrastructures use a network of interconnected devices, sensors and communications networks to enable the exchange, monitoring and control of data in real time which power energy management or transportation system as well as health-care systems among others (Smith & Anderson, 2024). The drivers of these advancements are the IoT devices, cloud computing and AI that together make it a seamlessly integrated, autonomous system. Smart infrastructures provide a multitude of optimization and sustainability opportunities, but in place with these innovations is an increasingly complicated cyber threat landscape offering potential risks for their security, stability & integrity.

Malware, ransomware, distributed denial-of-service (DDoS) attacks, phishing and advanced persistent threats (APTs), as well as other digital fraud activities targeting smart infrastructures are among the most prominent cyber threats. For example, malware might infiltrate servers across an infrastructure and result in operational chaos or breach the overall data security. Ransomware can shut down critical infrastructure by encrypting important data and then only unlocking it when demands are met. DDoS attacks create a situation in which network traffic overload makes services unable to serve the return legal users. APTs pose a different intimidating threat, the result of long-term focused operations undertaken by highly funded hackers targeting networks to siphon off specific data or to cripple systems over time.

Due to their interconnectivity, security concerns are specific to smart infrastructures and vary from traditional digital environments. Since most of these gadgets do not have solid security, their makers intend to offset the cost and versatility issues by offering them low prices after all remember they fall under connected devices called IoT (internet-of-things) for this very reason attackers essentially get a gateway. Once infiltrated, these vulnerabilities can be leveraged by attackers to move laterally through organizational networks and potentially compromise larger critical systems. An enormous scale of data is processed in real-time and stored over distributed networks enabled by massive adoption of cloud computing as well as the employment on smart infrastructures to capitalize every available information. This dependence adds more variables that bad actors can take advantage of to either steal data or tamper with it, which as leaders you need for efficient running.

An equally important issue is that these advanced, persistent threats cannot be mitigated by conventional cyber security techniques as they are sophisticated and changing. Most of the legacy systems were built when smart infrastructures with their complicated data flows became only a subject to emerge and are, therefore, not properly protected or badly adopted last year's tactics. As such, smart infrastructures need a multi-layer cyber security system that enables real time identification of threats and attacks followed by aggressive prevention against further exploitation or misuse with strong recovery measures instead (Chastain & Smith, 2024). Artificial intelligence (AI) and machine learning are also becoming essential in securing these systems by helping to process large amounts of data and detect any deviations. But as AI-driven approaches to security must adapt over time to meet the threat of emerging cybersecurity threats, it highlights how difficult it will be protect smart infrastructure against an expanded cyber landscape.

Figure 2. Points on understanding smart infrastructure and cyber threat landscape (Original)

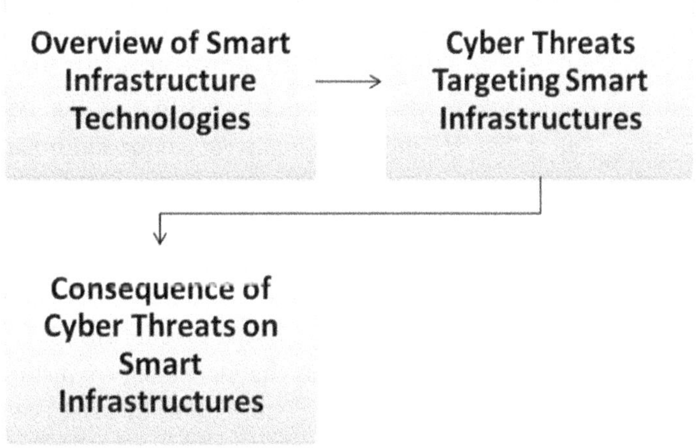

2.1 Overview of Smart Infrastructure Technologies

Smart infrastructures refer to the assemblage of advanced systems and units that can work effectively for efficiency, connectivity, and responsiveness in smart cities or industrial settings. They make use of Internet of Things (IoT), Artificial Intelligence (AI) and Big Data Analytics to get real-time data, process the data in various ways pronto so as to have applications like smart grids or intelligent transport systems or automated public services. Role of IoT devices and sensors: They collect somatic data on environmental conditions, infrastructure usage and energy consumption. This data is then analyzed using cloud computing power, and further predictive maintenance, resource optimization or even user experience enhancement are achieved with the help of AI algorithms.

Smart infrastructure technologies are designed to be interoperable with other systems, such as energy water and transportation thus leading towards holistic ecosystem. This could involve changing the light sequences as our smart traffic lights do based on congestion or distributing power usage around a grid to match real-time demand like how our smart grids balance electricity loads. Blockchain being a secure and transparent technology is also finding its use in the world of smart infrastructure. These technologies together underpin smart cities and industry 4.0, which in turn are seeking to engineer climates that can sustain livable urban/industrial life at a scale modern world requires.

2.2 Cyber Threats Targeting Smart Infrastructures

Because of how interconnected and data-driven most smart infrastructures are, they present a variety of cyber threats. Some common cyberattacks that you might hear more or less often include malware, ransomware, distributed denial-of-service (DDoS) attacks and advance persistent threats. Malware infects devices and networks, leading to outages or data leaks. Ransomware locks systems or datasets for ransom that is hard to afford in essential public services DDoS attacks flood critical services and the network infrastructure with more than excessive traffic, often making them completely inaccessible for smart cities where everything relies on seamless connectivity (Biplob et al., 2024).

APTs align with more advanced types of cyber threat in which a live attacker develops root long-term access to networks extracting data at their leisure or setting the stage for additional malicious activities. Smart infrastructures in which IoT devices are an integral part, especially the ones that come with little to no security implementation, make for a comparatively easy target, effectively serving as starting points from where attackers can hop on bigger networks. Further, remote data being stored in other places such as the cloud or across distributed networks is insecure and can be breached, leading to squandering of traceability/privacy sensitive personal user information not only that but also operationally critical datasets too. And disadvantaged by the security landscape is the increasing sophistication of cyber-attacks that could compromise or create havoc and cripple critical systems in a variety of industries with all smart companies on board.

2.3 Consequence of Cyber Threats on Smart Infrastructures

Cyber threats to such smart infrastructures can threaten the operational integrity, data security and public safety at scale. Failure in such critical infrastructures as energy grids, transportation networks or even water supply systems may ripple out with cascading impacts to a broader scale economy prospect, trust lost from society and possible fatalities. A healthcare system disrupted by ransomware could stop critical patient care, or DDoS attack on transportation infrastructure would snarl traffic and delay slowing emergency response times.

The privacy and security of citizens are also under significant threat from data breaches, operations attack as well unauthorized access to sensitive data (issues related surveillance theory), which can be used for personal or group interests in an unwarranted manner. In addition to an assault on a target where bad actors seek control, in the present day with important technology infrastructures being integrated into government and industrial operations (and days of future passed) said attack can have grave national security ramifications. Advanced persistent threats (APTs), which enable attackers to breach systems over a prolonged period of time, increasing the likelihood they might be used for wide-reaching espionage or manipulation. To deal with the above implications, we need strong cyber-security hence real-time threat detection and proactive response strategy, on the other hand resilient infra well equipped to counter heavy attacks in form of recovery what if instead build a robust system which can take down alerts before even trigger any alert. Smart infrastructures help to ensure the functionality, security and resilience of contemporary urban and industrial landscapes (Dodiya et al., 2024).

3. ARTIFICIAL INTELLIGENCE IN MALWARE DETECTION: OVERVIEW OF MALWARE DETECTION TECHNIQUES

Now with industry on the brink of this new era in security, we are seeing firsthand AI really revolutionizing how malware can be detected using intelligent and scalable methods. Many malware detection techniques in traditional fashion utilize signature-based identification and rule-based approach that deals with comparing incoming files or code to known signatures of previously identified threats, i.e., predefined rules. These techniques are good in detecting known threats, but not so efficient for identifying new or mutant malware because they are largely reactive due to subsequent signatures and hence limited with respect to zero-day attacks the arena of first generation AV. AI and ML detection provides an active approach to malware scanning by combining machine learning and deep learning coupled with anomaly-based techniques which can spot new malwares not based solely on the past data thereof.

The most widely known AI applications for malware detection is machine learning-based detection techniques. Machine learning models, trained on large datasets of benign and malicious code, are able to automatically learn to distinguish between normal software and malware. These models can rapidly realize questionable code patterns, file behaviors, and network activities which flag a possible malware threat. And for other types of machine learning methods, such as supervised where a model is trained on labeled data to recognize known properties about malware itself or unsupervised which can be used in identifying patterns that no one has seen before using passive knowledge i.e., without knowing anything concrete about the particular entity, etc.

The result enables deep learning as an advanced subset of machine-learning technologies that improve the quality of detecting malware by understanding complex patterns within large data structures like byte sequences in executable files. Neural networks like Convolutional neural network (CNN) and Recurrent Neural Network (RNN)s are good for detecting features that are easily missed by traditional methods (Daniel & Victor, 2024). Unlike signature or regular expression-based models, deep learning can extract significant features from the code and recognize a subtle change that separates malware applications from benign ones. Arms themselves with over 30 years of more than experience in the malware crawlspace, these models are highly adaptive the maintain accuracy by getting even better as time goes on and have seen every form of cyberattack

AI-based solution, Anomaly detection techniques they identify possible abnormalities in system behavior rather than look for a signature. It was used to successfully detect zero-day attacks, relying not on known signatures or rules but rather an ensemble of unusual activity thresholds. In a nutshell, AI-driven malware detection mechanisms offer an elevated intelligent and intuitive approach to discover such threats thus making them indispensable when it comes to fighting against complex natured next-generation malwares targeting smart infrastructures or any other virtual ecosystem.

3.1 Machine Learning and Deep Learning in Malware Detection

Machine learning and Deep learning models have revolutionized malware detection by being proactive against known and unknown threats. ML models such as supervised learning using a labeled dataset are used to identify known malware patterns that use identifiable characteristics, and ML detects them with a higher accuracy rate when coming across the same threats. Where the supervised learning mechanism falls is where unsupervised learning comes in handy in detecting unknown malware through unusual behavioral patterns. Deep learning algorithms, Neural Networks like Convolutional Neural Networks, and Recurrent Neural Networks do pattern recognition at extremely deep levels. With the usage of the incredibly complex structure and search and find structure, these pieces of applications detect hidden patterns, speeding detection processes up and enhancing the ability to adapt to modern malware tactics due to dynamic learning.

3.2 AI Behavioral Analysis of Malware Behavioral analysis using AI

It is another form of identifying malware by tracking deviations from typical system actions. Rather than relying just on known signature-based behaviors, AI-powered behavioral strategy concentrates on the strange actions that a malicious or potentially thousands of malware occurrences can show and do. The profile creation of positive, not malicious, behavior triggers a real-time alert on different alarms. Whether a file is characterized as a potential threat, examines behavioral files, the checking of documents for hazard activities, and communicates with the network server are all included. The learning algorithm will begin to understand the pattern as messages of the same type being similar. The behavioral statistics are the record of the blacklist in which the creation of an alert should be done (Harris, 2024).

4. AI FOR THREAT DETECTION AND PREVENTION IN NETWORKS

The evolving cyber-threat landscape, however, has proved the traditional network security incapable of addressing that and AI is completely reshaping threat detection as well as prevention in Network Security by providing advanced adaptive solutions. Due to these issues, legacy network security efforts that are rule and signature-based detection is in a constant game of catch up with zero-day exploits, APTs advanced persistent threats and polymorphic malware which perpetually changes shape to Spiderman itself away from the eyes prying your precious data. But AI takes a lot more adaptive, active security stance to your network with machine learning (ML), deep learning (DL) and data analytics that can establish threats in real-time.

The AI-driven threat detection systems that most organizations now rely on also depend upon machine learning models, which attempt to classify the terabytes of network traffic data such as ML-based malware recognition methods or request rate processing algorithms meant to detect Distributed Denial-of-Service (DDoS) attacks (Ojo et al., 2024). They can separate normal traffic from bad, and they do that by looking at network flows, behaviors of the packets etc. Supervised learning is good for creating an accurate classification of known threats learned from a large, labeled data set, and unsupervised model work basically in the indirect way by recognizing out any new cohort presented to it. Besides, reinforcement learning allow security systems to evolve their detection strategy over time by feedback regurgitated hence continually adapting from new threats.

Deep learning expands on this by detecting possible patterns in network traffic data that may not be picked up with traditional security systems. Convolutional Neural Networks (CNNs) and Recurrent Neural Networks (RNNs), for example, are extremely successful with sequential data and time-series data such as those types involved in identifying malicious patterns within continuous network flows. While DL models can improve the accuracy of threat detection this in turn reduces false positives and alerts enabling security teams to more effectively prioritize which threats are genuine, decreasing alert fatigue (Radanliev, 2024).

AI further boosts network threat prevention, with behavioral analysis. Systems will have baseline profiles of stateful networked behaviors that AI-driven platforms can point out when they detect a deviation, which could suggest nefarious activity. Zero-day threats have no signature or identifiable marker that a dinky traditional machine can use to capture them. So behavioral analysis is particularly important in these instances. For example, if an AI system detects that the volume of outbound traffic is unexpectedly high or notices unexpected connection attempts to unfamiliar servers or irregular patterns in data access by authorized services; it can identify and report these as suspicious behavior while activating countermeasures such as blocking/ isolating compromised nodes.

AI not only aids detection, but also automatically responds to threats in order to mitigate these safeguarding networks can respond in milliseconds once they detect potential danger. In some cases, automated responses may involve adjusting firewall rules, isolating infected devices or even rerouting network traffic to prevent infection spread (Thakur, 2024). Combining AI with traditional security measures, enterprises are better protected as they provide a more durable defensibility framework and can respond to threats in the current rapidly changing threat environment. It is not just about increasing the effectiveness of security, AI-driven threat detection and prevention also provide operational benefits as well that are critical underpinnings for securing sensitive data, maintaining network integrity and ensuring digital infrastructure continuity.

4.1 AI-Powered Network Intrusion Detection System (NIDS)

Modern day cybersecurity relies on AI-based NIDS alerting to the identification of malicious activity in a given network. Thanks to machine learning (ML) and deep learning algorithms, NIDS powered by AI are able to look through large volumes of network traffic data in search of anomalies or other warning signs that some ones is attempting a breach. The key difference between AI-based NIDS and the traditional system based on known attack signature files is its ability to identify new generation threats, even invisible for zero-day attacks. Works well in a supervised fashion with ML models trained on known attack datasets to classify malicious traffic, or unsupervised learning where anomalies are identified without any existing data. A more powerful neural network is implemented for the increasing ability to detect subtle data patterns through multiple layers of this networks that help in lowering false positives. As a result, AI-based NIDS critique the limitations of conventional approaches and offer more aggressive strategy for network security, which obviously can be very beneficial to organizations needing better defense against their ever-evolving cyber threats (Mahajan et al., 2024).

4.2 AI in Network Anomaly Detection Role

AI is used in network anomaly detection, which prevents and alerts anomalies causing potential threats. Introductory approach to anomaly detection, using pre-set rules and thresholds may overlook atypical or subtle irregularities. It does this by using machine learning to create profiles of your network behavior and then it monitors for any deviation from those "normal" behaviors. AI can identify unknown threats by deploying unsupervised learning models that give notice to anomalies like abnormal data transfers, unanticipated login times or suspicious traffic flows which may indicate a wider cyberattack. Deep learning algorithms, and recurrent neural networks (RNNs), in particular are well suited for time-series analysis which makes them perfect to identify subtle changes over a number of hours or even days. AI can provide adaptive anomaly detection in networks, enabling more accurate and responsive alerting to breaches before they happen or network failures occurring.

4.3 Predicting Threats using Reactive Analytics

AI-powered predictive analytics helps organization to predict and prevent cyber threats before their onset by pattern-based analysis of your network data. Using data from previous experiences, along with real-time ones, machine learning models can predict different trainers against various attacks over time. Most importantly, using predictive analytics tech security in the correlation of attack vectors to system vulnerabilities and network behavior identifies areas where high risk occurs which allows teams to prioritize prevention strategies. AI models, supervised learning ones in particular are very successful at finding the initial weak signals of potential threats allowing orgs to strengthen defenses before an actual attack occurs. Predictive analytics enables threat landscapes to evolve and improve in accuracy with time while leveraging reinforcement learning. All of this together helps organizations maintain a far stronger line of defense and protects them from falling prey to any cyber big break that can result in significant data theft, unauthorized network entry or even worse (Mohammed, 2024).

5. AI IN MOBILE SECURITY FOR THREAT DETECTION AND PREVENTION

Mobile security has seen a complete transformation with Artificial intelligence (AI), which provides advanced means to find out and avoid threats aimed at mobile devices specifically. The expansive reach, diverse application ecosystem and user data make the mobile landscape a special place for security challenges. These challenges have created an increased demand for AI-powered solutions that are capable of both detection and prevention, powered by real-time analysis to implement robust defense mechanisms ensuring devices are secure at the highest possible level. In the era of increasingly sophisticated mobile malware, phishing attacks and privacy issues, AI provides stronger security for threat detection, malware prevention and data protection in different types of appliances by hiding malicious activity between otherwise benign actions on devices.

In fact, mobile devices are under a series of special threats due to mobility and the likelihood that they would carry data even for personal use. Mobile devices like smartphones and tablets do not have the long-standing security measures in place such as with classical computers that use primarily known networks but are much more casual users of public Wi-Fi access points where they can be exposed to man-in-the-middle (MitM) attacks during which bad guys intercept communications between clients attempting to communicate (Lad, 2024). App-based threats are also against mobile users, malware is concealed in what appears to be the original app. These applications execute actions such as quietly extracting sensitive data, monitoring user activities or may also drop a further payload of malicious code to enslave the device.

Phishing attacks, extraordinarily active on mobile devices are another significant means of threat. Phishing attacks trick users into disclosing their sensitive information such as passwords or credit card number by pretending to be trusted entities. Malicious URLs and apps are much more difficult to detect on mobile platforms than a traditional desktop environment, masked as the URL shown in browsers is limited for viewing due to screen size whilst there may be no SSL indicator; making it an ideal medium where attackers can disguise their malicious content easily. The other big trend we saw is an increase in mobile ransomware attacks where the attackers encrypt or lock a device and won't unlock it or expose sensitive data on that device until they receive money to free up the user. As there are numerous threats that climb aboard the bus, mobile security cannot remain abounded as just a mere extension of network protection it needs to be a specialized practice capable of addressing device-specific challenges and attack vectors customized for all those different buses carrying passengers from one part of electronic forest to another.

Mobile malware continues to advance in order to avoid traditional security measures, but AI plays an important role in finding mobile malware and protects us from it. While signature-based detection identifies known threats, it does nothing to help with the many new and polymorphic malware variants that regularly change their code in order to evade discovery (Khan et al., 2025). But AI allows a more proactive approach since machine learning and deep learning algorithms can often detect malware signatures, such as patterns or behaviors that might indicate malicious activity even without explicit knowledge on how the specific code works. Due to its static nature, a behavior-based approach is often less effective at detecting previously unknown malware (zero-day threats), as they can only detect unusual activities of an app. However, machine learning models could be trained on larger benign and malicious behaviors datasets that can understand normal/ suspicious activity which makes it easier for them to recognize such zero-day malware types.

The important methods employed in AI-powered malware detection. Instead of just looking at static features or code structures AI models learn how the applications behave over time. When an application starts to request sensitive data requests, creating strange network connections or performing high-risk operations it will raise and alarm. This behavior analysis is particularly useful for identifying "fileless" malware, which does not leave traditional traces but instead manages everything in memory. This allows AI to identify malware that traditional, signature-based solutions might miss by detecting any abnormal behaviors. Deep learning, an AI subfield, improves malware detection even more because it recognizes intricate structures from mobile application data. For example, Convolution Neural Networks (CNNs) and Recurrent Neural Network (RNN-s) do a good job at identifying the smaller behaviors in huge datasets that can indicate malware. CNNs are looking at patterns in code sequences or binary files, while RNNs process user action/ network traffic over time useful for real-time anomaly detection. AI-based models have the ability to go through a large set of data and that too very quickly, hence they provide this speed and scalability which is appropriate when it comes to managing numerous apps even if there are so many other networks connected together as its base is mobile (Sharma et al., 2024).

Among the most crucial roles of AI in phone security is keeping user data safe, information that may be stored on or accessed through a smartphone. Mobile devices are rife with sensitive data from personal communications to financial and location details, they represent a veritable goldmine for cybercriminals.

Artificial Intelligence can help in monitoring app permissions and behaviors to detect unusual data access patterns. If an app tries to request access additional info e.g., after changing its types of calling functions from a low-permitted group, AI may also be able flag or block this activity. Similarly, AI can recognize login attempts that do not conform to the usual patterns of normal users by taking into account factors such as time or location where user logs in with his / her device and in cases when some aspect changes a warning may be generated. AI feature fingerprint/facial recog, to further prevent unauthorized user from possible breaching the device.

The strong weapon in the AI armor for data security on mobile devices is predictive analytics. They can predict security threats based on historical data and usage patterns, so that the users or security applications will come up with counter measures. For example, high-risk app categories or behaviors are subject to being caught in advance by AI technology and show comments when downloading. AI can also help with data encryption and manage access keys, as well as maintain the security of information when the device is lost or stolen. The example of AI reinforcement is related to the security analysis between mobile services and more where in detecting and blocking phishing attempts (Roshanaei et al., 2024). Utilizing natural language processing (NLP) and image recognition via AI-driven phishing detection to spot phony emails, messages, or websites that pretend they are legitimate. Securing vulnerable information, an area where AI can deeply dive into analyzing the content, language and copy of a message or website to certify its authenticity before a user interacts with it.

AI strengthens mobile security by improving the identification of malware, safeguarding user data and responding to emergencies with greater speed due to emerging threats. Due to the challenges of some aspects, AI provides adaptive and predictive solutions that learn through machine learning (ML), deep learning, analytics by using profiling when it comes to detection in a mobile-specific environment from an interconnected world as well because synthetic intelligence is required for securing particularly the modern way we interact with our digital devices.

6. ROLE OF AI IN IOT SECURITY FOR SMART INFRASTRUCTURES

The role of Artificial Intelligence (AI) as part of the Internet of Things (IoT) security is one aspect which cannot be overlooked for securing smart infrastructures. Smart devices proliferating in almost every industry, from smart cities and healthcare to industrial automation makes security a critical requirement (Hossain, 2024). AI can improve the security of IoT by leveraging sophisticated tools to identify, respond and eliminate threats in real-time, hence eliminating weaknesses posed between connected devices. Anomaly detection is one of the key features AI can play in IoT security. State of the art security often works on fixed rules but new or complex attacks towards IoT devices could hide no end in unlimited rule set. AI and in particular machine learning algorithms mine the huge quantity of data generated by IoT devices to create awareness around what we could call baseline behaviors. When data is streamed in real-time, AI constantly watches this dataset and if there are any deviations from the normal it raises exceptions on these. It is essential to catch such anomalies in real-time as you would not like unprivileged users having access or running malicious actions.

AI-based systems also help modern threat intelligence by correlating data from different sources. In other words, technology can analyze information conducted from a multitude of IoT sensors as well as user interactions and network traffic through big data analytics to ascertain new threats and attack vectors. This prepares Security Teams for responding quickly and more effectively when potential vulnerability is identified. Artificial intelligence (AI) is being increasingly leveraged to automate threat response as well. If an anomaly or potential threat is detected, AI systems can automatically initiate predetermined responses like quarantining compromised devices, adapting access contorts and alerting security staff.

AI helps with securing IoT devices allowing adaptive security. ML models are capable of learning from past incidents and accordingly tweak their detection algorithms adaptively to tackle the changing threat landscape. This flexibility is essential, considering that cyber threats rarely stay the same and static security measures can quickly fall behind (Jimmy, 2024). A Game Changer in IoT Security for Smart Infrastructures by detecting anomalies, improving threat intelligence, and deploying an automated response mechanism alongside adaptive security measures; AI will most effectively fortify the defense against cyber threats to preserve the integrity, availability and confidentiality of networked systems.

6.1 IoT Vulnerabilities and Threats in Smart Infrastructures

Smart infrastructures: IoT vulnerabilities are related to the implementation of weak security protocols, outdated software and lackluster device management in smart systems. Some IoT devices do not have a secure authenticating mechanism, subsequently they become soft targets for illegible access and exfiltration. Moreover, the number of connected devices is massive that forms an extensive attack surface which hackers can target. The remaining major risks would be realistic malware created to target and exploit devices in the IoT, either by shutting down machines or manipulating data. Another reason IoT presents a challenge to cybersecurity is because of the dynamic way in which these devices move around and change roles, meaning that one second, they are there displaying a presentation at an exhibition, the next connecting back within your network.

6.2 AI for IoT Security Detection and Prevention

In IoT, AI provides data to automatically detect and stop threats with its sophisticated analytical programs of machine learning. AI continuously watches the IoT networks, and therefore AI learns how it is expected to behave naturally because they decide what normal or abnormal behavior might pose as threats. This active control and response give the ability to monitor, report on current status of any point production data systems in your network as well has make real-time alerts automated responses if ever there is something catastrophic like infected user equipment. AI can recognize patterns across massive data sets from IoT sensors and devices more accurately so that the threat detection is much better focused on minimizing false positives. As new threat intelligence becomes available, machine learning can adapt and evolve to counter the vulnerabilities as they emerge. AI can go even further to streamline security protocols by removing repetitive actions from human workload and allowing the security team members to concentrate on more challenging problems. The incorporation of AI fuels IoT security mechanisms with extraordinary strength against threats to which protects and comforts smart infrastructures (Das et al., 2024).

7. CHALLENGES AND LIMITATIONS OF AI IN CYBERSECURITY

Adoption of Artificial Intelligence (AI) for cybersecurity has become increasingly widespread, but the implementation and effectiveness continue to be challenged with a number of constraints that AI-driven solutions are facing. If we are to have a nuanced cybersecurity strategy that enables us to fully reap the rewards from AI technology, then it is crucial for us to comprehend these issues (Hammad et al., 2024). AI is a promising tool to help solve cyber security challenges, but as with any technology we must tread carefully. Once these organizations address the aforementioned issues, they will be better placed to successfully and sustainably weave AI into their cybersecurity strategies.

7.1 Data Privacy and Ethical Issues

Addressing ethical issues and ensuring data privacy remains one of the foremost challenges in AI cybersecurity. AI systems routinely need large amounts of data to be trained well, and that data often contains personal information like images. That gives rise to questions about data ownership, storage and application, particularly where compliance with regulations like the General Data Protection Regulation (GDPR) is concerned. Data security is the utmost concern as ill-management of data can cause unauthorized data access, information leakage, and lost user seclusion. Similarly, AI algorithms have the risk of introducing bias and thereby promote unequal treatment or even profiling of people. It is now clear that AI in cybersecurity must be developed and deployed ethically such that the mitigative properties of systems do not involve user privacy or widespread misuse.

7.2 Technological Limitations and Reliability Issues

AI in cybersecurity has its limitations that may make us less willing to rely on them so fully. A machine learning model is only good as the data from which it learns, and if that training base uses flawed or unrepresentative examples then there are plenty of ways AI could be about to screw life up for us all. AI systems can be hit with both false positives and negatives identifying benign actions as threats or missing real ones. This inconsistency can result in alert fatigue punching security teams, which makes them numb for alarms and might not address actual threats. Worse, AI systems themselves are susceptible to adversarial attacks: malicious actors can tinker with inputs such that an AI is deceived (Mohammed et al., 2024).

7.3 Human Factor in AI-Based Cybersecurity

Yet, the people's peace remains a top obstacle in AI-powered cybersecurity. Human supervision is also required to analyze the outputs for making decisions and responding in case of incidents that may occur while AI can implement multiple processes. If you rely too heavily on AI, it can give a false sense of security leading to complacency amongst the security team. Moreover, there is no talent to address cyber-security as it relates to artificial intelligence and may take time for the organizations that are hiring qualified people (who can effectively manage and interpret AI system better) without skills. It is also important that employees are trained to understand the role of AI and its capabilities, in order for human expertise to be complementary with those technologies.

7.4 Cost and Scalability Perspective

The expenses and scale are big factors for any organization looking to use AI in cybersecurity. AI, on the other hand, has time and again proven to be an area for financial vampire requiring a lot of money not only upfront but overtime too in hardware (infrastructure), educational infrastructure and maintenance. Most notably, however, the demand of resources is likely to be prohibitive for smaller organizations in getting budgeting advanced AI technologies. As cyber threats are becoming more sophisticated organizations have to keep adapting their AI systems for new vulnerabilities. It can test budgets and resources in the relentless march to stay abreast of AI innovation, prompting some companies to delay or avoid altogether embarking down an integrated path (Tirulo et al., 2024).

Figure 3. Challenges and limitations of AI in cybersecurity (Original)

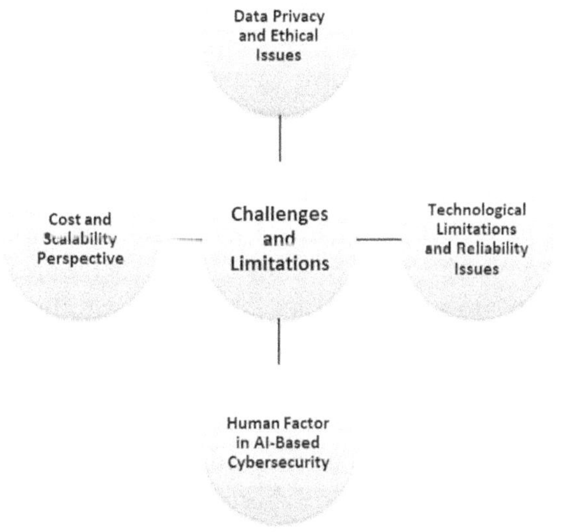

8. POLICY AND REGULATORY FRAMEWORK FOR AI-DRIVEN CYBERSECURITY IN SMART INFRASTRUCTURE

Considering that the use of Artificial Intelligence (AI) in cybersecurity, especially in smart infrastructures, is spreading like wildfire this rise to the need for a resilient policy and regulatory frameworks. These frameworks are important for responding to new challenges related to AI technologies and the security practices of interconnected systems (Alsuwayh, 2024). The growing complexity, and the interconnected nature of smart infrastructures from grids to transportation systems leaves them vulnerable to multiple types of cyber threats. It also requires comprehensive policies that bring a consistent manner to AI solutions—they need their cybersecurity issues addressed, too. This takes the form of writing out explicit rules on how exactly AI technologies can be used in a way that is both ethical and effective.

Regulators need to collaborate with cyber security professionals, industry and academia partners in setting up guidelines for promoting growth while protecting danger.

An example of a good policy structure is to lay down compliance requirements in AI applications for cybersecurity with regulatory standards. Authorities and regulators need to enforce industry-wide rules that stipulate how AI should be used in security. These standards cover matters like data privacy, algorithmic transparency, accountability and security. Businesses that use AI should be held to account through the disclosure of how their algorithms work, what data they used, and steps taken towards addressing biases (Andreoni et al., 2024). Such transparency not only helps create trust between users but also establishes accountability in case of system failures or breaches.

Such AI-driven cybersecurity strategies will also rely on improving collaboration and the sharing of information among different groups. Policymakers should establish a format where organizations can exchange threat intelligence and best practices or discuss lessons learned in implementing AI. This is a worthwhile joint effort that can provide organizations with key insights, in real-time, as to what future threats are coming and how they should be positioned to act defensively. As well as spurring AI research and mitigating regulatory issues, public-private partnerships are capable of delivering tremendous innovation.

In the policy framework, another pillar revolves around dealing with the ethics of AI in cybersecurity. It is essential that even as AI systems are becoming more and more autonomous, we maintain this oversight by humans to prevent anything unintended from creeping up (Rahaman et al., 2024). Policy makers should promote rules requiring humans to be directly involved in key decision making processes, especially those that might lead to security breach or an ethical conundrum. It is also important that developers and cybersecurity professionals be ethically educated in the applications of AI to teach them what concepts they should keep into account when deploying these technologies (Mudgal, 2025).

The policy framework for AI-driven cybersecurity will need to be both pliable and fast paced. New cybersecurity threats and technologies are common (Lal et al., 2024). Regulations ought to be reflective of this constant change so that they can evolve accordingly with time for updates and modifications. This flexibility is set to ensure policies continue supporting the solutions capable of addressing these complicated facets on AI and smart infrastructure cybersecurity (Arora et al., 2024). Stakeholders can ensure AI technologies fulfill their potential by adopting a holistic policy approach that is conducive to innovation, ensuring compliance with regulations, in particular the GDPR and maintaining cooperation through ethical considerations for collaboration within national borders.

9. CONCLUSION AND FUTURE SCOPE

Artificial Intelligence (AI) applications became a force to reckon which have dramatically evolved the way malware and threat detection systems can do much more than before just detect it. Artificial intelligence is able to analyze a multitude of data through machine learning algorithms that can determine patterns signifying malice, and this eventually helps the system detect threats in real time. Taking such an approach will limit the consequence of worst-case scenarios from data breaches until compromised systems AI plays a role in network security when it comes to securing networks from possible breaches through advanced intrusion detection systems which detect and alert the responsible party to any anomaly present on transmitted data. AI-based protection measures vary from dynamic threat assessment to keep user data safe and sound against potential infiltration by malware or phishing. Incorporating AI into cybersecurity systems for smart infrastructure strengthens security but also builds user confidence; thereby enabling more resistive and dependable neighboring services in a maze-like universe where all digital touch points are connected.

REFERENCES

Adil, M., Almaiah, M. A., Omar Alsayed, A., & Almomani, O. (2020, April 18). An anonymous channel categorization scheme of edge nodes to detect jamming attacks in wireless sensor networks. *Sensors (Basel)*, 20(8), 2311. DOI: 10.3390/s20082311 PMID: 32325646

Ali, S., Ali, A., Uzair, M., Amir, H., Bari, R. Z. A., Sharif, H., . . . Allaberdiev, S. (2024, July). Empowering Cybersecurity: CyberShield AI Advanced Integration of Machine Learning and Deep Learning for Dynamic Ransomware Detection. In *International Conference on Deep Learning Theory and Applications* (pp. 95-117). Cham: Springer Nature Switzerland. DOI: 10.1007/978-3-031-66705-3_7

Almaiah, A., & Almomani, O. (2020). An investigation of digital forensics for shamoon attack behaviour in FOG computing and threat intelligence for incident response. *Journal of Theoretical and Applied Information Technology*, 15, 98.

Almaiah, A. M. I. N., & Almomani, O. M. A. R. (2020). An investigator digital forensics frequencies particle swarm optimization for dectection and classification of apt attack in fog computing enviroment (idf-fpso). *Journal of Theoretical and Applied Information Technology*, 15, 98.

Almaiah, M. A., Al-Zahrani, A., Almomani, O., & Alhwaitat, A. K. (2021). Classification of cyber security threats on mobile devices and applications. In *Artificial intelligence and blockchain for future cybersecurity applications* (pp. 107–123). Springer International Publishing.

Almaiah, M. A., Almomani, O., Alsaaidah, A., Al-Otaibi, S., Bani-Hani, N., Hwaitat, A. K. A., Al-Zahrani, A., Lutfi, A., Awad, A. B., & Aldhyani, T. H. H. (2022). Performance investigation of principal component analysis for intrusion detection system using different support vector machine kernels. *Electronics (Basel)*, 11(21), 3571. DOI: 10.3390/electronics11213571

Almaiah, M. A., Dawahdeh, Z., Almomani, O., Alsaaidah, A., Al-Khasawneh, A., & Khawatreh, S. (2020). A new hybrid text encryption approach over mobile ad hoc network. [IJECE]. *International Journal of Electrical and Computer Engineering*, 10(6), 6461–6471.

Almaiah, M. A., Saqr, L. M., Al-Rawwash, L. A., Altellawi, L. A., Al-Ali, R., & Almomani, O. (2024). Classification of Cybersecurity Threats, Vulnerabilities and Countermeasures in Database Systems. *Computers, Materials & Continua*, 81(2).

Almomani, O. (2020). A feature selection model for network intrusion detection system based on PSO, GWO, FFA and GA algorithms. *Symmetry*, 12(6), 1046. DOI: 10.3390/sym12061046

Almomani, O. (2021). A Hybrid Model Using Bio-Inspired Metaheuristic Algorithms for Network Intrusion Detection System. *Computers, Materials & Continua*, 68(1).

Almomani, O., Almaiah, M. A., Alsaaidah, A., Smadi, S., Mohammad, A. H., & Althunibat, A. (2021, July). Machine learning classifiers for network intrusion detection system: comparative study. In *2021 International Conference on Information Technology (ICIT)* (pp. 440-445). IEEE.

Almomani, O., Alsaaidah, A., Shareha, A. A. A., Alzaqebah, A., & Almomani, M. (2024). Performance Evaluation of Machine Learning Classifiers for Predicting Denial-of-Service Attack in Internet of Things. *International Journal of Advanced Computer Science and Applications*, 15(1).

Alsuwayh, A. (2024). *Effectiveness of Artificial Intelligence (AI) Strategies Against Cyber Security Threats* (Doctoral dissertation, Marymount University).

Andreoni, M., Lunardi, W. T., Lawton, G., & Thakkar, S. (2024). Enhancing autonomous system security and resilience with generative AI: A comprehensive survey. *IEEE Access : Practical Innovations, Open Solutions*, 12, 109470–109493. DOI: 10.1109/ACCESS.2024.3439363

Arora, M. K., Lal, S., Singh, B., & Olyaee, M. (2024). Through an Energy Lens: Examining SDGs From a Policy Perspective. In Riswandi, B., Singh, B., Kaunert, C., & Vig, K. (Eds.), *AI Applications for Clean Energy and Sustainability* (pp. 320–343). IGI Global., DOI: 10.4018/979-8-3693-6567-0.ch016

Biplob, M. B., Mong Marma, S., & Akther, M. (2024). Securing Tomorrow's Digital World: Key Trends in Cyber security for 2024.

Camacho, N. G. (2024). The Role of AI in Cybersecurity: Addressing Threats in the Digital Age. *Journal of Artificial Intelligence General science (JAIGS) ISSN: 3006-4023, 3*(1), 143-154.

. Chastain, K., & Smith, J. (2024). *Cybersecurity Reinvented: the Integration of AI Defense Mechanisms* (No. 13307). EasyChair.

Daniel, S. A., & Victor, S. S. (2024). Emerging Trends in Cybersecurity for Critical Infrastructure Protection: A Comprehensive Review. *Computer Science & IT Research Journal*, 5(3), 576–593. DOI: 10.51594/csitrj.v5i3.872

Das, P., Gupta, I., & Mishra, S. (2024). Artificial intelligence driven cybersecurity in digital healthcare frameworks. In *Securing Next-Generation Connected Healthcare Systems* (pp. 213–228). Academic Press. DOI: 10.1016/B978-0-443-13951-2.00002-7

Dodiya, K. R., Jha, M., & Jha, S. (2024). Fortifying the Digital Forge: Unleashing Cybersecurity in the Interconnected World of Digital Manufacturing. In *Emerging Technologies in Digital Manufacturing and Smart Factories* (pp. 230-256). IGI Global.

. East, A., & Smith, J. (2024). *Defenders of the Cyber Realm: AI's Evolutionary Role in Cybersecurity* (No. 13308). EasyChair.

Hammad, A., Saleh, H. M., & Alomari, M. (2024). Advancements in Cybersecurity: Novel Approaches to Protecting Against Emerging Threats and Vulnerabilities. *CyberSystem Journal*, 1(1), 9–22. DOI: 10.57238/r15e5074

. Harris, S. S. B. A., & bin Zolkipli, M. F. (2024) The Evolution of Threat Intelligence: Trends and Innovations in Cyber Defense.

Hossain, M. T. (2024). *Privacy and Security for Trustworthy AI/ML in Multi-Agent Critical Infrastructures: An Analysis of Adversarial Dynamics and Protective Strategies* (Doctoral dissertation).

Jimmy, F. N. U. (2024). Cyber security Vulnerabilities and Remediation Through Cloud Security Tools. *Journal of Artificial Intelligence General science (JAIGS) ISSN: 3006-4023, 2*(1), 129-171.

. Kasowaki, L., & Ahmet, S. (2024). *Shielding the Virtual Ramparts: Understanding Cybersecurity Essentials* (No. 11700). EasyChair.

Khan, A., Jhanjhi, N., Abdulhabeb, G. A. A., Ray, S. K., Ghazanfar, M. A., & Humayun, M. (2025). Securing IoT Devices Using Generative AI Techniques. In *Reshaping CyberSecurity With Generative AI Techniques* (pp. 219–264). IGI Global.

. Lad, S. (2024). Cybersecurity Trends: Integrating AI to Combat Emerging Threats in the Cloud Era. *Integrated Journal of Science and Technology, 1*(8).

Lal, S., Arora, M. K., Riswandi, B. A., Singh, N., & Singh, B. (2024). Melding Artificial Intelligence and Remote Sensing Data for Real-Time Monitoring of Marine Biodiversity. In Riswandi, B., Singh, B., Kaunert, C., & Vig, K. (Eds.), *AI Applications for Clean Energy and Sustainability* (pp. 299–319). IGI Global., DOI: 10.4018/979-8-3693-6567-0.ch015

Mahajan, S., Khurana, M., & Estrela, V. V. (Eds.). (2024). *Applying Artificial Intelligence in Cybersecurity Analytics and Cyber Threat Detection*. John Wiley & Sons. DOI: 10.1002/9781394196470

Mohammed, A. A. A. (2024). Fortifying Digital Frontiers: A Survey on Enterprise Ransomware Resistance. *Nanotechnology Perceptions*, •••, 111–127.

Mohammed, Y. B., Badara, M. S., & Dan'azumi, H. (2024). An Intelligence-Based Cybersecurity Approach: A Review. *Journal of International Communication*, 4(1), 32–43.

Mudgal, A. (2025). Leveraging AI and ML for Proactive Threat Detection for E-Commerce. In *Strategic Innovations of AI and ML for E-Commerce Data Security* (pp. 281–322). IGI Global.

Ojo, B., Ogborigbo, J. C., & Okafor, M. O. (2024). Innovative solutions for critical infrastructure resilience against cyber-physical attacks. *World Journal of Advanced Research and Reviews*, 22(03), 1651–1674. DOI: 10.30574/wjarr.2024.22.3.1921

. Preston, R., & Smith, J. (2024). *Fortifying Cybersecurity: Exploring AI's Role as Guardians of the Virtual Gate* (No. 13310). EasyChair.

. Radanliev, P. (2024). Cyber diplomacy: defining the opportunities for cybersecurity and risks from Artificial Intelligence, IoT, Blockchains, and Quantum Computing. *Journal of Cyber Security Technology*, 1-51.

Rahaman, M., Bakkireddygari, S. S., Chattopadhyay, S., Gomez, A. L., Arya, V., & Bansal, S. (2024). Infrastructure and Network Security. In *Metaverse Security Paradigms* (pp. 108–144). IGI Global. DOI: 10.4018/979-8-3693-3824-7.ch005

Roshanaei, M., Khan, M. R., & Sylvester, N. N. (2024). Enhancing Cybersecurity through AI and ML: Strategies, Challenges, and Future Directions. *Journal of Information Security*, 15(3), 320–339. DOI: 10.4236/jis.2024.153019

Sharma, G., Malley, D. J., Parle, D., Akowua, K., & Padgaonkar, N. (2024, March). Analysis and Study of Intelligent Testbed for Safeguarding Nuclear and Defense Industry from AI-Enabled Cyberattacks. In *2024 IEEE International Conference on Interdisciplinary Approaches in Technology and Management for Social Innovation (IATMSI)* (Vol. 2, pp. 1-6). IEEE. DOI: 10.1109/IATMSI60426.2024.10502505

. Smith, J., & Anderson, J. (2024). *AI's Watchful Eye: Strengthening Cyber Defense as Guardians of the Virtual Gate* (No. 13302). EasyChair.

Thakur, M. (2024). Cyber security threats and countermeasures in digital age. [JASE]. *Journal of Applied Science and Education*, 4(1), 1–20. DOI: 10.54060/a2zjournals.jase.42

Tirulo, A., Chauhan, S., & Dutta, K. (2024). Machine learning and deep learning techniques for detecting and mitigating cyber threats in IoT-enabled smart grids: A comprehensive review. *International Journal of Information and Computer Security*, 24(3-4), 284–321. DOI: 10.1504/IJICS.2024.141601

Chapter 2
Proactively Approaching Cybersecurity With AI-Powered Malware Detection Is Essential

Spandan Agrawal
https://orcid.org/0009-0008-0013-2739
VIT Bhopal University, India

Lakshya Pandey
https://orcid.org/0009-0005-2468-4237
VIT Bhopal University, India

D. Lakshmi
https://orcid.org/0000-0003-4018-1208
VIT Bhopal University, India

ABSTRACT

The rapid increase in ransomware attacks has created a need for new cybersecurity methods. This research introduces a multi-faceted approach using Artificial Intelligence (AI), Machine Learning (ML), Deep Learning (DL), and Natural Language Processing (NLP) to improve the detection and prevention of ransomware attacks. It uses various AI and ML techniques to detect ransomware signatures, analyze system activities, and understand the evolving threat landscape. It can detect phishing attacks by analyzing email content and user behavior. It can also identify insider threats and assess the security posture of third-party vendors. By using these AI-powered solutions, organizations can strengthen their cybersecurity capabilities, detect threats at an earlier stage, and respond more effectively to cyber attacks. In the future, AI and ML will become more advanced in identifying and addressing complex cyber threats, such as Advanced Persistent Threats (APTs) and zero-day attacks.

DOI: 10.4018/979-8-3693-9919-4.ch002

1.0 INTRODUCTION

Quantum computers pose a threat to current security, necessitating new encryption methods. Adware generates income for developers by presenting ads in free software or apps. As cyber attackers become more advanced, conventional security measures struggle to keep pace. AI-powered malware detection is essential for proactive cybersecurity, addressing a growing range of digital threats. Along with technologies like Software-Defined Networking (SDN) and big data, the internet's growth presents significant challenges in protecting critical infrastructure. While deep learning (DL) enables advancements in areas like robotics and cyber defense, traditional methods like firewalls and intrusion detection systems need reinforcement to effectively identify modern cyber threats. The text also highlights the urgency of cybersecurity in cloud-based systems and explores the application of DL, ML, and Metaheuristics in modern cybersecurity practices Salem et al., (2024). The different types of cyber-attacks include malware, phishing, ransomware, and Denial-Of-Service (DoS) attacks. Understanding these attacks is crucial for developing effective prediction strategies and implementing appropriate security measures. The chapter also discusses the importance of predictive modeling in AI for predicting cyber threats and mentions federated learning and the FedAvg algorithm for training ML models Nadella & Gonaygunta (2024). Cybersecurity is an evolving field with increasing threats from sophisticated cybercriminals. Traditional solutions are struggling to keep up, but advancements in AI and ML offer hope. Global spending on cybersecurity is projected to surpass $1 trillion from 2017 to 2021. Researchers are exploring AI approaches to enhance cybersecurity while cybercriminals are also using AI for more sophisticated attacks. AI has been implemented in various areas, and its use in cybersecurity is gaining interest due to the substantial volume of data being generated Zeadally et al., (2020). The landscape of cyber threats is constantly changing, necessitating advanced technologies to identify and counter attacks. AI has become a critical tool for bolstering cybersecurity and enabling comprehensive detection of threats and automated response. This article examines the most recent progress in using AI to defend against cyber threats, focusing on ML, natural language processing, computer vision, and automation methods. Evaluating the top solutions from cybersecurity providers demonstrates a shift towards security platforms driven by AI that can contextualize threats, comprehend typical behavior, and take precise actions. Challenges regarding explainability, potential biases, and adversarial attacks targeting AI systems persist. Recommendations include creating robust training datasets, using ensemble models, enhancing explainability and accountability, and retaining human expertise oversight. Nevertheless, the potential for transformation through AI in cybersecurity makes it essential for organizations to incorporate it into their frameworks for detecting and responding to threats. With careful implementation, AI has the potential to significantly enhance cyber defenses in today's threat environment Huyen & Bao (2024). Taking a proactive approach to cybersecurity through AI-driven malware detection seeks to improve security by facilitating early threat detection, quick responses, enhanced threat intelligence, optimal resource use, flexibility, and minimizing risks and expenses. AI can evaluate large volumes of data to spot and recognize harmful activities, irregularities, and new threats in real-time, enabling immediate automated actions such as isolating systems or blocking traffic. Furthermore, AI can discern intricate patterns in threat data, foresee potential attacks, and automate routine security operations, allowing security teams to focus on more strategic tasks.

1.1 Machine Learning Algorithms

ML utilizes various algorithms to address data-related issues. Data scientists emphasize that no universal algorithm is optimal for all problems. The choice of algorithm depends on the specific situation, the number of variables, the most suitable model, and other factors. Let's quickly review some of the frequently used algorithms in ML.

1.1.1 Supervised Learning

Supervised learning involves the ML task of understanding a function that links an input to an output using example input-output pairs. It deduces a function from labeled training data that includes a set of training examples. Supervised ML algorithms are those that require external assistance. The input dataset is separated into train and test datasets. The training dataset contains the output variable that must be predicted or classified. All algorithms learn various patterns from the training dataset and apply them to the test dataset for prediction or classification Mahesh (2020).

1.1.2 Unsupervised learning

Unlabeled datasets are analyzed without human intervention, using a *data-driven process*. This method is extensively utilized to extract generative features, identify significant trends and structures, group results, and for exploratory purposes. Clustering, density estimation, feature learning, dimensionality reduction, finding association rules, and anomaly detection are some of the most common unsupervised learning tasks Sarker (2021).

1.1.3 Semi-Supervised Learning

Semi-supervised learning involves using both labeled and unlabeled data during training, falling between unsupervised and supervised learning. Incorporating unlabeled data with a small amount of labeled data can significantly enhance learning accuracy. Transductive learning aims to deduce correct labels for given unlabeled data, while inductive learning infers the correct mapping from one set to another. We can think of the learning problem as an exam and the labeled data as example problems solved in class Learning (2006).

1.1.4 Reinforcement Learning

Reinforcement Learning (RL) involves an AI agent learning an optimal strategy by trial and error, based on received reward signals. It mimics human and animal learning and is adaptable to various scientific and engineering fields. RL is effective for solving complex sequential decision-making tasks and presents opportunities for exploring new technological frontiers. Modern RL combines research from the psychology of human learning, optimal control solutions using Dynamic Programming, and temporal difference learning Shakya et al., (2023).

2.0 NEURAL NETWORK

Artificial Neural Networks (ANNs) have gained significant popularity as effective models for classification, clustering, pattern recognition, and prediction across various fields. Competing well with traditional regression and statistical models, ANNs are especially relevant in areas like AI, information security, big data, and cloud computing. Their performance can be evaluated through factors such as accuracy, processing speed, scalability, and fault tolerance. ANNs facilitate high-speed processing through parallel implementation, leading to advancements in applications such as image recognition and natural language processing. However, there is a pressing need for a systematic approach during the development phase to enhance ANN performance. This involves careful consideration of data sets, accuracy, preprocessing, and validation processes. Key challenges such as model robustness, transparency, extrapolation ability, and convergence issues also warrant further exploration. Despite these challenges, innovations like cognitive computing and deep learning continue to support the advancement of ANNs. Abiodun et al., (2018). The illustration in Figure 1 presents a comprehensive block diagram that outlines the structure and components of a Neural Network System. Figure 1 effectively showcases the various layers and connections involved, including input, hidden, and output layers, and the data flow through these components.

Figure 1. The block diagram of neural network system

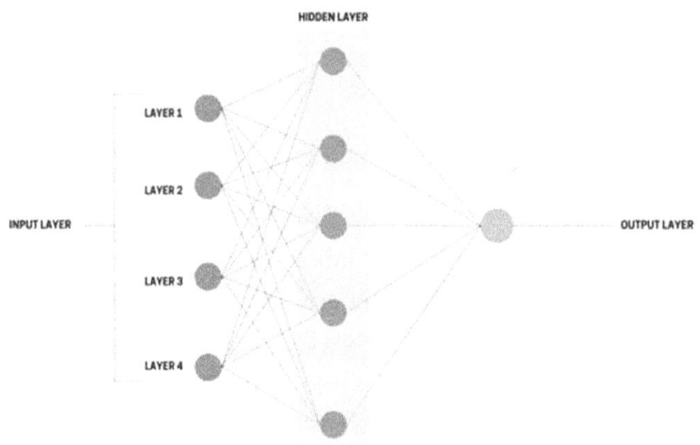

3.0 NATURAL LANGUAGE PROCESSING (NLP)

NLP emerged in the 1950s at the intersection of AI and linguistics, initially separate from text Information Retrieval (IR), which focused on scalable statistical methods for indexing and searching text. Over time, they have merged, requiring NLP researchers to expand their knowledge across diverse fields. Early approaches, like word-for-word Russian-to-English translation, struggled with homographs and metaphors, illustrated by the infamous mistranslation of “the spirit is willing, but the flesh is weak” to “the vodka is agreeable, but the meat is spoiled.” Chomsky's 1956 analysis of language grammar highlighted these complexities, leading to the development of the Backus-Naur Form (BNF) to specify context-free grammar, which is used to represent programming-language syntax through a set of derivation rules. Nadkarni (2011). Natural Language Processing can make computer interfaces easier for users. People could talk to computers in their language instead of learning technical commands. While coding has traditionally required specific programming languages, we want to challenge that idea. We believe that modern Natural Language Processing techniques can allow people to use natural language for programming ideas, at least to some degree. This could make programming more accessible for those who are not experts. Our goal is to show that Natural Language Programming is possible Mihalcea (2006).

4.0 ANALYSIS OF MALWARE BASED ON TEXT

Metamorphic malware is a particularly harmful type of malicious software that can alter its code as it spreads within a system. This capacity to continuously transform makes it extremely challenging to identify and eliminate using standard antivirus techniques. Metamorphic malware represents one of the most significant threats in the digital realm, as they are highly advanced and have reduced the efficacy of signature-based detection methods. Such types of malwares employ code obfuscation to perpetually evolve and assume various forms, rendering it impractical and unfeasible to maintain a thorough signature database that encompasses all variations. Consequently, no antivirus provider can assert 100% detection reliability, even for non-zero-day malware. When malware is encrypted or packed, performing static analysis becomes unfeasible. In these situations, dynamic analysis emerges as the most reasonable approach. However, the difficulty lies in figuring out how to automate behavior analysis for malware detection and how to quantify that behavior. An approach is needed to outline how to analyze dynamic reports and develop a model that can aid in making detection decisions Choudhary & Vidyarthi (2015). The field of malware analysis is actively researched and still faces many unresolved issues (refer to Egele, Scholte, Kirda, & Kruegel, 2012 for a comprehensive survey). The proliferation of both malware and harmless apps on smartphones has made it increasingly impractical for humans to manually analyze potentially harmful apps. This situation has reinforced the necessity for intelligent analysis methods to assist malware analysts in their daily tasks. For example, when dealing with a continuously increasing influx of malware samples, it would be highly beneficial to distinguish between minor variations of known samples and entirely new, unseen samples. Grouping samples into families, establishing their relationships, and studying the development of different "species" are highly desirable applications Suarez-Tangil(2014).

5.0 COMMUNICATION OF MALWARE COMMAND AND CONTROL (C&C)

Network administrators face a significant challenge in identifying botnets and advanced persistent threats. The command-and-control channel is a crucial element of such malware, allowing it to execute commands from its controller. Detecting these command-and-control channels could help thwart further malicious activities carried out by cyber criminals using malware. Malware detection in network traffic has traditionally relied on identifying specific patterns in packet payloads. However, modern bot writers now encrypt the command-and-control payloads, rendering pattern recognition less effective for detection. This paper focuses on an alternative approach, using a data mining method combined with applied classification algorithms to effectively detect anomalies in botnets and advanced persistent threats. After fine-tuning, the final testing on an unseen dataset resulted in a 0% false positive rate and a 100% malware detection rate for two examined malware threats, with promising results for other threats as well McLaren et al., (2017). There is a recent type of malicious software that enables criminals to remotely manipulate computers through Command & Control (C&C) channels. These channels are utilized for carrying out illicit activities using compromised computers, posing a risk to both the infected computer user and other network users. Detecting C&C channels on the network can help mitigate this threat. This thesis aims to enhance the capabilities for detecting web-based C&C channels. It includes a review of existing techniques for detecting C&C channels and an analysis of the behavior of web-based C&C channels. Based on these findings, we introduce three new methods for identifying HTTP and HTTPS-based C&C channels. We assess these methods and provide an overview of their effectiveness in detection Warmer (2011).

6.0 AI-POWERED MALWARE DETECTION TECHNIQUES

Ransomware attacks are exploiting the current global health crisis and targeting vulnerable systems in various sectors such as business, healthcare, education, insurance, banking, and government. Several strategies have been suggested to counter ransomware, but the ever-changing tactics of malware creators often evade security measures. While there are commercial tools available for ransomware analysis and detection, their effectiveness is uncertain. This document aims to propose a ransomware detection framework based on AI and to develop a detection tool (AIRaD) that utilizes a combination of static and dynamic malware analysis techniques. Dynamic binary instrumentation (DBI) is an effective method for examining and altering the behavior of active programs at the binary level. The PIN tool is utilized to perform dynamic binary instrumentation, while function call trace analysis is conducted with the help of the Cuckoo sandbox and Ghidra. Features obtained from the DLL, function calls, and assembly levels are analyzed through NLP and association rule mining techniques, which are subsequently fed into various machine learning classifiers. Support vector machine and Adaboost with J48 algorithms achieved the highest accuracy of 99.54% with a false-positive rate of 0.005 for a multi-level combined term frequency approach Poudyal & Dasgupta (2020, December).

7.0 DETECTION AND PREVENTION OF MALWARE IN REAL-TIME

One of the primary dangers faced by corporate networks comes from bots. Bots are programs that act as surrogates for users and perform automated tasks over the internet at a much faster pace than a human could. A group of maliciously used bots in a network is known as a botnet. Our innovative approach aims to identify and counter bots using a dual strategy, employing both a stand-alone and a network algorithm. The stand-alone algorithm operates independently on each network node, monitoring active processes and activating the network algorithm when it detects a suspicious process. The network algorithm then analyzes communications to and from the hosts to uncover bot patterns and signatures, which can be utilized by the stand-alone algorithm to stop bot processes at their inception Thakur et al., (2012). Figure 2 provides a comprehensive overview of various common techniques utilized for malware detection. The illustration highlights different approaches such as signature-based detection, which relies on known malware patterns, and heuristic-based detection which analyzes behaviors to identify potentially harmful activities.

Figure 2. Common techniques for malware detection

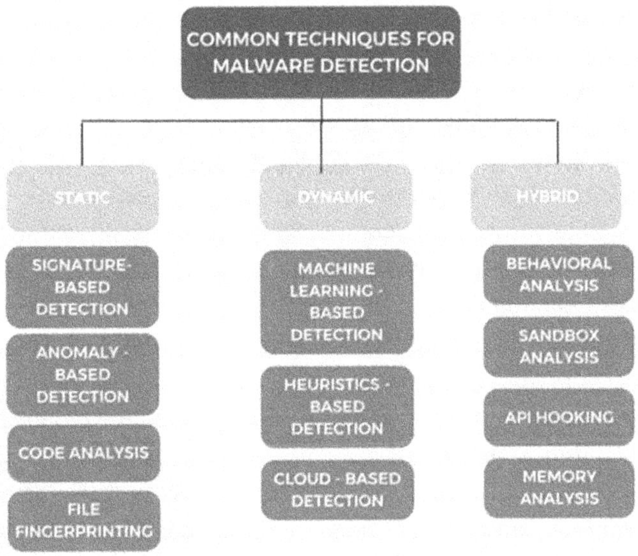

8.0 ADWARE

Adware, or ad-supported software, generates revenue for developers by displaying ads, typically in web browsers, and can be found on both computers and mobile devices. It often bundles with freeware or shareware, installing without user consent. While ad-supported software itself isn't illegal, malicious adware installed without permission is. Adware can track your browsing history to deliver targeted ads and may sell that data to third parties. Legitimate adware allows users to opt into advertisements to access free software, and it's generally developed by reputable companies. However, adware can pose threats, from annoying pop-ups to more severe issues like ad fraud, where malicious apps click ads or subscribe to users to paid services without consent. To remove adware, manual deletion may not suffice; using cybersecurity software is recommended for thorough cleanup.

9.0 FEDERATED LEARNING AND PRIVACY-PRESERVING AI

There has been significant progress in M) technologies, enabling practical applications of AI such as automatic speech recognition and computer vision. Nonetheless, we are currently confronted with two primary obstacles in AI adoption. One obstacle is that data across many industries remain fragmented and isolated. The other challenge is the growing necessity for privacy-preserving AI. Traditional AI methods that depend on centralized data gathering are insufficient to address these issues. Finding a way to resolve data fragmentation and isolation while adhering to privacy protection laws and regulations poses a significant challenge for AI researchers and practitioners. On the legislative side, lawmakers and regulatory agencies are establishing new regulations governing how data is handled and utilized. A notable problem is the implementation of the General Data Protection Regulation (GDPR) by the European Union in 2018. In the United States, the California Consumer Privacy Act will take effect in 2020. Additionally, China's Cyber Security Law, which came into force in 2017, has also enforced strict measures on data collection and transactions. With this evolving legal framework, the processes of data collection and sharing among different organizations are becoming increasingly difficult, if not entirely unfeasible. Furthermore, the sensitive nature of particular data (such as financial transactions and medical records) hinders free data flow and necessitates the existence of data silos. Due to factors like competition, user privacy, data security, and complex administrative procedures, even data integration within different departments of the same organization encounters significant obstacles. As traditional, intrusive methods of data collection and sharing are no longer permissible, consolidating data among various data owners is becoming exceedingly challenging. Data silos and privacy issues represent two of the most significant barriers to advancements in AI. Therefore, it is logical to explore solutions for developing ML models that do not depend on gathering data in a centralized location for model training. An appealing concept is to train a sub-model at each location using solely local data and then enable entities at different sites to exchange their respective sub-models to arrive at a consensus on a global model. To maintain user privacy and data confidentiality, the communication process is meticulously designed to prevent any site from reverse-engineering the private data of other sites. Simultaneously, the model is constructed as though the data sources were combined Cheng et al., (2020).

10.0 BEHAVIOR ANALYSIS

The last few decades have seen rapid advances in the computer and communication fields. While this progress has led to various techniques for creating virus programs, it has also made antivirus software essential for protecting data and files stored in computers or transmitted over networks. The development of antivirus software requires a thorough understanding of how computer viruses spread. The spread of virus codes in a network of interacting computers can be compared to the spread of infectious diseases in a population to some extent. Based on this analogy, certain classical epidemic models have been adapted to characterize the spread of computer viruses. The results obtained from these adaptations indicate that the long-term behavior of virus programs can be predicted. As far as we know, all existing models describing the spread of virus codes have been based on the assumption that a computer is uninfected at the time it connects to the Internet. However, this assumption does not align with the reality that some computers are already infected when they connect Yang & Yang (2012).

11.0 NETWORK SECURITY

The use of information technology has permeated every aspect of politics, economy, and culture in society. The information revolution has transformed global communication, spurred significant development in human society, and brought unprecedented attention to cybersecurity issues. Cybersecurity research has evolved through four main stages: idealized security design, passive defense, and auxiliary examination, active analysis and strategy development, and comprehensive perception and trend prediction. Against the backdrop of the intense global competition for digital control, discussions on cybersecurity situational awareness exhibit new characteristics in both academic study and industrialization. This paper conducts an in-depth review of the literature on cybersecurity situational awareness, beginning with an introduction to the research status at home and abroad, followed by the proposal of a logical analysis framework for cybersecurity situational awareness based on the data value chain perspective. The process consists of five consecutive stages: factor acquisition, model representation, measurement establishment, solution analysis, and situation prediction Li et al., (2019). The Internet of Things (IoT) represents the third stage of development in the global information industry, fostering closer collaboration between users, networks, and perception devices. However, potential security issues in IoT could lead to various damages and pose threats to human lives and properties. To enhance monitoring capabilities, emergency response, and prediction of IoT security trends, a new approach called network security situation awareness (NSSA) has been introduced. Its effectiveness, however, is constrained by its capacity to extract and assess security elements from diverse network security information sources. To address this challenge, this paper presents an IoT network security situation awareness model that utilizes a situation reasoning method based on semantic ontology and user-defined rules. Ontology technology offers a standardized and formalized description to resolve semantic inconsistencies in the IoT security domain. The paper proposes four key sub-domains to characterize an IoT security situation: context, attack, vulnerability, and network flow. Furthermore, user-defined rules can compensate for the limited descriptive capability of ontology, thereby enhancing the reasoning capacity of our proposed ontology model. Real-world IoT scenarios demonstrate that network security situation awareness, which employs our situation reasoning method, exhibits more comprehensive and powerful reasoning capabilities compared to traditional NSSA methods Xu et al., (2017).

12.0 RECONNAISSANCE ATTACK DETECTION VIA BOOSTING MACHINE LEARNING CLASSIFIERS

With the rise of Internet technologies, concerns regarding network security are increasing rapidly. One of the most challenging aspects of network security is ensuring its protection. To identify and detect any malicious activities within the network, numerous security measures have been implemented. IDS ranks among the most commonly used strategies to mitigate the impact of these attacks. Reconnaissance represents a typical attack in computer networks where the attacker collects extensive information about the target before launching an attack. ML classifiers are frequently employed to differentiate between normal and anomalous network traffic. This paper examines the detection of reconnaissance attacks using the following ML classifiers: Adaptive Boosting (AdaBoost), Gradient Boosting, Cat Boosting, and eXtreme Gradient Boosting (XGBoost) to assess which classifier is the most effective at identifying reconnaissance attacks. The evaluation metrics applied include accuracy, precision, F-measure, and True Positive. Experiments conducted on the UNSW-NB15 dataset reveal that the Cat Boosting classifier outperforms XGBoost, AdaBoost, and Gradient Boosting Almomani et al., (2023).

13.0 PROTECTION AGAINST CLOUD-NATIVE MALWARE

Cloud-native services refer to applications specifically designed and built to leverage the full potential of cloud computing environments. Cloud-native services face unique cybersecurity challenges due to their decentralized infrastructure. They are susceptible to a range of risks, including malware, DDoS attacks, and Man-In-The-Middle (MITM) attacks. Moreover, these services often handle sensitive data that must be protected from unauthorized access. Additionally, the dynamic and scalable nature of cloud-native services makes it difficult to maintain consistent security, as the deployment of new instances and infrastructure introduces new vulnerabilities. To address these challenges, effective security solutions are essential to mitigate potential threats while adapting to the characteristics of cloud-native services. Despite the extensive focus on security in the cloud, there has been a noticeable lack of research specifically dedicated to the security of cloud-native services. To fill this gap, this work represents the first comprehensive survey dedicated to exploring security in cloud-native services. It aims to conduct a thorough investigation of the aspects, features, and solutions associated with security in cloud-native services. It functions as a uniquely structured mapping study that connects key aspects to corresponding features and these features to various contemporary solutions. Additionally, it involves identifying potential open-source technologies capable of supporting the implementation of each explored solution. Finally, it demonstrates how these solutions can work together to establish each corresponding feature. The insights and findings of this work can be used by cybersecurity professionals, including developers and researchers, to enhance the security of cloud-native services Theodoropoulos et al., (2023). Using cloud-native architecture to build digital products is now widely accepted as the best approach for developing Internet-scale applications. While there are numerous advantages, engineers face challenges when managing these systems in production. It is typical to have thousands of components running that need active supervision. Managing these systems is complex because they require monitoring and automation to ensure that the correct versions of these components are deployed, operational, and functioning correctly. Cloud-native architecture must also be capable of responding to changes resulting from bug fixes, feature additions, or modifications to address security issues Mitchell et al., (2024).

14.0 SECURITY OF DATA IN THE CLOUD

Cloud computing is an evolving revolution in the IT industry, offering high performance, accessibility, cost-effectiveness, and numerous other advantages. It enables businesses to maximize capacity and capabilities without the need for new infrastructure, additional personnel, or software licensing. Customers can access vast data storage and faster computing over the internet through cloud computing, which involves moving database and application software to large data centers known as the cloud. Despite the benefits, concerns about the reliability of data management and services in the cloud have caused some companies to hesitate in deploying their businesses in this environment. One significant issue is data security, which poses a challenge to the adoption of cloud computing. This paper suggests a framework with various techniques and specialized procedures to effectively secure data from the owner to the cloud and then to the user. The proposed approach starts by classifying data based on three cryptographic parameters: Confidentiality (C), Availability (A), and Integrity (I). To protect data, the strategy includes using measures such as 128-bit SSL (Secure Socket Layer) encryption, with the option to increase to 256-bit if needed. In addition, MAC (Message Authentication Code) is used for data integrity checks, along with searchable encryption and dividing the data into three sections for storage in the cloud. This division provides extra protection and facilitates data access Sood (2012).

15.0 PERFORMANCE INVESTIGATION OF PRINCIPAL COMPONENT ANALYSIS FOR INTRUSION DETECTION SYSTEM USING DIFFERENT SUPPORT VECTOR MACHINE KERNELS

Computer attacks are becoming more diverse and frequent as data exchange on the Internet increases. Traditional antivirus and firewall solutions are no longer sufficient for ensuring complete security in both wired and wireless networks, necessitating multiple layers of protection. An Intrusion Detection System (IDS) is a vital layer, continuously monitoring applications to defend against potential threats. The main types of IDS include signature-based detection (misuse detection), anomaly detection, and hybrid IDS. Signature-based detection matches gathered data against known attack patterns, proving effective for recognized threats but unable to identify new ones. Anomaly detection creates a model of normal behavior to spot irregularities, capable of detecting unknown attacks but often generating false positives. Hybrid IDS combines the strengths of both methods. ML techniques enhance IDS effectiveness in signature-based, anomaly-based, and hybrid detection, focusing on high accuracy. Key ML types include supervised, unsupervised, and semi-supervised learning, with Support Vector Machine (SVM) being the most prevalent. SVM classifies data by determining support vectors and identifying the optimal hyperplane for new data points. For non-linear classification, SVM can use various kernel functions. Feature selection is crucial in IDS, improving classification by identifying relevant features while removing redundant ones to maintain accuracy. Principal Component Analysis (PCA) is a popular unsupervised algorithm that reduces dimensionality, condenses variables while retaining key characteristics, and enhances computational efficiency Almaiah et al., (2022).

16.0 ACCURACY AND PRECISION OF MODELS

Accuracy and precision are critical metrics in evaluating the performance of ML models, yet they are often mistakenly used interchangeably. Understanding their differences is key to accurately assessing a model's predictive effectiveness. Accuracy refers to the proportion of correct predictions, both true positives and true negatives—among the total number of cases examined. It provides a broad overview of how often the model is right in its predictions. However, it can be misleading in scenarios where the data is imbalanced or when the implications of incorrect predictions vary significantly. In contrast, precision focuses specifically on the instances where the model predicts a positive result. High precision indicates that if the model claims a case is positive, there is a high likelihood that this assertion is correct. Nevertheless, precision does not consider how many actual positive cases were missed—known as false negatives. This is particularly important in applications where the cost of false positives is high, such as in spam filtering or medical diagnoses, where unnecessary interventions can have significant consequences. When striving for a comprehensive understanding of a model's performance, consider the context of your application. Assessing both accuracy and precision allows for a more nuanced evaluation, enabling you to choose the most appropriate metric to align with your specific goals and the potential consequences of false positives and false negatives. By doing so, you optimize your ML model's effectiveness according to the unique demands of your task.

17.0 AI-DRIVEN THREAT INTELLIGENCE

Table 1 lists some of the key features of AI-driven threat intelligence. The specific capabilities and benefits will vary depending on the tools and technologies used.

Table 1. AI-driven threat intelligence

Feature	Description	Example
Real-time threat detection	Identifies emerging threats as they occur, enabling rapid response.	Detecting a new malware variant as soon as it appears online.
Advanced anomaly detection	Uses AI algorithms to detect unusual patterns in network traffic or user behavior that may indicate a threat.	Identifying a sudden spike in login attempts from an unusual location.
Automated threat hunting	Uses AI to search for hidden threats within networks and systems.	Finding dormant malware that has evaded traditional detection methods.
ML-based threat classification	Categorizes threats into different types, such as malware, phishing, or ransomware.	They are automatically classifying new malware samples based on their behavior and characteristics.
Automated incident response	Triggers predefined actions to contain and mitigate threats.	It was automatically blocking malicious IP addresses or quarantining infected systems.
Continuous learning and adaptation	AI models can learn from new data and adapt to evolving threat landscapes.	Updating threat models to account for new vulnerabilities or attack techniques.

18.0 DEEP LEARNING-BASED NETWORK INTRUSION DETECTION FOR UNMANNED AERIAL VEHICLES (UAV)

Unmanned Aerial Vehicles (UAVs) have experienced considerable growth across a range of applications, such as surveillance, reconnaissance, and data gathering. However, the growing dependence on network connectivity makes UAVs vulnerable to potential cyber threats. Network intrusion detection systems (NIDS) play a crucial role in protecting the communication channels of UAVs. This paper introduces an innovative method to improve the security of UAV networks through the use of deep learning-based NIDS. The suggested system harnesses the power of deep neural networks to effectively identify and categorize network intrusions. We investigate the use of CNNs for feature extraction alongside RNNs for modeling sequences. The network undergoes training on an extensive dataset designed to simulate various attack scenarios to guarantee strong detection performance. Our experimental findings illustrate the effectiveness of the deep learning-based NIDS for UAVs. The system achieves high detection rates while maintaining low false-positive occurrences, making it appropriate for real-world scenarios. Additionally, the model shows adaptability to new attack techniques, as it can continuously learn and enhance its detection abilities. The proposed deep learning-based NIDS not only bolsters the cybersecurity of UAVs but also adds to the overall safety and reliability of UAV operations. As UAVs are more frequently incorporated into critical infrastructure and autonomous systems, the significance of strong network security measures cannot be emphasized enough. This research marks a notable advancement in ensuring the integrity and security of UAV networks in a fast-changing digital environment Ahmad et al., (2024).

19.0 AI-POWERED ETHICAL HACKING

In today's era of advanced digitalization and constant change, AI-driven chatbots represent a significant technological advancement. This type of chatbot showcases exceptional innovation worldwide in terms of efficiency and interaction across various domains. The transition from basic automated scripts to advanced natural language processing systems like Chat GPT marks a noteworthy progression in conversational technology. Nonetheless, this innovation comes with specific cybersecurity threats, as AI plays a dual role in both enhancing and compromising digital security. This research investigates the potential risks associated with AI chatbots and outlines suitable strategies for mitigation. This paper highlights the existing risks, threats, and implications posed by these digital assistants, and examines effective methods to diminish these risks and safeguard personal data and sensitive information. By integrating current research and viewpoints, it aims to present a comprehensive view of the challenges and opportunities that AI chatbots bring to the cybersecurity landscape. This serves as a foundation for developing my PhD proposal, which focuses on an Intelligent Chatbot that merges the latest large language models with its databases, ensuring a safe, practical, and user-friendly interface Syed & ES (2024).

20.0 FUTURE TRENDS AND INNOVATIONS

The intersection of AI and cybersecurity is rapidly progressing, leading to significant advancements and new risks. Several key trends and innovations are worth monitoring. These networks can produce highly complex and elusive malware variations that can evade traditional detection systems. Malware can learn and adapt in real time, making detection and management more challenging. AI can create particularly convincing phishing tactics that exploit human vulnerabilities. It can analyze extensive data sets to identify anomalies and potential threats that might escape human analysts' attention. AI can improve routine tasks, such as isolating compromised devices and fixing security vulnerabilities, ultimately enhancing response times. It can monitor user behavior patterns to identify possible breaches or suspicious activities. Ethical hackers can leverage AI to simulate attacks and identify system weaknesses before they can be exploited by malicious actors. The incorporation of AI in cybersecurity raises ethical concerns, including the risk of widespread surveillance and the potential for misuse. As AI-driven malware becomes more advanced, cybersecurity professionals will have to continuously adapt their strategies to stay proactive. The collection and analysis of large data sets for cybersecurity might raise privacy issues. The future of AI in the cybersecurity realm is likely to be characterized by an ongoing battle between attackers and defenders. As AI technologies advance, we can expect the rise of even more sophisticated malware along with innovative cybersecurity solutions. It will be crucial to address the ethical and privacy challenges associated with these technologies to ensure their responsible application in protecting our digital environment. The rapid rise of ransomware attacks poses significant challenges for traditional cybersecurity methods, necessitating new approaches for effective detection and response.

This study proposes a comprehensive strategy that employs AI to enhance the identification, analysis, and prevention of ransomware attacks. By integrating ML, DL, and NLP techniques, this strategy aims to establish a strong defense mechanism against the advanced methods employed by ransomware attackers. Our method involves using both supervised and unsupervised ML algorithms to identify ransomware signatures and unusual behaviors that could indicate upcoming attacks. Notably, CNNs are utilized to detect patterns in file structures and network traffic associated with ransomware. RNNs, particularly Long Short-Term Memory (LSTM) networks, are used to analyze time-series data of system activities, identifying anomalies that may suggest ransomware execution. NLP techniques are included to assess threat intelligence from unstructured text sources, such as dark web forums and phishing emails, allowing the extraction of relevant Indicators of Compromise (IOCs) and a more comprehensive understanding of the evolving threat landscape. Methods like sentiment analysis and topic modeling further enhance our predictive capabilities by revealing emerging ransomware trends and the motivations of the involved actors Maddireddy et al., (2021).

21.0 REAL-WORLD APPLICATIONS AND CASE STUDIES

The use of AI in healthcare has revealed significant opportunities for innovation in public health during the COVID-19 pandemic. Various AI-driven initiatives have been implemented within the broader community through joint efforts. It is essential to comprehend the recent advancements and their limitations to anticipate and have confidence in any upcoming trends related to AI-based solutions. Further research is needed to investigate the scalability of these solutions for managing future pandemics and to enhance strategic readiness against emerging COVID-19 variants alongside other global health crises Nawaz et al., (2022).

21.1 XAI for Cyber Security of Smart Transportation

The rise of advanced technologies such as Software-Defined Networks (SDNs), IIoT, Blockchain, AI, and Vehicular Ad Hoc Networks (VANETs) has led to increased operational complexity while effectively integrating smart transportation systems. Nevertheless, these systems can face security issues that expose them to potential intrusions. Furthermore, security challenges in transportation technology impact the AI models used. Key transportation infrastructures like Wireless Sensor Networks (WSN), Vehicle-to-everything communication (V2X), VMS, and Traffic Signal Controllers (TSC) have already been targeted or remain vulnerable to hacking attempts. To counteract these cyber threats and safeguard the smart transportation system, AI-enabled IDS have recently been introduced. Although AI has shown remarkable advancements in enhancing the performance of smart transportation systems over the last few years, the use of explainable AI (XAI) techniques is still necessary, as XAI can help the smart transportation system monitor factors like driver behavior, accident causes, and vehicle conditions Zhang et al., (2022). To protect our digital devices, networks, and information from cyber threats, individuals, companies, and governments need to keep investing in cyber security Admass et al., (2024).

22.0 STUDYING AI, ML, DL, AND NLP MODELS IS CRUCIAL FOR SEVERAL KEY REASONS

AI/ML/DL/NLP are driving innovation across industries, from autonomous vehicles and medical diagnostics to personalized education and financial predictions. These technologies excel at solving complex problems that humans struggle with, such as analyzing vast datasets, identifying intricate patterns, and making accurate forecasts. This has profound implications for fields like healthcare, climate science, and finance. Furthermore, they stimulate economic growth by creating jobs, enhancing productivity, and fostering the development of new sectors. Notably, these technologies can significantly contribute to addressing global challenges such as climate change, poverty, and disease by providing valuable insights and enabling more effective solutions. Finally, studying these models deepens our understanding of the world by offering novel approaches to data analysis, knowledge extraction, and informed decision-making.

23.0 ADVERSARIAL ATTACKS ON AI SYSTEMS

As public and academic interest continues to grow regarding the evolving role of machine learning in the health information economy, a unique and previously obscure category of vulnerabilities within machine-learning systems may become significant. These vulnerabilities permit a minor, strategically crafted modification in how inputs are presented to a system, which can drastically change its output, leading it to confidently reach incorrect conclusions. The advanced methods used to compromise otherwise dependable machine-learning systems—known as adversarial attacks—have primarily attracted the attention of researchers in computer science thus far. However, the complex web of often conflicting interests presents in the healthcare sector, coupled with the potential for substantial financial impacts stemming from the outputs of these systems, suggests a range of challenges. We outline the potential motivations that different stakeholders in the healthcare system might have for employing adversarial attacks and initiate a discussion on how to address them. Rather than deterring ongoing innovations in medical machine learning, we advocate for the proactive collaboration of medical, technical, legal, and ethical professionals to foster efficient, widely accessible, and effective healthcare that machine learning can facilitate Finlayson et al., (2019).

24.0 ENHANCING IOT INTELLIGENCE: A TRANSFORMER-BASED REINFORCEMENT LEARNING METHODOLOGY

The growth of the IoT has resulted in a vast increase in data generated by connected devices, creating both opportunities and challenges for intelligent decision-making in complex settings. Conventional RL methods frequently find it difficult to effectively utilize this data due to their constrained capacity to process and interpret the complex patterns and relationships that are typical in IoT applications. A new framework that combines transformer architectures with Proximal Policy Optimization (PPO) to tackle these issues. By utilizing the self-attention mechanism associated with transformers, our method enhances the ability of RL agents to comprehend and operate in dynamic IoT environments, resulting in more effective decision-making processes. We showcase the effectiveness of our approach across a range of IoT applications, including smart home automation and industrial control systems, demonstrating significant improvements in decision-making efficiency and adaptability. Our contributions consist of a thorough examination of the transformer's role in handling diverse IoT data, an extensive assessment of the framework's performance in various settings, and a comparison against traditional RL approaches. The findings reveal substantial progress in empowering RL agents to navigate the intricacies of IoT ecosystems, emphasizing the potential of our method to transform intelligent automation and decision-making within the IoT domain Rjoub et al., (2024).

25.0 CONCLUSION

AI is transforming industries by enhancing efficiency through innovative applications, particularly in conjunction with IoT. This integration allows for better data sensing and transfer between interconnected devices, improving tasks across various sectors, such as agriculture—where AI optimizes soil assessment and crop management—and weather forecasting, which helps predict conditions to mitigate disasters. The collaboration of AI, IoT, and smart devices is vital in enhancing cybersecurity. As IoT adoption grows, addressing cyber threats becomes crucial. AI is expected to aid cybersecurity professionals quickly identifying and counteracting attacks, minimizing potential losses. Everyday examples, like spam email detection, highlight the importance of cybersecurity, especially in critical areas like healthcare. Cybersecurity safeguards systems from threats that compromise data confidentiality, integrity, and availability. It faces challenges from hackers, state actors, and internal risks, with key issues revolving around advanced cyber-attacks, AI-driven malware, and vulnerabilities in IoT and cloud security. Despite these challenges, innovations like quantum computing and enhanced AI capabilities offer promising solutions for future cybersecurity efforts.

25.1 Future Scope

Taking a proactive stance on cybersecurity by utilizing AI-powered malware detection is essential for bolstering security through early identification of threats, swift response, enhanced threat intelligence, effective resource management, flexibility, and minimized risks and expenses. AI is particularly adept at examining large datasets to uncover subtle patterns, facilitating timely recognition of threats and allowing for immediate automated actions. By evaluating threat information, AI can offer crucial insights into the methods employed by attackers, aiding organizations in understanding and adapting to changing threats. Additionally, AI can streamline routine security operations, allowing security teams to concentrate on more strategic matters. This proactive methodology, fueled by AI, empowers organizations to transition from reactive to proactive, significantly enhancing their capacity to ward off cyber threats.

REFERENCES

Abiodun, O. I., Jantan, A., Omolara, A. E., Dada, K. V., Mohamed, N. A., & Arshad, H. (2018). State-of-the-art in artificial neural network applications: A survey. *Heliyon*, 4(11), e00938. DOI: 10.1016/j.heliyon.2018.e00938 PMID: 30519653

Admass, W. S., Munaye, Y. Y., & Diro, A. A. (2024). Cyber security: State of the art, challenges, and future directions. *Cyber Security and Applications*, 2, 100031. DOI: 10.1016/j.csa.2023.100031

Ahmad, W., Almaiah, M. A., Ali, A., & Al-Shareeda, M. A. (2024, April). Deep Learning Based Network intrusion detection for unmanned aerial vehicle (UAV). In *2024 7th World Conference on Computing and Communication Technologies (WCCCT)* (pp. 31-36). IEEE.

Almaiah, M. A., Almomani, O., Alsaaidah, A., Al-Otaibi, S., Bani-Hani, N., Hwaitat, A. K. A., Al-Zahrani, A., Lutfi, A., Awad, A. B., & Aldhyani, T. H. (2022). Performance investigation of principal component analysis for intrusion detection system using different support vector machine kernels. *Electronics (Basel)*, 11(21), 3571. DOI: 10.3390/electronics11213571

Almomani, O., Almaiah, M. A., Madi, M., Alsaaidah, A., Almomani, M. A., & Smadi, S. (2023, October). Reconnaissance attack detection via boosting machine learning classifiers. In *AIP Conference Proceedings* (Vol. 2979, No. 1). AIP Publishing. DOI: 10.1063/5.0174730

Cheng, Y., Liu, Y., Chen, T., & Yang, Q. (2020). Federated learning for privacy-preserving AI. *Communications of the ACM*, 63(12), 33–36. DOI: 10.1145/3387107

Choudhary, S. P., & Vidyarthi, M. D. (2015). A simple method for detection of metamorphic malware using dynamic analysis and text mining. *Procedia Computer Science*, 54, 265–270. DOI: 10.1016/j.procs.2015.06.031

Finlayson, S. G., Bowers, J. D., Ito, J., Zittrain, J. L., Beam, A. L., & Kohane, I. S. (2019). Adversarial attacks on medical machine learning. *Science*, 363(6433), 1287–1289. DOI: 10.1126/science.aaw4399 PMID: 30898923

Huyen, N. T. M., & Bao, T. Q. (2024). Advancements in AI-Driven Cybersecurity and Comprehensive Threat Detection and Response. *Journal of Intelligent Connectivity and Emerging Technologies*, 9(1), 1–12.

. Learning, S. S. (2006). Semi-supervised learning. *CSZ2006. html, 5*, 2.

Li, Y., Huang, G. Q., Wang, C. Z., & Li, Y. C. (2019). Analysis framework of network security situational awareness and comparison of implementation methods. *EURASIP Journal on Wireless Communications and Networking*, 2019(1), 1–32. DOI: 10.1186/s13638-019-1506-1

Maddireddy, B. R., & Maddireddy, B. R. (2021). Evolutionary Algorithms in AI-Driven Cybersecurity Solutions for Adaptive Threat Mitigation. *International Journal of Advanced Engineering Technologies and Innovations*, 1(2), 17–43.

Mahesh, B. (2020). Machine learning algorithms-a review. *International Journal of Science and Research (IJSR).Internet.*, 9(1), 381–386.

McLaren, P., Russell, G., & Buchanan, B. (2017, July). *Mining malware command and control traces. In 2017 Computing conference*. IEEE.

Mihalcea, R., Liu, H., & Lieberman, H. (2006). NLP (natural language processing) for NLP (natural language programming). In *Computational Linguistics and Intelligent Text Processing: 7th International Conference, CICLing 2006, Mexico City, Mexico, February 19-25, 2006.* [Springer Berlin Heidelberg.]. *Proceedings*, 7, 319–330.

. Mitchell, B. S., Chandnani, A., Carter, J., Roumelioti, D., & Mancoridis, S. (2024). Malware Detection in Cloud Native Environments.

Nadella, G. S., & Gonaygunta, H. (2024). Enhancing Cybersecurity with Artificial Intelligence: Predictive Techniques and Challenges in the Age of IoT. *International Journal of Science and Engineering Applications*, 13(04), 30–33.

Nadkarni, P. M., Ohno-Machado, L., & Chapman, W. W. (2011). Natural language processing: An introduction. *Journal of the American Medical Informatics Association : JAMIA*, 18(5), 544–551. DOI: 10.1136/amiajnl-2011-000464 PMID: 21846786

Nawaz, F. A., Khan, A. R., & Boillat, T. (2022). AI-enhanced solutions during COVID-19: Current trends and future innovations. *Annals of Medicine and Surgery (London)*, 80, 80. DOI: 10.1016/j.amsu.2022.104158 PMID: 35855874

Poudyal, S., & Dasgupta, D. (2020, December). AI-powered ransomware detection framework. In *2020 IEEE Symposium Series on Computational Intelligence (SSCI)* (pp. 1154-1161). IEEE. DOI: 10.1109/SSCI47803.2020.9308387

Rjoub, G., Islam, S., Bentahar, J., Almaiah, M. A., & Alrawashdeh, R. (2024). Enhancing IoT Intelligence: A Transformer-based Reinforcement Learning Methodology. *arXiv preprint arXiv:2404.04205.* DOI: 10.1109/IWCMC61514.2024.10592607

Salem, A. H., Azzam, S. M., Emam, O. E., & Abohany, A. A. (2024). Advancing cybersecurity: A comprehensive review of AI-driven detection techniques. *Journal of Big Data*, 11(1), 105. DOI: 10.1186/s40537-024-00957-y

Sarker, I. H. (2021). Machine learning: Algorithms, real-world applications and research directions. *SN Computer Science*, 2(3), 160. DOI: 10.1007/s42979-021-00592-x PMID: 33778771

Shakya, A. K., Pillai, G., & Chakrabarty, S. (2023). Reinforcement learning algorithms: A brief survey. *Expert Systems with Applications*, 231, 120495. DOI: 10.1016/j.eswa.2023.120495

Sood, S. K. (2012). A combined approach to ensure data security in cloud computing. *Journal of Network and Computer Applications*, 35(6), 1831–1838. DOI: 10.1016/j.jnca.2012.07.007

Suarez-Tangil, G., Tapiador, J. E., Peris-Lopez, P., & Blasco, J. (2014). Dendroid: A text mining approach to analyzing and classifying code structures in android malware families. *Expert Systems with Applications*, 41(4), 1104–1117. DOI: 10.1016/j.eswa.2013.07.106

Syed, F. M., & ES, F. K. (2024). AI-Powered Security for Internet of Medical Things (IoMT) Devices. *Revista de Inteligencia Artificial en Medicina*, 15(1), 556–582.

Thakur, M. R., Khilnani, D. R., Gupta, K., Jain, S., Agarwal, V., Sane, S., Sanyal, S., & Dhekne, P. S. (2012). Detection and prevention of botnets and malware in an enterprise network. *International Journal of Wireless and Mobile Computing*, 5(2), 144–153. DOI: 10.1504/IJWMC.2012.046776

Theodoropoulos, T., Rosa, L., Benzaid, C., Gray, P., Marin, E., Makris, A., Cordeiro, L., Diego, F., Sorokin, P., Girolamo, M. D., Barone, P., Taleb, T., & Tserpes, K. (2023). Security in Cloud-Native Services: A Survey. *Journal of Cybersecurity and Privacy*, 3(4), 758–793. DOI: 10.3390/jcp3040034

Warmer, M. (2011). *Detection of web based command & control channels* (Master's thesis, University of Twente).

Xu, G., Cao, Y., Ren, Y., Li, X., & Feng, Z. (2017). Network security situation awareness based on semantic ontology and user-defined rules for Internet of Things. *IEEE Access : Practical Innovations, Open Solutions*, 5, 21046–21056. DOI: 10.1109/ACCESS.2017.2734681

Yang, L. X., & Yang, X. (2012). Propagation behavior of virus codes in the situation that infected computers are connected to the Internet with positive probability. *Discrete Dynamics in Nature and Society*, 2012(1), 693695. DOI: 10.1155/2012/693695

Zeadally, S., Adi, E., Baig, Z., & Khan, I. A. (2020). Harnessing artificial intelligence capabilities to improve cybersecurity. *IEEE Access : Practical Innovations, Open Solutions*, 8, 23817–23837. DOI: 10.1109/ACCESS.2020.2968045

Zhang, Z., Al Hamadi, H., Damiani, E., Yeun, C. Y., & Taher, F. (2022). Explainable artificial intelligence applications in cyber security: State-of-the-art in research. *IEEE Access : Practical Innovations, Open Solutions*, 10, 93104–93139. DOI: 10.1109/ACCESS.2022.3204051

Chapter 3

Art of Network Monitoring and Security Enhancement Using AI-Driven Tools

G. Pradeep Kumar
https://orcid.org/0000-0002-9381-2889
Velammal Educational Trust, India

B. Sridevi
Velammal Educational Trust, India

P. Suveetha Dhanaselvam
Velammal Educational Trust, India

K. Kavitha
Velammal Educational Trust, India

P. Karthikeyan
https://orcid.org/0000-0001-8515-7370
Velammal Educational Trust, India

B. Karthikeyan
Velammal Educational Trust, India

ABSTRACT

This paper explores the "Art of Network Monitoring and Security Enhancement Using AI-Driven Tools," examining how artificial intelligence (AI) is revolutionizing network security by enhancing threat detection, incident response, and overall network resilience. Traditional security measures often struggle to keep pace with the dynamic nature of modern threats, leading to increased vulnerability and potential for significant disruption. AI, with its ability to analyse vast amounts of data, identify patterns, and make predictions, offers a powerful solution to these challenges. This paper delves into various AI/ML techniques, such as machine learning, deep learning, and natural language processing, and their applications in network security, including threat detection, intrusion prevention, incident response, and network traffic analysis. By embracing AI-driven solutions, organizations can effectively address the challenges of the evolving threat landscape and protect their critical assets in the digital age.

1. INTRODUCTION

In today's hyper-connected world, networks are the lifeblood of businesses, enabling seamless communication, data flow, and operations. However, this interconnectedness also brings significant security challenges. The rise of sophisticated cyber threats, such as advanced persistent threats (APTs), ransomware, and zero-day exploits, demands a proactive and adaptive approach to network security.

DOI: 10.4018/979-8-3693-9919-4.ch003

Traditional security measures, often relying on static rules and signatures, are increasingly struggling to keep pace with the dynamic nature of these threats. Artificial Intelligence (AI) Huang et al. (2016), Sharafaldin et al. (2018) emerges as a transformative force in this landscape, revolutionizing how we monitor and secure our networks. AI-powered solutions leverage advanced algorithms and machine learning techniques to analyse massive volumes of network data, identify anomalies, and predict potential threats with unprecedented accuracy. By continuously learning and adapting, these systems can detect and respond to cyber attacks in real-time, surpassing the limitations of human analysts. AI-based network security encompasses a wide range of applications, including anomaly detection, threat hunting, intrusion detection, malware detection, and vulnerability assessment. By embracing AI-driven solutions, organizations can enhance their security posture, improve threat detection and response capabilities, and ultimately minimize the impact of cyber attacks on their operations.

The evolving threat landscape in AI-based network monitoring and security presents a dynamic and challenging environment. Cybercriminals are increasingly leveraging AI to craft sophisticated attacks, including AI-generated malware, AI-powered phishing, and AI-driven DDoS attacks. These attacks are becoming more complex and sophisticated, utilizing zero-day exploits, advanced persistent threats, and supply chain attacks. This arms race necessitates continuous adaptation of AI-based security solutions, demanding ongoing research and development to stay ahead of evolving threats. Furthermore, the ethical implications of AI in cyber security, including the potential for misuse and the need to address bias, require careful consideration.

The modern threat landscape is characterized by:

- **Sophistication:** Cyber attacks have become more sophisticated, employing advanced techniques like zero-day exploits, ransom ware, and targeted attacks.
- **Velocity:** Threats evolve rapidly, with new vulnerabilities and attack vectors emerging constantly.
- **Volume:** The sheer volume of network traffic and security alerts is overwhelming for human analysts, making it difficult to identify and respond to critical threats in a timely manner.
- **Stealth:** Advanced persistent threats (APTs) can remain undetected within a network for extended periods, enabling attackers to exfiltration sensitive data or disrupt critical operations.

These factors underscore the urgent need for innovative security solutions that can effectively address the evolving threat landscape.

2. LIMITATIONS OF TRADITIONAL NETWORK SECURITY

Traditional network security measures, while essential, face significant limitations in today's evolving threat landscape. These limitations stem from inherent design constraints, the rapid evolution of cyber attacks Kumar et al. (2021), Jahani & Rahmati (2021) and the increasing complexity of modern networks.

2.1. Signature-Based Detection:

Reliance on Known Threats: Many traditional security tools, such as antivirus software and intrusion detection systems (IDS) Chandola et al. (2009), rely heavily on signature-based detection. This approach involves identifying and blocking known threats based on pre-defined patterns or signatures.

Ineffectiveness Against Novel Attacks: Signature-based detection is inherently limited in its ability to identify and respond to novel or zero-day attacks. These attacks exploit previously unknown vulnerabilities and do not have pre-existing signatures. As a result, they can often bypass traditional defenses undetected.

Limited Pro activeness: Signature-based detection is primarily reactive. It relies on identifying known threats and then updating security measures accordingly. This approach struggles to proactively identify and prevent emerging threats.

2.2. False Positives and Negatives:

High False Positive Rates: Traditional security tools often generate a high number of false positives. This occurs when normal network activity is mistakenly identified as malicious. The constant stream of false alarms can overwhelm security teams, hindering their ability to investigate and respond to genuine threats.

Missed Threats: Conversely, traditional systems can also miss critical threats, leading to delayed response times and increased risk. This can occur when attacks evade signature-based detection or when the system fails to recognize subtle anomalies.

2.3. Limited Visibility and Context:

Lack of Comprehensive Visibility: Traditional security tools often provide limited visibility into network traffic and user activity. This lack of comprehensive context makes it difficult to understand the overall security posture and identify potential threats.

Difficulty in Correlating Events: Traditional systems struggle to correlate events across different security domains, such as network traffic, endpoint activity, and user behaviour. This makes it challenging to understand the full scope of an attack and determine the appropriate response.

2.4. Manual Analysis and Response:

Time-Consuming and Error-Prone: Analysing large volumes of security logs and alerts manually is time-consuming, tedious, and prone to human error. This can delay threat identification and response, increasing the potential impact of an attack.

Difficulty in Keeping Pace: The volume and complexity of cyber threats are constantly increasing. Manual analysis struggles to keep pace with this rapid evolution, making it difficult to effectively identify and respond to emerging threats.

2.5. Difficulty in Adapting to Change:

Slow Response to New Threats: Traditional security solutions often require manual updates to address new threats. This can lead to delays in protection and increase the risk of exploitation.

Limited Scalability: As networks become more complex and dynamic, traditional security solutions may struggle to scale effectively. This can lead to performance issues and reduced effectiveness.

2.6. Reliance on Perimeter Security:

Shifting Threat Landscape: The traditional focus on perimeter security, such as firewalls, is becoming increasingly ineffective in today's interconnected world. With the rise of remote work, cloud computing, and mobile devices, the network perimeter has become more fluid and less defined.

Exploitation of Weaknesses: Attackers are increasingly exploiting vulnerabilities within the network perimeter, such as weak passwords, unpatched software, and social engineering attacks.

2.7. Lack of Proactive Threat Hunting:

Reactive Approach: Traditional security measures primarily focus on reacting to known threats. They lack the proactive capabilities to actively hunt for and investigate potential threats Li et al. (2018).

Increased Risk of Advanced Threats: This reactive approach increases the risk of advanced persistent threats (APTs) remaining undetected within a network for extended periods, enabling attackers to exfiltrate sensitive data or disrupt critical operations.

2.8. Difficulty in Integrating with Modern IT Environments:

Challenges with Cloud and Mobile: Traditional security solutions may struggle to effectively protect modern IT environments, such as cloud computing and mobile devices. This can create gaps in security coverage and increase the risk of attack.

Lack of Visibility and Control: Integrating traditional security tools with modern IT environments can be challenging, leading to limited visibility and control over security posture.

2.9. Skills Gap:

Lack of Skilled Personnel: Implementing and managing traditional security solutions requires skilled personnel with expertise in security technologies and best practices. However, there is a significant shortage of skilled cyber security professionals.

Difficulty in Adapting to New Technologies: As new technologies and threats emerge, the skills and knowledge required to effectively manage network security are constantly evolving. This requires ongoing training and development for security teams.

2.10. Cost Considerations:

High Costs: Implementing and maintaining traditional security solutions can be expensive, requiring significant investments in hardware, software, and personnel.

Limited Return on Investment: In some cases, traditional security measures may not provide a sufficient return on investment, especially in the face of increasingly sophisticated and evasive threats

3. THE RISE OF AI IN NETWORK SECURITY

AI, with its ability to analyse vast amounts of data, identify patterns, and make predictions, offers a powerful solution to the challenges of modern network security. Key AI/ML techniques LeCun et al. (2015), LeCun et al. (1998) applied in network security include:

3.1. Machine Learning (ML):

Machine learning (ML) empowers AI-based network security by enabling computers to learn from data and identify patterns. This allows for the detection of anomalies, such as unusual traffic patterns or suspicious user behaviour that may indicate malicious activity. ML algorithms can analyse vast amounts of network data, identifying subtle deviations from normal operations that might be missed by human analysts. This proactive approach enhances threat detection, reduces false positives, and enables faster response times to security incidents, ultimately improving the overall security posture of an organization.

Figure 1. AI based network monitoring and security

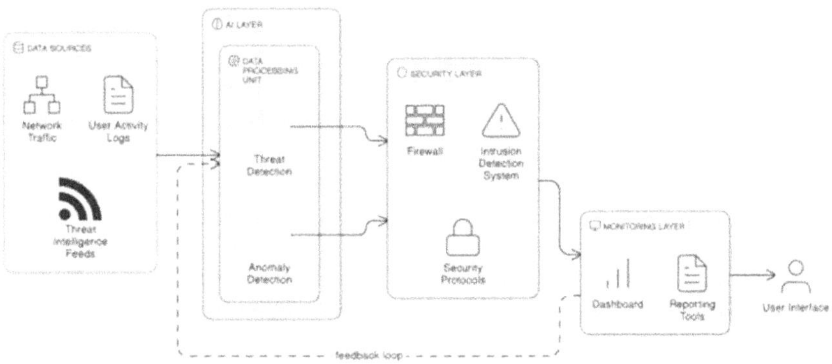

3.1.1. Supervised Learning:

Trains models Ghorbani (2014) on labelled data (e.g., known malware, normal traffic patterns) to classify new data as malicious or benign. Techniques include:

- **Classification:** Categorizing network traffic as malicious or benign.
- **Regression:** Predicting the likelihood of a security incident.

3.1.2. Unsupervised Learning: Identifies patterns and anomalies in network traffic without prior labelling. Techniques include:

- **Clustering:** Grouping similar network activities, potentially identifying unusual behaviour.
- **Anomaly detection:** Detecting deviations from normal network behaviour, such as unexpected traffic spikes or unusual communication patterns.

3.2. Deep Learning:

Deep learning, a subfield of artificial intelligence, has emerged as a powerful tool for enhancing network monitoring and security. By leveraging deep neural networks with multiple layers, deep learning algorithms can analyse complex patterns and relationships in network data, enabling more accurate and sophisticated threat detection.

3.2.1. Convolutional Neural Networks (CNNs)

- Excel at analysing image-like data, such as network traffic patterns visualized as heat maps or spectrograms.
- Can effectively identify spatial and temporal patterns within network data.
- Used for tasks like:
    - Intrusion Detection: Identifying malicious traffic patterns within network flows.
    - Malware Classification: Analysing malware byte code or network behaviour for classification.
    - Anomaly Detection: Detecting unusual traffic patterns or deviations from normal network behaviour.
        - Example: A CNN could analyse network traffic data to identify patterns associated with specific types of malware, such as ransom ware or botnet communication.

3.2.2. Recurrent Neural Networks (RNNs)

- Designed to process sequential data, such as time series data.
- Can capture temporal dependencies and long-term patterns within network traffic.
- Types of RNNs:
    - Long Short-Term Memory (LSTM) networks: Effective for handling long-term dependencies in sequential data.
    - Gated Recurrent Units (GRUs): Simpler than LSTMs, offering a good balance between performance and complexity.
        - Example: An RNN could analyse network logs to detect evolving attack patterns, such as the progression of an intrusion within a network over time.

3.2.3. Auto encoders

- Unsupervised learning models that learn to reconstruct input data.
- Used for anomaly detection by identifying instances that cannot be accurately reconstructed.
- Can learn compressed representations of normal network traffic.
    - Example: An auto encoder could be trained on normal network traffic. When presented with anomalous traffic (e.g., a malware infection), the auto encoder would struggle to reconstruct it, indicating a potential threat.

3.2.4. Generative Adversarial Networks (GANs)

- Comprised of two neural networks: a generator and a discriminator.
- Can generate synthetic network traffic data that mimics real-world patterns.
- Used for:
    - Anomaly Detection: Generating synthetic normal traffic and comparing it to real-time traffic to identify deviations.
    - Threat Simulation: Generating realistic attack scenarios for testing and evaluating security defenses.

Figure 2. GAN based network architecture

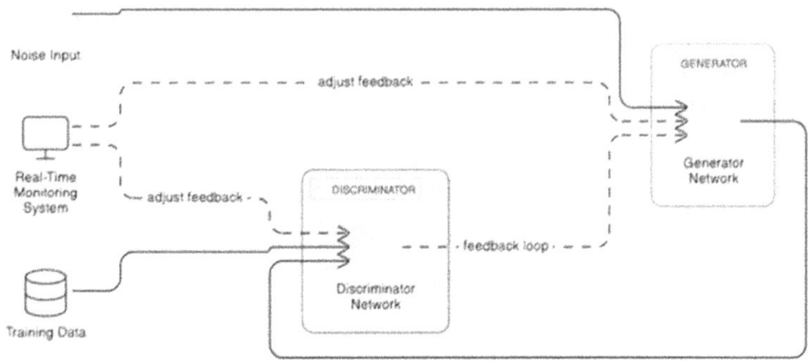

- Example: A GAN could generate synthetic normal network traffic. Security analysts could then use this synthetic data to train and evaluate intrusion detection systems.

3.2.5. Graph Neural Networks (GNNs)

- Designed to analyse graph-structured data, such as network topologies.
- Can identify vulnerabilities in network infrastructure by analysing relationships between devices and nodes.
- Used for:

- Network Vulnerability Assessment: Identifying critical nodes and potential attack paths within a network.
- Botnet Detection: Identifying interconnected devices within a botnet.
    - Example: A GNN could analyse the relationships between devices on a network to identify critical nodes that, if compromised, could significantly impact the overall network security.

3.3. Natural Language Processing (NLP):

Natural Language Processing (NLP) Bishop (2002) plays a crucial role in enhancing AI-based network monitoring and security. By enabling machines to understand and interpret human language, NLP empowers organizations to leverage textual data for improved threat detection, incident response, and overall security posture.

3.3.1. Threat Intelligence Analysis:

- **Extracting Key Information:** NLP algorithms can analyse threat intelligence feeds, security advisories, and research papers to extract key information, such as indicators of compromise (IOCs), threat actor tactics, techniques, and procedures (TTPs), and emerging threats.
- **Identifying Trends and Patterns:** By analysing large volumes of threat intelligence data, NLP can identify emerging threats and trends, enabling organizations to proactively address potential risks.
- **Correlating Information:** NLP can correlate information from various threat intelligence sources to gain a more comprehensive understanding of the threat landscape.

3.3.2. Phishing Detection:

- **Analysing Email Content:** NLP algorithms can analyse the content of emails, including the sender, subject, and body, to identify potential phishing attempts.
- **Detecting Malicious URLs and Attachments:** NLP can detect malicious URLs and attachments within emails by analysing their content and context.
- **Identifying Social Engineering Tactics:** NLP can identify social engineering tactics used in phishing emails, such as urgency, fear, and impersonation.

3.3.3. Security Log Analysis:

- **Extracting Relevant Information:** NLP can extract relevant information from security logs, such as error messages, event timestamps, and user actions.
- **Identifying Anomalies:** By analysing the language used in security logs, NLP can identify anomalies that may indicate malicious activity.
- **Correlating Events:** NLP can correlate events across different security logs to gain a better understanding of the scope and impact of security incidents.

3.3.4. **Vulnerability Assessment:**

- **Analysing Security Advisories:** NLP can analyse security advisories and vulnerability reports to identify potential vulnerabilities and their potential impact.
- **Prioritizing Remediation Efforts:** NLP can help prioritize remediation efforts by analysing the severity and likelihood of exploitation for different vulnerabilities.

4. AI-DRIVEN NETWORK SECURITY SOLUTIONS

AI is transforming network security across various domains are,

4.1 AI-Powered Intrusion Detection Systems (AI-IDS)

AI-powered intrusion detection systems (AI-IDS) Kaufman et al. (2002) represent a significant advancement in network security. These systems leverage the power of artificial intelligence, specifically machine learning and deep learning algorithms, to go beyond traditional signature-based detection methods.

4.1.1 How AI-IDS Work:

Figure 3. AI powered intrusion detection system

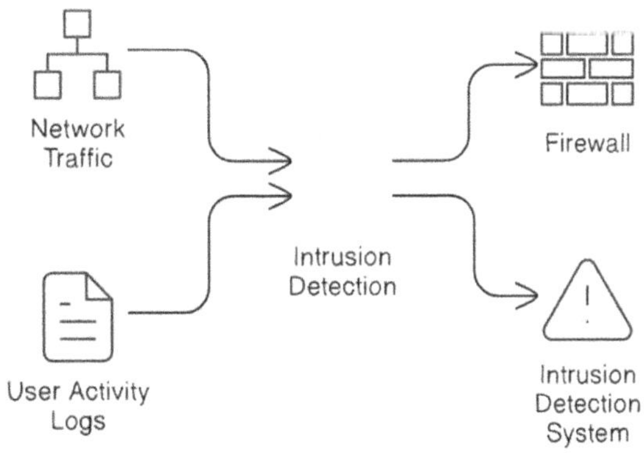

Data Collection and Analysis: AI-IDS continuously monitor network traffic, system logs, and user activities, collecting vast amounts of data. This data is then processed and analysed using advanced algorithms.

Anomaly Detection: AI algorithms are trained to identify deviations from normal network behaviour. This includes identifying unusual traffic patterns, unexpected spikes in activity, or unauthorized access attempts. By analysing historical data and establishing baseline behaviour, AI-IDS can detect anomalies that might indicate malicious activity.

Machine Learning and Deep Learning: AI-IDS employ various machine learning techniques, such as:

- o **Supervised Learning:** Trains models on labelled data (known attacks and normal traffic) to classify new data as malicious or benign.
- o **Unsupervised Learning:** Identifies patterns and anomalies in network traffic without prior labelling.
- o **Deep Learning:** Utilizes neural networks to analyse complex patterns and relationships in network data, enabling the detection of sophisticated and evolving threats.

Real-time Threat Detection: AI-IDS can analyse network traffic in real-time, providing immediate alerts when suspicious activity is detected. This allows for rapid response to threats, minimizing potential damage.

Key Advantages of AI-IDS:

- **Enhanced Threat Detection:** AI-IDS can detect novel and zero-day attacks that traditional signature-based systems might miss.
- **Reduced False Positives:** By analysing complex patterns and behaviours, AI-IDS can minimize false alarms, reducing alert fatigue and improving the efficiency of security teams.
- **Proactive Threat Hunting:** AI-IDS can proactively search for and investigate potential threats, enabling organizations to take pre-emptive action.
- **Improved Accuracy and Efficiency:** AI-IDS can analyse vast amounts of data quickly and accurately, identifying threats that might be missed by human analysts.
- **Continuous Learning and Adaptation:** AI-IDS can continuously learn and adapt to new threats, improving their detection capabilities over time.

4.2. Malware detection and prevention:

AI algorithms Sharma et al. (2018) can effectively identify and classify malicious software, including polymorphic malware that constantly changes its form.

- o **Phishing detection:** AI can analyse emails and websites to identify and block phishing attempts.
- o **Botnet detection:** AI can identify and disrupt botnets by analysing communication patterns and identifying command-and-control servers.

4.3. Incident Response and Remediation:

- **Automated Incident Response:** AI can automate routine incident response tasks, such as isolating infected systems, blocking malicious traffic, and deploying countermeasures. This frees up security teams to focus on more complex and critical issues.
- **Threat Hunting:** AI algorithms can analyse vast amounts of data to identify and investigate potential threats that may have evaded initial detection. This proactive approach allows organizations to address threats before they can cause significant damage.
- **Root Cause Analysis:** AI can help pinpoint the root cause of security incidents by analysing historical data, identifying patterns, and correlating events. This accelerates the investigation process and enables faster remediation.

- **Vulnerability Prioritization:** AI can prioritize vulnerabilities based on their severity, potential impact, and likelihood of exploitation. This allows security teams to focus their remediation efforts on the most critical issues.
- **Forensics and Investigation:** AI can assist in forensic investigations by analysing system logs, network traffic, and other relevant data to reconstruct the timeline of an attack and identify the attacker's tactics, techniques, and procedures (TTPs).

Benefits of AI-Driven Incident Response:

- **Faster Response Times:** AI can automate many incident response tasks, enabling faster response times to security incidents.
- **Improved Efficiency:** AI can automate routine tasks, freeing up security teams to focus on more strategic initiatives.
- **Enhanced Accuracy:** AI can analyse large volumes of data more accurately than humans, reducing the risk of human error.
- **Proactive Threat Hunting:** AI can proactively identify and investigate potential threats, enabling organizations to prevent attacks before they occur.
- **Reduced Mean Time to Resolution (MTTR):** By accelerating the incident response process, AI can significantly reduce the time it takes to resolve security incidents.

Challenges and Considerations:

- **Data Quality and Availability:** The effectiveness of AI-driven incident response depends heavily on the quality and availability of data.
- **Model Interpretability:** Understanding how AI models arrive at their conclusions is crucial for building trust and ensuring responsible use.
- **Integration with Existing Tools:** Integrating AI-driven solutions with existing security tools and processes can be complex.

4.4. Network Traffic Analysis:

AI-powered network traffic analysis Roy et al. (2019) revolutionizes how organizations monitor and understand the flow of data across their networks. By leveraging advanced algorithms and machine learning techniques, AI can analyse massive volumes of network data, identify anomalies, and provide valuable insights into network behaviour.

Figure 4. AI based network traffic analysis

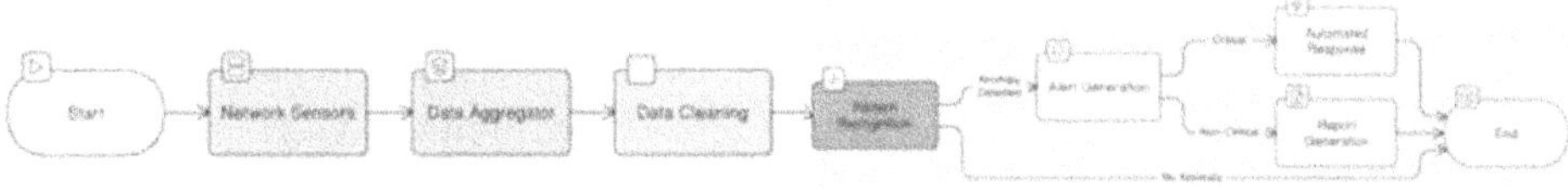

- **Anomaly Detection:** AI algorithms can identify deviations from normal network behaviour, such as unusual traffic patterns, unexpected spikes in activity, or unauthorized access attempts. This helps detect potential security threats and performance issues.
- **Performance Monitoring and Optimization:** AI can analyse network traffic patterns to identify bottlenecks, predict future traffic demands, and optimize network resource allocation. This ensures optimal network performance and user experience.
- **Capacity Planning:** AI can forecast future network traffic needs based on historical data and current trends. This enables organizations to proactively plan for future capacity requirements and avoid performance degradation.
- **Security Threat Detection:** AI can analyse network traffic to identify malicious activities, such as malware infections, data exfiltration, and denial-of-service attacks. This enhances the effectiveness of intrusion detection systems and improves overall network security.
- **User Behaviour Analysis:** AI can analyse user behaviour patterns to identify potential insider threats or unusual activity that may indicate malicious intent.

Benefits of AI-Driven Network Traffic Analysis:

- **Enhanced Threat Detection:** AI can detect sophisticated and evolving threats that traditional methods might miss.
- **Improved Network Performance:** AI can optimize network performance by identifying and resolving bottlenecks.
- **Proactive Capacity Planning:** AI can help organizations plan for future network needs, ensuring adequate capacity and avoiding performance issues.
- **Reduced Operational Costs:** AI can automate many network management tasks, reducing the need for manual intervention and freeing up IT staff for other critical tasks.
- **Data-Driven Decision Making:** AI provides valuable insights into network behaviour, enabling data-driven decision making and proactive network management.

Challenges and Considerations:

- **Data Quality and Availability:** The effectiveness of AI-driven network traffic analysis depends heavily on the quality and availability of data.
- **Model Interpretability:** Understanding how AI models arrive at their conclusions is crucial for building trust and ensuring responsible use.
- **Integration with Existing Tools:** Integrating AI-driven solutions with existing network management tools can be complex.

5. BENEFITS OF AI-DRIVEN NETWORK SECURITY

AI-driven network security offers several significant benefits. Firstly, it enhances threat detection by identifying novel and sophisticated attacks, including zero-day exploits and advanced persistent threats (APTs) Russell et al. (2018), that traditional methods often miss. Secondly, AI significantly improves accuracy by reducing false positives, minimizing alert fatigue, and enabling security teams to focus on critical threats. This, in turn, leads to faster response times to security incidents, minimizing potential damage and reducing business disruption. Furthermore, AI empowers proactive threat hunting Moor et al. (2004), enabling organizations to identify and investigate potential threats before they can cause significant harm. Finally, by automating many routine security tasks, AI frees up security teams to focus on more strategic initiatives, such as threat intelligence analysis and vulnerability management, leading to a more proactive and resilient security posture.

- **Enhanced threat detection:** AI can effectively detect novel threats, including zero-day exploits and advanced persistent threats that traditional methods often miss.
- **Improved accuracy and reduced false positives:** AI algorithms can significantly reduce false positives, minimizing alert fatigue and enabling security teams to focus on critical threats.
- **Faster response times:** AI can automate many security tasks, enabling faster response times to security incidents.
- **Proactive threat hunting:** AI can proactively identify and investigate potential threats, enabling organizations to prevent attacks before they occur.
- **Improved operational efficiency:** AI can automate many routine security tasks, freeing up security teams to focus on more strategic initiatives.
- **Increased network resilience:** By enhancing threat detection and response capabilities, AI can significantly improve the overall resilience of network infrastructure.

6. CHALLENGES AND CONSIDERATIONS

- **Data quality and availability:** The effectiveness of AI-driven security solutions depends heavily on the quality and availability of training data. Obtaining sufficient high-quality data can be challenging.
- **Model interpretability:** Many AI/ML models Tavallaee et al. (2009) are complex and difficult to interpret. Understanding how a model arrives at a particular decision is crucial for building trust and ensuring responsible use.
- **Bias and fairness:** AI models can inherit biases from the data they are trained on, leading to unfair or discriminatory outcomes. It is essential to ensure that AI-driven security solutions are unbiased and fair.
- **Ethical considerations:** The use of AI in network security raises ethical concerns, such as privacy, surveillance, and the potential for misuse.
- **Skill gap:** Implementing and managing AI-driven security solutions requires specialized skills and expertise. There is a growing need for skilled cyber security professionals with knowledge of AI and machine learning.

7. FUTURE DIRECTIONS

- **Advancements in AI/ML:** Continued advancements in AI/ML techniques, such as deep learning and reinforcement learning, will further enhance the capabilities of network security solutions.

- **AI-driven threat intelligence:** AI can be used to analyse and correlate threat intelligence Kumar et al. (2011) from various sources, providing a more comprehensive understanding of the threat landscape.
- **AI-powered security orchestration and automation:** AI can automate many security tasks, such as incident response and remediation, improving operational efficiency and reducing the burden on security teams.
- **Explainable AI:** Research and development LeCun et al. (2015) in explainable AI will improve the transparency and interpretability of AI models, building trust and confidence in their decisions.

8. CONCLUSION

In conclusion, AI is revolutionizing network security by providing powerful tools for detecting and responding to threats, improving operational efficiency, and enhancing overall network resilience. By embracing AI-driven solutions Huang et al. (2016), organizations can effectively address the challenges of the evolving threat landscape, including the rise of sophisticated attacks, the increasing complexity of networks, and the growing volume of security data. While challenges such as data quality, model interpretability, and ethical considerations must be carefully addressed, the potential benefits of AI in network security are significant. As AI technology continues to advance, we can expect to see even more innovative and effective solutions for protecting critical infrastructure and ensuring a secure digital future.

REFERENCES

Akoglu, A. (2018). Natural Language Processing (NLP) Applications in Cyber security. *IEEE Security and Privacy*, 16(1), 70–75.

Bishop, M. (2002). *Computer and Network Security*. Addison-Wesley.

Chandola, V., Kumar, V., & Banerjee, P. (2009). Anomaly Detection: A Survey. *ACM Computing Surveys*, 41(3), 1–58. DOI: 10.1145/1541880.1541882

Ghorbani, A. (2014). Phishing Detection Using Machine Learning and Natural Language Processing. *IEEE Transactions on Information Forensics and Security*, 9(6), 969–980.

Huang, Y., Zhang, X., & Wang, X. (2016). A Deep Learning Approach to Network Intrusion Detection. *IEEE Transactions on Neural Networks and Learning Systems*, 58(5), 3481–3492.

Huang, Y., Zhang, X., & Wang, X. (2016). A Deep Learning Approach to Network Intrusion Detection. *IEEE Transactions on Neural Networks and Learning Systems*, 58(5), 3481–3492.

Jahani, M., & Rahmati, M. (2021). Malware Detection Using Deep Learning: A Survey. *Journal of Computer and System Sciences*, 116, 1–37.

Kaufman, C., Perlman, R., & Speciner, M. (2002). Network Security: Private Communication in a Public World. Prentice Hall.

Kumar, S., Yadav, S., & Singh, S. K. (2011). A Survey on Network Security: Techniques, Attacks, and Challenges. International Journal of Computer Applications, 29(10), 09-16.

Kumar, Y. V., Poornachandra, S., & Kumar, C. S. (2021). Deep Learning for Intrusion Detection: A Survey. *Artificial Intelligence Review*, 34(1), 1–33. PMID: 32836651

LeCun, Y., Bengio, Y., & Hinton, G. (2015). Deep Learning. *Nature*, 521(7553), 436–444. DOI: 10.1038/nature14539 PMID: 26017442

LeCun, Y., Bengio, Y., & Hinton, G. (2015). Deep Learning. *Nature*, 521(7553), 436–444. DOI: 10.1038/nature14539 PMID: 26017442

LeCun, Y., Bottou, L., Bengio, Y., & Haffner, P. (1998). Gradient-Based Learning Applied to Document Recognition. *Proceedings of the IEEE*, 86(11), 2278–2324. DOI: 10.1109/5.726791

Li, Y., Han, S., & Ren, Y. (2018). Network Anomaly Detection with Long Short-Term Memory Networks. *IEEE Access : Practical Innovations, Open Solutions*, 6, 14137–14147.

Moor, J. (2004). *The Ethics of Artificial Intelligence*. Cambridge University Press.

Roy, S., Majumdar, A. K., & Ghosh, S. K. (2019). AI for Cybersecurity: A Survey. *IEEE Access : Practical Innovations, Open Solutions*, 7, 56986–57017.

Russell, S., Norvig, P., & Tegmark, M. (2018). AI, Ethics, and the Future of Humanity. *Science*, 361(6407), 890–891.

Sharafaldin, S., Lazarevic, A. L., & Borodovsky, L. A. (2018). Intrusion Detection Using Recurrent Neural Networks. *Computers & Security*, 76, 100–116.

Sharma, R. K. (2018). Artificial Intelligence and Machine Learning in Cybersecurity. *International Journal of Engineering and Advanced Technology*, 8(2), 142–146.

Tavallaee, M., Bagheri, E., Lu, W., & Ghorbani, A. A. (2009). A Survey of Machine Learning for Network Security. *Computer Networks*, 54(3), 491–510.

Chapter 4
Autoencoder-Based Anomaly Detection for Cyber Threat Monitoring

Abinaya Devi
https://orcid.org/0000-0002-3736-6386
Mepco Schlenk Engineering College, India

Manoj Kumar Prabhakaran
Mepco Schlenk Engineering College, India

J. S. Prasanna Kumar
Mepco Schlenk Engineering College, India

J. Nithish Kumar
https://orcid.org/0009-0009-2679-9635
Mepco Schlenk Engineering College, India

ABSTRACT

To identify and defend networks against attacks such as Distributed Denial of Service (DDoS), Probe assaults, Remote-to-Local (R2L), and User-to-Root (U2R), the Intrusion Detection System (IDS), we used autoencoders and machine learning algorithms. We applied label encoding on the NSL KDD-99 dataset. To address class imbalances, many autoencoder models are used along with the generation of synthetic data via a Conditional Tabular Generative Adversarial Network (CTGAN). To extract ensemble features, autoencoder models like SNDAE, SAE, and SSDAE are coupled. Prior to training, dimensionality reduction is implemented. The collected characteristics are concatenated and utilized to train various classifiers (Random Forest, KNN, and SVM-OVO). A testing dataset is used to evaluate the trained model. A comparison is made between the classifiers and the ensemble model output.

DOI: 10.4018/979-8-3693-9919-4.ch004

INTRODUCTION

Network intrusion or cyber threat refers to unauthorized or malicious attempts to compromise the security of a computer network or system. It involves various activities aimed at gaining unauthorized access, stealing sensitive information, disrupting functions, or causing damage to digital infrastructure. Cyberthreats encompass a wide range of techniques, including malware, phishing, denial-of-service attacks, and exploitation of software vulnerabilities. These dangers highlight the critical need for cyber-security measures in the modern, interconnected world by posing serious risks to people, corporations, and even entire nations.

Sophisticated and persistent attacks by state-sponsored actors or organized cybercrime groups have increased. There has been a noticeable rise in supply chain attacks, where cybercriminals target software vendors or suppliers to penetrate multiple organizations simultaneously. Due to the increased vulnerabilities brought about by the Internet of Things (IoT) rapid expansion which took use of weak IoT devices to cause enormous distributed denial-of-service (DDoS) assaults, have become more common and it is given by Amanullah MA et. al. (2020). Cyber attackers have shifted towards more sophisticated techniques, such as fileless malware that operates in system memory and zero-day exploits targeting previously unknown vulnerabilities, making detection and prevention more challenging. Cybercriminals leveraged the COVID-19 pandemic, launching phishing attacks, creating fake websites, and spreading misinformation to exploit the uncertainty and increased remote work scenarios. These trends collectively demonstrate the growing sophistication and diversity of network intrusions over the past decade, necessitating continual advancements in cybersecurity practices to mitigate risks and protect against evolving threats.

An essential part of cybersecurity infrastructure is a network intrusion detection system (NIDS), which keeps an eye on network traffic in order to spot any unusual or hostile activities. In order to identify potential dangers, it continuously analyzes data that is moving via a network. NIDS monitors network packets and patterns in real-time to spot unusual activity or recognized threat signatures Habeeb RAA et. al. (2019). It makes use of a number of detection techniques, including anomaly-based detection, which finds departures from typical network behavior, and signature-based detection, which compares network traffic to a database of known attack patterns. An intrusion detection system (NIDS) can identify possible threats and send out notifications, automate replies, or notify cybersecurity staff for additional investigation and mitigation. It serves as a proactive defense system, assisting in the prevention or reduction of the effects of cyberattacks by offering early warning signals and facilitating rapid response to potential threats within a network environment Amanullah MA et. al. (2020).

Machine learning algorithms, in particular deep learning models like recurrent neural networks and convolutional neural networks, can evaluate large amounts of network data to uncover complex patterns and abnormalities Kim H et. al. (2016). This makes it possible to detect sophisticated threats that might elude conventional signature-based systems with greater accuracy. Machine learning models are flexible and can pick up new information. They are more resilient to uncertain assaults and previously undetected intrusion attempts because they can constantly refresh their understanding of network traffic patterns and emerging threats. Deep learning algorithms can be trained to differentiate between normal network behavior and abnormal activities, reducing false alarms Kim J et. al. (2017). This helps cybersecurity teams focus on genuine threats rather than being overwhelmed by numerous false positives. Deep learning excels at recognizing intricate patterns within network traffic, allowing it to identify anomalies that might be subtle or hard to detect using rule-based or signature-based systems Tang TA et. al. (2016). These methods scale to process and analyze data in real time over vast networks without sacrificing efficiency, making them effective at handling the massive volumes of network data generated in current networks. Machine learning can enable NIDS to perform behavioral analysis by learning typical network behaviors and identifying deviations from these norms, even in encrypted traffic, which is vital as encryption becomes more prevalent. While deep learning and machine learning enhance NIDS capabilities, it's important to note that they're not without challenges. They require extensive training data, may be susceptible to adversarial attacks, and their black-box nature can make it challenging to interpret why certain decisions are made. Nonetheless, their potential for significantly improving the effectiveness of NIDS against sophisticated cyber threats makes them an invaluable asset in modern cybersecurity strategies.

Since end-to-end encryption has become so popular, it has become more challenging for conventional NIDS to scan encrypted traffic for possible threats. Modern networks have become more complex, incorporating cloud services, IoT devices, and diverse architectures (e.g., hybrid, multi-cloud) Dong B et. al. (2016). NIDS faces challenges in effectively monitoring and analyzing traffic across these diverse and distributed environments Hinton GE et. al. (2006). Attackers have started leveraging adversarial techniques to evade detection by NIDS. The sheer volume of network data generated, coupled with the need for real-time analysis, poses challenges for NIDS. Processing and analyzing large datasets in real time to identify anomalies without introducing latency or missing critical threats is a significant challenge Alrawashdeh K et. al (2016). Understanding the context of network traffic is crucial for accurate threat detection. However, discerning malicious intent from legitimate activities requires contextual awareness, which can be challenging for NIDS, especially in complex network environments. Despite advancements, NIDS can still produce false positives, leading to alert fatigue Alrawashdeh K et. al (2016). Sorting through numerous alerts to identify genuine threats remains a challenge for cybersecurity teams.

MAIN FOCUS OF THE CHAPTER

- A number of cyberattack techniques, such as Distributed Denial of Service (DDoS), Probe attacks, and User-to-Root (U2R) and Remote-to-Local (R2L) intrusion attempts, have the ability to disrupt services, compromise sensitive data, and affect the availability and integrity of network resources.
- The dynamic nature of cyber-attacks often proves to be too much for conventional intrusion detection systems to keep up with.
- They might not be able to quickly identify and neutralize sophisticated attacks with enough accuracy, particularly when there are disparities in class and some attack types are more common than others.
- Class imbalances create a major intrusion detection challenge when specific attack types are underrepresented in the dataset.
- The primary source of the low accuracy for U2R and R2L labels observed in prior work is the class imbalance resulting from much fewer samples for probe, U2R, and R2L.
- In order to detect and defend networks against attacks such as Distributed Denial of Service (DDoS), Probe assaults, Remote-to-Local (R2L) and User-to-Root (U2R), the Intrusion Detection System (IDS), autoencoders and machine learning techniques were used.
- As in section III, Label encoding technique was utilized to preprocess NSL KDD-99 dataset.
- In section III, S-NDAE, SAE and SSDAE autoencoder models are employed in conjunction with the creation of artificial data using a Conditional Tabular Generative Adversarial Network (CTGAN) in order to overcome class imbalances.

- Autoencoder models such as SNDAE, SAE, and SSDAE are linked in order to extract ensemble characteristics.
- Dimensionality reduction is applied before training.
- A variety of classifiers, including Random Forest, KNN, and SVM-OVO, are trained using the concatenated attributes that have been gathered.
- A testing dataset is used to evaluate the trained model. The results of the classifiers and the ensemble model are compared in section IV.

BACKGROUND AND LITERATURE REVIEW

Khaled Alrawashdeh & Carla Purdy (2016) performed binary classification in an intrusion detection system by implementing the Restricted Boltzmann Machine (RBM) and Deep Belief Network (DBN). It can avoid overfitting. It improves the accuracy rate on U2R.It is expensive to train. It leads to false positives. Using a Deep Neural Network (DNN), Sasanka Potluri & Christian Diedrich (2016) carried out binary classification in an intrusion detection system. It helps debug and troubleshoot hence the neural network is easy to understand. It requires a large data to train. It is prone to overfitting. Bo Dong & Xue Wang (2016) used Restricted Boltzmann Machine and Support Vector Machine to conduct binary classification in an intrusion detection system (SVM-RBM). It can evaluate big sets of data. RBM helps in increasing the accuracy of SVM. It can lead to overfitting which can lead to poor performance on unseen data. The network is very complex hence it is difficult to understand. Syed Ali Raza Zaidi, Mounir Ghogho, Des McLernon, Lotfi Mhamdi, and Tuan A Tang. (2016) used a Deep Neural Network (DNN) to conduct binary classification in intrusion detection systems. In software network data patterns change frequently as it can learn to adapt to network traffic. It is inexpensive to train. It is difficult to interpret the decisions. It is prone to overfitting. Yao Wang, Wan-dong Cai, and Peng-Cheng Wei (2016) used stacked denoising autoencoder to achieve binary classification in an intrusion detection system. It provides high-speed testing which does not consume more time. It helps to capture intricate and deep patterns in JavaScript testing. It takes a long training time which is time-consuming. FiscCarlos Garcia Cordero, Sascha Hauke, Max Miihlhauser & Mathias Hert (2016) performed binary classification in an intrusion detection system by implementing a Replicator Neural Network (RNN). The method is unsupervised, meaning it doesn't rely on labeled data for training. This allows it to adapt to various network conditions without requiring extensive labeled datasets. It is not very effective against a wide range of attacks. A false positive is possible. Deep Neural Network (DNN) implementation was used by Min-Joo Kang & Je-Won Kang (2016) to conduct binary classification in an intrusion detection system. It is suitable for real-time monitoring of vehicular networks. DNN enhances detection accuracy. It depends on the quality of data hence it is complicated for real-time monitoring. It is not suitable for new attacks. Using a Deep Neural Network (DNN), Jin Kim, Nara Shin, Seung Yeon Jo, and Sang Hyun Kim (2017) carried out binary classification in an intrusion detection system. It automatically learns complex features from raw data. It can adapt to changing attack methodologies. It trained on one network environment might not transfer well to another due to differences in data distributions or attack patterns. Using the Support Vector Machine (SVM) Algorithm, **Chao** Liu1, Jing Yang, and Jinqiu Wu (2020) carried out binary classification in an intrusion detection system. Sorting and preprocessing data based on URLs for normalization helps in preparing data for analysis and model creation, potentially contributing to improved accuracy. It does not focus on a wide range of attacks. It highly depends on the quality of data hence it is not possible for real time approach. Binary classification was carried out in an intrusion detection system by Zhendong Wang, Yaodi Liu, Daojing He, and Sammy Chan (2021) using the Stacked Denoising Autoencoder. It handles gradient sparseness issues. Optimization helps in effective training. Complex structure with a large number of parameters. Long training time for large datasets hence it is not possible for real-time intrusion detection. Using an LSTM-RNN classifier, Jihyun Kim, Jaehyun Kim, Huong Le Thi Thu, and Howon Kim (2016) carried out binary classification in an intrusion detection system. Long-term storage and retrieval of information is facilitated by the memory cells found in LSTMs, which enables them to recall intricate relationships in sequences. Overfitting can occur when the model memorizes noise in the training data rather than learning general patterns. A Web intrusion detection system with feature analysis and SVM optimization utilizing HMM and SVM algorithms was carried out by Liu C, Yang J, and Wu J in 2020. HMM algorithm is Suitable for Modeling Sequential Data, Flexibility, and Probabilistic Framework. In HMM algorithm the main demerits are Sensitivity to Model Parameters, Assumption of Independence, and Difficulty in learning Long Term Dependencies. The SVM algorithm is Suitable for Dimensional Data and global optimization and is effective in non-linear Spaces. The SVM algorithm's main demerits are sensitivity to noise, Computational Complexity, Black box Nature, and Limited Scalability. Devaraju S. and Ramakrishnan S. (2014) compared neural network-based intrusion detection systems with the KDD dataset. Neural networks are helpful for Pattern Recognition, Adaptability, Feature Learning, Non-Linearity, and Generalization. In Neural networks, the main disadvantages are Data Imbalance, Accurate Computational Complexity, Overfitting, Interpretability, Sensitivity to Hyperparameters, Data Preprocessing Challenges, and Limited Anomaly Detection Capability Gao N, Gao L, Gao Q, Wang H. (2014) performed DBN. DBN is useful in Feature Training, Generative Model, and Pre-Training. DBN model is not helpful for Computational Complexity, Limited Interpretability, and Data Requirements. Deep neural network self-training based on unsupervised learning and dropout was carried out by Lee HW, Kim NR, and Lee JH (2017). Deep Belief Network (DBN)-based Int J Fuzzy Logic Intel Syst. Deep Neural Network is the main advantage for Feature Training, Generative Models, and Pre-Training. Deep Neural Network's main demerits are Computational Complexity, Limited Interpretability, and Data Requirements. Fuzzy clustering and artificial neural networks were used in Wang G, Hao J, Ma J, and Huang L.'s (2010) novel intrusion detection method. ANN is suitable for Soft Assignment, Handling Noisy Data, Flexibility, and Applicability to a Variety of Domains. In ANN main disadvantages are Sensitivity to an initialization time, Computational Complexity, Interpretability, and Determining the Number of Clusters. Fuzzy Clustering is suitable for Non-linearity, Adaptability, Parallel Processing, and Generalization. In Fuzzy Clustering main demerits are Data Requirements, Computational Complexity, Black Box Nature, Hyper-Parameter Tuning, and Vulnerability to Adversarial Attacks. A deep learning-based DDoS detection system in software-defined networking (SDN) was implemented by Niyaz Q, Sun W, and Javaid AY (2016). DDos detection system in sdn model is helpful for Centralized Network Control, Programmability, Improved Network Automation, Dynamic Resource Allocation, Enhanced Security, and Open Standards.DDOS detection system in sdn model is not helpful for Complexity during Implementation, Dependency on Network Infrastructure, Security Concerns, Skillset Challenges, Interoperability Issues, and Performance Concerns. JAM project which has main advantages for Customization to Business Context, Optimized Resource Allocation, Risk Mitigation, Adaptability to Changing Threats, and Prioritization of Alerts. In the JAM project main disadvantages are Complexity in Model Development, Subjectivity in Cost Assignments, Data Limitations, Changing Business Environments, Difficulty in cost quantification, Trade-off Challenges, and Resistance to Change. In 2019, Habeeb RAA, Nasaruddin F, Gani A, Hashem IAT, Ahmed E, and Imran M. processed huge data in real-time to find anomalies. It is suitable for Timely Detection, Improved Accuracy, Dynamic Thresholds, Reduced Time to Action, Efficient Resource Utilization, Continuous Monitoring, Enhanced Situational Awareness, and Scalability. Real-time big data processing for anomaly detection is not suitable for Complexity, Data Quality and Cleansing, Latency Concerns, Resource Intensiveness, Model Complexity, Limited Historical Context, Security and Privacy Concerns, Continuous Monitoring Overhead. Deep learning and big data technologies for IoT security were carried out by Amanullah MA, Habeeb RAA, Nasaruddin F, Gani A, Ahmed E, Ninar ASM, Akim NM, and Imran M. in 2019. Big data technologies for IoT security are suitable for Anomaly Detection, Complex Pattern Recognition, Automatic Feature Learning, Real-time Monitoring, and Adaptability. In Big Data Technologies for IoT security main demerits are Data Requirements, Computational Resources, Interpretability, Scalability, real-time processing, Data Fusion, Historical Analysis, Data Privacy Concerns, Complexity, Latency, and Security of Big Data Infrastructure.

Table 1. Comparing the suggested S-NADE method's performance (%) with the KDD Cup '99 dataset

Study	Method used	Performance			
		Accuracy	Precision	Recall	F1-Score
Kim et al	LSTM	96.93	-	-	98.88
Gao et al	DBN	93.49	-	-	-
Wang et al	Fuzzy Clustering	96.75	-	-	-
Qazi et al	SNDAE with SVM	99.65	99.99	99.85	99.55

PROPOSED METHOLOGY

1. Dataset

A structured collection of data known as a dataset is the basis for numerous types of analysis, modeling, and decision-making. Researchers and practitioners use the NSL-KDD dataset to develop and evaluate machine learning algorithms and IDS systems that can distinguish between probable intrusions and normal network traffic. Researchers can test and train intrusion detection models using this labeled data, which helps evaluate the model generality, accuracy, and efficacy.

NSL-KDD 99: NSL-KDD 99 is the upgraded and modified version of the KDD CUP 99 dataset. There are 42 features in the dataset. It makes a clean division between typical and unusual traffic. Two sets of 1,48,519 records make up this collection. 1,18,815 (80%) records from the training set and 29,704 (20%) records from the test set. It mostly consists of the attack labels for probe, U2R (User to Root), R2L (Root to Local), and DDOS (Distributed Denial-of-Service). Attacks such as back, land, Neptune, pod, smurf, and teardrop are among the DDOS. U2R encompasses rootkit, load module, perl, and buffer overflow. R2L comprises of the following attacks: ftp write, guess passwd, imap, multihop, phf, spy, warezclient, and warezmaster. The investigation encompasses port sweep, nmap, ipsweep, and satan assaults. The KDD CUP 99 dataset is replaced with the NSL-KDD dataset. Thirty-one distinct assault labels are mapped to five attack methods: probing attack, DDOS, U2R, R2L, and normal. Additionally, it has a standard label that does not denote an attack.

2. Data Preprocessing

The Figure 1 presents the flow of our proposed work which includes preprocessing, data generation, feature extraction and classifiers. The dataset is divided into a 20% testing set and an 80% training set. Both training and testing set are passed to preprocessing step is the class imbalance in the NSL-KDD dataset, Label encoding, and data generation can be implemented. String-valued features can be converted into numerical representations using a label encoder. It laid the foundation for subsequent processing. The scarcity of training samples for specific attack types (U2R, R2L, and probe) can be solved by implementing CTGAN (Conditional Tabular Generative Adversarial Networks) for data generation. A conditional tabular GAN typically consists of a discriminator network and a generator network, just like a conventional GAN. To direct the generating process, conditional GANs provide extra conditioning information to both the discriminator and the generator. The generator's objective is to produce artificial samples that, when conditioned on specific characteristics, resemble real data. Its goal is to reduce the discrepancy between the generated samples' discriminator's prediction and 1 (which denotes actual data). The generator equation can be represented as:

$$GminEz \sim pz(z), c\left[log(1 - D(G(z,c),c))\right]\# \quad (1)$$

The generating network is represented by G in equation 1, while the discriminator network is represented by D. Random noise sampled from latent space is represented by z. The c represents the conditioning samples. The synthetic samples produced by the generator with conditioning variables c are represented by G(z,c). D(G(z,c),c) represents the discriminator's output when evaluating the generated samples with conditioning variables c. The discriminator's objective is to differentiate between real and synthetic samples. Its goal is to accurately identify synthetic samples as false (predicting 0) and real samples as real (predicting 1). The discriminator equation can be represented as:

$$DmaxEx{\sim}pdata(x|c)[logD(x,c)]+Ez{\sim}pz(z),c[log(1-D(G(z,c),c))] \quad (2)$$

In the equation 2, x represents real values from the training data. c represents conditioning variables. $pdata(x \mid c)$ represents the distribution of real data conditioned on c. D(x,c) represents the discriminator output when evaluating real samples x with conditioning variables c. CTGAN ability to learn the data underlying distribution enabled the creation of synthetic samples mirroring the characteristics of existing minority attack data. This data generation can balance the dataset, mitigating the bias inherent in imbalanced classes and potentially improving the generalizability and accuracy of trained intrusion detection models.

a. Feature extraction using autoencoders

In machine learning and signal processing, raw data is converted into a more condensed and useful representation known as features through a process called feature extraction. Using autoencoders for feature extraction, the input data is compressed into a lower-dimensional representation that extracts important features. Multiple layers of encoding are used in this procedure to encode the input data into a latent space, which is then decoded to recover the original input. The autoencoder reduces dimensionality while maintaining pertinent information by learning to extract meaningful features from the data during training. The encoded representations that are obtained can be used as short feature vectors for machine learning applications including anomaly detection and classifications.

Figure 1. System diagram

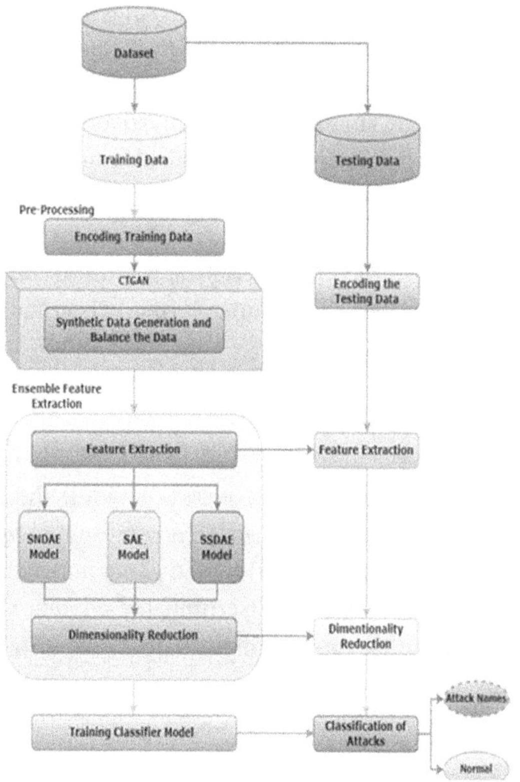

3. Stacked Non-Symmetric Deep Autoencoder (S-NDAE)

The Figure 2 presents the S-NDAE model. S-NDAE is an unsupervised learning network that refers to a Stacked Non-Symmetric Deep Autoencoder. "Stacked" implies that multiple layers of autoencoders are combined. Every layer in the stack uses the output of the layer before it as its input. By stacking layers, the model can be trained to acquire hierarchical representations of the input data, which may enable it to capture more intricate and abstract properties. The stacked autoencoder receives the encoded data as input. Learning a concise representation of typical network traffic is the autoencoder job. The input data must be mapped to a lower-dimensional representation using the autoencoder's encoder network. Every layer of the encoder in a stacked architecture creates a fresh, usually more abstract representation of the input data. Simple features may be captured by lower levels, whereas more complicated and abstract features are captured by higher layers. A lower-dimensional abstract representation of the input data must be transferred to the input data. Simple features may be captured by lower levels, whereas more complicated and abstract features are captured by higher layers.

Figure 2. S-NDAE model

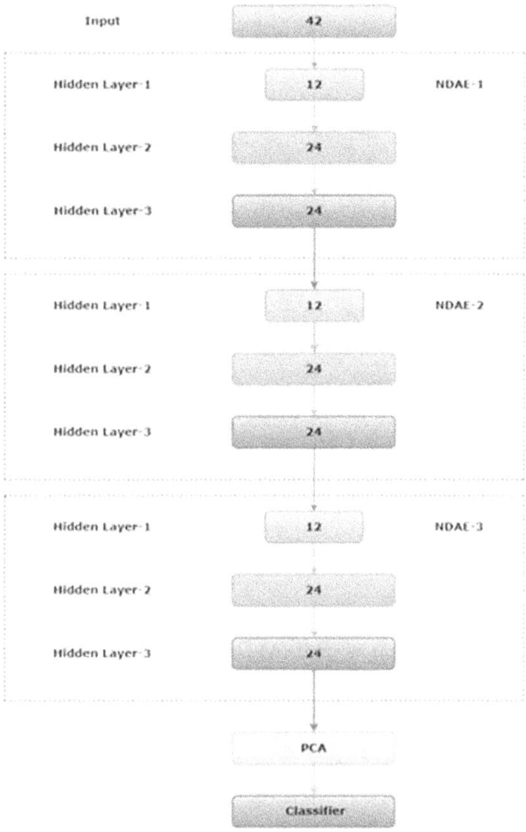

Every layer in the encoder pulls features that are applicable to the current task, which might be recording patterns that represent typical network behavior in the context of network intrusion detection. Since they don't need labeled examples of typical and intrusive data, they are taught autonomously. Based on the input, the model learns how to represent the incoming data. The data's intrinsic structure will be effectively captured by the learned representation (features), rendering it susceptible to abnormalities or intrusions. The output of one of the autoencoder's last layers functions as the feature vector, or representation, of the input data, once the autoencoder has been trained. To detect network intrusions, this feature vector can be fed into a later classification model. The proposed SNDAE model layer can be represented as:

$$z_i = \sigma(W_i \cdot z_i - 1 + b_i) \qquad (3)$$

In this instance, z_i indicates the input data at layer I in its encoded form. σ is the activation function symbol. W_i is the weight matrix representation for the i-th layer. It contains the weights that you will learn throughout the training session. $z_i - 1$, which serves as the input for the i-th layer, is a representation of the output of the (i-1) layer. b_i represents the bias vector for the i-th layer. The formula can be used to determine the output vector.

$$\hat{x} = \sigma(W_{output} \cdot h_{final} + b_{output}) \quad (4)$$

Here $\hat{x}$ denotes the output of the final layer in the SNDAE. In the context of an autoencoder, x is often the reconstructed output or the encoded representation of the input data. σ represents the activation function. *Woutput* represents the weight matrix of the final layer. *hfinal* denotes the output of the n-th layer, serving as the input to the final layer. *boutput* denotes the bias vector for the final layer. It contains biased terms associated with each neuron in the final layer.

Figure 3. SAE model

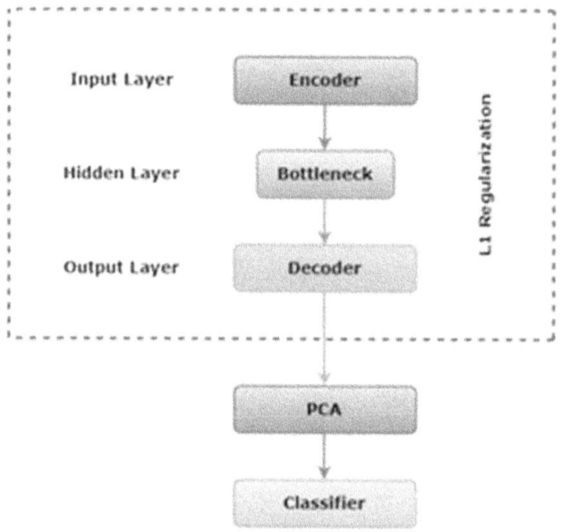

4. *Sparse Autoencoder (SAE)*

Figure 3 presents the SAE model and it is implemented along with two autoencoder models. The input and output layers of the sparse autoencoder model are larger than the hidden layer. The first layer to be added to the model is the input layer. It is completely connected (Dense) and contains a ReLU activation function. A ReLU activation function and twenty units comprise the second layer, which is a hidden layer. Additionally, this layer has L1 regularization with a 10e-5 regularization strength. L1 regularization helps in inducing sparsity in the model The output layer is the third tier. It is a fully linked layer that is appropriate for multi-class classification and has a softmax activation function. The number of units and the number of unique classes in the target variable y are equal. The model's compilation consists of the categorical cross-entropy loss (suited for multi-class classification), the Adam optimizer, and accuracy as the training metric. Using the labels and training data, the model is trained. The hidden layer equation input layer can be shown as

$$z[1] = \sigma(W[1]x + b[1]) \quad (5)$$

z[1] is the output of the hidden layer. σ represents the activation function of ReLU. The first layer's weight matrix (input to hidden layer) is W[1]. The bias vector for the first layer is b[1].

$$\hat{y} = softmax(W[2]z[1] + b[2]) \# \quad (6)$$

$\hat{y}$ is the predicted output. The softmax function is used because it is suitable for multi-class classification. The weight matrix for the second layer, which is concealed from the output layer, is W [2]. The bias vector for the second layer is B [2].

5. *Stacked Symmetric Deep Autoencoder (SSDAE)*

The Figure 4 presents the stacked symmetric deep autoencoder model implemented in the ensemble feature extraction along with other autoencoder models. The encoder layer, which has the ReLU activation function, comprises the first three layers. The next three layers are the decoder layer, which has a linear activation function and the same number of units as the input. The second autoencoder is an encoder layer with an activation function. The second autoencoder's decoder layer shares the same number of units and a linear activation function as the encoder layer that came before it. The output layer has the same number of units as the input layer and a linear activation function. One way to depict the encoder layer transition is as

$$z[1] = ReLU(W[1]x + b[1]) \# \quad (7)$$

x is the input vector to the first autoencoder. Z [1] is the output of the encoder layer. ReLU represents the ReLU activation function W [1] and b [1] are the weight matrix and bias vector for the first layer, respectively. The transformation in the decoder layer can be represented as:

$$\hat{x} = W[2]z[1] + b[2]\# \quad (8)$$

$\hat{x}$ is the decoder layer reconstructed output. The weight matrix and bias vector for the second layer are denoted by W [2] and b [2], respectively. The same encoder layer equation is implemented for the second autoencoder as z[2], and the decoder layer equation is denoted as $\hat{x}[2]$, utilizing weight matrix W[3], bias vector b[3] for the encoder layer, and W[4], b[4] for the decoder layer. This process continues similarly for the encoder and decoder layers of the third autoencoder, with W[5], b[5] for the encoder and W[6], b[6] for the decoder, along with $\hat{x}[3]$ in the module. The seventh layer represents the final output.

$$\hat{x}[final] = W[7]\hat{x}[3] + b[7]\# \quad (9)$$

It stands for the finished product. The last layer weight matrix and bias are represented by W[7] and b[7].

Figure 4. SSDAE model

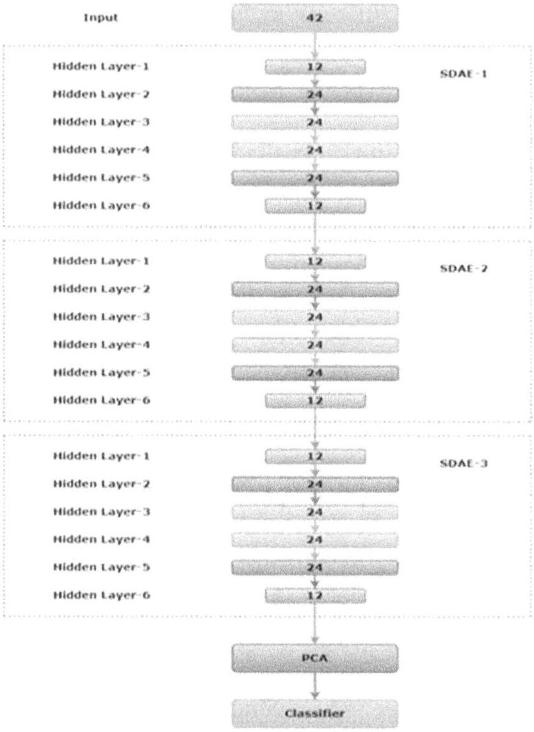

a. Ensemble feature extraction

By combining the advantages of several autoencoder architectures, ensemble feature extraction produces a reliable and thorough representation of the input data. Ensemble feature extraction is a technique that improves the complexity and richness of the extracted features by utilizing a variety of autoencoder models, each specifically created to capture distinct characteristics of the input. By using this method, the ensemble is able to extract more correlations and patterns from the data, which results in feature representations that are both discriminative and informative. The ensemble feature extraction approach provides a comprehensive picture of the data by merging the encoded representations from S-NDAE, SAE, and SSDAE. This enhances performance in downstream machine learning tasks like classification, clustering, or anomaly detection.

b. Support Vector Machine (SVM)

For applications involving regression and classification, Support Vector Machine is a supervised learning technique. After being encoded, the features from the S-NDAE, SAE, and SSAE are fed into a Support Vector Machine (SVM) classification model. SVM is well known for its ability to effectively discriminate between classes in high-dimensional spaces. Principal Component Analysis, a dimensionality reduction technique that identify and removes less informative features iteratively, is used to increase the discriminative power of the Support Vector Machine (SVM). Through the extraction and selection of pertinent features, the combined S-NDAE and SVM-PCA architecture seeks to improve the efficacy and accuracy of intrusion detection systems by strengthening the model's capacity to identify minute anomalies within intricate network data. The SVM decision function's formula is

$$f(x) = (\Sigma^{N} a_i y_i K(x_i, x) + b) \qquad (10)$$

The decision function output, f(x), in this case indicates the class of the input sample x. *ai* represents the Lagrange multiplier for the i-th support vector. *yi* indicates the class label of the i-th support vector. The kernel function, represented by the symbol K (*x*i, x), quantifies how similar each support vector is to the input sample. The term "b" is biased. SVM-OVO (one vs one classifier) is used for multi-class classification.

c. Random Forest

During training, the Random Forest classifier creates a large number of decision trees and outputs the class for classification. It is an ensemble learning technique. It works on the basis of random feature selection and bagging. Decision trees serve as the fundamental building pieces of a Random Forest. A decision tree makes judgments at each node by recursively dividing the dataset into subsets according to the values of the input features. Every leaf node stands for a regression output or class. In classification problems, the final prediction is the class that each individual tree predicts to be the most frequent. The Random Forest classifier is used after PCA because it reduces dimensionality, which is crucial for enhancing performance.

d. K-nearest neighbors (KNN)

The k-Nearest Neighbors (k-NN) algorithm is a nonparametric instance-based learning method for classification and regression issues. It uses the predominate class as the basis for its classification predictions. The dataset is split into training and validation sets multiple times, and the average performance over folds is assessed for different values of k. By going through this procedure, it becomes easier to determine which value, k, best optimizes the model's ability to generalize to new data.

RESULTS AND DISCUSSION

The performance of models like Stacked non-symmetric deep autoencoder, sparse autoencoder, and stacked symmetric autoencoder is analyzed and recorded individua. The model is executed in the Google Colab platform with T4GPU. The Turing architecture from NVIDIA, on which the T4 GPU is based, is made to balance features, speed, and power efficiency for a range of computational applications, such as high-performance computing, machine learning, and deep learning. It is based on the new NVIDIA

Turing TM architecture and is housed in an energy-efficient, tiny PCIe form factor that consumes only 70 watts. The evaluation metrics are stated below.

Accuracy is the percentage of all connections the IDS correctly classifies, whether normal or malicious. A high accuracy score suggests the system makes mostly accurate calls. The formula for accuracy is represented as:

Accuracy = (TP + TN)/Total Samples (11)

The TP represents True Positive and TN represents True Negative. These both are divided by total samples. Precision measures the proportion of those the IDS labels as malicious that are. Precision tells you how often the system's red flags are genuine alarms, not false cries. A high precision score means the IDS accurately identifies real threats without raising too many false alarms, reducing unnecessary panic. The equation for precision is represented as:

Precision = TP/(TP + FP) (12)

The true positive in this equation is divided by the sum of the true positives and false positives. Recall reveals the percentage of actual malicious connections the IDS successfully detects. A high recall score reduces the possibility that the system may miss numerous legitimate threats and hence potential attacks. The formula for recall can be represented as:

Recall = TP/(TP + FN) (13)

The recall score is calculated by divided the true positive with the total sum of true positive and false negative. The F1-score combines recall and precision into a single metric. It strikes a balance between accurately identifying threats and minimizing false alarms, giving a single, concise picture of the IDS's overall performance. A high F1 score shows the system effectively catches threats without unnecessarily disrupting normal operations. The formula for F1-score is represented as:

F1 Score = 2.(Precision . Recall)/(Precision + Recall) (14)

In this equation the F1 score is obtained by dividing double the multiple of precision and recall with the total sum of precision and recall.

The NSL-KDD 99 dataset, which has five labels normal, ddos, probe, u2r, and r2l. The findings that are recorded are obtained via training and classifying the NSL-KDD 99 dataset using ENSEMBLE models and classifiers KNN, Random Forest, and SVM.

Table 2. Implementation result of balanced NSL-KDD 99 with Ensemble-SVM

Using Ensemble-SVM				
Target Labels	**Accuracy**	**Precision**	**Recall**	**F1-Score**
DDOS	99.65	99.86	99.71	99.78
NORMAL	99.88	99.91	99.78	99.85
PROBE	99.59	99.21	99.35	99.29
R2L	98.81	96.96	98.80	97.88
U2R	68.18	32.61	65.15	44.12

TABLE 2 shows that the accuracy for DDOS is much higher. Normal, probe attacks too show better performance. But U2R and R2L performance is much reduced than other labels. These causes occur due to GAN-generated data which has been slightly balanced using CTGAN.

Figure 5. Bar graph of ensemble-SVM model for balanced NSL-KDD 99

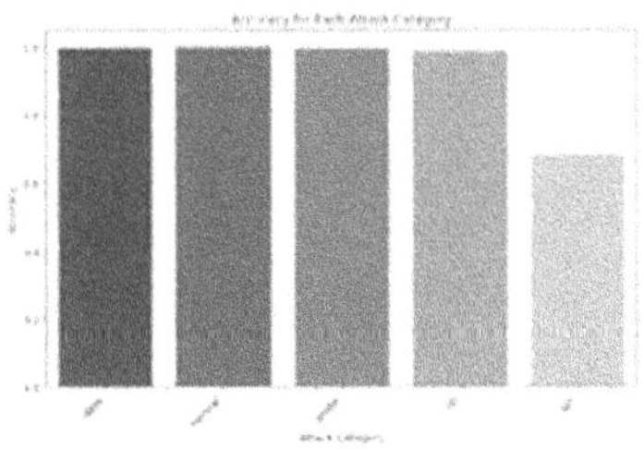

Figure 5 presents the bar graph in which the DDOS, normal, U2R, R2L and probe are represented in which the U2R label is well below 0.8 and it is slightly above 0.6. The other labels are much greater than 0.8 and slightly below 1.0.

Table 3. Implementation result of balanced NSL-KDD 99 with Ensemble-Random forest

Using Ensemble-Random Forest				
Target Labels	**Accuracy**	**Precision**	**Recall**	**F1-Score**
DDOS	99.80	99.94	99.83	99.87
NORMAL	99.91	99.97	99.90	99.94
PROBE	99.78	99.48	99.76	99.63
R2L	99.52	97.21	99.56	98.35
U2R	81.82	60.00	80.70	69.23

TABLE 3 shows that the accuracy for normal is much higher than for other labels. DDOS, probe, and R2L attacks too show better performance. U2R performance is much reduced than other labels.

Figure 6. Bar graph of ensemble-random forest for balanced NSL-KDD 99

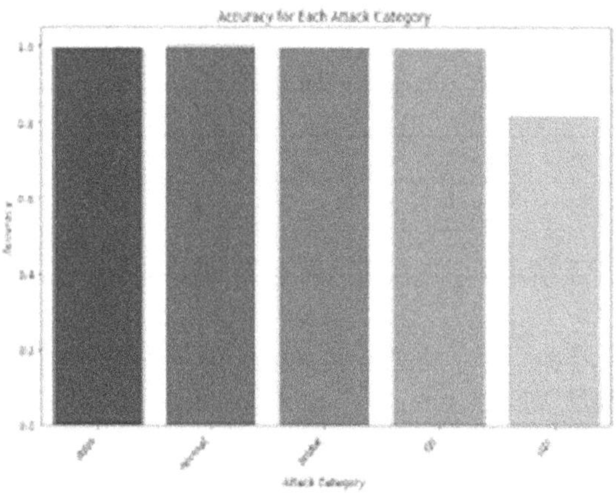

Figure 6 presents the bar graph in which the DDOS, normal, U2R, R2L and probe are represented in which the U2R label is slightly above 0.8. The other labels are much greater than 0.8 and slightly below 1.0.

Table 4. Implementation of balanced NSL-KDD 99 with Ensemble-KNN

Using Ensemble-KNN				
Target Labels	**Accuracy**	**Precision**	**Recall**	**F1-Score**
DDOS	99.80	99.34	99.80	99.57
NORMAL	99.82	99.66	99.84	99.74
PROBE	98.63	93.93	98.63	96.22
R2L	98.55	80.85	98.50	88.83
U2R	70.74	98.24	70.74	95.73

Table 4 shows the results of testing the trained Ensemble-KNN model in which the NORMAL label obtains high-level accuracy compared to DDOS which is slightly lesser than NORMAL. The U2R label is lesser than other labels with a 70 percentage of the value.

Figure 7. Bar graph of ensemble-KNN model for balanced NSL-KDD 99

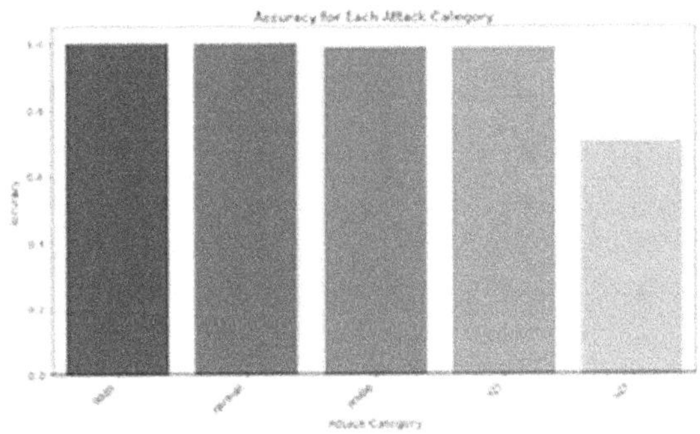

Figure 7 presents the testing result of the trained ensemble-KNN model in which u2r is in the middle of the range between 0.6 and 0.8. The other labels are well much higher as they are slightly less than 0.1. The DDOS, normal, probe, r21 have obtained values above 95 percent. Each label may have a very slight difference between them.

Table 5. Comparison of Ensemble method with different classifiers

Models	Accuracy	Precision	Recall	F1-score
Ensemble-SVM	99.67	99.66	99.60	99.65
Ensemble-Random Forest	99.78	99.75	99.74	99.76
Ensemble-KNN	95.87	96.37	95.88	95.72

Table 5 represents the comparison between the ensemble method with different classifiers. Compared to that Ensemble-Random Forest gives much higher accuracy, precision, recall, and F1-score value. Ensemble-SVM is slightly lesser than Ensemble-Random Forest. The Ensemble-KNN gives very much lesser performance compared to the other models.

Figure 8. Bar graph of ensemble-SVM for balanced NSL-KDD 99

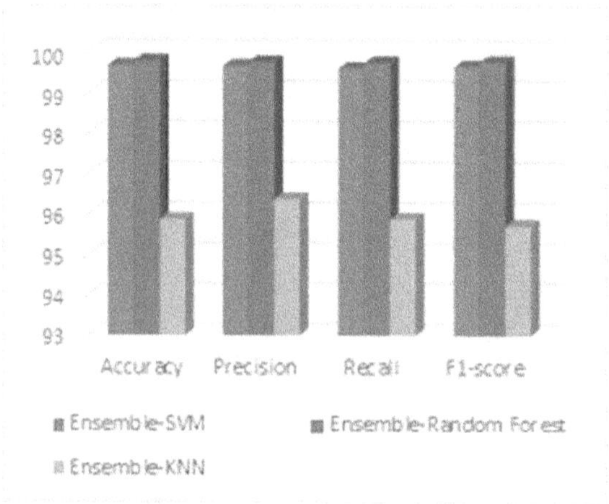

Figure 8 presents the testing result of various trained ensemble-models. The Ensemble models compared are Ensemble-SVM, Ensemble-Random Forest and Ensemble KNN. The Ensemble-Random Forest shows better performance in accuracy compared to Ensemble-KNN and Ensemble-SVM. The Ensemble-KNN shows least performance in accuracy, precision, recall and F1-score. The Ensemble-Random Forest shows better performance in all evaluation metrics.

Table 6. Comparison between accuracy of labels of proposed method and base model

Labels	Method	DDOS	NORMAL	PROBE	R2L	U2R	TOTAL
Qazi et al	SNDAE with SVM	99.92	95.89	99.24	19.31	21.45	99.65
Proposed Work	**Ensemble with Random Forest**	**99.80**	**99.91**	**99.78**	**99.52**	**81.82**	**99.78**

Table 6 represents the comparison of the accuracy values of each method. The proposed work shows a significant increase in U2R and R2L even though the accuracy values for some labels are less than the base model. The proposed work provides better performance in Probe, U2R, and R2L labels. Due to the less samples in the unbalanced data, it shows poor performance for SNDAE-SVM model. The proposed model may show slight less performance in DDOS labels but it provides significant increase in all other labels.

Figure 9. Bar graph of comparison between base model and proposed work

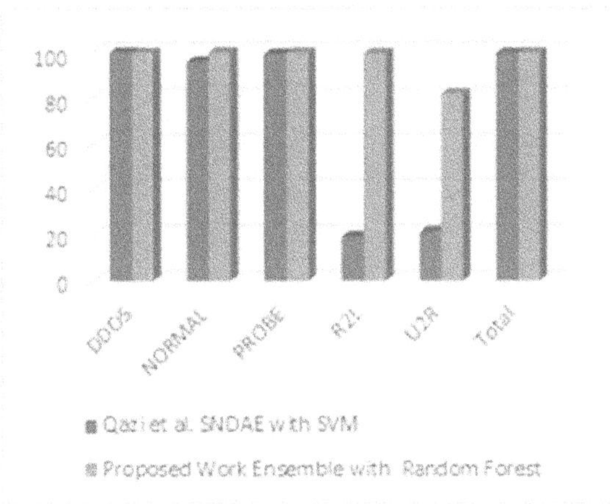

Figure 9 presents the testing outcome of the comparison between the base model and the suggested work. While the SNDAE-SVM model performs well overall, it performs horribly in the U2R and R2L categories. It is because there are less samples in the dataset for the R2L and U2R attacks. The balanced dataset used by the suggested approach enhances the evaluation metrics as a whole. Conditional Tabular GAN (CTGAN) balances the dataset by equating the total number of attack labels with the count of normal labels.

Table 7. Comparison between Ensemble methods with feature extraction and without feature extraction

Models	Accuracy	Precision	Recall	F1-score
SVM	96.27	96.44	96.29	96.20
Ensemble-SVM	**99.67**	**99.66**	**99.60**	**99.65**
RF	98.86	98.92	98.88	98.86
Ensemble-RF	**99.78**	**99.75**	**99.74**	**99.76**
KNN	92.12	92.43	92.34	91.68
Ensemble-KNN	**95.87**	**96.37**	**95.88**	**95.72**

Table 7 represents the comparison between SVM and Ensemble-SVM, Random Forest and Ensemble-RF, KNN, and Ensemble-KNN. The Ensemble models in each classifier shows better performance than the classifiers without feature extraction models.

Table 8. Experimental results of proposed work and other research methods

Study	Wang et al.	Kim et al	Qazi et al	Proposed Work
Method	Fuzzy clustering	LSTM	SNDAE with SVM	Ensemble with Random Forest
Accuracy	96.75	97.54	99.65	99.78
Precision	-	97.69	99.64	99.75
Recall	-	-	99.66	99.74
F1-score	-	98.95	99.63	99.76

Table 8 represents the different experimental results of previous research models. The Fuzzy clustering method provides an accuracy of 96.75. The LSTM approach shows the performance of 97.54. The base research model provides an accuracy of 99.65. The Proposed work slightly shows better results than the SNDAE-SVM model. The Ensemble-Random Forest method shows better results in all evaluation metrics than the SNDAE-SVM.

CONCLUSION AND FUTURE WORK

NSL-KDD 99 was the Network Intrusion Detection System employed in this study. The NSL-KDD 99 is split between a 20% testing set and an 80% training set. It has 1,48,519 samples and 43 features. There are 31 attack labels in the NSL-KDD 99 dataset, categorized into 4 attack methods and 1 normal label. Impressively, the Ensemble with Random Forest achieves 99.78% accuracy, 99.75% precision, 99.74% recall, and a 99.76% F1 score, outperforming other approaches. When compared to the SNDAE-SVM model, these findings strengthen and increase the dependability of our suggested method. Our findings show that better performance results from utilizing the combined strength of S-NDAE, SAE and SSDAE models in an ensemble framework, especially when Random Forest is used. This effectively addresses issues with intrusion detection by increasing prediction accuracy while maintaining a balanced trade-off between precision and recall.

REFERENCES

Alrawashdeh, K., & Purdy, C. (2016). Toward an online anomaly intrusion detection system based on deep learning. In: *Proceedings of the 15th IEEE international conference on machine learning and applications (ICMLA)*. IEEE; p. 195–200. DOI: 10.1109/ICMLA.2016.0040

Amanullah, M. A., Habeeb, R. A. A., Nasaruddin, F., Gani, A., Ahmed, E., Ninar, A. S. M., Akim, N. M., & Imran, M.. (2020). Deep learning and big data technologies for IoT security. *Computer Communications*, 151, 495–517. DOI: 10.1016/j.comcom.2020.01.016

Cordero, C. G., Hauke, S., Mühlhäuser, M., & Fischer, M. (2016, December). Analyzing flow-based anomaly intrusion detection using replicator neural networks. In 2016 14th Annual Conference on Privacy, Security and Trust (PST) (pp. 317-324). IEEE.

Devaraju, S., & Ramakrishnan, S. (2014). Performance comparison for intrusion detection system using neural network with kdd dataset. *ICTACT J Soft Comput*, 4(3), 743–752. DOI: 10.21917/ijsc.2014.0106

Dong, B., & Wang, X. (2016). Comparison deep learning method to traditional methods used for network intrusion detection. In: *Proceedings of the 8th IEEE international conference on communication software and networks (ICCSN)*. IEEE; p. 581–5.

Gao, N., Gao, L., Gao, Q., & Wang, H. (2014). An intrusion detection model based on deep belief networks. In: *Proceedings of the international conference on advanced cloud and big data*. p. 247–52. DOI: 10.1109/CBD.2014.41

Habeeb, R. A. A., Nasaruddin, F., Gani, A., Hashem, I. A. T., Ahmed, E., & Imran, M.. (2019). Real-time big data processing for anomaly detection: A survey. *International Journal of Information Management*, 45(4), 289–307. DOI: 10.1016/j.ijinfomgt.2018.08.006

Hinton, G. E., & Salakhutdinov, R. R. (2006). Reducing the dimensionality of data with neural networks. *Science*, 313(5786), 504–507. DOI: 10.1126/science.1127647 PMID: 16873662

Kang, M. J., & Kang, J. W. (2016). Intrusion detection system using deep neural network for in-vehicle network security. *PLoS One*, 11(6), e0155781.

Kim, J., Kim, J., Thu, H. L. T., & Kim, H. (2016). Long short term memory recurrent neural network classifier for intrusion detection. In: *Proceedings of the international conference on platform technology and service (PlatCon)*. IEEE; p. 1–5. DOI: 10.1109/PlatCon.2016.7456805

Kim, J., Shin, N., Jo, S. Y., & Kim, S. H. (2017). Method of intrusion detection using deep neural network. In: *Proceedings of the IEEE international conference on big data and smart computing (BigComp)*. IEEE; p. 313–6.

Lee, H. W., Kim, N. R., & Lee, J. H. (2017). Deep neural network self-training based on unsupervised learning and dropout. *Int J Fuzzy Logic Intell Syst*, 17(1), 1–9. DOI: 10.5391/IJFIS.2017.17.1.1

Liu, C., Yang, J., & Wu, J. (2020). Web intrusion detection system combined with feature analysis and SVM optimization. *EURASIP Journal on Wireless Communications and Networking*, 33(1), 2020. DOI: 10.1186/s13638-019-1591-1

Niyaz, Q., Sun, W., & Javaid, A. Y. 2016 A deep learning based ddos detection system in software-defined networking (SDN). *CoRR. vol. abs/*1611.07400.

Potluri, S., & Diedrich, C. (2016). Accelerated deep neural networks for enhanced intrusion detection system. In: *Proceedings of the IEEE 21st international conference on emerging technologies and factory automation (ETFA).* IEEE*;* p. 1–8. vol. DOI: 10.1109/ETFA.2016.7733515

Tang, T. A., Mhamdi, L., McLernon, D., Zaidi, S. A. R., & Ghogho, M. (2016). Deep learning approach for network intrusion detection in software defined networking. In: *Proceedings of the international conference onwireless networks and mobile communications (WINCOM).* IEEE*;* p. 258–63. DOI: 10.1109/WINCOM.2016.7777224

Wang, G., Hao, J., Ma, J., & Huang, L. (2010). A new approach to intrusion detection using artificial neural networks and fuzzy clustering. *Expert Systems with Applications*, 37(9), 6225–6232. DOI: 10.1016/j.eswa.2010.02.102

Wang, Y., Cai, W. D., & Wei, P. C. (2016). A deep learning approach for detecting malicious JavaScript code. *Security and Communication Networks*, 9(11), 1520–1534. DOI: 10.1002/sec.1441

Wang, Z., Liu, Y., He, D., & Chan, S. (2021). Intrusion detection methods based on integrated deep learning model. computers & security, 103, 102177.

KEY TERMS AND DEFINITIONS

Autoencoders: A type of neural network used for unsupervised learning that compresses data into a lower-dimensional representation and then reconstructs the original input. Used for feature extraction in IDS.

Conditional Tabular Generative Adversarial Network (CTGAN): A GAN-based model specifically designed for generating synthetic tabular data, used to balance the class distribution in imbalanced datasets.

SNDAE (Stacked Nonlinear Denoising Autoencoder): A type of autoencoder that is trained to reconstruct inputs corrupted by noise, enhancing the learned features and improving robustness.

SAE (Sparse Autoencoder): An autoencoder variant that encourages sparsity in the hidden layer, extracting useful, compressed features with fewer active neurons.

SSDAE (Stacked Sparse Denoising Autoencoder): A hybrid model combining sparse and denoising autoencoders for efficient feature extraction from noisy, high-dimensional data.

Chapter 5
Malicious Anomaly Detection and Prediction Using Prophet Luminol and RNN

R. Suganya
New Horizon College of Engineering, India

Sashikanth Reddy Avula
Nitte Meenakshi Institute of Technology, India

Balasubramanian Prabhu Kavin
https://orcid.org/0000-0001-6939-4683
SRM University, India

Priyan Malarvizhi Kumar
University of North Texas, USA

Jeeva Selvaraj
Jain University, India

Gan Hong Seng
Xi'an Jiaotong-Liverpool University, China

ABSTRACT

Machine learning (ML) has brought about many advancements in today's world which is benefiting humans and machines. Because of the growth of digital services, malicious anomalies have increased on the transmission media. This has compromised crucial and important data of several organizations and companies. Vulnerabilities in network have increased in recent years and problems such as loss of data have increased. The process of detecting anomalies in network traffic becomes very important activity. An effective system for detection of these anomalies should be utilized to stop such attacks. Machine learning mechanisms for anomaly detection can prove to be the most accurate and best form of detecting malware or botnets on network so that we can prevent further threats. In this work one can understand the new implementation methods for anomaly detection. By importing python libraries and building ML models, one can learn certain outliers and different anomalies presence.

DOI: 10.4018/979-8-3693-9919-4.ch005

I. INTRODUCTION

The internet houses large numbers of personal and professional data that becomes vulnerable to certain attackers. Due to the vast usage of the internet by humans' personal data is being compromised which is causing data breaches and economic losses. Recently Facebook, which is the social media hub, lost several million dollars because of

hacking. Several methods have already been utilized in detecting anomalies such as artificial intelligence methods as well as statistical analysis. But anomaly detection involves the analysis of several attributes of the network which makes it complicated. The complex method takes a longer time for identifying the anomalies by which the attack has already been undertaken. In total, three classifications of anomalies which include,

1. Collective anomaly: These anomalies are very identical to the usual data points. Meanwhile, the series of data points present on the whole dataset are very similar, and these are nothing but collective anomalies. An independent anomaly cannot be considered as a problem, but altogether certain abnormalities noticed could be considered as collective anomalies.
2. Point anomaly: Point Anomalies are referred as the most basic form. Unlike collective anomalies they are independent points and they are more abnormal than the normal data and can be easily identified.
3. Contextual anomaly: All the data points representing unusual context are known as contextual anomalies.

Few clarifications have been considered and implemented over the years such as intrusion and fraud detection using some specific software tools and firewalls. Though these are effective it has not given complete protection on attacks over the network thus the study for better methods is undertaken regularly. In this study we can see the usage of recurrent neural networks. RNN is the best suited algorithm to make predictions on time series data. Although the computations are a little on the slower side the RNN because of its memorizing capabilities has proved its worth in detection of anomalies in network traffic. Thus, it is importantly required to have faster and better methods for anomaly detection is needed.

The research study is to understand how the increase in the usage of digital services has enhanced the overall growth of vulnerabilities and the impact of it on today's world. Vulnerabilities can be able to create a disastrous effect in an organization and loss of valuable information including data leaks. This will be problematic for the implementation and progress of any organization or business. Thus, implementation of prediction models helps companies to predict and identify the vulnerabilities affecting their performance and growth. This will help them to take the necessary measures in preventing future data leaks and loss of information. The research will give an efficient approach of predicting vulnerabilities by using machine learning models to help in future development of better and more efficient techniques to prevent vulnerabilities and predict threats occurring at IP workstations as well as network servers of organizations and companies.

Deep learning (DL) and machine learning (ML) techniques have shown promise in a number of anomaly detection applications in recent years, including cybersecurity. Recurrent Neural Networks (RNNs), Prophet, and Luminol are three of these methods that have shown to be effective in identifying and forecasting malevolent abnormalities. The combination of these methods, their functions in anomaly detection, and their potential synergies for increased precision and predictive power are all covered in this introduction.

1. Malevolent Trends in Cybersecurity:

A malicious anomaly is a divergence from a system or network's typical operating behavior brought about by deliberate acts like malware, hacking attempts, denial of service (DoS) assaults, or insider threats. These abnormalities frequently show up as odd network traffic spikes or dips, odd login attempts, strange system activity, or odd patterns of data access. The difficulty in identifying these malevolent abnormalities resides in differentiating between anomalies that are harmless and those that pose real risks. In order to detect abnormalities in real-time, cybersecurity requires extremely accurate systems that can continuously monitor and analyze network logs, user behavior, system performance, and other data sources, (Alshamkhany *et al.*, 2020).

2. The Prophet's Function in Identifying and Predicting Anomalies:

Facebook created Prophet, an open-source forecasting tool made to work with time-series data that includes noise, seasonality, and complex trends. It works especially well with time-series data that is produced by network traffic, system logs, or performance indicators and contains a lot of seasonal patterns and trends. Prophet is a great option for identifying time-series anomalies in cybersecurity because of its exceptional resilience to missing data and ability to adapt to trend changes over time.

3. Luminol's Function in Identifying Anomalies:

LinkedIn created the open-source anomaly detection and correlation library known as Luminol. Its goal is to find patterns in time-series data and link them to other occurrences or irregularities in relevant measures. Because of this, Luminol is particularly helpful in complex systems that monitor several data streams concurrently. By identifying correlations between anomalies in various data sources, one can get a more comprehensive picture of possible security risks, (Shafee, 2020).

4. Using Recurrent Neural Networks (RNN) to Predict Anomalies:

One kind of deep learning architecture called recurrent neural networks (RNNs) performs very well for processing sequential data, including time-series data. RNNs can simulate temporal dependencies and patterns throughout time because of their ability to remember past time steps. Because they can understand intricate temporal correlations between data points, they are therefore well-suited for anomaly identification and prediction in time-series data.

5. Combining Prophet, Luminol, and RNN for Predicting and Detecting Malicious Anomalies:

While Prophet and Luminol work well for identifying and elucidating abnormalities in time-series data, RNNs are superior at understanding intricate temporal relationships and forecasting future occurrences. A more complete approach for identifying and forecasting malevolent abnormalities in cybersecurity may result from combining these tools:

Prophets can be used to predict future trends, find deviations from the expected behavior of time-series data, and model the expected behavior.

Luminol has the ability to detect and correlate anomalies in real-time across several system parameters, facilitating the linking of anomalies.

By learning intricate patterns from past time-series data, RNNs can be trained to predict future dangerous events.

II. LITERATURE SURVEY

By the evolution of internet devices, vulnerabilities on the network are also evolving quite rapidly. Botnets being a major threat to our network, that can be detected easily with the implementation of appropriate machine learning models like Naïve Bayes, KNN, SVM and Decision Tree. These ML models were introduced on a dataset acquired from University of New South Wales (UNSW) which yielded results of 99.89% Testing Accuracy, 100% Recall, 100% Precision and 100% score in detection of malicious network traffic activity giving us an idea that Decision Tree algorithm could be an optimal solution used in classifying anomalies which occur, (Alshamkhany *et al.*, 2020). Few attacks from botnets include Distributed Denial of Service (DDOS), Spamming, Click Fraud, Identity Theft and Phishing Attacks. To counter such attacks and vulnerabilities it is very important to incorporate two host-based detection techniques inclusive of a hybrid methodology, one in which botnets are detected at the host level and the other where corrupted hosts are detected. Both techniques have equal perks, and both prove their efficiency in detecting botnets, (Shafee, 2020). To enhance the detection of rate of malicious traffic in a network, deep neural networks are incorporated along with the support of hierarchical attention mechanisms.

The hierarchical attention technique consists of a detection model known as HAGRU which is a hierarchical attention gated recurrent unit which combines the feature information of almost three hierarchies, (Alabadi & Celik, 2020). Results obtained from the HAGRU model have helped in performing category recognition and also helped in efficiently selecting rich features even in unbalanced and smaller datasets. The only drawback of the model was that it was not able to perform well with larger datasets similar to how it was performing among smaller datasets. The study conducted in Alabadi and Celik (2020) using the repository of NSL - KDD dataset can able to achieve 98% F- score in categories of DoS, normal, probe but in the category of U2R the F-score was only 87.86% which was able to give us the advantages and disadvantages while performing malicious anomaly detection using HAGRU model. Another widely deployed neural network algorithm in detection of anomalies is CNN. The network has been executed along with unified cross framework that supports end-to-end and cross-checking process for anomaly detection is seen being used for obtaining best solutions for botnet detection. CNN has the capability to also work on real-time models by detecting botnets coming in and out of traffic during data transmission, (Elmrabit *et al.,* 2020).

Using some datasets experimental analysis was performed in a high-performing computing facility known as ALICE at the University of Leicester. The results by this Experiment were evaluated by performance metrics which stated that Random Forest model provided the best performance, and Naive Bayes provided the least performance out of the twelve machine learning models used, (Qian, Sun, & Cui, 2021). Another important classifier used for anomaly detection is the SVM- C classification model. Techniques such as feature extraction using statistical laws and linear projection are being deployed along with ML models to assist in deriving the best parameters which could be useful for classification. The SVM-C further helped in analyzing and classifying the attributes with development and implementation of BCD method. The results obtained from using the PBB method have paved the way to give deeper understanding of by what means the parameters in SVM-C react to the dataset, (Tyagi & Kumar, 2021). Although the best methods of DNN are utilized in various models, still there are a few misclassified traffic in the prediction results due to which we can observe loss of information which will prove vulnerable for various situations. The recent methods of detection of anomalies include the incorporation of a two-level anomaly detection system which is grounded on DNN and association analysis. To enhance anomaly detection an intrusion identification mechanism was designed which delivered high performance in detecting malicious traffic and proving that the Apriori algorithm is capable of mining rules between discrete features and normal labels. This process could be utilized in filtering the classifying traffic and falling down the false positive rate. The two-way detection system employed includes only two steps such as classification and filtering giving better accuracy and precision on the detection model, (Nicolas-Alin, 2020).

Internet of Things based smart devices have been utilized in recent times for anomaly detection and as these devices have a higher edge for cyber threats and thus it is highly important to establish an intrusion detection. This method can give a quick, automatic and accurate comparison between benign and malicious traffic. IoT detection systems give better efficiency even if feature reduction techniques such as PCA are not used. A combination of 7 lightweight features were used in identifying attacks such as DDoS, DoS, Reconnaissance, and Information Theft along with IoT system and Random Forest (RF) algorithm which produced 99.99% accuracy, (Haq & Singh, 2018). Even though IoT driven smart devices and applications are widely deployed and used in detecting the purpose of having multiple sensors for collection of information. They are always prone to vulnerabilities; these determinations were obtained by studying the IoT-23 dataset, (Hoang & Nguyen, 2018). Malicious bots found in the communication channel have the ability to run programs automatically once executed in a computer system. Similar to such an attack is the attack of zombie bots which can be controlled remotely by an attacker and a bot can be controlled by a botmaster or a bot controller. Malicious bots have the capacity to tamper confidentiality and authenticity of a network or system. In a pool of zombies, this is so difficult to figure out the bots which are corrupting the system and thus it requires the usage of high- end ML algorithms and a hybrid approach of detection, (Amini *et al.,* 2019).

The IDS-based solution in anomaly detection uses signatures over the network which is less effective because of the adaptability of botnets which have sophisticated code updating and evasion techniques. A machine level botnet detection model was used to determine better accuracy and results over the DGA and FF botnet dataset, (Manikandakumar & Karthikeyan, 2019). Malicious bots and botmasters work ok becoming a threat to the network and infiltrate into the system to gather information, they also make changes to control the data as well as target it. A systematic approach of hierarchical X-Means clustering algorithm and rule-based classification is selected to protect loss of data and information from this attack. The main advantage of X-Means algorithm is that it has the best intra cluster cohesion and can create ample distances between each cluster by choosing the best cluster-based method for diverse numbers of K's. Two important rules such a pseudo-bot properties table and time difference entropy can be utilized to recognize the time order of cluster flows and the clusters which have the entropy less than 95 percent indicated normal traffic this is compared to protocol signatures knows as NetBIOS and DNS to finally give us better understanding of how fuzzy logic with contribution of ML algorithms were used in detection of anomalies in network traffic, (Ahsan & Nygard, 2020).

Anomalies in a network can be categorized in different forms namely point anomalies, collective anomalies, collective anomalies, and contextual anomalies. Anomalies can not only be categorized based on their nature but also can be divided into operation events, flash crowds, measurement anomalies, and network attacks. A novel approach of CNN and Long Short Term which is a hybrid algorithm is considered while performing intrusion detection. The bidirectional algorithm was able to obtain an accuracy of 99.70% on the SL KDD dataset. It also produced accurate results on real time data as well, (Manikandakumar, Sharmi, & Devi, 2015). There are several issues researchers are facing during the development of applying ML techniques, especially deep learning algorithms on wireless communication networks. Route deciding, Network Security, Channel Assignment, Network Optimization, Signal management and network management operations can act as the major influencing factors that are assisting us to resolving the issues faced in detecting anomalies over a wireless communication network, (Tahereh *et al.,* 2020). Applications over the internet are prone to major security threats such as phishing attacks, cross-site scripting attacks, denial of service attacks and many more. Thus, a unified determination method for detection of anomalies could be utilized to safeguard the web applications from internal and external attackers, (Manikandakumar & Kasrthikeyan, 2023). GBAD is a fraud detection technique also used in identifying, analyzing and most importantly synthesizing several approaches for anomaly detection.

The classification framework will give a systematic probe for researchers to get more insights and understanding on the benefits of GBAD techniques. This will help in gaining the better insights of network's nature and anomalies types. The GBAD technique played a major role in detection when vulnerabilities were faced during the fintech software which is also a financial analysis software used by several companies. The same problems were faced by Cambridge Analytica when it decided to use Facebook data for fraud detection. Thus, the GBAD method in OSN's and helped companies and organizations in anomaly detection providing better performance in network traffic, (Ring *et al.,* 2019). A tool known as IDS is used for identifying malicious behavior of network traffic by identifying unauthorized users with the assistantship of all the information gathered. The major drawback in this system is that the IDS can only detect anomalies only when it has been executed on the system and cannot prevent them while the attack is taking place, nor can it detect anomalies very early during the attack. Thus, early detection of malware can be taken care of by deep neural networks supported classifiers. The DNN model helps in training the network data by a supervised method and also will perform feature learning rather than using the existing features. This has already been used in earlier approaches of anomalies detection techniques. A new metric known as earliness is introduced to evaluate how fast an attack can be detected, (Zhiqiang *et al.,* 2021). There are nearly 15 properties that were identified and they all categorized into 5 categories later which included: Nature of the data, General Information, Data volume, Evaluation and Recording Environment. Depending on the listed parameters one will be able to decide which dataset can be best suited for research. Some traffic generators are being used to create a synthetic network and adapt to different network scenarios along with this overfitting of a model that should be prevented while detecting anomalies. Anomalies can be found in URL's as well; thus, a word embedded method is used by which the vector expression of URL can be learned automatically by joining both characters along with the word. A design of DCNN is used for malicious URL detection and pooling of parameters are adjusted for feature extraction which depends on the depth of the current convolution layer and length of the input vector. The experiments conducted on DGA URL, and real URL experiments helped in designing and contributed in building an efficient model for detection of anomalies in network traffic.

III. PROPOSED METHODOLOGY

The primary objective of this proposed work is to understand the techniques like prophet and luminol and RNN to identify the anomalies present in the network. Outliers clearly show abnormalities in the network and thus can be considered as potential threats. The proposed methodology will help in identifying these outliers by representing them in the form of graphs, the necessary steps can be taken to prevent malicious bots in the network as given in Figure 1.

The process of detecting and predicting malicious anomalies through the use of Prophet, Luminol, and Recurrent Neural Networks (RNNs) is depicted in the diagram. The first step is to open the dataset, which is made up of time-series data that was probably taken from network traffic, system logs, or user behavior related to cybersecurity. Following data visualization and analysis, this information is examined more closely. This is an important step that helps reveal patterns, trends, and seasonal fluctuations and facilitates the identification of probable anomalies in the following phase.

The diagram's central theme is anomaly detection and prediction, which makes use of a variety of methods to spot odd behavior. Whereas Luminol focusses on real-time anomaly detection and correlation across several system indicators, Prophet is utilized for time-series forecasting and identifying departures from anticipated trends. In the meanwhile, RNNs are used to identify long-term relationships in sequential data, which makes it possible to forecast future anomalies by using patterns from the past. For RNNs, a sub-dataset is built to focus on relevant characteristics and certain timeframes, ensuring the model is trained efficiently.

The last phase is to generate the observed and forecasted findings. This covers the instantaneous anomaly detection from Prophet and Luminol, as well as the future anomaly predictions from the RNN model. These findings enable real-time detection and proactive protection against malicious activities by providing cybersecurity professionals with useful information to monitor and mitigate potential assaults. This integrated strategy ensures a comprehensive plan for anomaly detection and prediction in dynamic, complex systems.

A. Data Set Selection

Data Set Selection is the first and most important process of implementing a machine learning model. For experimenting and testing purposes, the data are obtained from a public repository under the computer network security domain. The created dataset is called the computer networking traffic data which comprises the live track of communication traffic data collected over the period of years. There are 21K rows in the collected dataset which contains IPs of 10 local workstations collected over a period of three months. Almost 50% of these IPs were vulnerable and were attacked by botnets at some time during the three-month period. Each row in this traffic dataset has four columns which include the following attributes. When putting any machine learning model into practice, choosing the appropriate dataset is an essential first step. One of the most crucial elements of the entire process is the quality, relevance, and structure of the dataset, all of which have a substantial impact on the model's performance. The dataset utilized in this context was taken from a public repository that falls under the computer network security area in order to facilitate experimentation and testing. This dataset provides information on network traffic over a given time period and is intended to mimic real-world cybersecurity issues. The collection, known as computer networking traffic data, is made up of an extensive history of communication traffic data that was gathered over a number of years.

There are 21,000 rows in this dataset, and each row represents a distinct piece of information on network activity. Ten local workstations connected to a computer network are included in the data, which was gathered over a three-month period. These workstations were monitored to log their activities and functioned as the main hubs for network connectivity. The primary advantage of the dataset is its capacity to accurately depict real-world cybersecurity problems; during the course of the monitoring period, botnet attacks were detected on almost 50% of the workstations' IP addresses, which were proven to be vulnerable. This establishes a strong basis for anomaly identification and prediction based on machine learning and offers a useful insight into harmful behaviors. The date column is defined as date and is in yyyy-mm-dd format and contains data from 2006-07- 01 to 2006-09-30

Figure 1. Flow chart of implementation

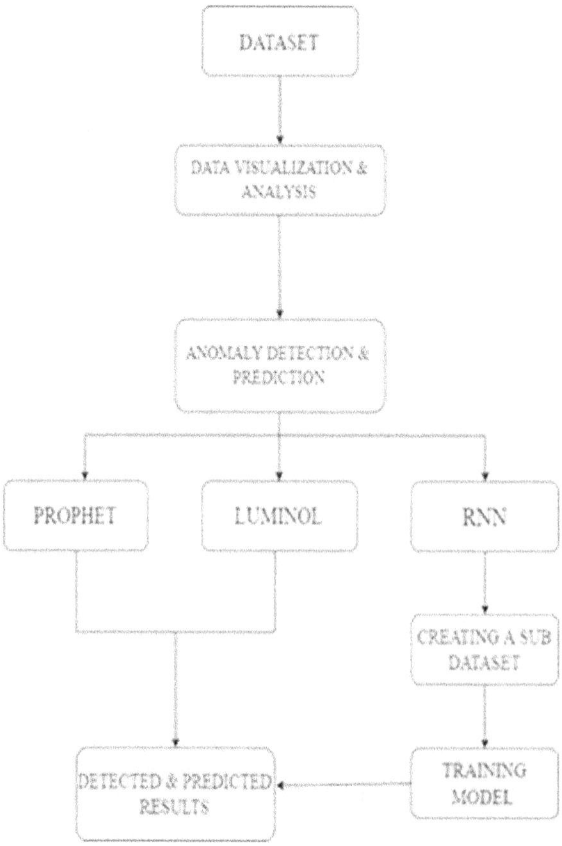

- Local IP: Local IP in dataset is termed as l_ipn it is coded in integer numbers and has values from 0-9 where these values are the 10 local workstations.
- Remote ASN: The remote ASN is denoted by r_asn and helps in identifying the remote ISP which is the remote internet service provider. The ASN which is the autonomous system number remains unique to every connection made by the network endpoint.
- Flow: The flow is represented by "f" which is total number counting of connections for a particular day in network.

Dataset used has 4 parameters which simple and straight forward that helps in decreasing the complexity of the overall model for implementation. The four parameters mentioned are general for all the organizations keeping more than one IP workstation for their networks. Large organizations such as schools and colleges run on an independent setup for network access and they use their own IP Pools & Autonomous system number. This helps them to differentiate the networks from one IP workstation to another. Such network architecture could be utilized by several organizations hence the dataset with these 4 parameters has been chosen to develop a prediction model. This strategy can be handled by the organizations following such network configurations.

B. Data Visualization and Analysis

Data Visualization and Analysis is the process of identifying the unique data points present in the given data. By Analysis and visualization, there are 20,803 rows and 4 columns which do not contain any missing values. The data available is 92 days and the unique local ip is given as 10 and remote asn is 2005. The minimum and maximum flow count per day is 1 and 784234 per day. Histograms and graphs were plotted to get the connection flow aggregate across both the local ip and remote asn for each day.

C. Anomaly Detection and Prediction

1) Prophet

Prophet techniques are helpful for demonstrating the data in a time series in which non-linear data flow can be fit daily, weekly and yearly. Prophet is very vigorous to missing values and change in data points, but majorly it acts very good at detecting outliers.

2) Luminol

Luminol is a python library which is lightweight and could be utilized for the analysis of data in time series. The major functionalities that luminol is supportive of are anomaly correlation and detection. The specific feature of the luminol library is that it will not be dependent on existing predefined values but rather it is capable of assigning individual data points with anomaly score. With the help of those scores, it is able to find and identify the anomalies in an easy manner.

3) RNN – Recurrent Neural Networks

RNN is one of the popular deep learning based neural network algorithms. In RNN the nodes are connected in the methods of the directed graph or an undirected graph in subject with a temporal sequence. The biggest advantage in the usage of this one is that it has a capability of memorizing about its past unlike other algorithms which rely on only present conditions. Now let us understand the three important auxiliary features undertaken during the implementation of RNN in predicting the flow of network traffic.

a) Create a sub dataset: The first auxiliary function is to develop two independent lists. One list is used for holding all the features and the next one is for the target for the model.
b) Train Model: All the 10 local IPs are trained by a single RNN.
c) Predict the flow: The flow of the network based on each local workstation is predicted using the trained model.

IV. RESULTS AND PREDICTIONS

The graphs which were plotted based on prophet had red color dots which indicated potential anomalies. Similarly in the case of luminol library the red dots were the anomalies in the network. The RNN was used to predict how IP flow will evolve in time using approximation entropy; the results and predictions of all the three methods of detection and prediction can be seen in Figure 2.

Figure 2. Graph showing the IP flow and anomaly detection

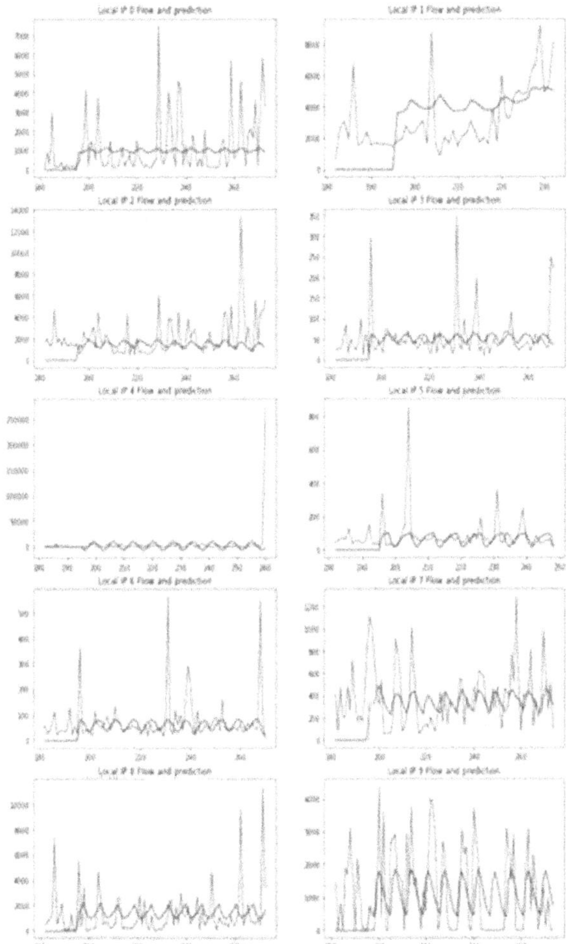

Figure 3. ApEn variation in comparison with the different Ip stations

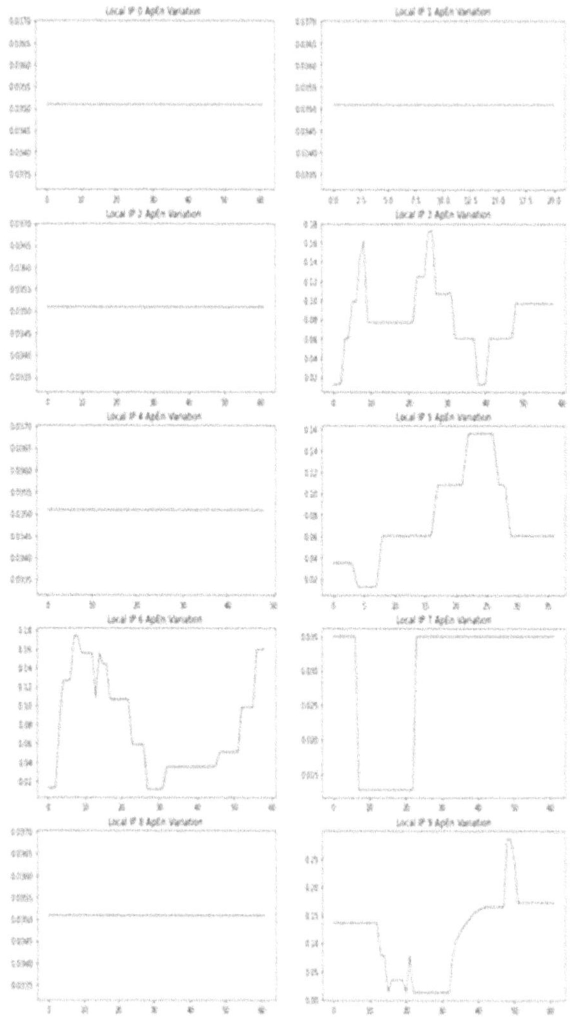

The Approximate entropy (ApEn) is a popular statistical approach that is useful and essential to recognize the regularity and unpredictability of the fluctuations consisting over time-series data. All the time series kind of data will be following the repetitive patterns of variations in them and the ApEn gives us the likelihood and similar patterns that were observed as illustrated in Figure 3. In case, time series data are having lesser repetitive pattern, then it will for sure have a smaller ApEn. Although a process that is less predictable has a much higher ApEn. The ApEn is determined by the given equation below where 'm' is the positive integer and r is the real positive number.

$$\text{ApEn} = \Phi^{m}(r) - \Phi^{m+1}(r)$$

VI. CONCLUSION

The study shows us one such way of detecting the anomalies of a network as well as predicting how the flow would evolve for future security benefits and preventing vulnerabilities in traffic. The data-set chosen was obtained from a public repository and contained more than 20K rows and 4 columns. Prophet and Luminol libraries were used to distinguish the anomalies present and the RNN was helpful in predicting the further evolution of the flow using approximation entropy. Future scope of the project will involve the real time detection of anomalies and finding high accuracy models and best detecting predicting models for detection of anomalies in network traffic. The developed model is mostly specific for networking devices having multiple IP workstations and requires the remote asn to access them. The prediction model can help large organizations such as schools, colleges, and companies etc. which uses similar network architecture for smooth functioning.

REFERENCES

Ahsan, M., & Nygard, K. E. (2020, March; Vol. 69). Convolutional Neural Networks with LSTM for Intrusion Detection. In CATA.

Alabadi, M., & Celik, Y. (2020, June). Anomaly detection for cyber-security based on convolution neural network: A survey. In *2020 International Congress on Human-Computer Interaction, Optimization and Robotic Applications (HORA)* (pp. 1-14). IEEE.

Alshamkhany, M., Alshamkhany, W., Mansour, M., Khan, M., Dhou, S., & Aloul, F. (2020, November). Botnet attack detection using machine learning. In 2020 14th International Conference on Innovations in Information Technology (IIT) (pp. 203-208). IEEE.

Amini, P., Azmi, R., & Araghizadeh, M. (2019). Analysis of Network Traffic Flows for Centralized Botnet Detection. *Journal of Telecommunication.*, 11, 7–17.

Elmrabit, N., Zhou, F., Li, F., & Zhou, H. (2020, June). Evaluation of machine learning algorithms for anomaly detection. In 2020 international conference on cyber security and protection of digital services (cyber security) (pp. 1-8). IEEE.

Haq, S., & Singh, Y. (2018, December). Botnet detection using machine learning. In *2018 Fifth International Conference on Parallel, Distributed and Grid Computing (PDGC)* (pp. 240-245). IEEE.

Hoang, X. D., & Nguyen, Q. C. (2018). Botnet Detection Based On Machine Learning Techniques Using DNS Query Data. *Future Internet*, 10(5), 43. DOI: 10.3390/fi10050043

Ma, Q., Sun, C., Cui, B., & Jin, X. (2021). A novel model for anomaly detection in network traffic based on kernel support vector machine. *Computers & Security*, 104, 102215.

Manikandakumar, M., & Karthikeyan, P. (2019). *A Comprehensive Study on Internet of Things Security: Challenges and Recommendations, Handbook of Advancing Consumer-Centric Fog Computing Architectures*. IGI Global.

Manikandakumar, M., & Karthikeyan, P. (2023). Weed classification using particle swarm optimization and deep learning models. *Computer Systems Science and Engineering*, 44(1), 913–927. DOI: 10.32604/csse.2023.025434

Manikandakumar, M., Sharmi, K. M., & Devi, S. S. (2015). Analyzing spam messages and detecting the zombies using spam count and percentage-based detection algorithm. *International Journal of Applied Engineering Research: IJAER*, 10(55), 1284–1289.

Pourhabibi, T., Ong, K. L., Kam, B. H., & Boo, Y. L. (2020). Fraud detection: A systematic literature review of graph-based anomaly detection approaches. *Decision Support Systems*, 133, 113303.

Ring, M., Wunderlich, S., Scheuring, D., Landes, D., & Hotho, A. (2019). A survey of network-based intrusion detection data sets. *Computers & Security*, 86, 147–167.

Sarao, P. (2019). Machine learning and deep learning techniques on wireless networks. *International Journal of Engineering Research & Technology (Ahmedabad)*, 12(3), 311–320.

Shafee, A. (2020, October). Botnets and their detection techniques. In *2020 International Symposium on Networks, Computers and Communications (ISNCC)* (pp. 1-6). IEEE.

Stoian, N. A. (2020). Machine learning for anomaly detection in iot networks: Malware analysis on the iot-23 data set (Bachelor's thesis, University of Twente).

Tyagi, H., & Kumar, R. (2021). Attack and anomaly detection in IoT networks using supervised machine learning approaches. *Revue d'Intelligence Artificielle*, 35(1), 11–21. DOI: 10.18280/ria.350102

Wang, Z., Ren, X., Li, S., Wang, B., Zhang, J., & Yang, T. (2021). A malicious URL detection model based on convolutional neural network. *Security and Communication Networks*, 2021(1), 5518528.

Chapter 6
A Framework for Insider Threat Detection Using Role-Based Profile Assessment and Threshold

Qais Al-Na'amneh
https://orcid.org/0009-0008-3034-7693
Applied Science Private University, Jordan

Mahmoud Aljawarneh
https://orcid.org/0000-0003-2003-6310
Applied Science Private University, Jordan

Rahaf Hazaymih
Jordan University of Science and Technology, Jordan

ABSTRACT

Insider threats are a major worry for organizations and governments. Insiders often have significant knowledge of an organization's architecture, making traditional intrusion detection systems ineffective. Sophisticated measures are needed to analyze internal behaviors and assess potential threats. The insider threat has started to represent a significant growing challenge for organizations and companies This chapter dives into the nature of insider threats in general, with a special focus on the malicious insider psychological factors exploring their causes and impacts, and how that can help predict and prevent such incidents. In comparison, providing and examining real-world cases and providing suggestions on how to deal with them .Furthermore, this chapter proposes a framework approach for detecting insider threats. The model is built on a layered method that connects the real world, measurements, and parameters to assess the likelihood of an insider threat.

DOI: 10.4018/979-8-3693-9919-4.ch006

INTRODUCTION

Insider threats pose a high risk and significant growing challenges for organizations and companies alike. This is a huge concern, as such incidents are rising worldwide. What distinguishes them from another type of attacks is that, unlike external attacks that often capture much more media attention, insider threats come from deep within the organization and deal with exploiting the very trust and access the organization grants to their employees and members to cause harm or damage to an organization's infrastructure or operations (Alzaabi & Mehmood, 2024). Hackers used the employees' legitimate credentials with direct access to critical systems and data in addition to the reputational damage the company endures from such incidents (Yilmaz & Can, 2024).

As organizations increasingly rely more on digital infrastructures, the attack surface for insider threats has expanded greatly. In modern work environments that are characterized by remote work,(Song et al., 2024) cloud computing such as an environment where most company data is stored digitally and not on paper, the lines between insider and outsider threats often blur, especially when external actors compromise internal credentials.

Below are notable security incidents that an insider caused:

1. Police Service of Northern Ireland (PSNI) - 2023: This insider breach involved an employee accidentally posting sensitive data of over 10,000 officers and civilian staff. The data included names and ranks, which were quickly disseminated by dissident groups. The exposure lasted only a couple of hours but caused significant concern for those in intelligence roles (Pete O'Doherty, 2023).
2. The Verizon data breach occurred when an employee improperly accessed a file containing personal information of over 63,000 colleagues. The breach was discovered in December 2023, but unauthorized access took place in September. The compromised data included names, addresses, Social Security numbers, and compensation details. (Al-Na'amneh et al., 2024; Toulas, 2024).
3. March 2019, Capital One bank: a bank with fifty-two thousand employees at the time of the attack (Al-Shehari et al., 2024) suffered from a massive data breach that made headlines, it resulted in over one hundred million customers having their data records exposed, including their financial information(Padiet et al., 2024).
4. 2020 Twitter: the famous social media company that employed 5500 employees at the time (A. Singh et al., 2024) the company suffered from an attack that happened by utilizing phone-based social engineering, hackers managed to get Twitter employee login credentials. At first, they managed to compromise login information for lower-level employees who did have access to the administrative tools needed for the attack. After more efforts, based on those first credentials, hackers were able to reach and compromise the individuals who had the needed access to the administrative tool to perform the planned attack (Duan et al., 2024)
5. 2019 Desjardins: a Canadian bank with forty-eight thousand employees and seven million members and clients (AlQahtani et al., 2024) was a victim of a data breach caused by a malicious insider who exfiltrated confidential data of 4.2 million clients (Aljaidi et al., 2023).

Most importantly, since prevention is better than curing, the main topic in this chapter is the psychological and other factors involved that can make it easier to detect a possible insider threat and prevent it beforehand from different insider threat sources as shown in Table 1. Certain behavior patterns as explained in Table 2 can be observed by managers that might indicate and help with predicting potential insider threats before they happen and that is called the psychological model.

Table 1. Insider threat sources

Malicious insider	Compromised insider	Neglect insider	Insider colluders	3rd party insiders
Saboteurs: employees who have access and intentionally want to harm the organization Thieves: insiders who steal sensitive data for their own personal gains	Unwitting Accomplices: employees who are helping the attack without realizing they are Account Compromise: when an outsider manages to get an insiders credentials	Careless Users: insiders who unintentionally harm the organization because of their incompetence (phishing for example) Inadvertent Disclosures: employees who accidently reveal secret info by sending emails to the wrong address	Collaborators: insiders who work side by side with an outsider sharing the info through blackmailing or for monetary gains	Contractors/Vendors: organizations and/or individuals who have been given access to the company's systems but cause problems due to their malicious intent or lack of knowledge

Table 2. Some of the psychological indicators

Indicator	Description
Disgruntlement	Employee showing, he is not satisfied in his current position given and feels like he deserves better. Which potentially makes him hold grudges
Not Accepting Feedback	He/she has a hard time accepting any given critic about his/her work and takes everything given on a personal level. hardly admits any mistakes
Anger Management Issues	Regularly shows anger at the management or his coworkers
Disengagement	Keeps everything to himself. Similarly to an introvert
Disregard for Authority	Doesn't respect rules. Sees himself as being above them
Stress	Appears to be having emotional, and/or physical and/or mental stress
Performance	Previously Received a corrective action based on his poor performance
personal Issues	employee is unable to separate his personal issues outside of work and rather carries it over with him to the workplace
Self-Centeredness	Employee shows little to know care about other employees and focuses on himself only while disregarding the interests of others around him
Confrontational	Known for showing aggressive behaviors and can be involved to bullying his coworkers and intimidating them
Lack of Dependability	Employee does not value his words and is unworthy of trust
absenteeism	Employee is frequently absent from his commitment at work

(Tao et al., 2024)

Those who are working in management or HR can use that information to better understand the nature of the threat or the threat indicators that can be reported to cybersecurity officers

The Main contribution of this study can be indicated as follows:

- Propose a new framework to identify potential malicious insiders using user activity data (i.e. profiling). The framework gets the following values for each user to detect a malicious insider-based metric parameter
- Discussion and comparison of the range of possible activities that an insider may conduct to achieve their expected daily workload, rather than being restricted to only the activities that are deemed as an attack. By doing so, acquire a richer picture of an attack which may reveal insiders' motives and facilitate our understanding of their behavior.
- The evaluation framework detects a malicious insider based on some factors.
- Proposes a framework approach for detecting insider threats. The model is built on a layered method that connects the real world, measurements, and parameters to assess the likelihood of an insider threat.

The remainder of the paper is structured as follows. The second Section discusses the literature in the field by evaluating the related work. The third Section explains the methodology and proposes an architecture framework to identify potential malicious insiders using the user activity data. The fourth Section presents the experimental results and their discussion. Finally, the conclusion and future work presented in section five.

LITERATURE REVIEW

Insider threats once considered a lesser concern compared to external attacks, have evolved into a significant cybersecurity risk. These threats stem from individuals within an organization who intentionally or unintentionally compromise its security. Recent improvements in insider threat detection frameworks emphasize the integration of user and role-based profiling to improve detection accuracy. The previous studies seem to have focused on either preventing the insider threat or constructing mitigation frameworks, but they seemed to have ignored thinking about coming up with a solution on the spot to fix the alerting psychological traits before they cause an incident.

In this interconnected world where practically nowadays all companies and organizations rely on internet-based services, cyber threats are becoming a real concern, and many companies have started to dedicate some of their budgets to counter cyber threats. One of the most prevalent threats is insider threats (Rao, 2024). What makes this threat especially interesting is that no matter how big a budget the company dedicates to and builds sophisticated defensive frameworks against outside attacks, it won't be of any benefit once the hackers gain insider administrative credentials. Insider threat or what can be referred to as "the invisible enemy within" is generally defined as "malicious actions performed by an insider in a secure environment often resulting in harm to the organizations' system, electronic fraud and information theft."(Hong et al., 2023)

According to this report, over the past five years, 76% of organizations involved have detected insider threat activities. A study by Clearswift (Pal et al., 2023)reports that 58% of reported security incidents were because of insider threats. What might explain why this topic is worthy of attention and why it has been gaining a lot of momentum recently is the existing studies on insider threat detection and mitigation have engaged a wide variety of approaches in trying to understand this very complicated phenomenon of insider threats within organizations.

(Li et al., 2023)developed one behavioral model that analyzed employee attitudes, emotions, motivations, and behaviors for the isolation of high-risk individuals who may become insider threats. In the pilot study, this work proved to have predictive accuracy regarding the model, but attendant ethical and privacy concerns had to be considered while fielding systems such as these.

Building on this, (Al-Na'amneh et al., 2023) went further to conduct a mixed-method study with interviews, questionnaires, and behavioral monitoring to elicit deep insight into insider threat motivations and behaviors. These results showed that the drivers of insider threats were basically dissatisfied with financial gain, and divided loyalties. These factors call for a multifaceted approach applicable to technical and human factors.

As far back as 2012, Pfleeger and Caputo wrote a conceptual piece that provided a comprehensive framework of understanding behind the drivers of insider threats and mitigation strategies, informed by psychological and organizational factors. It underlined the need for a multidisciplinary approach to meeting this challenge. Although not empirically validated, the model represents a useful theoretical base for further research (Asha et al., 2023).

(Randive et al., 2023) analyzed 23 insider threat incidents by applying a retrospective case study approach to understand how such incidents could be facilitated by behavioral, technical, and organizational factors. This research provided insight into common patterns and warning signs of insider threats, emphasizing the need for proactive monitoring and intervention. However, the findings were limited to the specific historical cases examined and may not be directly generalized in other organizational contexts.

Also, it is worth noting that over the last couple of years, the number of insider threat incidents increased by 47% (Al-Mhiqani et al., 2020). A methodology proposed by (Le & Zincir-Heywood, 2021) uses the Isolation Forest Algorithm to examine variations in user conduct within equivalent jobs, to detect irregularities suggestive of insider threats. When compared to conventional methods, this approach demonstrated higher dependability, especially when it came to differentiating between benign and harmful activity within the same job roles (Randive et al., 2023). Another system, called E-Watcher, was created by (Steingartner et al., 2021). It uses a hybrid model that combines statistical analysis and machine learning to handle problems like bias and overfitting. On the CERT dataset, it achieved a detection accuracy of 98.48% (AlSlaiman et al., 2023). Furthermore, (Laila et al., 2024) introduced the CATE model, which combines transformers and convolutional attention to evaluate sequential and statistical user data. This greatly enhances the identification of insider threats by identifying temporal linkages that are frequently missed by previous models (Al Mamlook et al., 2023). With an AUC of 0.9730, the BRITD model by (Kim et al., 2019) demonstrates its effectiveness in a variety of threat scenarios. It focuses on time-aware behavioral rhythm analysis, embedding time information into behavioral features. The work in (M. Singh et al., 2019) proposed insider threat detection by using deep learning techniques to analyze users' communication and build a profile for each individual. This profile is compared with the baseline profile to detect the anomalies and generate threat ranking based on those detected anomalies and user's role and their access rights allowing for proactive detection of potential threat insider. The work in (AlSlaiman et al., 2023) employed Hidden Markov models to detect insider threats and used the sequences and query sensitivity score to come up with a usage profile for each job role. The produced profile worked as the baseline for the detection of anomalous user action to effectively identify the insider attack for the relational database users.

The authors in (Padiet et al., 2024) address the critical issue of insider threats by proposing a user-centric approach to detect malicious activities through download logs. By leveraging machine learning and anomaly detection techniques, the study identifies patterns indicative of insider threats, achieving a high accuracy rate with the RandomTree classifier. This research offers practical solutions for enhancing organizational security, particularly in the context of increased remote work, and contributes valuable insights into the field of information security. A model utilizing graph neural networks was presented by (Jaradat et al., 2023) to abstract user features into heterogeneous graphs. This model captures implicit user relationships and improves detection performance significantly.

The authors in (Nasir et al., 2021) proposed a deep learning approach, based on 'LSTM-Autoencoder' for insider threat detection focusses on behavioral analysis, monitoring the actions of users within the network. By understanding normal user behavior, the model can more effectively identify deviations that suggest insider threats. This approach tried to identify the anomalies in network traffic that may indicate insider threats. Network packet inspection has been used for insider threat detection, while honey pot sensors have been used as s decoy within the company's local network to detect insiders.

The authors in (Haq et al., 2022) presents a NLP and deep learning hybrid approach model using Word2vec LSTM and GLoVe LSTM with promising results in reducing the false alarm rates. The integration of NLP with deep learning models has shown promise in various domains, including cybersecurity. NLP techniques, such as Word2vec and GLoVe, are used to convert textual data into meaningful vector representations, which can then be processed by deep learning models like LSTM (Long Short-Term Memory) networks. LSTM networks are particularly effective for sequence prediction tasks due to their ability to capture long-term dependencies in data. The study primarily focuses on analyzing historical data. Implementing these models for on-the-spot real-time detection of insider threats remains a challenge. The researchers in (Khan et al., 2022) explore the factors influencing unintentional insider threats in cybersecurity, emphasizing the role of decision-making, task complexity, and organizational dynamics. Through interviews and grounded theory, it identifies key themes such as lived experience, acquired knowledge, task complexity, speed of incidents, and emotional responses. The study proposes a framework based on the Epidemiological Triangle, focusing on user vulnerabilities, process effectiveness, resource allocation, knowledge sharing, and fluctuating vulnerabilities. This framework aims to provide actionable recommendations for organizations to identify, intervene, and mitigate unintentional insider threats, highlighting the importance of continuous improvement and a culture of empowerment.

(Legg et al., 2015) present an effective multi-faceted approach for insider threat detection using a combination of anomaly detection and visual analytics. The system is able to detect insider threats by assessing each user based on three levels of alerts: policy violations and previously recognized attacks, threshold-based anomalies, and deviation-based anomalies. The system employs a three-structured profiling approach to capture the details of activities conducted by each user and their respective job roles. This approach provides a rich description of user behavior, allowing for a comprehensive assessment of potential threats. The combination of these three levels of alerts ensures a robust detection mechanism that can identify a wide range of insider threats, but human analyst involvement can delay responses.

(Salem et al., 2024) provides a new framework for understanding insider threats, emphasizing the need for a multidisciplinary approach and continuous monitoring to detect and prevent IP theft. This research highlights the importance of considering both psychological and socio-technical factors in developing effective insider threat detection and prevention strategies.

While no system can be given 100% assurance and immunity from attacks (Lad, 2024). We suggest that companies dedicate a part of their budget to hiring a psychologist that works with HR utilizing the psychological indicator model to help with providing guidance and advice on how to deal with the employees that show bad alarming traits that require attention to help start on spot procedure that prevents the employees from initiating bad action.

In Conclusion, these studies show how useful it is to combine advanced machine learning approaches, role-based profiling, and user behavior analysis when creating frameworks for the detection of insider threats.

METHODOLOGY

In this section, we aim to identify potential malicious insiders using user activity data. The application gets the following values for each user to detect a malicious insider-based metric parameter. To tackle the complicated and unpredictable problem that an insider threat may pose, we created an analytical framework for insider threat detection that exists in the actual world and correlates with insider danger. Examples of insider behavior include system activity logs, building access records, physical behavior, and psychological mentality.

The approach we use involves identifying specific aspects of the issue's space that can provide valuable data for investigation. Many elements will have several distinguishing characteristics. Insider threats may have varying attack incentives, such as financial gain or competitive advantage.

1. **Login time**: The time the user logged into the system. Unless it differs from the user's typical schedule, the user's 15:00 login time does not raise any immediate concerns. The user signed in during usual business hours.
2. **Access count**: The number of times a user accesses the system within a certain period. Twenty times did the user log into the system. Based on the user's past conduct and the standards for the 'admin' role, it may be determined whether this is uncommon. For instance, it can be concerning if administrators log in less frequently than usual.
3. **Data accessed**: The quantity or type of data accessed by the user. There were 1000 data units accessed by the user. Although administrators frequently have more access to data, this could be regarded as high. It might be suspected, though, if 1000 units is noticeably more than usual for this admin or more than what users in this role usually access.
4. **User's role**: in the organization (for example, administrator, user, or guest): The user often gets additional access rights as an “admin.” But increased standards are also accompanied by increased scrutiny. If this behavior is unusual for administrators, there may be reason for concern.
5. **A threshold**: is a set boundary that distinguishes between normal and suspicious behavior. Since the threshold is set at 2, even a slight departure from typical behavior may raise questions. The available data indicates increased data usage and access, which might surpass this limit if the user usually logs in less frequently or accesses less data.

A user could possibly be considered a malicious insider if they display the following behaviors whereas Algorithm 1 presents the pseudocode

Algorithm 1 Pseudo-code of the Detect malicious insider threat algorithm

```
1. Initialize typical behavior for different roles:


typical_access_counts = {'admin': 8, 'user': 5, 'guest': 2}
```

```
typical_data_accessed = {'admin': 400, 'user': 100, 'guest': 20}

working_hours_start = 9 // Represents 9:00 AM

working_hours_end = 18 // Represents 6:00 PM

2. Convert login_time to a datetime object.

Extract the hour from the login_time.

3. Check Access Count:

If access_count > (typical_access_counts[role] * threshold):

Set is_malicious = True

Set reason = "Access count is unusually high for the role."

Return is_malicious, reason

4. Check Data Accessed:

If data_accessed > (typical_data_accessed[role] * threshold):

Set is_malicious = True

Set reason = "Data accessed is unusually high for the role."

Return is_malicious, reason
```

```
5. Check Login Time:

If login_hour < working_hours_start OR login_hour >= working_hours_end:

o Set is_malicious = True

o Set reason = "Login time is outside typical working hours."

o Return is_malicious, reason

If none of the above conditions are met:

Set is_malicious = False

Set reason = "No suspicious activity detected."

Return is_malicious, reason
```

Figure 1 shows how to make decisions based on access count, data accessed, and login time to identify possible Malicious insiders. started entering Data by the user (user_id, login_time, access_count, data_accessed, role, threshold) After that Verify the Access Count (Examine the difference between the user's access count and the usual access count multiplied by the threshold for their role).

Also, calculate whether access counts as suspicious or not. Moreover, Verify the Accessed Data (Examine how much data the user accesses concerning how much data is typically accessed for their role, multiplied by the threshold). Also, Verify the User's Login Time to See If It Is Outside of Typical Working Hours. Mark as Suspicious if it is outside of business hours. Go on to the following check if it's within business hours. Finally, the user is designated as a Potential Malicious Insider if any checks are reported as suspicious.

Figure 1. Proposed flow chart insider threat detection

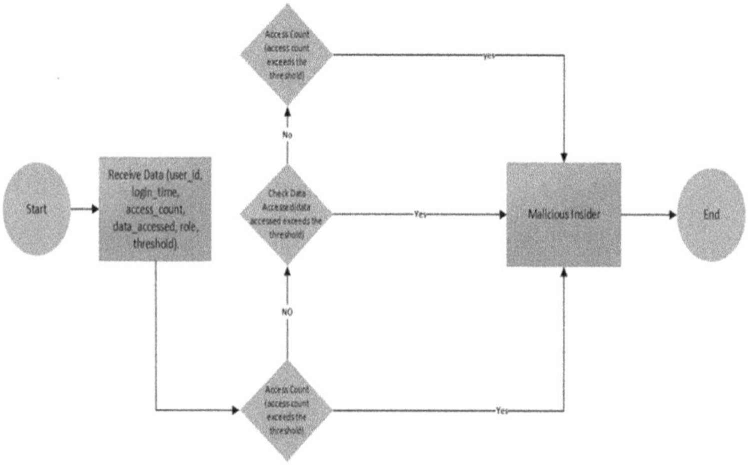

To evaluate the proposed approach whether a user is a possible insider threat, consider several scenarios depending on changes in the provided data (user_id, login_time, access_count, data_accessed, role, threshold). For each scenario, we'll evaluate the user's threat potential and explain our reasons

A. Scenario 1:

The subject in this scenario is “admin1”, who signs in on “August 10, 2024, at 10:00 AM”. The administrator has access to 5 different pieces of data during the session, for a total of 300 information units. The function of the administrator is designated as admin, and typical activity monitoring is triggered by a specified threshold of three accesses

- Access Count: An administrator typically has 5 access, which is normal, especially when compared to the 3 thresholds (an administrator's typical access count maybe 8 * 3 = 24.
- Data Accessed: Since administrators usually manage higher volumes of data, 300 units of data accessed by an admin is likewise within a fair range.
- Time of Login: The login period falls during standard business hours.

Finally, Normal administrative activity No threat was found. The administrator behaves within the expected parameters.

B. Scenario 2:

In this scenario, on” August 10, 2024, at 2:00 PM”, the user known as “user123” logs in. The user accesses 15 data items and retrieves a total of 100 information units, a marked increase in activity over normal. The role of the user is held by the user, and the usual activity threshold is set at two accesses.

- Access Count: 15 accesses by an ordinary user is a lot, especially in comparison to the threshold (5 * 2 = 10 is the typical access count for users). This can point to questionable actions.
- Data Accessed: A user's 100 units of data access are normal and unremarkable on their own.
- Time of Login: The login period falls during standard business hours.

Finally, High access by a regular user is a potential threat. The user accesses the system more frequently than usual.

C. Scenario 3:

In this scenario, on “August 10, 2024, at 4:00 PM”, the user “guest789” signs in. The guest user accesses two data items out of the entire 150 units of data, which is unusual behavior. This user has been assigned the role of guest, with a typical activity threshold of two data accesses.

- Access Count: Two guest accesses are normal and cause no cause for concern.
- Data Accessed: It is very unusual for a guest to access 150 units of data. Typically, guests shouldn't handle a lot of data and have restricted access. This greatly surpasses the average amount of data accessed by a guest, which might be approximately 20 * 2 = 40
- Time of Login: The login period falls during standard business hours.

Finally Unusual Data Access by Guest High risk. The guest has significantly more access to data than is appropriate.

D. Scenario 4:

In this scenario, on” August 10, 2024, at 11:00 PM”, the user known as” admin2” logs in. The administrator accesses six data items and retrieves 400 units of information, indicating a high degree of activity. The user has three accesses as the typical activity threshold, and their role is “admin”. The fact that the login happened outside of usual business hours gives the examination of the administrator's actions a new perspective.

- Access Account: Six accesses by an administrator are within a fair range
- Data Accessed: An administrator typically accesses 400 units of data.
- Time of Login: The login period is not during ordinary business hours. Administrators may work late on occasion, but frequent access afterhours could raise suspicions.

Finally, Off-hours administrative access A potential threat. Accessing the system outside of working hours is suspicious.

E. Scenario 5:

In this scenario, on” August 10, 2024, at 11:00 AM”, user “admin3” signs in. The administrator retrieves 8 data items and 1500 units of information in this session, an exceptionally high volume of data access. The “threshold” for typical activity is set at three accesses, and the user's role is “admin”.

This scenario demonstrates an instance of data access that is much higher than the average administrator usage limitations.

- Access Count: An administrator typically has eight accesses.
- Data Accessed: Even for an admin, 1500 data units accessed is a very high number. This could mean that the administrator is accessing more data than is necessary because it surpasses the normal amount of data accessed, which could be 400 * 3 = 1200.
- Time of Login: The login period falls during standard business hours.

Finally, Excessive data access by the administrator A potential threat. The administrator has access to an unusually huge amount of data.

After implementing scenarios Figure 2 provides an extended study of how each scenario deviates from predicted norms, assisting in identifying which scenarios provide a larger risk of insider threats.

Figure 2. Data and access deviation from threshold

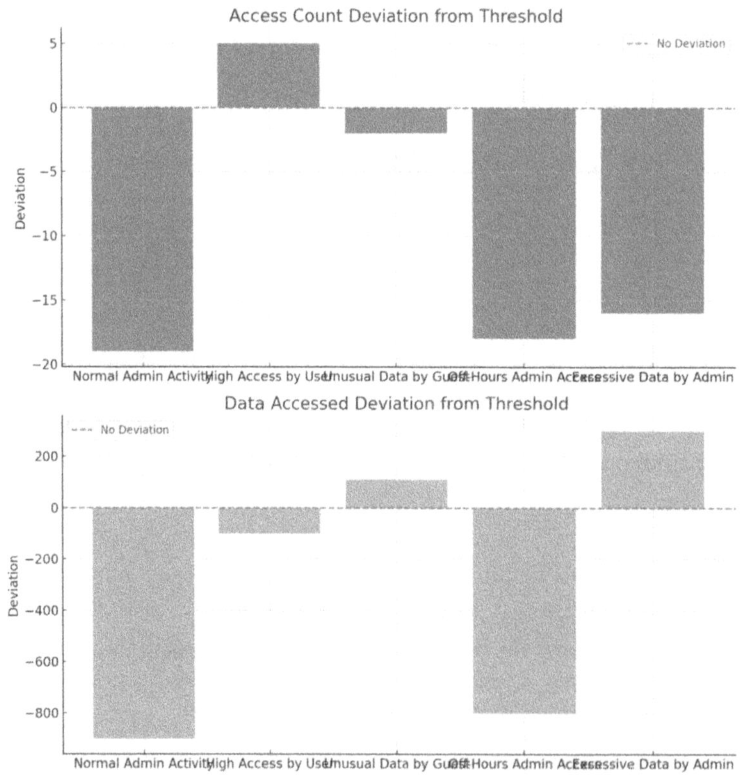

Also, Figure 3 shows a 7-day trend analysis that identifies tendencies for each position. While most roles, such as administrator, user, and analyst, adhere to standard working hours, the supervisor and developer roles' continuous late-night activity raises suspicions. Such patterns could imply either a requirement for after-hours labor or a hint of aberrant conduct that requires more scrutiny.

Figure 3. Long time trends over 7 days

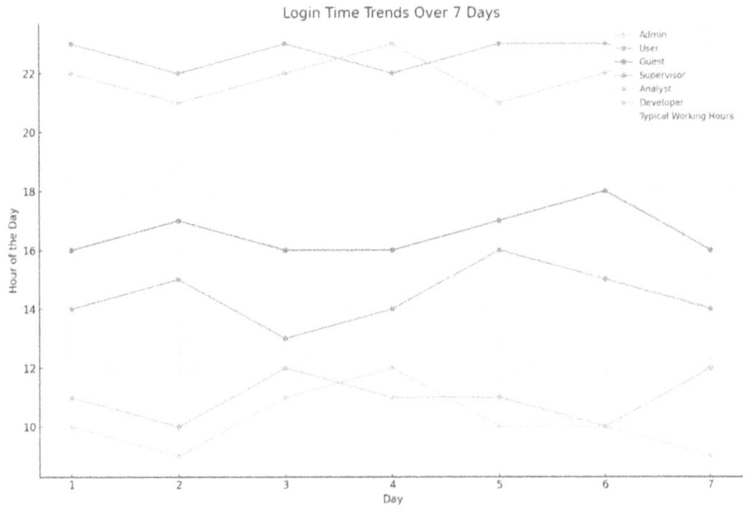

Figure 4 shows aids in identifying roles—especially those that log in outside of regular business hours—that can display odd login behavior. These trends might call for additional research to confirm that after-hours access is appropriate and required.

Figure 4. Login time comparison across roles

Now explain how various jobs behave concerning system access and data usage, these graphs make it easier to identify roles that, based on their behavior patterns, may be more vulnerable to insider threats as shown in Figure 5

Figure 5. Extended data accessed comparison

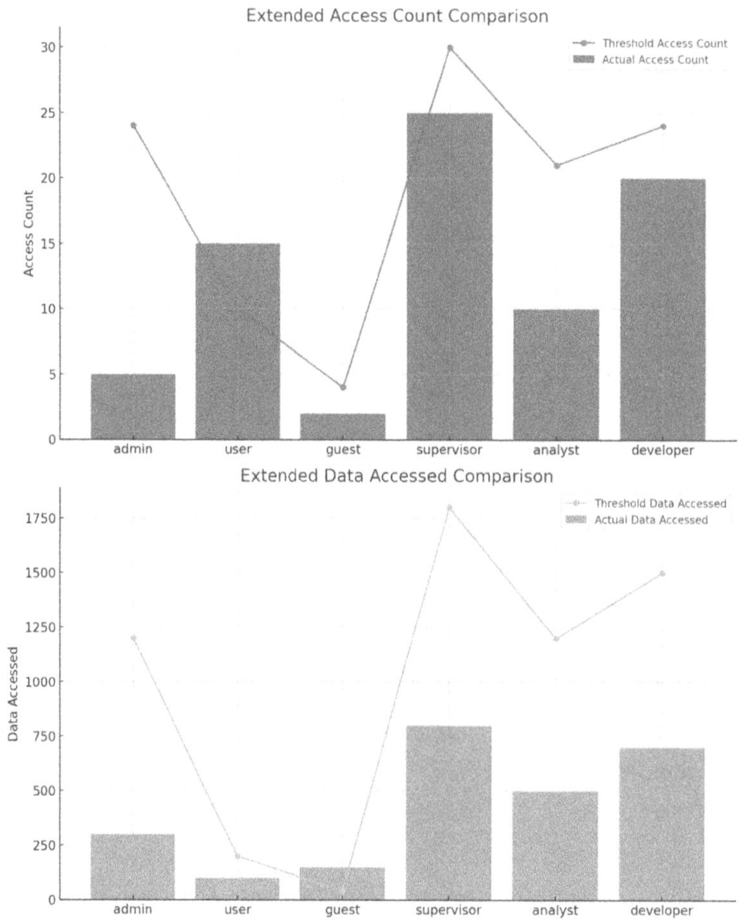

CONCLUSION AND FUTURE WORK

Insider threats remain a significant concern, capable of causing devastating financial losses and reputational damage. Despite substantial investments in cybersecurity, achieving a system that is 100% secure from cyber-attacks is generally accepted as impossible. Vulnerabilities can still be exploited, especially through sophisticated and targeted attacks. No system can be entirely foolproof. However, there are ways to mitigate these threats. In the case of insider threats, incorporating technical defensive strategies and measures is crucial. Additionally, employing a psychological model, with a psychiatrist working closely with the HR department, can provide much-needed guidance. This approach can help mitigate insider threats and greatly reduce the chances of such incidents occurring. Furthermore, this chapter proposes a framework approach for detecting insider threats. The model is built on a layered method that connects the real world, measurements, and parameters to assess the likelihood of an insider threat. Moreover, Future research can extend the proposed system by integrating a proactive deep-learning approach. This integration can enhance the protection against insider threats by providing on-the-spot actions and more detailed analysis for real-time threat detection.

REFERENCES

Al Mamlook, R. E., Nasayreh, A., Gharaibeh, H., Aljaidi, M., Al-Na'amneh, Q., & Alzu'bi, D. others, & Abdeltawab, A. (2023). Fine-Tuning Pre-Trained Models for Automated Analysis of Ophthalmic Imaging in Diagnosing Eye Diseases. *2023 24th International Arab Conference on Information Technology (ACIT)*, 1–6.

Al-Mhiqani, M. N., Ahmad, R., Zainal Abidin, Z., Yassin, W., Hassan, A., Abdulkareem, K. H., Ali, N. S., & Yunos, Z. (2020). A review of insider threat detection: Classification, machine learning techniques, datasets, open challenges, and recommendations. *Applied Sciences (Basel, Switzerland)*, 10(15), 5208. DOI: 10.3390/app10155208

Al-Na'amneh, Q., Aljaidi, M., Gharaibeh, H., Nasayreh, A., Al Mamlook, R. E., & Almatarneh, S. others, & Husien, A. S. (2023). Feature Selection for Robust Spoofing Detection: A Chi-Square-based Machine Learning Approach. *2023 2nd International Engineering Conference on Electrical, Energy, and Artificial Intelligence (EICEEAI)*, 1–7.

Al-Na'amneh, Q., Nasayreh, A. N., Al Mamlook, R., Gharaibeh, H., Alsheyab, A. M., & Almaiah, M. (2024). Improving Memory Malware Detection in Machine Learning With Random Forest-Based Feature Selection. In R. Assessment & C. for Cybersecurit (Eds.), *IGI Global* (pp. 96–114). . DOI: 10.4018/979-8-3693-2691-6.ch006

Al-Shehari, T., Rosaci, D., Al-Razgan, M., Alfakih, T., Kadrie, M., Afzal, H., & Nawaz, R. (2024). Enhancing Insider Threat Detection in Imbalanced Cybersecurity Settings Using the Density-Based Local Outlier Factor Algorithm. *IEEE Access : Practical Innovations, Open Solutions*, 12, 34820–34834. DOI: 10.1109/ACCESS.2024.3373694

Aljaidi, M., Alsarhan, A., Al-Fraihat, D., Al-Arjan, A., Igried, B., & El-Salhi, S. M. others, & Al-Na'amneh, Q. (2023). Cybersecurity Threats in the Era of AI: Detection of Phishing Domains Through Classification Rules. *2023 2nd International Engineering Conference on Electrical, Energy, and Artificial Intelligence (EICEEAI)*, 1–6.

AlQahtani, R., Farooq, H. M., & Khoraidly, A. (2024). Sentiment Clustering: A Hybrid Approach for Insider Threat Detection. *International Journal of Simulation–Systems, Science & Technology, 25*(1).

AlSlaiman, M., Salman, M. I., Saleh, M. M., & Wang, B. (2023). Enhancing false negative and positive rates for efficient insider threat detection. *Computers & Security*, 126, 103066. DOI: 10.1016/j.cose.2022.103066

Alzaabi, F. R., & Mehmood, A. (2024). A review of recent advances, challenges, and opportunities in malicious insider threat detection using machine learning methods. *IEEE Access, 12*, . , 30907–30927.

Asha, S., Shanmugapriya, D., & Padmavathi, G. (2023). Malicious insider threat detection using variation of sampling methods for anomaly detection in cloud environment. *Computers & Electrical Engineering*, 105, 108519. DOI: 10.1016/j.compeleceng.2022.108519

Duan, S. M., Yuan, J. T., & Wang, B. (2024). Contextual feature representation for image-based insider threat classification. *Computers & Security*, 140, 103779. DOI: 10.1016/j.cose.2024.103779

Haq, M. A., Khan, M. A. R., & Alshehri, M. (2022). Insider threat detection based on NLP word embedding and machine learning. *Intelligent Automation & Soft Computing*, 33(1), 619–635. DOI: 10.32604/iasc.2022.021430

Hong, W., Yin, J., You, M., Wang, H., Cao, J., Li, J., others, & Man, C. (2023). A graph empowered insider threat detection framework based on daily activities. *ISA Transactions, 141*, . , 84–92.

Jaradat, A. S., Nasayreh, A., Al-Na'amneh, Q., Gharaibeh, H., & Al Mamlook, R. E. (2023). Genetic optimization techniques for enhancing web attacks classification in machine learning. *2023 IEEE Intl Conf on Dependable, Autonomic and Secure Computing, Intl Conf on Pervasive Intelligence and Computing, Intl Conf on Cloud and Big Data Computing, Intl Conf on Cyber Science and Technology Congress (DASC/PiCom/CBDCom/CyberSciTech)*, 130–136. DOI: 10.1109/DASC/PiCom/CBDCom/Cy59711.2023.10361399

Khan, N. J., Houghton, R., & Sharples, S. (2022). Understanding factors that influence unintentional insider threat: A framework to counteract unintentional risks. *Cognition Technology and Work*, 24(3), 393–421. DOI: 10.1007/s10111-021-00690-z PMID: 34725543

Kim, A., Oh, J., Ryu, J., Lee, J., Kwon, K., & Lee, K. (2019). SoK: A Systematic Review of Insider Threat Detection. *Journal of Wireless Mobile Networks, Ubiquitous Computing and Dependable Applications*, 10(4), 46–67.

Lad, S. (2024). Harnessing Machine Learning for Advanced Threat Detection in Cybersecurity. *Innovative Computer Sciences Journal, 10*(1).

Laila, D. A., Al-Na'amneh, Q., Aljaidi, M., Nasayreh, A. N., Gharaibeh, H., Al Mamlook, R., & Alshammari, M. (2024). Enhancing 2D Logistic Chaotic Map for Gray Image Encryption. In R. Assessment & C. for Cybersecurit (Eds.), *IGI Global* (pp. 170–188). .

Le, D. C., & Zincir-Heywood, N. (2021). Exploring anomalous behaviour detection and classification for insider threat identification. *International Journal of Network Management*, 31(4), e2109. DOI: 10.1002/nem.2109

Legg, P. A., Buckley, O., Goldsmith, M., & Creese, S. (2015). Automated insider threat detection system using user and role-based profile assessment. *IEEE Systems Journal*, 11(2), 503–512. DOI: 10.1109/JSYST.2015.2438442

Li, X., Li, X., Jia, J., Li, L., Yuan, J., Gao, Y., & Yu, S. (2023). A high accuracy and adaptive anomaly detection model with dual-domain graph convolutional network for insider threat detection. *IEEE Transactions on Information Forensics and Security, 18*, . , 1638–1652.

Nasir, R., Afzal, M., Latif, R., & Iqbal, W. (2021). Behavioral based Telecommunication Systems, using deep learning. *IEEE Access : Practical Innovations, Open Solutions*, 9, 143266–143274. DOI: 10.1109/ACCESS.2021.3118297

Padiet, P., Islam, R., & Khan, M. A. (2024). Users' Scenario-Base for Analysing Insider Threat Detection Based on User's Downloads Activity Logs. *Future of Information and Communication Conference*, 457–472.

Pal, P., Chattopadhyay, P., & Swarnkar, M. (2023). Temporal feature aggregation with attention for insider threat detection from activity logs. *Expert Systems with Applications*, 224, 119925. DOI: 10.1016/j.eswa.2023.119925

Pete O'Doherty, C. V.-P. (2023). *"Protecting From Within" A review commissioned by the Police Service of Northern Ireland (PSNI) and the Northern Ireland Policing Board (NIPB), into the PSNI data breach.*

Randive, K., Mohan, R., & Sivakrishna, A. M. (2023). An efficient pattern-based approach for insider threat classification using the image-based feature representation. *Journal of Information Security and Applications*, 73, 103434. DOI: 10.1016/j.jisa.2023.103434

Rao, S. D. P. (2024). *HARNESSING AI FOR EVOLVING THREATS: FROM DETECTION TO AUTOMATED RESPONSE.* Journal of Science Technology and Research (JSTAR).

Salem, A. H., Azzam, S. M., Emam, O. E., & Abohany, A. A. (2024). Advancing cybersecurity: A comprehensive review of AI-driven detection techniques. *Journal of Big Data*, 11(1), 105. DOI: 10.1186/s40537-024-00957-y

Singh, A., Rakhra, M., Singh, D., Kaur, B., & Kaur, H. (2024). Improving Insider Threat Detection with User and Role-Based Behavior. *2024 11th International Conference on Reliability, Infocom Technologies and Optimization (Trends and Future Directions)(ICRITO)*, 1–6.

Singh, M., Mehtre, B. M., & Sangeetha, S. (2019). User behavior profiling using ensemble approach for insider threat detection. *2019 IEEE 5th International Conference on Identity, Security, and Behavior Analysis (ISBA)*, 1–8.

Song, S., Gao, N., Zhang, Y., & Ma, C. (2024). BRITD: Behavior rhythm insider threat detection with time awareness and user adaptation. *Cybersecurity*, 7(1), 2. DOI: 10.1186/s42400-023-00190-9

Steingartner, W., Galinec, D., & Kozina, A. (2021). Threat defense: Cyber deception approach and education for resilience in hybrid threats model. *Symmetry*, 13(4), 597. DOI: 10.3390/sym13040597

Tao, X., Lu, S., Zhao, F., Lan, R., Chen, L., Fu, L., & Jia, R. (2024). User Behavior Threat Detection Based on Adaptive Sliding Window GAN. *IEEE Transactions on Network and Service Management*, 21(2), 2493–2503. DOI: 10.1109/TNSM.2024.3355698

Toulas, B. (2023). *Verizon Insider Data Breach hits over 63,000 employees.*

Yilmaz, E., & Can, O. (2024). *Unveiling Shadows: Harnessing Artificial Intelligence for Insider Threat Detection. Engineering, Technology & Applied Science Research, 14(2), 13341-13346* (Vol. 14). ngineering, Technology & Applied Science Research.

Chapter 7
Attacks Detection and Mitigation of IoT Using Machine Learning Model

Qais Al-Na'amneh
https://orcid.org/0009-0008-3034-7693
Applied Science Private University, Jordan

Mohammed Almaiah
https://orcid.org/0009-0008-9785-485X
University of Jordan, Jordan

Saja Smadi
Yarmouk University, Jordan

Rahaf Hazaymih
Jordan University of Science and Technology, Jordan

Laheeb Alabadi
Applied Science Private University, Jordan

ABSTRACT

The RPL protocol has been increasingly used in low-loss networks and Internet of Things networks in recent years. The RPL protocol is exposed to many attacks that affect the network performance and disrupt the connection. In this study, a machine learning-based intrusion detection system (IDS) was developed to distinguish between benign and malicious attacks. Ensemble learning was applied by stacking three models: Random Forest, Gradient Boosting, and Linear SVC with hyperparameter optimization using Random search CV. The proposed approach was applied to version number, Decreased rank, and Hello Flooding database. The results obtained indicate that this approach provides a reliable and effective solution to protect networks from attacks, and it also sought to achieve a balance between detection accuracy and computational efficiency. The proposed model achieved an accuracy of 98% for HF database, 97% for VN database, and 95% for DR database.

DOI: 10.4018/979-8-3693-9919-4.ch007

1 INTRODUCTION

The Internet of Things (IoT) is a network of interconnected devices that interact and send data via the internet. It is a groundbreaking technology that links numerous physical items to the internet, allowing them to gather, share, and analyze data. These gadgets, which range from household appliances to industrial gear, are equipped with sensors and software that gather and send data. IoT allows devices to collaborate seamlessly, resulting in smarter decision-making, automation, and improved user experiences. Smart home systems (Almusaylim et al., 2019), for example, may control lighting, temperature, and security, whilst industrial IoT can enhance production processes and provide predictive maintenance. IoT encompasses a wide range of disciplines, including smart homes, cities, healthcare (Chithaluru et al., 2020), manufacturing, and agriculture, where sensors and embedded devices collect data to improve operations, improve decision-making, and enhance user experiences.

As defined. As more devices connect via IPv6, the Internet of Things (IoT) becomes increasingly important for tracking the external environment. Due to restricted resources, Low-Power and Lossy Network (LLN) routers cannot use typical routing protocols such as OSPF, RIP, AODV, or DSR. The Routing Protocol for Low Power and Lossy Networks (RPL) addresses these challenges, but it is susceptible to specific assaults, necessitating the development of systems to detect and prevent them (Raghavendra et al., 2022) .

Researchers are working to improve security in IoT-enabled smart systems, notably the network layer, which is extremely sensitive to network and routing assaults. IoT devices provide real-time monitoring and control, which improves operational efficiency in industries and healthcare. However, their extensive adoption raises security concerns, since the large number of linked devices might become cyberattack targets. To fully understand the potential of IoT, key challenges must be overcome, including ensuring device compatibility and handling the huge volumes of data collected. The authors in (Choukri et al., 2020) present a machine learning-based intrusion detection system for the Internet of Things to better monitor network connections and detect attackers. The system selects and classifies features using a genetic recursive feature selection method and a fuzzy k-nearest neighbor classifier, collecting maximum accuracy while minimizing false positives. The paper compares this system to existing intrusion detection algorithms, measuring accuracy, recall, and F1-score for performance comparisons.

The Low Power Lossy Network Routing Protocol (Zahra et al., 2022) is susceptible to attacks from both outside and insider nodes. To protect the network, encryption and authentication are used. Malicious nodes masquerading as legitimate nodes, known as rank assaults (RA), can pose a significant hazard. RA is based on the rank property, which is required for choosing parents in the RPL topology. (Zahra et al., 2024) A malicious node can change its rank value and cause neighboring nodes to transmit data, assuming it is the best parent as shown figure 1. The RPL protocol cannot detect RA because it considers that all nodes in the network conform with protocol requirements.

Figure 1. The network architecture of Contiki

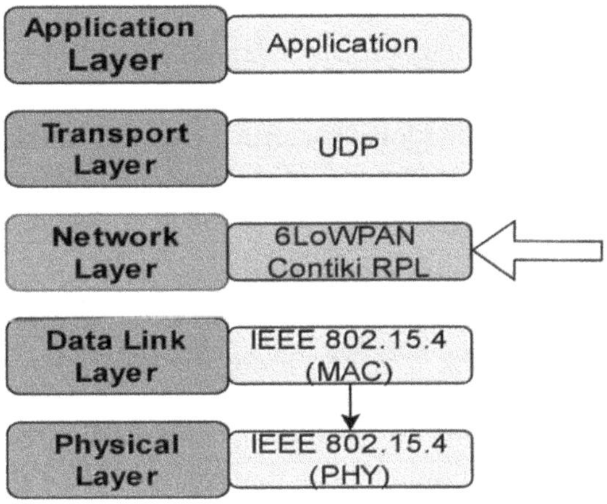

The Internet of Things (IoT) poses substantial security issues, especially in low-power and lossy networks (RPL) for data exchange. The research (Rouissat et al., 2024) introduces MC-MLGBM, a lightweight multiclass classification-based attack detection model that is RPL-specific and sensor-network-inherited. The model detects multiclass classification-based attacks using a unique dataset, optimum feature selection, and a light gradient boosting machine-based technique. Experiments show the model's performance using measures such as the confusion matrix, accuracy, precision, and recall. Multiclass measures such as cross-entropy, Cohn's kappa, and Matthews correlation coefficient is also used to evaluate and reduce bias (Hkiri et al., 2024).

(Qureshi et al., 2020) provides a novel machine learning (ML) model for applied by stacking three models Random Forest, Gradient Boosting, and Linear SVC with hyperparameter optimization using Random search CV. The model is trained on a self-created dataset and achieves good accuracy, detection rate, and performance. A new dataset is created, including RPL-specific IoT node modes.

The remaining paper is organized as follows: Section 2 reviews the relevant existing literature, Section 3 presents the methodology and proposed model, Section 4 recounts the experimental results, and Section 5 discusses the conclusion, the limitations of this work, and future research direction.

2 RELATED WORK

Due to the lack of security, we face in Internet networks in addition to the various attacks that Internet of Things networks are exposed to, this paper proposes a method to counter attacks that RPL is exposed to, especially the DIO attack. The distillation algorithm was used to implement the attack, and a measure was proposed to protect the network from this type of attack through a lightweight countermeasure Sahay (Tahar et al., 2024).

This paper presents a method to protect RPL-based networks through an intrusion detection system (IDS). The proposed ELG-ID (Ensemble Learning) system is used in parameter optimization and stacking. The genetic algorithm is used for feature selection. The proposed approach is applied to three databases: decreased rank, version number, and DIS flooding attacks. The proposed approach achieves results of 99.83%, 99.18%, and 99.66% for decreased rank, version number, and DIS flooding respectively (Osman et al., 2024).

This paper proposed an approach to detect decreased rank attacks due to the increasing attacks on IoT networks. The attacks involve small variables in their characteristics and behavior, so it was necessary to find a robust approach to detect small mutational variables. The ANN model was used to detect this type of attacks. They first preprocessed the database and then used the Random Forest model to extract the features and finally used the Artificial neural network model to perform the classification process. The proposed model achieved an AUC-ROC scores of 97.14% on the IRAD database (Osman et al., 2021).

This study (Qureshi et al., 2020) presented an approach to detect threats to PRL-based IoT networks. It identifies four types of attacks: Version number attack, HELLO-Flood attack, Black hole attack, and Sinkhole attack. The proposed approach was implemented in two stages: the first stage is threshold modification, where genetic programming was used to increase the number of features and then the best one is chosen among them to produce threshold data for each type of attack. The second stage is attack detection, where the features are analyzed to finally evaluate this approach through the Cooja simulator.

This study (Sahay et al., 2020) proposed a system using RPL known as 6LOWPAN. It provides DODAGs with one or more non-cyclic graphs. The version number is given to ensure that there are free paths to the root nodes of each DODAG. The version number is incremented by the root node in case of a discrepancy. Sometimes a malicious node announces the wrong version number in the control message. Therefore, an approach is proposed to detect such attacks.

This paper (Sahay et al., 2020) proposed an approach to detect RPL-based routing attacks. A Graph Convolution Network is included with the document network to learn and capture the latent state of each node within the network. To perform traffic prediction, short-term and long-term memory and neural networks are used. Blockchain technology is used to create a set of secure channels that enable us to access the network data. The proposed approach achieved an accuracy of 94.5%.

The authors in (Mehdi et al., 2023) focus on weaknesses in security in the Routing Protocol for Low-power and Lossy Networks (RPL), which leaves IoT networks open to attacks such as the Hybrid Rank Attack (HRA). By advertising higher and lower rank values in control messages, HRA manipulates RPL, seriously impairing network performance and interfering with regular network operations. The paper provides a cutting-edge intrusion detection system with a distributed, lightweight countermeasure technique that is tailored especially for Internet of Things networks (IOT). Simulation-based evaluations indicate the suggested approach only necessitates a tiny increase in RAM utilization of 1.05%, while reducing control overhead by 68.7% and energy consumption by 61.83%. With this technology, network performance is preserved against HRA threats while security is enhanced.

The study (Amal et al., 2024) work with weaknesses in the RPL protocol in Internet of Things networks, especially in relation to the Hello Flood attack. Using the Cooja simulator and four group mobility models, the paper examines how the attack impacts RPL networks. The authors discovers that the Hello Flood assault substantially lowers throughput, increases average power use, increases the total delay, and decreases the ratio of packet delivery after examining key performance parameters. where the conclusions indicate that further security precautions must be taken to protect RPL-based IoT networks in mobile applications.

(Mohammed et al., 2023), paper discuss that for devices with constrained resources, the Routing Protocol for Low-power and Lossy Networks (RPL) is a protocol that makes IPv6 communication easier. To control network topology, it makes use of a Destination Oriented Directed Acyclic Graph (DODAG).

However, because RPL lacks the tools to monitor parent node behavior, it is vulnerable to attacks. there are two major types of rank attacks that can disrupt a network's topology and performance are Rank Attack Type 1 (RA1) and Rank Attack Type 2 (RA2). The authors suggest the statistically based Anomaly Detection Scheme (SARPL), that employs statistical methods, to recognize and diminish these threats. Simulation experiments show that SARPL can detect RA1 assaults quite well and can detect RA2 attacks with a detection rate of approximately 93%. The application of SARPL significantly enhances network performance metrics.

(Mehdi et al., 2023) IoT networks are expanding quickly, which poses problems for their effectiveness and quality, especially for their edge and core networks. One well-known routing protocol at the edge of the Internet of Things (IoT) that was created to satisfy the needs of limited IoT devices is the Routing Protocol (RPL). RPL is still vulnerable to security breaches with the goal to compromise the traffic, topology, and node resources. It has been suggested to use a lightweight countermeasure along with a new silent dropped rank attack against RPL-Contiki. As a result of the malicious node that was planted, the inquiry reveals that about half of the current nodes were drawn to it, increasing control overhead and overall energy usage. Although the modified rank attack showed no effect on the PDR, it generated a 45% increase in latency if compared to the attack-free scenario, making it a serious threat to IoT RPL-based networks.

while (Musa et al., 2024) discuss that Network security is increasingly a worry with the proliferation of Internet of Things (IoT) devices, especially concerning the Routing Protocol for Low-Power and Lossy Networks (RPL). Given its open nature and limited resources, the RPL is susceptible to a variety of threats. The false alarm rates of current intrusion detection systems are quite high. This study presents the Ensemble Learning-based Intrusion Detection System (ELG-IDS), which detects three RPL internal attacks: version number, lower rank, and DIS flooding attacks. It does this by using stacking and extreme parameter optimization. The findings for version number, rank attack, DIS flooding, and ELG-IDS demonstrate an excellent accuracy of 99.18%, 99.38%, 99.66%, and 97.90%, correspondingly, with an average accuracy of 97.90% in the multi-classification mode.

The work (Alekha et al., 2023) introduces a centralized approach to protect the rank computation process from sinkhole nodes. The expectation maximization technique is used by the authors of this study to cluster nodes into groups of the same rank, improving efficiency and security. By spreading only valid ranks, the rank distribution will be guaranteed by the sink's signature. The suggest approach requires more network activity between settling nodes but is protected against sinkhole nodes, according to the results of the experimental validation. This work extends to the overall understanding of IoT security by addressing the specific problem of sinkhole attacks in IoT systems. Also, it offers strategies and information to fortify network defenses against an extensive spectrum of invasion methods.

Cyberattacks against the Internet of Things have become more complex as more intelligent gadgets are linked to the internet. The study (Thiyagu et al., 2022) aims to identify wormhole attacks against the technology that powers most Internet of Things devices and sensors, Routing Protocol for Low Power and Lossy Networks (RPL). A proposed deep learning-based advanced gated recurrent unit (AGRU) network model is compared with one support vector machine and logistic regression using varied weight states and node power consumption. The study's commitment and expectations are validated by the outcomes, and the model's predictions and assurances on IoT security and source success are accurate as shown in Table 1.

Table 1. Summary of previous studies

Ref.	Model	Attacks Detected	Dataset	Accuracy
[7]	LR, NB, ANN, EM, DT	VN, HF, BH	UNSW-NB15, KDD-99, WSN-DS, RPL-NIDDS17	93%
[8]	ANN	DRA, VN, HF	IRAD	97.14%
[9]	Neural network	WP, VN, HF	KDD-99	97.52%
[10]	Bernoulli RBM, SVM, DT, LR	VN	IoT-LLN	98%
[11]	LSTM, GCNN, FNN	routing attacks	Real-time (Cooja)	94.50%
[12]	Lightweight Countermeasure Algorithm	Hybrid Rank Attack (HRA)	The study gives the MC-MLGBM model, which generates a new dataset using several network models, however there are no specifics regarding the dataset used for training and testing.	68.7% reduction in control overhead, 61.83% reduction in energy usage, and 1.05% increased RAM utilization.
[19]	SRF-IoT	identifying rank and blackhole attacks.	Whitefield RPL Routing Attack Dataset IoT-23 Dataset, Bot-IoT Dataset, Contiki-NG RPL Dataset,NS-3 IoT Network Attack Dataset	92.8%
[20]	Hybrid Deep Learning (Supervised and Semi-Supervised)	DIS, Rank, Wormhole	IoTR-DS	98% (known traffic), 95% (unknown traffic)
[21]	Hybrid Deep Learning (LSTM and Deep Belief Network)	Multiple RPL attacks	200K traffic samples	98.93% recall, 2.16%, 5.73%, and 6.06% improved accuracy over LGBM, LSTM, and DBN respectively
[22]	Federated Transfer Learning-assisted Customised Distributed IDS (FT-CID)	RPL intrusions	RPL-IIoT dataset	85.52%

3. METHODOLOGY

In this section, we will present an approach based on applying machine learning techniques to databases related to intrusion detection systems (IDS). The proposed methodology uses machine learning models to build a high-accuracy model. We applied leveraging ensemble learning (stacking) to three models: Random Forest, Gradient Boosting, and Linear SVM, in addition to improving the hyperparameters by applying the random search technique to reduce the time taken for implementation. Figure 2 illustrates the proposed approach for implementing an intrusion detection system that distinguishes between malicious and benign attacks.

Figure 2. Proposed methodology

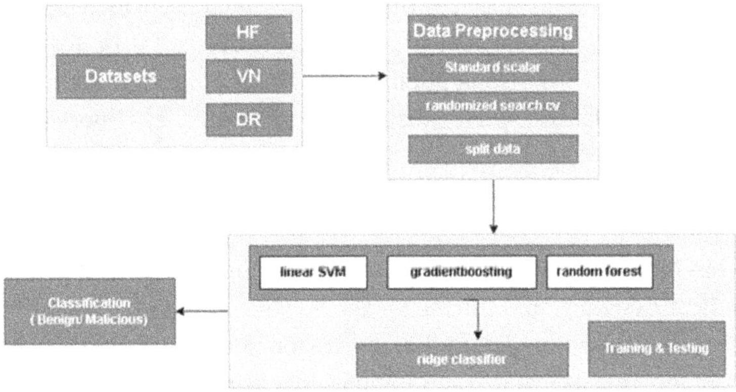

3.1 Dataset description

Three different databases were used: Version Number, Decreased Rank, and Hello Flooding. The Version Number database contained 1955 records [19], the Decreased Rank database contained 3609 records, and the Hello Flooding database contained 1474 records. The total number of features in the three databases was 16 as shown in table 2 and they will be used to determine whether the attack is benign (0) or malicious (1) (Yahya et al., 2023).

Table 2. Description of features

features	Description
Source Mote	A distinct number for every mote
Destination Mote	identical to the source mote's number
Packet Count:	the total number of source motes in the frame lasting one second.
Source Mote Ratio	(Source: Packet/Mote Count). -second-time interval.
Destination Mote Ratio	(Mote Count/Packet Count at Destination)
Source Mote Duration	the total of all packet durations sent inside a frame of one second, from source to destination.
Destination Mote Duration	the total of all packet durations that the destination received inside the frame of one second.
Total Packet Duration	It is the total of every packet's time within a frame of one second.
Total Packet Length	It is the total of each packet's length inside a frame of one second.
Source Packet Ratio	(Total Packet Length / Sum of Source Packet Length).
Destination Packet Ratio	(Total Packet Length / Sum of Dest. Packet lengths).
DIO Message Count	DIO message counts in the frame of one second.
DIS Message Count	number of DIS messages within a one-second time frame.
DAO Message Count	DAO message count in the one-second frame
Other Message Count	all the messages—aside from DIO, DIS, and DAO—count.

3.2 Data Preprocessing

A set of pre-processing steps was applied to the three databases, which consisted of dividing the databases into 80% for training to build and improve the model and 20% for testing to evaluate the performance of the final model. We also applied feature scaling through StandardScalar. This step is important for the scale of input data related to sensitive algorithms such as Sport Vector Machine (SVM).

3.3 Model Selection

Three traditional machine learning models were selected as the base models for the stacking ensemble: Random Forest, Gradient Boosting, and Linear SVM.

Random Forest: A supervised model used in regression and classification tasks. It creates a set of decision trees and randomly selects features and samples for each decision tree. Random Forest performs well despite dealing with default values and can reduce the risk of overfitting by averaging the ensemble of trees. In classification, it takes a majority vote, while in prediction, it calculates the average values of all the trees to perform the final prediction and decide (Kowsalyadevi et al., 2023).

Gradient Boosting: A robust model is built with a series of weak learners, designed so that each learner can handle the mistakes made by the previous learner. It can perform complex tasks and handle various loss functions. It calculates the gradient at each step for the current predictions and then uses them to create a new model to minimize the loss (Nasr et al., 2022).

Linear SVC: It is a type of support vector machine classifier used to deal with large databases. Linear SVC is characterized by its efficiency and speed, especially in dealing with data that requires linear separation by finding the best hyperplane that separates two classes. The margin represents the distance between the closest data point for each class and the hyperplane, and the model aims to maximize this margin (Al-Na'amneh et al., 2024).

The Ridge model was selected as a meta-model to combine the predictions of the three base models. The ridge classifier is computationally efficient and penalizes large parameters to avoid overfitting, which is useful in stacking a set of models. Ridge makes the final prediction by taking the outputs of the three base models (Aljaidi et al., 2023).

Algorithm: Machine Learning-Based Intrusion Detection for RPL Attacks

```
Input: Dataset containing network traffic features, including both malicious and benign activities

Output: Classification model capable of distinguishing between malicious and benign attacks

Steps:
```

1. Data Preprocessing: Load the dataset from the CSV file, split the dataset into 80% for training and 20% for testing, and normalize the feature data using StandardScaler.

2. Model Selection: Select base models for the ensemble:

Model 1: Random Forest Classifier

Model 2: Gradient Boosting Classifier

Model 3: Linear SVC

Choose the Ridge Classifier as a meta-model to aggregate predictions from the base models.

3. Hyperparameter Optimization: Define hyperparameter search spaces for each base model, use RandomizedSearchCV for efficient hyperparameter tuning, use 3-fold cross-validation to assess model performance on different subsets of the training data and perform parallel processing (n_jobs=-1)

4. Training the Model: Train the stacking ensemble model using the training data.

5. Model Evaluation: Test the optimized model on the testing dataset to evaluate its performance.

End

3.4 Hyperparameter Optimization

randomsearchcv was used to perform hyperparameter optimization to improve the performance of the stacking model. This technique is characterized by its ability to balance between finding optimal parameters and computational efficiency (Jaradat et al., 2023). specified the parameter values in each model such as the number of trees in Random Forest, the regularization parameter in Linear SVC, and the learning rate for Gradient Boosting as shown in Table 3. Random search was applied to perform 10 iterations in addition to 3-fold cross-validation to verify the model performance and to speed up the optimization process, all CPU cores were considere (Al-Na'amneh et al., 2023).

Table 3. Parameters description

parameter	parameter values
n_estimators (RF)	randint(100, 300)
Learning rate (GB)	[0.01, 0.1]
C (linear SVC)	[0.1, 1]

3.5 Performance models

Developing a machine learning model in the field of intrusion detection to distinguish between malicious and benign attacks is of utmost importance. To evaluate the proposed machine learning model developed, several metrics were used: precision as shown in equation (4), recall as shown in equation (3), F1 score as shown in equation (2), and accuracy as shown in equation (1). These metrics will provide a comprehensive view of the model's ability to identify valid attacks while minimizing false positives and false negatives (Gharaibeh et al., 2023).

$$Accuracy = \frac{TP + TN}{TP + FP + FN + TN} \tag{1}$$

$$\mathrm{F1-score} = 2 \times \frac{\mathrm{precision} \times \mathrm{recall}}{\mathrm{precision} + \mathrm{recall}} \tag{2}$$

$$\mathrm{recall} = \frac{\mathrm{TP}}{\mathrm{TP} + \mathrm{FN}} \tag{3}$$

$$\mathrm{precision} = \frac{\mathrm{TP}}{\mathrm{TP} + \mathrm{FP}} \tag{4}$$

4 RESULTS AND DISCUSSION

The proposed machine learning model was evaluated using a set of performance metrics for intrusion detection using three test datasets designed to distinguish between malicious and benign network traffic attacks. The aim was to evaluate the model to accurately and efficiently distinguish between these two types of traffic. The results of the models were as shown in Table 4.

Table 4. Model performance for three datasets

Datasets	Accuracy	Precision	Recall	F1-score
HF	98%	99%	99%	99%
VN	97%	100%	95%	97%
DR	95%	98%	94%	96%

Figure 3 shows the results of the model for each of the three databases. The proposed model achieved results on the version number database with an accuracy of 97%, precision of 100%, recall of 95%, and F1 score of 97% and on the decreasing rank database with an accuracy of 95%, precision of 98%, recall of 94% and F1 score of 96% while the results when applying the model to the Hello Flooding database were accuracy of 98%, precision of 99%, recall of 99% and F1 score of 99%.

Figure 3. Model performance on different datasets

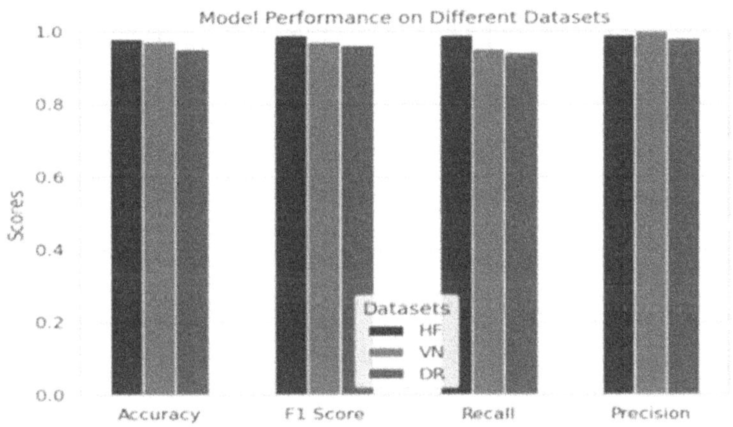

Now, Figure 4 shows the version number confusion matrix where the matrix shows the relationship between the benign attack category (0) and the malicious attack category (1) where the number of records that were correctly classified as benign attacks was 169 and incorrectly classified as 11 while the number of records that were correctly classified as malicious attacks was 211 and incorrectly classified as 0.

Figure 4. Confusion matrix for version number database

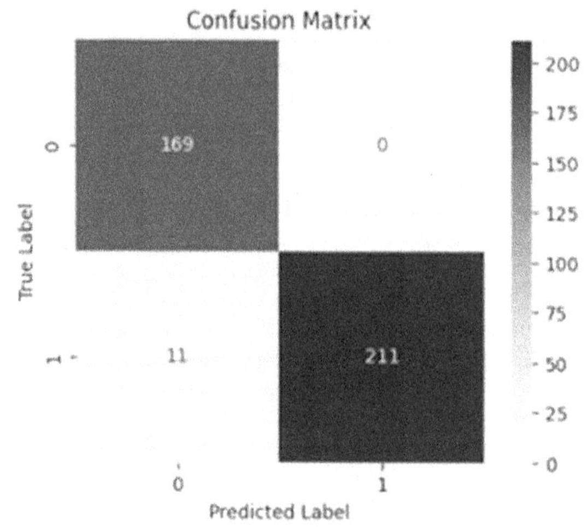

Figure 5 shows the confusion matrix for the version number where the number of records that were correctly classified as benign attacks was 228 and incorrectly classified as 28, while the number of records that were correctly classified as malicious attacks was 457 and incorrectly classified as 9.

Figure 5. Confusion matrix for decreased rank database

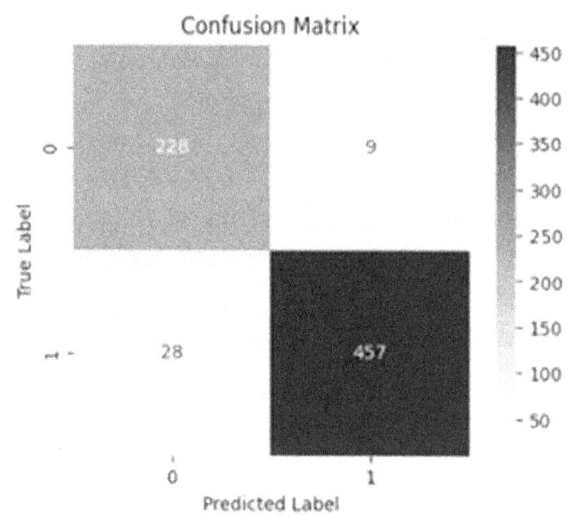

Figure 6 shows the Hello Flooding confusion matrix where 33 records were correctly classified as benign attacks and 2 were incorrectly classified as malicious attacks, while 257 records were correctly classified as malicious attacks and 3 were incorrectly classified as malicious attacks.

Figure 6. Confusion matrix for Hello Flooding database

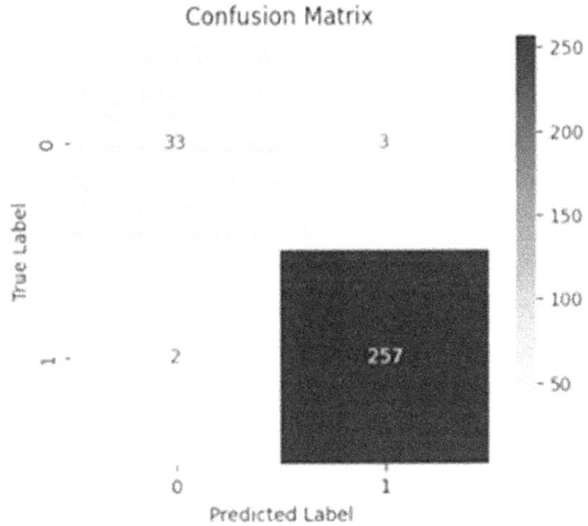

Comparison with Related Studies

Many related studies on the topic of detecting malicious or benign attacks and classifying them used machine learning and deep learning models, but our proposed model outperformed all studies shown in the table Table (1), where our model (stacking model for Decrease Rank Attack) achieved accuracy reached 95%, Precision 98%, Recall 94% and F1-Score 96%, Also (stacking model for Hello Flooding Attack) achieved accuracy reached 98%, Precision 99%, Recall 99% and F1-Score 99% and (stacking model for Version Number Attack) achieved accuracy reached 97%, Precision 100%, Recall 95% and F1-Score 97% compared to the studies described, as there is Study No. 1, they used the DNN and DBN model, and their results were 96%, as well as Study No. 2, they used SVM, RF, NB, and DT, and they got an accuracy of 96.1%, and Study No. 3 used more than one model Machine learning sand their results were 96.1%, and the last study used GCNN, LSTM, and FNN with an accuracy of 94%, Table (5) shows a comparison between most studies on IoT attack prediction with our proposed study,

Table 5. Comparison with related studies

NO.	Reference	Model	Results
1	(Thamilarasu & Chawla, 2019)	DNN and DBN	Accuracy: 96%
2	(Yavuz, Ünal, & Gül, 2018)	SVM, RF, NB, and DT	Accuracy: 96.1%
3	(Osman M. H., 2024)	NB, DT, LR, ANN, and EM	Accuracy: DT: 93%
4	(Kamel & Elhamayed, 2020)	CNN	Accuracy: 96.1%
5	(Sahay R., Geethakumari, Mitra, & Sahoo, 2020)	GCNN, LSTM, and FNN	Accuracy: 94%
This study	**Our Proposed (Stacking Models)**	**Decrease Rank Dataset**	**Accuracy: 95%**
		Hello Flooding Dataset	**Accuracy: 98%**
		Version Number Dataset	**Accuracy: 97%**

5 CONCLUSION AND FUTURE WORK

In this study, we proposed an approach to detect three types of attacks. Detecting these attacks is very important to ensure the reliability and security of IoT networks. RPL attacks threaten IoT networks due to the limited resources of these networks. A machine learning model was applied to detect intrusions and distinguish between malicious and benign attacks. Ensemble learning was applied by stacking three models: Random Forest, Gradient Boosting, and Linear SVC. The ridge model was used as the meta-model and optimized the parameters. The proposed model achieved promising performance when applied to the version number, Decreased rank, and Hello Flooding database. The proposed model achieved an accuracy of 98% for the HF database, 97% for the VN database, and 95% for the DR database. Future research will focus on using more advanced techniques such as deep learning to improve the efficiency and accuracy of attack detection in IoT networks. We will also generalize our proposed model to study other types of attacks.

REFERENCES

Al-Na'amneh, Q., Aljaidi, M., Gharaibeh, H., Nasayreh, A., Al Mamlook, R. E., Almatarneh, S., . . . Husien, A. S. (2023, December). Feature Selection for Robust Spoofing Detection: A Chi-Square-based Machine Learning Approach. In *2023 2nd International Engineering Conference on Electrical, Energy, and Artificial Intelligence (EICEEAI)* (pp. 1-7). IEEE. DOI: 10.1109/EICEEAI60672.2023.10590243

Al-Na'amneh, Q., Nasayreh, A. N., Al Mamlook, R., Gharaibeh, H., Alsheyab, A. M., & Almaiah, M. (2024). Improving Memory Malware Detection in Machine Learning With Random Forest-Based Feature Selection. In *Risk Assessment and Countermeasures for Cybersecurity* (pp. 96–114). IGI Global. DOI: 10.4018/979-8-3693-2691-6.ch006

Al Sawafi, Y., Touzene, A., & Hedjam, R. (2023). Hybrid deep learning-based intrusion detection system for RPL IoT networks. *Journal of Sensor and Actuator Networks*, 12(2), 21.

Aljaidi, M., Alsarhan, A., Al-Fraihat, D., Al-Arjan, A., Igried, B., El-Salhi, S. M., . . . Al-Na'amneh, Q. (2023, December). Cybersecurity Threats in the Era of AI: Detection of Phishing Domains Through Classification Rules. In *2023 2nd International Engineering Conference on Electrical, Energy, and Artificial Intelligence (EICEEAI)* (pp. 1-6). IEEE.

Almusaylim, Z. A., & Zaman, N. (2019). A review on smart home present state and challenges: Linked to context-awareness internet of things (IoT). *Wireless Networks*, 25(6), 3193–3204. DOI: 10.1007/s11276-018-1712-5

Amal, H. (2024, June 06). Sami, Alqurashi., Omar, Ben, Bahri., Mouna, Karmani., Hamzah, Faraj., Mohsen, Machhout. (2024). Performance Evaluation of Mobile RPL-Based IoT Networks under Hello Flood Attack. *Electronics (Basel)*, 13(11), 2226. Advance online publication. DOI: 10.3390/electronics13112226

Chithaluru, P., Al-Turjman, F., Kumar, M., & Stephan, T. (2020). I-AREOR: An Energy-Balanced Clustering Protocol for Implementing Green IoT in Smart Cities. *Sustainable Cities and Society*, 61, 102254. DOI: 10.1016/j.scs.2020.102254

Choukri, W., Lamaazi, H., & Benamar, N. (2020, December). RPL rank attack detection using Deep Learning. In *2020 International Conference on Innovation and Intelligence for Informatics, Computing and Technologies (3ICT)* (pp. 1-6). IEEE DOI: 10.1109/3ICT51146.2020.9311983

Gharaibeh, H., Aljaidi, M., Nasayreh, A., Al-Na'amneh, Q., Jaradat, A. S., Samara, G., & Al Mamlook, R. E. (2023, December). Deep Feature Extraction Framework Based on DNN for Enhancing Mirai Attachment Classification in Machine Learning. In *2023 2nd International Engineering Conference on Electrical, Energy, and Artificial Intelligence (EICEEAI)* (pp. 1-5). IEEE. DOI: 10.1109/EICEEAI60672.2023.10590608

Ioulianou, P. P., Vassilakis, V. G., & Shahandashti, S. F. (2022). A trust-based intrusion detection system for RPL networks: Detecting a combination of rank and blackhole attacks. *Journal of Cybersecurity and Privacy*, 2(1), 124–153.

Jaradat, A. S., Nasayreh, A., Al-Na'amneh, Q., Gharaibeh, H., & Al Mamlook, R. E. (2023, November). *Genetic optimization techniques for enhancing web attacks classification in machine learning. In 2023 IEEE Intl Conf on Dependable, Autonomic and Secure Computing, Intl Conf on Pervasive Intelligence and Computing, Intl Conf on Cloud and Big Data Computing, Intl Conf on Cyber Science and Technology Congress (DASC/PiCom/CBDCom/CyberSciTech) (pp. 0130-0136)*. IEEE.

K., Kowsalyadevi., N.V., Balaji. (2023). IoBTSec-RPL: A Novel RPL Attack Detecting Mechanism Using Hybrid Deep Learning Over Battlefield IoT Environment. International journal of computer networks and applications, DOI: 10.22247/ijcna/2023/223317

Mehdi, R. (2023). Implementing and evaluating a new Silent Rank Attack in RPL-Contiki based IoT networks. *Journal of Electrical Engineering*, 74(6), 454–462. DOI: 10.2478/jee-2023-0053

Mishra, A. K., Puthal, D., & Tripathy, A. K. (2023, May). A secure rpl rank computation and distribution mechanism for preventing sinkhole attack in iot-based systems. In IEEE INFOCOM 2023-IEEE Conference on Computer Communications Workshops (INFOCOM WKSHPS) (pp. 1-6). IEEE.

Mohammed, A., Alqarni., Sajjad, Hussain, Chauhdary. (2023). A Security Scheme for Statistical Anomaly Detection and the Mitigation of Rank Attacks in RPL Networks (IoT Environment). DOI: 10.48084/etasr.6433

Musa, O. (2024, January). Na, Fei, Zhu., Fawaz, Mahiuob, Mohammed, Mokbal. (2024). An ensemble learning framework for the detection of RPL attacks in IoT networks based on the genetic feature selection approach. *Ad Hoc Networks*, 152, 103331. Advance online publication. DOI: 10.1016/j.adhoc.2023.103331

Nasr, R. (2022). Customised Intrusion Detection for an Industrial IoT Heterogeneous Network Based on Machine Learning Algorithms Called FTL-CID. *Sensors (Basel)*, 23(1), 321–321. DOI: 10.3390/s23010321 PMID: 36616920

Osman, M., He, J., Mahiuob, F., Mokbal, M., & Zhu, N. (2021). Artificial Neural Network Model for Decreased Rank Attack Detection in RPL Based on IoT Networks. *International Journal of Network Security*, 23, 496–503.

Osman, M. H., He, J., Zhu, N., & Mokbal, F. M. M. (2024). An ensemble learning framework for the detection of RPL attacks in IoT networks based on the genetic feature selection approach. *Ad Hoc Networks*, 152, 103331. DOI: 10.1016/j.adhoc.2023.103331

Qureshi, K., Rana, S., Ahmed, A., & Jeon, G. A. (2020). novel and secure attacks detection framework for smart cities industrial internet of things. *Sustainable Cities and Society*, 61, 102343. DOI: 10.1016/j.scs.2020.102343

Raghavendra, T., Anand, M., Selvi, M., Thangaramya, K., Kumar, S. S., & Kannan, A. (2022). An intelligent RPL attack detection using machine learning-based intrusion detection system for Internet of Things. *Procedia Computer Science*, 215, 61–70. DOI: 10.1016/j.procs.2022.12.007

Sahay, R., Geethakumari, G., Mitra, B., & Sahoo, I. (2020). Efficient Framework for Detection of Version Number Attack in Internet of Things. In *Advances in Intelligent Systems and Computing*. Springer International Publishing.

Sahay, R., Geethakumari, G., & Mitra, B. J. (2020). A holistic framework for prediction of routing attacks in IoT-LLNs "Mehdi, Rouissat., Mohammed, Belkehir., Allel, Mokaddem., Merahi, Bouziani., Ibrahim, S., Alsukayti. (2024). Exploring and mitigating hybrid rank attack in RPL-based IoT networks. *Journal of Electrical Engineering*, 75(3), 204–213. DOI: 10.2478/jee-2024-0025

Tahar, G. E. (2024). Lightweight Mitigation Against DIO Suppression Attack In RPL-Based IoT Networks. *In 2024 6th International Conference on Pattern Analysis and Intelligent Systems (PAIS)*, (pp. (pp. 1-6). IEEE.).

Thiyagu, T., & Krishnaveni, S. (2022, December). RPL Attacks Detection and Prevention in IOT Networks with Advanced GRU Deep Learning Algorithm. In 2022 Smart Technologies, Communication and Robotics (STCR) (pp. 1-5). IEEE.

Zahra, F., Jhanjhi, N. Z., Brohi, S. N., Khan, N. A., Masud, M., & AlZain, M. A. (2022). Rank and wormhole attack detection model for RPL-based internet of things using machine learning. *Sensors (Basel)*, 22(18), 6765. DOI: 10.3390/s22186765 PMID: 36146111

Chapter 8

Analysis for Detection and Mitigation of Version Number Modification Attack in the Internet of Things

Qais Al-Na'amneh
https://orcid.org/0009-0008-3034-7693
Applied Science Private University, Jordan

Laith Alzboon
https://orcid.org/0000-0002-7715-9306
Applied Science Private University, Jordan

Walid Dhifallah
https://orcid.org/0000-0003-1368-9612
University of Gabes, Tunisia

Ayoub Alsarhan
https://orcid.org/0000-0001-9075-2828
Hashemite University, Jordan

Rahaf Hazaymih
Jordan University of Science and Technology, Jordan

Mohammed Alshinwan
Applied Science Private University, Jordan

Rabia Emhamed Al Mamlook
Trine University, Libya

ABSTRACT

The connectivity of devices and the ability to collect massive amounts of data, the Internet of Things (IoT) has radically changed networking. However, security and privacy issues still exist, especially in networks with limited resources. In IoT applications, the RPL routing protocol is frequently used for routing; However, version number attacks represent a security issue. Considering sensor node mobility IoT has evolved into IoET (internet of Everything), which encompasses all electronic devices, including body sensor networks, VANETs, and smart grid stations. This paper studies the effects of version number attacks on RPL networks. To detect rogue nodes, save overhead, and improve security in lossy and low-power networks, a version number modification approach is proposed as well as to demonstrate how to create and test these attacks using COOJA and Contiki-NG.

DOI: 10.4018/979-8-3693-9919-4.ch008

I. INTRODUCTION

Version Number Attacks (VNAs) pose a significant internal threat to RPL-based networks, but there is a dearth of research on the specific tasks that lead to excessive energy use. Node hyperactivity is not attributed to loops or local and global fixes in this paper. In the first scenario, hostile nodes initiate their "trick timer" in response to the maximum number of VN incrementations. The outcomes support the RPL-Contiki working theory (Belkhira et al., 2024)

Version Number Modification Attack: This internal attack occurs when a DODAG tree's version number is changed from lower to higher. Nodes begin creating a new DODAG tree when they get the DIO message with a higher version number. This leads to a network topology that is neither optimal nor consistent, which raises control overhead and packet loss (Kaur, 2019).

Instead of developing a data-level WSN implementation, we refactored a security-focused project to evaluate attacks on the RPL protocol in Contiki.

Figure 1. Contiki network layer

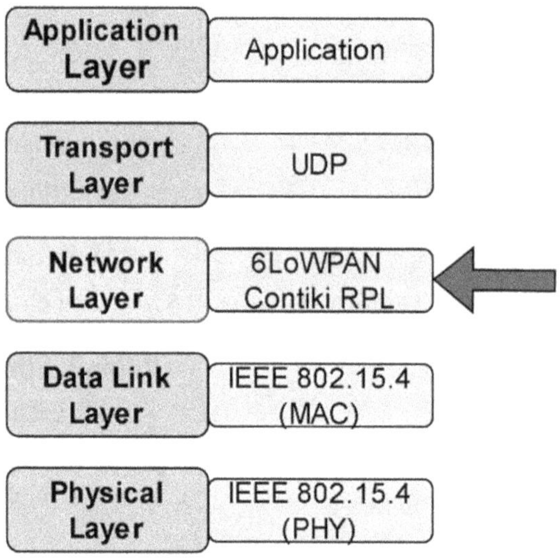

Figure 1 shows the Contiki network stack, with the attacked layer, Cooki simulations will be able to easily incorporate testing of malicious nodes, and the results of specific attacks will be evaluated and displayed. It includes experimentation, design and implementation of the framework and RPL attacks. Terminology is used throughout the document to describe attackers, normal nodes, and the DODAG root. The study was divided into three sections: introduction, experiments, and conclusion.

The DODAG version number can be altered by writers in a "version attack," which renders the system unstable and vulnerable to Denial of Service (DoS) attacks (Dey & Ghosh, 2024) .

For use in IoT and Wireless Sensor Networks (WSNs), RPL is a distance-vector routing protocol. It satisfies resource-constrained device and application needs and is straightforward and interoperable. A Destination Oriented Directed Acyclic Graph (DODAG) serves as the foundation for the protocol's topology, and each node is given a version number and rank value. Five control messages are used to maintain the topology of the RPL network, and Objective Functions (OF) are used to determine the best path (Tassorelli et al., 2024) .

For devices with limited resources, RPL protocol security is essential; yet research on rank and version number assaults has shortcomings, such as security issues, multiple attacks, and an inability to identify and counteract them (A. Almusaylim et al., 2020). By raising the root node's DODAG version number, the RPL version number attack worsens network performance. This causes higher control overhead, routing loops, energy consumption, problems with channel availability, and packet delivery failure (Almusaylim et al., 2020) . This work provides a security approach to stop DODAG attacks, like pretending to be a root and raising the Version Number or allowing an internal attacker to publish a falsely lowered Rank value (Dvir et al., 2011).

The suggested method uses root DODAG random numbers to construct hash chains for rank and version number; it works well in simulations but could cause resource depletion in LLN networks (Boudouaia et al., 2020). As part of an organized plan to enhance RPL security, the authors present two simple techniques. The first technique uses information messages from the nodes to fill a table with information about each network node, which is managed by the root. The root performs checking methods and notifies the nodes when it detects unauthorized rank modifications. The second approach is carried out in nodes, where each node possesses a checking table containing neighbor IDs, rankings, and version numbers. The receiving node computes a probability value and decides whether to update the version number based on the conducted probability value (Eddine Khalfoune & Beghdad, 2024)

Figure 2 shows how network assaults are classified, with attacks indicated in blue frames. Malicious nodes that use a lot of memory, power, and energy fall into the first group. These nodes might disrupt the availability of the network by causing congested links or downed nodes to last longer. This can be accomplished by forcing lawful arrest agencies to engage in needless activities.

Figure 2. Attack taxonomy targeting RPL networks (version number modification)

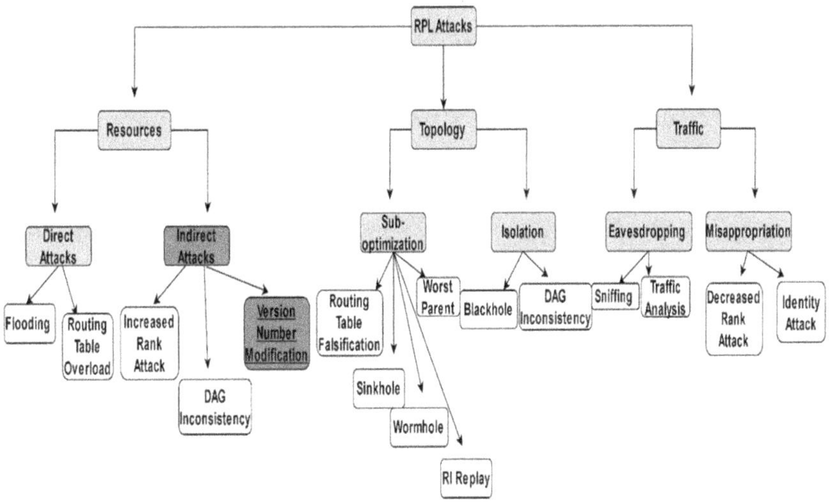

Figure 2 shows direct and indirect attacks are two subcategories of network attacks. While direct attacks lead to overloading, indirect attacks involve malicious nodes that produce overloading. The goal of attacks against RPL network topology is to disrupt normal operations, which may lead to node isolation. This may be followed by node isolation and branch performance. Attacks on network traffic can give rise to rogue nodes that can eavesdrop on or impersonate trusted nodes and cause information leakage. These attacks can be divided into two categories: passive eavesdropping and contract theft. These attacks may result in insufficient performance and network convergence.

Version Number Modification: The version number may rise due to the DODAG's root, necessitating pointless graph rebuilds. To deliver a fresh DIO, the root resets its trickle timer and updates the invalid DIO. Normal nodes, on the other hand, start global repairs by unplugging their parents and updating their new parent with the received DIO.

Figure 3. Version number modification attack

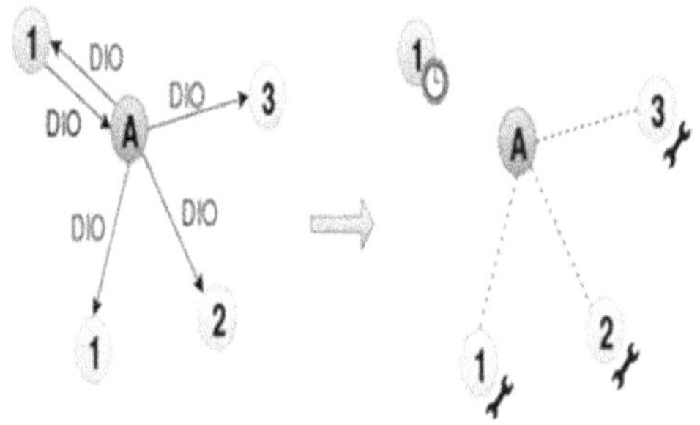

Version attack the red one has an increase of 1, whereas the DIO in black as shown in Figure 3

Mitigation use Hash operations are used for authentication in Amit Dvir's VeRa mechanism, which is intended to stop hostile nodes from unjustly increasing version numbers, however it doesn't seem to be included in Contiki RPL. Also to mitigate form attack use strategies like TRAIL (Trust Anchor Interconnection Loop) and VeRa (Version Number and Rank Authentication) can be implemented to counter these attacks. This work provides a better understanding of the different attack vectors.

Through this effort, we will gain a better understanding of the different species. The observed parameters and the study environment are explained in Section II. The results are tabulated in Section III. By linking the observations, Section Four explains the findings and assists in the conclusion-making process. The results of the case study are concluded in Section V. Finally, Section VI attempts to guide how to further develop work to examine attacks more comprehensively on.

Figure 4 shows a Version Number attack: Manipulating or advertising fake version numbers to force genuine nodes out of the Destination Oriented Directed Acyclic Graph (DODAG) structure and create instability in the network is known as a Version Number (Traffic I Disruption) attack. This can lead to network fragmentation, routing loops, and node overload, which can also expose the network to secondary attacks such as sinkholes or blackhole.

Figure 4. Version number attack

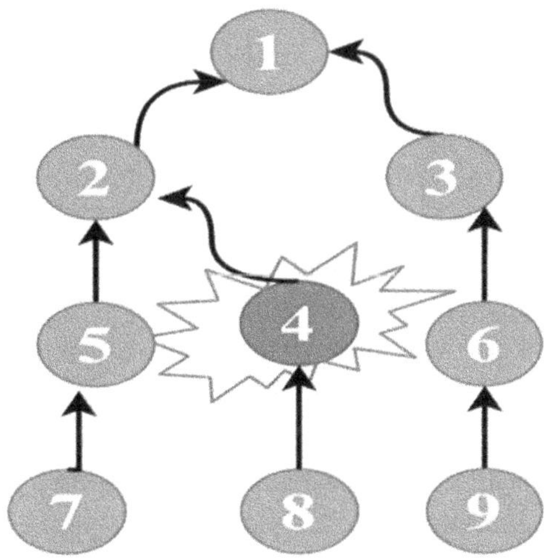

The observed parameters and the study environment are explained in Section II. The results are tabulated in Section III. By linking the observations, Section Four explains the findings and assists in the conclusion-making process. The results of the case study are concluded in Section V. Finally, Section VI attempts to guide how to further develop work to examine attacks more comprehensively.

II. RELATED WORK

Using a networked control system testbed for man-in-the-middle (MITM) attacks, the study shows how well-encrypted control systems detect attacks. Based on a threshold-based approach, the MITM-attack detection method works well in real-time situations. The possibility of creating different attack-detection strategies based on variations in processing time is also covered in the paper (Kosugi et al., 2024)

The usage of deep learning models is expanding across industries, raising the possibility of harmful assaults. Model owners can generate numerous versions of their models with varying attack qualities to guard against these losses without having to alter the design of the model. This can be accomplished by selecting the best-hidden distributions and adding parameterized hidden distributions to training data (Ding et al., 2024)

With an emphasis on packet delivery, latency, and power consumption, the study investigates how well Low-Power Wireless Personal Area Networks (RPL)-based Internet of Things networks function under attack. Version assaults are widespread, and traditional security procedures are ineffective in contexts with limited resources. The goal of this research is to enhance secure Internet of Things applications (Sharma et al., 2023).

Although the Routing Protocol for Low Power and Lossy Networks (RPL) of the Internet of Things (IoT) is a promising technology, it is susceptible to attacks such as Version Number Attacks. This work introduces VeNADet, a novel assault detection technique that is built into the Cooja Simulator. According to the study, VeNADet improves RPL security by detecting Version Number Attacks with a high True Positive rate and a low false alarm rate (Anitha, 2021)

The most dangerous flaw in web application security is SQL injection, which may seriously harm databases, web apps, and the server. This article offers a unique defense against SQL injection attacks by categorizing them according to how this vulnerability is used. The technique has been shown to be effective against all varieties of SQL injection threats by means of widely used tools and security datasets. The findings demonstrate a high detection accuracy rate of SQL injection attacks (Dalai & Jena, 2017).

Interactive communication across heterogeneous networks is made possible by the Internet of Things (IoT), yet topological assaults can be launched against the RPL routing protocol as it stands. This work demonstrates the security and effective computational cost and energy consumption of a lightweight Identity Based Offline–Online Signature-based system to resist version number and rank spoofing attacks. It also evaluates the vulnerabilities of RPL (Nikravan et al., 2018)

The security of code models with trigger injections, such CodeBERT and CodeT5, against hidden backdoor attacks is tested in this study using Afraidoor. The findings indicate that when Afraidoor is applied to two downstream jobs and three commonly used code models, it is less likely to be recognized than baseline approaches. The results draw attention to security vulnerabilities and urge more research to build more robust defenses (Abu Laila et al., 2024)

For low-power and lossy (RPL) networks, routing protocol is one of the key technologies driving the increasing popularity of the Internet of Things (IoT). However, RPL is vulnerable to potential intrusions that may compromise network security. To understand these risks, testing and experimentation on reference implementation are required (Al-Na'amneh et al., 2024)

This research (Rouissat et al., 2024) investigates and counteracts the Hybrid Rank Attack (HRA) in Internet of Things (IoT) networks based on Routing Protocol for Low-power and Lossy Networks (RPL). By showing higher and lower rank values in control messages, the exploit manipulates RPL, impairing network functionality and severely degrading performance. To measure the effect of HRA on important network parameters such as energy consumption, latency, memory footprint, packet delivery ratio, and exchanged messages, the authors carried out a number of in-depth tests. To combat HRA, they suggested a brand-new intrusion detection system combined with a simple countermeasure algorithm. Simulation-based assessments demonstrated that the method-maintained network efficiency by drastically lowering control overhead and usage of energy.

The study (Hebbaka Shivanajappa et al., 2024) addresses the security issues brought on by the Internet of Things, cloud computing, and Internet's explosive growth. By highlighting how vulnerable the "Routing Protocol for Low power and Lossy networks" (RPL) is to intrusions and unauthorized access, it draws attention to the necessity of an intrusion detection system (IDS) to detect and thwart assaults on Internet of Things (IoT) communication devices. The novel strategy that the authors recommend is the Graph Neural Network (GNN) method GCNConv, which logs edge and node attributes in a graph. The experimental validation of the proposed IDS by the RADAR dataset shows that the GCNConv method outperforms the existing state-of-the-art methodologies in several performance measures, indicating its application in identifying routing risks in the Internet of Things.

This paper (Verma et al., 2024) discusses issues and solutions related to the Routing Protocol for Low-power Lossy Networks (RPL) in Internet of Things (IoT) applications. It highlights the role that LLNs play in the digital transformation process as well as the danger that comes with the Destination Advertisement Object (DAO) control messages that RPL sends. The authors recommend using the "Li-MSD" low-impact mitigation strategy to address this problem. Li-MSD uses a blacklisting strategy to decrease attacks and restore RPL network operation. Simulation results show that Li-MSD performs better than previous approaches, indicating that it could be a helpful tool for bolstering network security against DAO attacks by insiders. The article's conclusion emphasizes the importance of RPL in the Internet of things and the risks posed by DAO insider attacks.

The paper (Kowsalyadevi & Balaji, 2023) discusses the importance of IoT technology in the context of the Internet of Battlefield Things (IoBT). The Routing Protocol for insufficient-Power and Lossy Networks (RPL) is a lightweight protocol that is essential for Internet of Things applications, but its inadequate security features expose it to several forms of attacks. This paper discusses a novel technique named IoBTSec-RPL to mitigate these vulnerabilities. It uses a hybrid Deep Learning model to identify multiple attack types that target RPL in IoBT settings. The model exceeds previous models in terms of accuracy and has a great recall rate of 98.93% in spotting numerous RPL attacks.

While in This study (Rouissat et al., 2023), addresses the security vulnerabilities associated with Internet of Things (IoT) networks because of their constrained computational and energy resources, as well as their limited capabilities. It presents a novel attack known as Destination Information Object Flooding (DIOF), in which a malicious node propagates false information and transmits an excessive amount of DIO control messages, thereby impairing network performance. assaults using denial-of-service assaults reduce energy consumption, delay, control overhead, and packet delivery ratio. The paper suggests a technique called DIOF-Secure RPL (DSRPL), which can detect and neutralize DIOF assaults in a timely manner. It also reduces usage of energy and network overhead by more than 80% while preserving acceptable QoS levels.

Moreover, in IoT Smart Grid Networks, the paper (Guan et al., 2023) analyzes the vulnerability of the Routing Protocol for Low-Power Lossy Networks (RPL). The researchers suggest a hybrid deep neural network method for attack detection and classification that combines Bidirectional Long Short-Term Memory (BiLSTM) networks with Convolutional Neural Networks (CNN). To solve the data imbalance, the method offers the use of feature augmentation, preprocessing, and the Synthetic Minority Oversampling Technique (SMOTE). When applied to a simulated IIoT network under several attacks and to a dataset including nine commercial IoT devices that were targeted by two botnets, the CNN-BiLSTM technique performs better than alternative methods in both examples. The results were 89% recall, 89% F1-score, 89% precision, and 91% accuracy.

Also, in this study (Alsukayti & Alreshoodi, 2023) shows the significant security risks that RPL networks face, particularly about internal routing attacks. The paper emphasizes the need for more research on these attacks, especially when attack scenarios get more complex and deployment scales increase. In-depth experimental research of several routing attacks on RPL networks is provided in this study, which reveals that even simple assaults can significantly reduce network stability and Quality of Service (QoS) performance. The analysis indicates that there is a potential for over 200% increase in energy consumption and control traffic overhead, along with a possible loss of over 90% in QoS performance and topological stability. Based on the authors, understanding these impacts is crucial for developing security fixes that improve the protocol's.

To organize networks in a tree-like structure, the Routing Protocol for Low power and Lossy networks (RPL), which was created for the Internet of Things (IoT), is discussed in this research (Ghaleb et al., 2023). An attribute named Rank, which represents each node's location in relation to the root, is present in every RPL network node. Attacks could be made against this Rank, which is important for routing decisions. The Rank system can be abused by a malicious node, which would cause the network harm by making it appear as though it is closer to the root. The research performed several detailed simulations to demonstrate how this assault deteriorates network performance. To counteract this vulnerability and avert the decreased rank attack, the paper proposes a new secure objective that uses sure nodes cannot improperly claim a higher rank.

(Khan et al., 2023) discusses IoT network security concerns, particularly with Sybil attacks. The study highlights the shortcomings of RPL security, the susceptibility of low-power devices, and the flaws in traditional protocols. It recommends using centralized, cooperative Random Password Generation (RPG) to defend RPL-based IoT networks from Sybil attacks. The detection methodology matches the keys and constant IDs of interacting nodes after validating their passwords, whereas the prevention method uses a delivery delay ratio to restrict sensor node participation in communication. When compared to dispersed protection systems, the simulation results show better throughput, average delivery latency, detection rate, and performance.

(Thiyagu & Krishnaveni, 2022) addresses wormhole attacks on the Routing Protocol for Low Power and Lossy Networks (RPL) to address the increasing occurrence of assaults on the Internet of Things (IoT). Internet of Things networks are better protected against attacks thanks to the authors' advanced gated recurrent unit (AGRU) deep learning model, which accurately recognizes possible risks. The model's performance is evaluated with conventional approaches such as One Support Vector Machine and Logistic Regression using measures like weight states and node power consumption. The results show that IoT security prediction has become more accurate and efficient, particularly when it comes to reducing mistake rates associated with monitoring RPL flood attacks. This approach greatly improves the overall dependability of Internet of Things networks and contributes to IoT security.

III. ADOPTED METHODOLOGY

Due to its scalability and energy efficiency, the RPL protocol is widely used in Internet of Things (IoT) networks. This study aims to develop a reference application for executing attacks against this protocol. It provides a comprehensive introduction to the RPL protocol, reviews common attacks, and demonstrates how to use Cooja and Contiki-NG to implement and test these attacks. The main objective is to enhance the robustness of RPL-based networks against malicious actors (Aljaidi et al., 2023).

A version number attack involves a malicious node manipulating or arbitrarily increasing the version number of the Destination-Oriented Directed Acyclic Graph (DODAG). In the RPL protocol, the version number indicates changes or updates in the network topology. By sending false higher version numbers, the attacking node forces other nodes to reform the DODAG, causing disruptions in the network topology and forcing nodes to recalculate their routing paths.

This malicious behavior can have several detrimental effects on network performance. Firstly, repeated manipulation of version numbers leads to constant network reconfiguration, increasing energy consumption of IoT nodes and causing resource overload. Secondly, this attack can result in routing loops and suboptimal paths, thereby increasing network latency and reducing overall efficiency. Finally, by disrupting the DODAG structure, the malicious node can cause packet loss or severe delays, compromising the integrity and reliability of the network (Aljaidi et al., 2023).

The version number manipulation attack typically unfolds in two phases. In the first phase, the malicious node sends falsified DODAG Information Object (DIO) messages with a manipulated version number, prompting neighboring nodes to leave the current DODAG and form a new structure, thus disrupting the normal topology. In the second phase, the node continues to emit false version numbers, maintaining network instability and exacerbating congestion and routing efficiency issues (Jaradat et al., 2023).

Figure 5 illustrates a scenario where 40 nodes have formed a DODAG and are operating normally. Conversely, Figure 5 depicts the same scenario under a version number manipulation attack initiated by node 10, demonstrating how this malicious node disrupts the RPL routing structure by broadcasting false version numbers.

The simulation runs for 47,000 seconds in each scenario, during which nodes exchange data and control information. A normal scenario serves as a baseline, aiding in understanding the deviation of certain parameter values in attack-present scenarios. The impact of malicious activity on the arrival delay of data packets at the receiving node is analyzed, as an increase in packet delay may indicate the presence of attacking nodes. Furthermore, the packet delay from node 10 (the malicious node) is compared to that from other nodes in a normal scenario, highlighting the impact of malicious behavior on packet delays from this node. Scenario 2 (with attack) is compared to Scenario 1 (without attack) in terms of frequency and distribution of DIO messages, to determine if malicious activity disrupts the exchange of these crucial messages for path stability.

Figure 5. Positioning of sensor nodes concerning the sink node

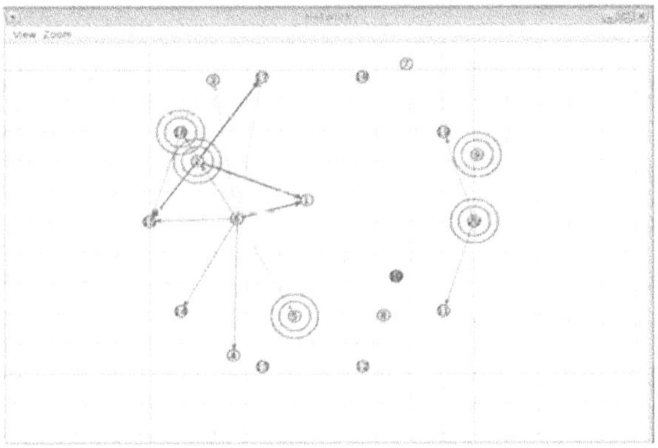

Figure 6. Version number attacks (node 10)

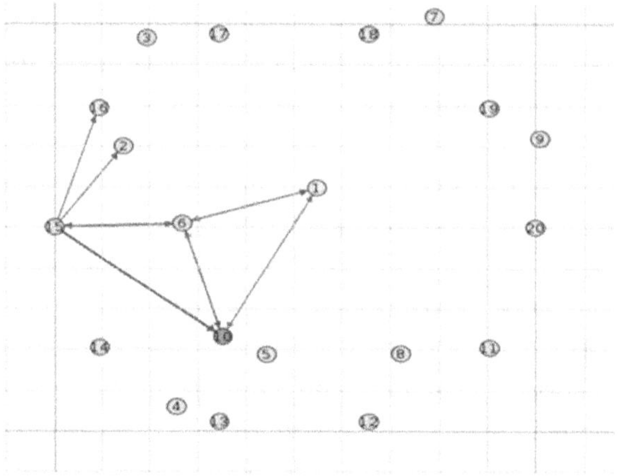

IV. OBSERVATION

Figure 6 displays a graph representing the data flow and packet transmission frequency in a normal network scenario. Figure 7 illustrates the network flow in a scenario with version number attacks, where a malicious node manipulates the version number to disrupt the network routing process by causing frequent reorganizations of the dodag structure.

Figure 7. Normal packet transmission frequency

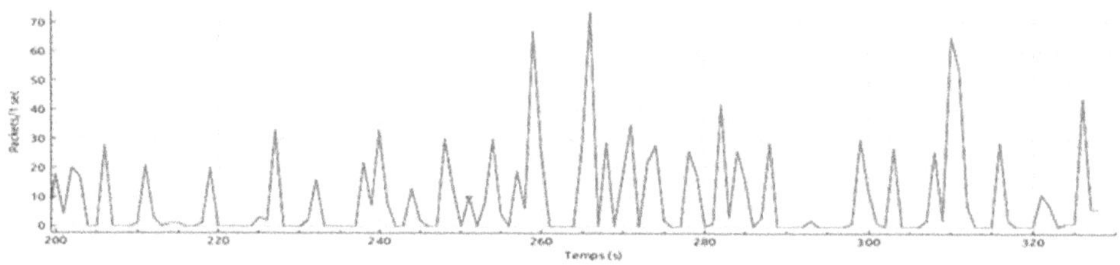

Figure 8. Malicious packet transmission frequency

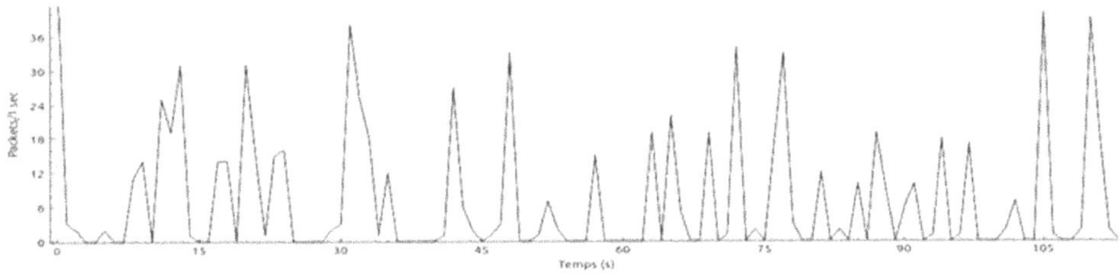

V. RESULTS DISCUSSION

The collected data includes the number and timestamps of DIO messages sent by each node. This information enables the calculation and assessment of DIO message frequency. Table 1 provides a summary of the number of DIO messages exchanged in different scenarios. An increase in the number of DIO messages exchanged signals instability in the routing topology. By analyzing the DIO messages sent by individual nodes, we can determine whether specific nodes have detected this instability and attempted to stabilize the network by sending their own DIO packets. The normal network scenario serves as a baseline for comparison with other scenarios, as shown in Table 1.

In Scenario 2, node 10 is the malicious node, initiating a version number attack by broadcasting a falsified, higher version number. Nodes 8, 9, and 12 are affected, misled into leaving the original DODAG structure, which causes instability in the network.

Table 1. Scenes with DIO packets released

Node	**Scenario1**	**Scenario2**
2	79	24
3	54	44
4	77	71
5	64	22
7	85	54
8	33	87
10/6/15	55	77
14	58	64
11	87	66
Total DIO Messages	592	509

The Contiki RPL protocol exchanges various control messages between transmitting and receiving nodes to establish a network topology. Nodes exchange control information to generate DODAG Information Object (DIO) messages. The version number of the DODAG helps nodes identify changes in the network structure, while the round-trip time (RTT) of these packets helps estimate the distance to neighbors. The frequency of DIO messages decreases once the topology stabilizes.

By analyzing the rate and frequency of DIO messages emitted by nodes in different scenarios, it becomes evident that the introduction of malicious activity by node 10 in Scenario 2 led to network instability experienced by all nodes. Scenario 2 showed an overall increase in the number of DIO messages. As illustrated in Figure 4, data from Scenario 2 demonstrated that all nodes emitted a higher number of DIO messages compared to the clear network scenario.

However, the total number of DIO messages in Scenario 2 was lower than in Scenario 1. This suggests that although node 10 in Scenario 2 maliciously manipulated the version number, causing the network to reorganize, it disrupted the DODAG structure by forcing nodes to form a new topology. Other nodes had to readjust their routing paths frequently, resulting in an increased frequency of DIO messages to restore stability to the topology.

This observation is reinforced by Figure 9, which shows that node 10 in Scenario 1 took much longer to emit the same number of DIO messages as the attacking node in Scenario 2. Examining the DIO messages from node 10 in Scenario 2, it emitted the first 100 DIO messages in a much shorter time compared to Scenario 1, as illustrated in Figure 10. This indicates that the version number attack disrupted the network topology and caused temporary instability that required frequent adjustments to routing paths by non-malicious nodes.

Thus, impacts the stability of the RPL network, leading to an increased frequency of control messages and constant topology readjustments, which degrade the overall network performance.

Figure 9. Comparison of DIO messages for malicious/affected nodes

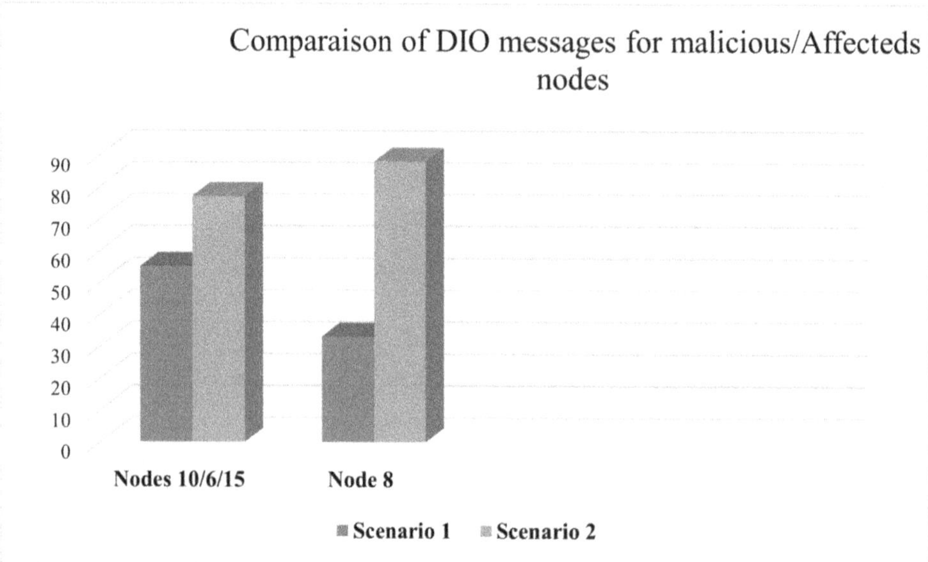

Figure 10 in Scenario 2, data packets from the malicious node (Node 10) experienced significantly higher delays compared to its counterpart in Scenario 1. The delay for packets from Node 10 was about 4.3 times greater than that of Node 12 in Scenario 1. This increased packet delay was not confined to the malicious node's data; non-malicious packets, both near and far from the malicious node, also faced higher delays in Scenario 2. All nodes in Scenario 2 experienced substantially higher delays compared to other scenarios.

Figure 10. DIO messages over time in different scenarios

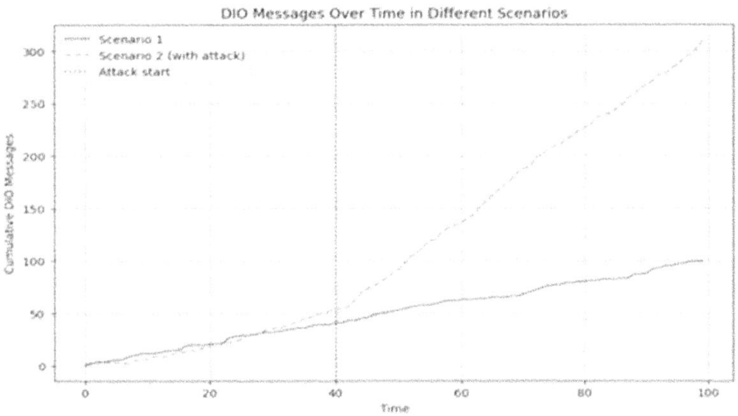

The primary cause of these packet delays was likely due to instability caused by the version number attack. The malicious node (Node 10) frequently triggered reconfigurations of the DODAG by sending DIO messages with a manipulated version number, causing nodes to reorganize the network. This frequent reorganization led to buffered queues where packets waited to be processed while the sink node generated and handled DIO packets, attempting to stabilize the network topology. Extended waiting times could lead to packet expiration due to the time-to-live (TTL) setting. Additionally, the sink node did not release any data packets, and the malicious node in Scenario 2 suppressed forwarding any self-generated data packets.

The total number of packets received at the sink node was recorded for each scenario. Packet loss could occur due to prolonged waiting times in the buffer queue, being dropped by the malicious node, or might have been mitigated if the simulation had run for a longer period.

VI. CONCLUSIONS

According to a chapter, network performance and reliability in RPL-based 6LoWPAN networks can be greatly impacted by a reduced rank attack having a substantial impact on network performance, according to the study's assessment of Random Point Loading (RPL) performance in static and mobile settings. This finding emphasizes the need for strong security measures in dynamic and mobile network environments. This makes the system relevant for modern IDS design. The experimental results show a considerable decrease in packet delivery rate, an increase in end-to-end packet delay, and higher power consumption.

VII. LIMITATIONS AND FUTURE WORK

The authors address the limitations and shortcomings of previous efforts on rank and version number attacks by proposing two lightweight approaches in their combined solution to increase RPL security.

Future research endeavors to develop and put into place a system that safeguards RPL-based networks from coordinated attacks, which have the potential to inflict immense harm because the existing literature lacks default defense lines.

REFERENCES

Abu Laila, D., Al-Na'amneh, Q., Aljaidi, M., Nasayreh, A. N., Gharaibeh, H., Al Mamlook, R., & Alshammari, M. (2024). *Simulation of Routing Protocols for Jamming Attacks in Mobile Ad-Hoc Network.*, DOI: 10.4018/979-8-3693-2691-6.ch013

Al-Na'amneh, Q., Nasayreh, A. N., Al Mamlook, R., Gharaibeh, H., Alsheyab, A. M., & Almaiah, M. (2024). *Improving Memory Malware Detection in Machine Learning With Random Forest-Based Feature Selection.*, DOI: 10.4018/979-8-3693-2691-6.ch006

Aljaidi, M., Alsarhan, A., Al-Fraihat, D., Al-Arjan, A., Igried, B., El-Salhi, S. M., Khalid, M., & Al-Na'amneh, Q. (2023). Cybersecurity Threats in the Era of AI: Detection of Phishing Domains Through Classification Rules. *2023 2nd International Engineering Conference on Electrical, Energy, and Artificial Intelligence (EICEEAI)*, 1–6. https://doi.org/DOI: 10.1109/EICEEAI60672.2023.10590011

Almusaylim, Z. A., Alhumam, A., Mansoor, W., Chatterjee, P., & Jhanjhi, N. Z. (2020). Detection and mitigation of rpl rank and version number attacks in smart internet of things.

Almusaylim, Z. A., Alhumam, A., Mansoor, W., Chatterjee, P., & Jhanjhi, N. Z. (2020). *Detection and Mitigation of RPL Rank and Version Number Attacks in Smart Internet of Things.* https://doi.org/DOI: 10.20944/preprints202007.0476.v1

Alsukayti, I. S., & Alreshoodi, M. (2023). RPL-Based IoT Networks under Simple and Complex Routing Security Attacks: An Experimental Study. *Applied Sciences (Basel, Switzerland)*, 13(8), 4878. DOI: 10.3390/app13084878

Anitha, A. A. (2021). VeNADet: Version Number Attack Detection for RPL based Internet of Things. *Solid State Technology*, 64(February).

Belkhira, H. S. A., Belkheir, M., Rouissat, M., Mokaddem, A., Lorenz, P., Boukhobza, M. A., Salmi, A., & Kouar, A. (2024). Comprehensive Examination of Version Number Attacks in IoT Networks: Nodes Hyperactivity as Specific Criterion. *Open Information Science*, 8(1), 20220165. Advance online publication. DOI: 10.1515/opis-2022-0165

Boudouaia, M. A., Ali-Pacha, A., Abouaissa, A., & Lorenz, P. (2020). Security Against Rank Attack in RPL Protocol. *IEEE Network*, 34(4), 133–139. DOI: 10.1109/MNET.011.1900651

Dalai, A. K., & Jena, S. K. (2017). Neutralizing SQL Injection Attack Using Server Side Code Modification in Web Applications. *Security and Communication Networks*, 2017, 1–12. DOI: 10.1155/2017/3825373

Dey, D., & Ghosh, N. (2024). *iTRPL: An Intelligent and Trusted RPL Protocol based on Multi-Agent Reinforcement Learning.*

Ding, W., Bhagoji, A. N., Zhao, B. Y., & Zheng, H. (2024). Towards Scalable and Robust Model Versioning. *2024 IEEE Conference on Secure and Trustworthy Machine Learning (SaTML)*, 592–611. https://doi.org/DOI: 10.1109/SaTML59370.2024.00036

Dvir, A., Holczer, T., & Buttyan, L. (2011). VeRA - Version Number and Rank Authentication in RPL. *2011 IEEE Eighth International Conference on Mobile Ad-Hoc and Sensor Systems*, 709–714. https://doi.org/DOI: 10.1109/MASS.2011.76

Eddine Khalfoune, A., & Beghdad, R. (2024). Securing RPL-Based Networks Against Version Number and Rank Attacks. *Acta Informatica Pragensia*, 13(3), 340–358. DOI: 10.18267/j.aip.234

Ghaleb, B., Al-Dubai, A., Hussain, A., Ahmad, J., Romdhani, I., & Jaroucheh, Z. (2023). (POSTER) Resolving the Decreased Rank Attack in RPL's IoT Networks. *2023 19th International Conference on Distributed Computing in Smart Systems and the Internet of Things (DCOSS-IoT)*, 65–67. https://doi.org/DOI: 10.1109/DCOSS-IoT58021.2023.00018

Guan, Y., Noferesti, M., & Ezzati-Jivan, N. (2023). CNN-BiLSTM-Based Classification of RPL Attacks in IoT Smart Grid Networks (Industry Track). *Proceedings of the 24th International Middleware Conference: Industrial Track*, 29–34. https://doi.org/DOI: 10.1145/3626562.3626832

Hebbaka Shivanajappa, M., Maidanahalli Seetharamaiah, R., Viswaraju Sai, B., Jakkanahally Siddegowda, A., & Kuppanna Rajuk, V. (2024). An Intrusion Detection System against RPL-based Routing Attacks for IoT Networks. *Indonesian Journal of Electrical Engineering and Computer Science*, 34(2), 1324. DOI: 10.11591/ijeecs.v34.i2.pp1324-1335

Jaradat, A. S., Nasayreh, A., Al-Na'amneh, Q., Gharaibeh, H., & Al Mamlook, R. E. (2023). Genetic Optimization Techniques for Enhancing Web Attacks Classification in Machine Learning. *2023 IEEE Intl Conf on Dependable, Autonomic and Secure Computing, Intl Conf on Pervasive Intelligence and Computing, Intl Conf on Cloud and Big Data Computing, Intl Conf on Cyber Science and Technology Congress (DASC/PiCom/CBDCom/CyberSciTech)*, 0130–0136. https://doi.org/DOI: 10.1109/DASC/PiCom/CBDCom/Cy59711.2023.10361399

Kaur, J. (2019). An ultimate approach of mitigating attacks in RPL based low power lossy networks. arXiv preprint arXiv:1910.13435.

Khan, M. A., Rais, R. N., & Khalid, O. (2023). Collaborative Detection and Prevention of Sybil Attacks against RPL-Based Internet of Things. *Computers, Materials & Continua*, 77(1), 827–843. DOI: 10.32604/cmc.2023.040756

Kosugi, A., Teranishi, K., & Kogiso, K. (2024). Experimental Validation of the Attack-Detection Capability of Encrypted Control Systems Using Man-in-the-Middle Attacks. *IEEE Access : Practical Innovations, Open Solutions*, 12, 10535–10547. DOI: 10.1109/ACCESS.2024.3353289

Kowsalyadevi, K., & Balaji, N. V. (2023). IoBTSec-RPL: A Novel RPL Attack Detecting Mechanism Using Hybrid Deep Learning Over Battlefield IoT Environment. *International Journal of Computer Networks and Applications*, 10(4), 637. DOI: 10.22247/ijcna/2023/223317

Nikravan, M., Movaghar, A., & Hosseinzadeh, M. (2018). A Lightweight Defense Approach to Mitigate Version Number and Rank Attacks in Low-Power and Lossy Networks. *Wireless Personal Communications*, 99(2), 1035–1059. DOI: 10.1007/s11277-017-5165-4

Rouissat, M., Belkehir, M., Mokaddem, A., Bouziani, M., & Alsukayti, I. S. (2024). Exploring and mitigating hybrid rank attack in RPL-based IoT networks. *Journal of Electrical Engineering*, 75(3), 204–213. DOI: 10.2478/jee-2024-0025

Rouissat, M., Belkheir, M., Alsukayti, I. S., & Mokaddem, A. (2023). A Lightweight Mitigation Approach against a New Inundation Attack in RPL-Based IoT Networks. *Applied Sciences (Basel, Switzerland)*, 13(18), 10366. DOI: 10.3390/app131810366

Sharma, G., Grover, J., & Verma, A. (2023). Performance evaluation of mobile RPL-based IoT networks under version number attack. *Computer Communications*, 197, 12–22. DOI: 10.1016/j.comcom.2022.10.014

Tassorelli, C., Onishchenko, K., Halker Singh, R. B., Duan, M., Dupont-Benjamin, L., Hemstock, M., Voller, C., McAllister, P., Nahas, S. J., Gandhi, P., & Ailani, J. (2024). Comparative efficacy, quality of life, safety, and tolerability of atogepant and rimegepant in migraine prevention: A matching-adjusted indirect comparison analysis. *Cephalalgia*, 44(2), 03331024241235156. Advance online publication. DOI: 10.1177/03331024241235156 PMID: 38410850

Thiyagu, T., & Krishnaveni, S. (2022). RPL Attacks Detection and Prevention in IOT Networks with Advanced GRU Deep Learning Algorithm. *2022 Smart Technologies* [STCR]. *Communication and Robotics*, 1–5, 1–5. Advance online publication. DOI: 10.1109/STCR55312.2022.10009350

Verma, A., Verma, S. K., Pandey, A. C., Grover, J., & Sharma, G. (2024). Li-MSD: A lightweight mitigation solution for DAO insider attack in RPL-based IoT. *Future Generation Computer Systems*, 159, 327–339. DOI: 10.1016/j.future.2024.05.032

Chapter 9
Semantic Search for IoT-Based Object Recognition Using Clustering and Classification

R. Prasath
https://orcid.org/0000-0002-6346-1301
RMK College of Engineering and Technology, India

V. Vasantha Kumar
https://orcid.org/0000-0002-5752-7175
KCG College of Technology, India

V. Jaisankari
https://orcid.org/0000-0001-9960-0003
AMET University, India

R. Sivasubramani
RMK College of Engineering and Technology, India

ABSTRACT

A search engine helps retrieve information from large datasets using data retrieval techniques. Enterprise search engines analyze diverse organizational data, while open-source engines focus on customization. For code acquisition, data (code, docstrings) is processed into pairs for training models. Optimizations like B-tree-based P2P indexing and syntax-aware tokenization improve efficiency. Real-time object recognition requires at least 10 fps, which may be achievable with newer Intel NCS versions. The system also scales well for IoT applications, achieving 80% accuracy.

INTRODUCTION

A web search engine is a common example, but as stated earlier, search engines are part of the various applications such as customized search and enterprise search. "Search Engine" was coined and first used to indicate a particular hardware intended for the text search. Because of the convergence of Internet of

DOI: 10.4018/979-8-3693-9919-4.ch009

Things and Machine Learning prompted large scope for the broad and informative data analysis (Janani R, Vijayarani S, 2019)(Ambhika et al 2024). IoT generates massive amounts of data every day from the various connected objects. Machine Learning helps in extracting the hidden correlations between the data. Machine Learning also helps in building the best prediction model by analyzing the existing data by applying various existing algorithms(Lakumarapu et al 2024)(Subha et al 2024). Many existing search engines namely Google, Bing and Yahoo come in various variants which reflect the applications designed for web search upgraded to crawl many terabytes of data by reducing the response time to fewer milliseconds for all queries all over the world. A typical and inevitable application to search large text repositories is the Search Engine. There are many categories of search engines involving the general-purpose search engines and customized search engines. Long ago the term search engine was commonly used to indicate a specific hardware for searching text. The enterprise search engines must be capable of processing a large variety of information sources inside the organization and leverage the knowledge as a product of information mining and searching. Data mining is a domain of extracting the related patterns which leads to the knowledge representation by means of applying the data mining techniques prominently clustering and classification(Maheshwaran et al 2024). Open-source search engines are one more significant type of systems with varied design goals compared to the commercial search engines. These systems are many and one can get links to these for data recovery. Modern search engines are not under estimated in their capability. Knowledge mining is a fast job for gathering information from the internet (Gulnashin et al 2019)(Kushwaha N, Pant M 2018). Unluckily, this tremendous capability cannot be used at every place. Searching is not readily available if the searing object is not the text data. Further, strict keyword searches will not allow users to extract information in a knowledgeable way. That is to say that the vital information is missing in the search results. Figure 1 below shows what is interconnected within an organization.

Figure 1. Interconnected things in an organization

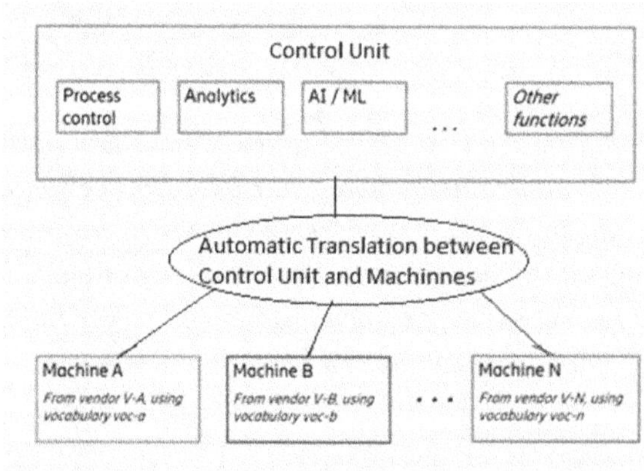

The above figure depicts the power of semantic search along the keywords, where the chances of getting the information by the user are increased for what they are looking. The advantages of the semantic search are manifold to name it allows developers to search code in the repositories in-spite of unaware of the syntax or predicting the correct syntax or words (Garg N, Gupta R 2018). Necessarily this approach can be generalized for the IoT-based connected objects including the images, sounds and other things one cannot even though off(Venketbabu et al 2024). The aim is to correlate code to natural language vector space, in which (code, text) ordered pairs describing the same context will be the close relatives, but the unrelated (code, text) ordered pairs will be estimated using cosine similarity. There exist many methods to arrive at the same point but we have demonstrated how to take a pre- trained model and tune the model to achieve the extracted frames form the code and to extract the hidden features in the natural language vector space (Karaa et al 2016). This process is carried out in five stages. These stages are illustrated in the following figure and will be the road map for the progress through the work. The figure below represents IoT-based semantic search architecture.

Figure 2. Architecture of IoT- based semantic search

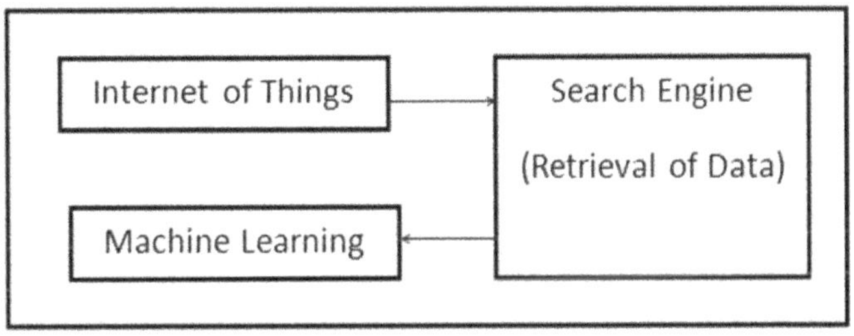

Step 1: Extract the files from database.
Step 2: Build a model that predicts a string from code such as code encoder.
Step 3: Build language model such as sentence Encoder.
Step 4: Tune code encoder to map code into a shared vector space with natural language.
Step 5: Create a Sprightly search.

Since 1980s, Henry Holec formally put forward the concept of "learner autonomy", and then autonomous learning has aroused the extensive attention of academic field at home and abroad, especially in the field of foreign language studies. Scholars began to transfer their academic research focus from the traditional study on how teachers teach to the study on how learners learn (Janani R, Vijayarani S 2019). Cultivation of autonomous learning ability and lifelong learning ability is regarded as one of the goals of modern education. In 1990s, foreign academic research achievements of learner autonomy have been introduced, which attracted many scholars in educational and foreign language teaching fields. With the development of higher education in, practice of the reform of college teaching has been put into effect nationwide. The cultivation of learning ability has been put in a very important position. To solve the existing problems in college teaching, the Ministry of national education put forward the reform scheme of college Teaching. In July 2007, the national ministry of education issued "College Curriculum Requirements", which ruled that the goal of college teaching is to cultivate student's comprehensive ability, especially listening and speaking ability. So, they could communicate effectively in their study, meanwhile enhance their autonomous learning ability, and improve the comprehensive cultural literacy. To meet the needs of social development and international exchanges, the new teaching model should depend on modern information technology, especially network technology as the support (Gulnashin et al 2019). Teaching and learning could not be controlled by time and place and then develop in the direction of individualization.

The primer focal point of Cognitive Reasoning (CR) makes the specialists going about as PUs to screen task of unutilized range and dynamic access from authorized band in remote organizations. The CR network innovation being a boundless innovation upgrades the organization utilization and makes the wasteful access of the range to be appropriately used in the organization. Additionally, notwithstanding different weaknesses (Kushwaha et al 2018) and security assault, the CR network is helpless towards different organization penetrate action performed by dangers. Range effectiveness is a main consideration to think about the usage in powerful access. Range assignment the board is included to be of four capacities like Sensing, Decision, Mobility and Sharing. The stochastic game hypothesis approach controls the sticking assault in the normal control channel and offers the control messages. These normal control messages (Garg N, Gupta R 2018) can give mindful, access and sharing of channel, distinguishing neighbors and range the board. A circulated normal control channel is expected to begin the activity for each unit to dissect and satisfy these tasks. The most far reaching assault occurring in the actual layer is sticking assault which transcendently occurs at actual layer and it ought to be checked right away. Game hypothesis approach is a numerical demonstrating that assists us with breaking down the collaboration among coherent players, and makes the capacity to apply the procedure to a solitary player or client and between various clients in a staggered order to anticipate the movement or occasion going through in networks. Multi-specialist support learning calculation used to recognize sticking among CR climate. Dynamic and occasion observing in unique conditions make complex in Cognitive radio organizations.

Sticking assault in Cooperative range detecting (Karaa et al 2016) in CR is truly challenging to improve execution. Game hypothetical model assume a significant part in identifying Jamming in CR to improve security. The stochastic game hypothesis was displayed between unlicensed SU and gatecrashers. Dependable productive telecom and information correspondence in psychological radio organizations range designation (Guinard, Trifa, & Wilde, 2010) is finished utilizing numerous stations that depended on the utilization checking and send control messages from different cases of time as per jammer procedure. It foresees the sticking assault by jumping among the multi-access channels and gathering of networks(Lin et al 2016). Secure Authentication instrument (Jara 2014) gave privacy and uprightness among the PU in CR. Bunching system used to bunch the touchy hubs in Cognitive Reasoning. Information capture assault was forestalled utilizing dynamic range portion dependent on CASG displaying (Thakran 2013).Discrete-time part of the way noticed Markov choice interaction (Janani & Vijayarani, 2019) sped up secure correspondence in CRN.

What is self-ruling realizing? Self-governing learning is an advanced learning mode relating to the conventional responsive learning. Accepting understudies as the primary piece of the investigation, cause them to accomplish the learning targets through the examination, autonomous investigation, practice, creation, question and different strategies. Up to this point, the name and meaning of self-ruling learning isn't totally bound together (Davoodi et al 2013). It has different names like autonomous learning, student independence, self-coordinated learning, self-access learning, etc. Self-sufficient taking in began from grown-up schooling toward the finish of 1960s in Europe. Since 1970s, the specialists of unknown dialect schooling start to focus on independent learning in unknown dialect instructing. By the 1980s, Henri Holec initially gives acquaintance of self-sufficient learning hypothesis with the field of unknown dialect educating (Ruta et al 2012). He imagines that self-sufficient learning is “assuming responsibility for their own learning capacity”, which incorporates the three key elements of self-ruling learning capacity: learning objectives, self-observing and self-assessment. Since set forward the idea of self-ruling learning, various researchers have various meanings of student self-governance according to alternate points of view (Compton et al 2012). Little thinks about that self-governing learning is the students' mental response to their learning content and learning measure. It is an autonomous, basic reasoning, dynamic and free activity capacity. Students are answerable for their own learning during the time spent 1autonomous learning; in the learning method, students can choose and assess their own learning input. Self-ruling learning strategy ought to be arranged or it has arrived at the level of computerization of the self-sufficient learning after work out. Learning time is customary and productive and self-ruling learning understudies ought to know about their learning results (Kamilaris et al 2011). They can make the appropriate observing of the interaction of independent learning and can be drive to establish physical and social climate which is helpful for learning.

OBTAIN THE DATA

In this stage, data collection is done from the open source GitHub data warehouse and deposited in the Big Query. The GitHub is a trustable data repository for all types of data science projects. The data that is stored in Big Query is perfect for the data retrieval using the SQL queries to retrieve the required files and the metadata on these files for further analysis. Instructions for the retrieval of these files are provided for the users, these data entities are represented in the form of (code, docstring) pairs (Zhou et al 2016). To make it to work the code needs to be the developed at the top level methods or functions. These pairs are used in the form of training data for the code capture model, which is a tremendous task. Fortunately, Python library possess a package called AST which helps in capture functions, methods and docstrings (Lin et al 2016)(Jara et al 2014). The data stored in the Big Query is prepared for modeling, training, validation and testing. The files are also managed to keep track of the original (code, docstring) pair. Then, the same model is applied to the code which does not have the docstring and it is saved separately since it is needed to search for code as well. These series of the stages are to extract the necessary information from the data applying the Machine Learning.

A raw corpus is created and a set of rules based on the corpus is framed to classify whether the crawled text document matches or not.

A classification strategy is used to classify the extracted dataset to see that whether it belongs to a specified class or not. In the process supervised Machine Learning methods are used(Sudha et al 2024)(Maithili et al 2024). Training data is very essential to run the supervised model. Training data involves manually collected data from various sources across multiple objects. After which, the training data holds the current dataset tagged to represent the category of the file. This training data is used to run the supervised model. A single application of this model on crawled data can classify a new document that it belongs to which specific category among all extracted.

TRAIN A PROTOTYPE TO CIPHER THE NATURAL LANGUAGE PHRASES

The materials in this stage a mechanism is created for representing code as a vector, next there is a need for a similar mechanism for encode the natural language phrases present in doc string and search queries. There exists a numerous general-purpose model that created high-quality phrase embeddings called sentence embeddings. The proposed work gives a great overview in the field of sentence embeddings. One of the examples is Google's Universal Sentence Encoder works well in many applications and is available on TensorFlow Hub, (Jara et al., 2014). There are many ways of sentence embeddings, which ranges from the simple methods to say word vector averaging to the more sophisticated methods used in the construction of universal sentence embeddings. In this work Natural Language model is used to create embeddings for sentences. While building the language model, it is important to carefully consider the corpus used for the training.

Ideally it will be helpful to use the corpus that have a similar domain to the underlying problem so that it can adequately capture the relevant semantics and vocabulary. An example of a correct corpus would be the stack overflow data, as it is an open forum where much discussion takes place on the code. This is suboptimal, since the discussion about the stack overflow often contains more semantic information than that contained in single-line documentation strings. After the language pattern is trained the next task is to apply that pattern to embedded every sentence (Zhu et al 2013)(Davoodi et al 2013). A simple method could be to capture the hidden pattern of a language such as concrete pooling method. The architectural design for Sprightly Semantic Search is shown in the following Figure 3:

Figure 3. System architecture for sprightly semantic search

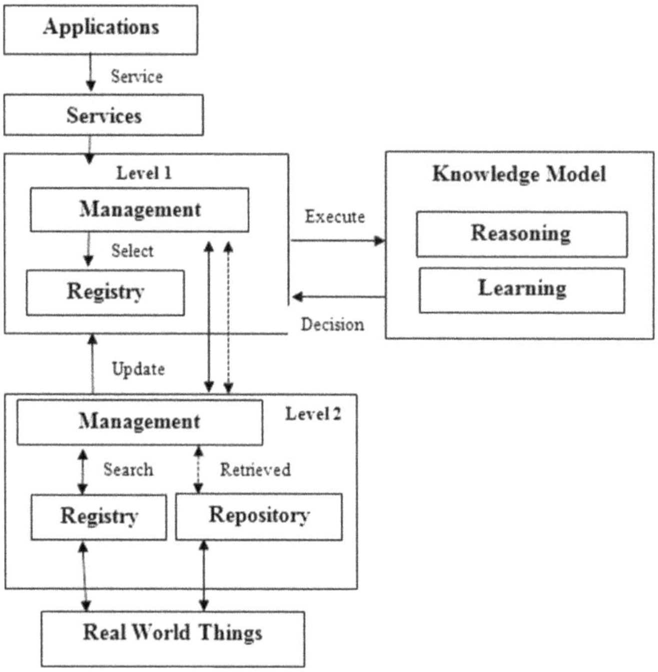

This pattern is used to measure embedding skills based on text or object similarity and is an excellent method for evaluating sentence embedding. In many cases, measuring the quality of the embedding using common benchmarks are among the one described here. However, most of the data is domain- specific, so the universal benchmarks probably not suitable for this problem. Unfortunately, the set of open source tasks for this domain has not yet been created. In the absence of such a bottom-up task, one needs to take care of sensibly checking whether these embeddings possess semantic information by observing the similarities among phrases that are known to be identical . Note that this is an integrity check only. This is a more rigorous approach to measure the impact of this embedding on various ground tasks, thereby giving a more objective impression of the quality of the embedding.

BUILD A SUMMARIZER USING A P2P MODEL

Model-to-pattern formatting is to capture code theoretically similar to the GitHub Issue. Summarizer previously offered, except that use Python code in place of issue body and docstrings in place of issue names. Code, on the other hand, is not a natural language, unlike GitHub issue text. Domain-specific optimizations like Tree-Based P2P model and Syntax- aware Tokenization (Kamilaris et al 2011) (Sailaja et al 2021) can be included to fully utilize the data in the code. In the proposed method the information is kept straightforward and the code in written in plain English. It should be mentioned that there are other methods which can be employed to develop a feature extractor for code (Guinard et al 2010) besides training the P2P model to extract code. The dataset can be trained, for instance, and discrimination can be used as a feature extractor. The subsequent figure 4 shows the procedure for building a summarizer using a P2P model:

Actual input -> Data collected from user (tokenized code)

Original output -> After each test method, cleaning the user instances (Actual Document)

Predicted output -> Clean up the data after each test.

Figure 4. Procedural diagram for build a summarizer

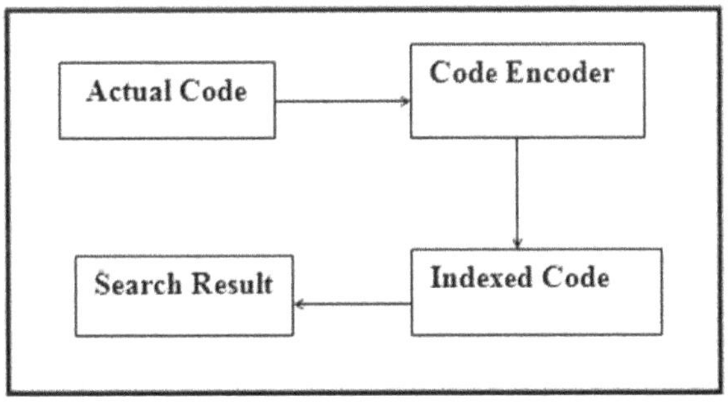

In this part, the philosophy for the examination primarily alludes to investigating reason, research questions, research instruments, and information assortment. The fundamental reason for the general plan is to reply, "in an overall way, how the framework ought to be figured it out". Accordingly, the general plan is likewise called "diagram plan" or "primer plan". Another significant errand in the general plan stage is to plan the construction of the product, that is, to figure out which modules each program is made out of, and the connections among these modules.

It is important to explore the circumstance of system which is independent figuring out how to help the examination. Just the training can test hypothesis. Through the examination of non-English significant understudies self-governing learning circumstance, we can find out about the getting capacity and level of the undergrads learning, and investigate the connection between the capacity of independent learning and understudies' sexual orientation and calling. As indicated by the aftereffect of examination and the genuine circumstance of our school, the information gives a premise and reference to showing change in our college, and investigates the powerful strategies and approaches to further develop the understudies self-governing learning capacity (Pfisterer et al 2011).

There are a wide range of sorts of techniques to gather the information in student self-sufficiency, like meeting, perception, poll, and journal, etc. (Madhu et al 2011). Contrasted and meeting and perception, poll takes less time and it is an effective and helpful technique to explore in college. In this examination, the survey is intended to research the circumstance of independent learning under network climate (Pschorr et al 2010). The investigation objects were non-English significant understudies who learned English in school. The poll contains an aggregate of 16 inquiries, which are isolated into four sections. The initial segment is the fundamental individual data; The subsequent part is undergrads' arrangement and utilization of self-sufficient learning under the organization climate; The third part is the abstract and target factors which impact the organization autonomous learning under the organization environment (such as close to home drive, the learning climate in school and equipment gear, etc.); The fourth part is whether the organization can assist understudies with their examination (Guinard et al 2010). Quick improvement of local area development in online interpersonal organization (OSN) spur the specialists to dissect the client premium that could profit the designated and social advertising throughout the timeframe (Perez et al 2010) and furthermore help the clients in interpersonal organization to get data or individuals from their own advantage into one's local area. Significant factor for being a gathering or local area is a common interest. Interpersonal organization gives a gathering to individuals to speak with old companions, relatives and to discover new companions who are of comparative interest, however the interests of individuals differ throughout the timeframe as the client interest can change because of the segment, transient and spatial construction of individuals.

However individuals include in interpersonal organization for diversion and unwinding, they likewise rely upon it for social event valuable data identified with the subject of interests. However, the data that is accessible locally are the interests of the banner (one who post the data) than the beneficiary and furthermore there is tons of data flooding step by step in network. Along these lines, separating the data that intrigues the client has gotten obligatory. This load of impediments is on the grounds that the individuals locally are not of comparative interest of the client. As an option many interests based organizations like Pinterest, Quora Flipora, and so on, are thrived these days. Yet, they do have their own disadvantage that the reliability of the data and the distributer is a question mark. Hence having comparative intrigued people as a piece of the local area will remember us from this load of issues and the subsequent SN can be protected and valuable.

To have the comparable intrigued people with regards to the local area, care should be taken while tolerating or raising companion demand. Companion idea by the informal communities today depends on the simple presence of common companion between two uses through primary examination. Yet, the shared companion may as have late become a companion of a common companion to mishandle the targeted. Along these lines, chart structure based investigation will not be useful (Ahad et al 2022) for the consideration of new client to the local area or to discover the clients of comparable premium in light of the fact that the SN are developed and supported with various sort of connections. Incorporation of new client to the local area will be protected and helpful if the new companion is trustable and of comparable interest. Such comparative interest of the client can be processed from client profiles.

Different order based theoretical techniques like AVL tree, Formal Concept Analysis (FCA) models however exist, it has its own disadvantage that it could dissect just on static client interest. As the client interest in SN is dynamic, sensible derivation can be made through the progressive semantic Modeling from the social client profile utilizing ontological strategy. However, the ontological pecking order is constructed semantically it could bring just the presence of the tag in the specific space. Yet, point Modeling utilizes allocation which is the unaided stochastic model which examinations the likelihood of specific subject of interest for the client from the recurrence of the word expression. Accordingly subject Modeling will mirror the truth of client interest even more definitely than the various leveled semantic Modeling. In this way the proposed study dealt with semantic Modeling to process the clients of comparative intrigue and assess its precision.

Figure 5. Design framework

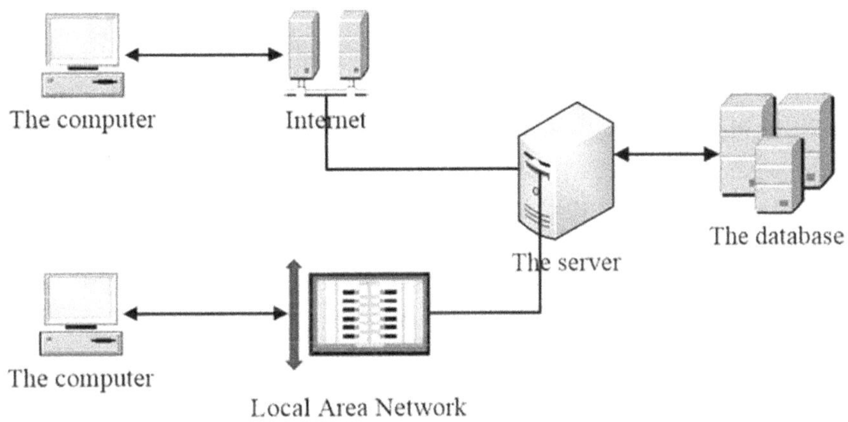

Numerous works had been done in the writing to break down the client interest in network for the business and individual necessities. Client's advantage in SN can be surmised by primary investigation, applied Modeling and semantic Modeling. Primary component put together interest deduction depends with respect to the fame, comparability and association strength (tie strength) with social neighbors. Differing patterns in client interest can be perceived and followed by examining label frequencies across time.

Catchphrase based idea displaying are addressed utilizing progressive relationship. The various leveled relationship that exists between ideas is depicted by super-idea and sub-idea. Each individual from a sub-idea is an individual from super-idea. In applied model client interest deduction can be addressed utilizing static model and dynamic model. The static model might be executed utilizing FCA and similitude by Jaccard record and the powerful model can be addressed utilizing semantic demonstrating utilizing philosophy in light of the fact that the assorted relationship that exists inside interpersonal organization can't be addressed utilizing the chart structure like FCA.

Profile based cosmology can be made for different ideas and properties by considering different settings as properties of framework and properties of archive assortment. For instance, fostered a client profile based recommender framework to suggest online scholastic examination paper utilizing ontological strategy. The metaphysics made altogether centers around static client qualities. However, the unique conduct of the clients is the innate idea of OSN. Subsequently understanding the elements of gatherings of people is a characteristic objective for network investigation. The disadvantage of absence of semanticity can be defeated utilizing the ontological technique. The Water Resource Component (WRC) cosmology developed which portrays the center idea and the connection between the water asset segments utilizing metaphysics.

The subject closeness between the substances of informal community administrations is combined utilizing the strategy for semantic bunches. Theme Modeling is a quickly developing part of insights which process the likelihood of words in a record to the subject and extent of point to the report, which could assess the % of client premium in a specific archive in an area. Client interest based SN is built from the web-based media exercises like remarks and tweets. The proposed framework utilizes the order based semantic model and point model from the communication data that the client divide between themselves to discover the clients of comparable interest.

SEMANTIC MODELLING IN MACHINE LEARNING

Data set innovation is the center innovation and significant establishment in the turn of events and development of data framework. The data set of a lot of information associated with the framework as indicated by certain model to sort out, give and keep up with the information stockpiling and recovery works, the data framework can meet the application necessities of clients for information stockpiling, recovery and support. The data set is the key of each piece of the data framework. The capacity design and improvement procedure of information straightforwardly decide the information legitimacy, honesty and inquiry effectiveness. If the data set plan is sensible straightforwardly affects the effectiveness of program advancement. In the information base plan cycle of the framework, the data set plan follows the accompanying standards As much as conceivable to guarantee information consistency and uprightness. The framework the board stage incorporates the landing page and the section news, the declaration, the strategy, etc. data scattering framework, every sort of utilization. Client and executive rights the board, situation log see, data set reinforcement framework, etc. G, working frameworks, data sets, or middleware .Use Windows, Linux, or Unix as working frameworks. Receive huge information bases that adjust to JDBC or ODBC, like Sql-Server2005 and Oracle, utilizing Resin or WebSphere or WebLogic as middleware.

Figure 6. Semantic modelling in machine learning

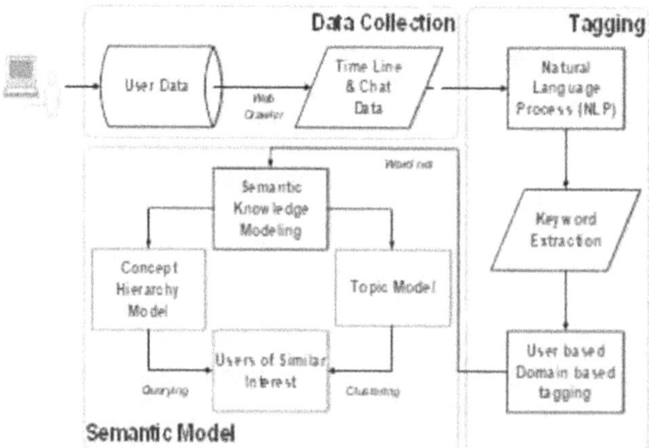

Semantic modelling (SM) dependent on client conduct is pointed towards demonstrating the unique idea of client interest in interpersonal organization and to feature the semantic connection that exists among clients utilizing two methodologies: I) Concept chain of command model utilizing cosmology and ii) Topic model. Contribution for SM is the content information that was traded between clients during visits and remarks. Idea based various leveled connections for cosmology is addressed utilizing an express applied portrayal of human information through the phrasings associated with correspondence. Cosmology indicates the conceptualization of the space as far as ideas, traits and relations, which is coordinated as a taxonomical tree where every hub addresses an idea and every idea is a specialization of its folks. Hence the metaphysics based comparative interest gathering will feature the truth of client conduct.

Subject displaying is the measurable probabilistic model that processes the probabilities of the words in the point as for the absolute reports in a comparing space that could assess the client interest exactly.

The technique that is most generally acknowledged and effectively executed for building ontologies was planned. The current work receives the altered rendition of this technique as offered beneath to plan and carry out client interest metaphysics. Development of client interest cosmology includes the accompanying advances: 1) Defining the reason and prerequisite of philosophy 2) Data assortment 3) Data cleaning and change 4) Ontology building and 5) Rule based deduction.

The reason for client interest philosophy is to display the semantic relationship that exists among the clients' advantage. Clients' advantage has been isolated into various areas of interest as indicated by the system characterized. The development of the metaphysics requires the labels/watchwords shared by the clients to show their inclinations, various areas of interest and the apparatus to build the philosophy.

Information utilized for this examination is the clients' timetable and visit meetings of the FB interpersonal organization. An engaged web crawler is intended to gather the people's information from Facebook (FB) utilizing the diagram API stage given by the FB engineers. The information given by the FB is in the .txt design which contains text, pictures, recordings, URL, exceptional characters, and so on The gathered timetable and visit meetings incorporate the usernames and client ids, writings of remarks and talks, and date and season of the content, and so forth Such commotion inclined information ought to be cleaned and changed into the structure reasonable for additional preparing.

The information gathered from FB is uproarious as it contains URLs, uncommon characters, and rehashed letter words, stop words, words in different tense t(book, booking, booked) and short messages, and so forth These pointless components should be eliminated or changed into the structure reasonable for metaphysics building. This information cleaning and change is a consecutive interaction where yield from one cycle is given as a contribution to the following. The gathered client interest information is pre-handled and changed into watchwords for additional preparing utilizing natural language processing procedures.

Subject displaying is a probabilistic model for noticing the reasonable point that happens in a bunch of given records. SM is a sort of subject displaying approach that characterizes the similitude of words in a point against the record as a two layer Bayesian likelihood as p(word | theme) and p(topic | report). The proposed SM model considers clients' conversational data like the talk and remarks as reports.

SM builds the corpus from the arrangement of reports and thinks about each archive as a mix of subjects and themes as a multinomial conveyance over the words. For each word circulation in the point and subjects in the report, likelihood is processed dependent on the rehashed example of words in the corpus in this manner forcing semantic instinct for the theme. From the standard of whole likelihood and the suspicion of restrictive freedom likelihood of word to the archive is given by the eqs. (1) and (2) from which the SM figures the point likelihood.

$$p(topic) = p(t/d) \tag{1}$$

$$p\left(\frac{w}{d}\right) = \sum_{t \in T} p(t/d)\, p(w/t) \quad (2)$$

Where w, t, d, t is the words, topics, documents and total number of topics respectively.

$$p(\text{domainwise topic}) = \frac{\text{number of domain words per topic}}{\text{total number of words per topic}} * \mathrm{p}(\text{topic}) \quad (3)$$

$$\mathrm{p}(\text{domain topic}) = \mathrm{R}_{\max}(\mathrm{p}(\text{domainwise topic}) \quad (4)$$

IMPLEMENTATION OF SPRIGHTLY SEARCH

The P2P is fine tuned to model so that it estimates the docstrings embedding rather than the docstrings themselves. All layers are freeze after training the model for the frozen version and train the model over a long period of time, (Maithili et al., 2024). This will be very helpful in the model's further improvement for the quoted task. To assess how well this strategy applies to data we haven't previously encountered, we also vector code without docstrings. In order to create a search index, we want the code to be represented in the form of a vector at the end. We utilize the k text library to pre- process this data using the same techniques we learnt in training, (Maheshwaran et al., 2024) (Pschorr et al., 2010). Map code for the natural language's vector space using the P2P model. We can proceed to the final step now that the vectorized code has been collected. The figure 7 illustrates how to insert these vectors into the search index so that the nearest neighbors are readily found. Nmslib is a useful Python package for quicker neighborhood searches. To benefit from speedier searches while using nmslib, the search index must be pre-computed.

Figure 7. Clustering graph of semantic search

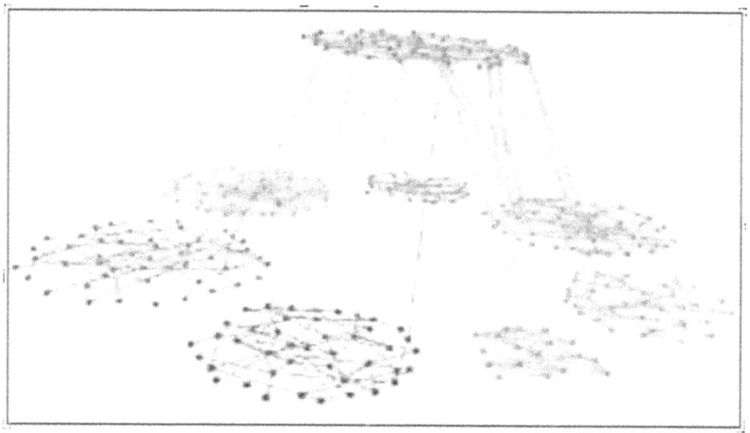

After creating the search index from the code vector, we need a way to convert the string (query) to a vector using the proposed model. To facilitate this process, we have provided a utility class called P2P under lang_model_utils.py. Finally, once after converting the string to a query vector, it is easy to get the nearest neighbors of that vector. A search index provides two elements.

RESEARCH METHODOLOGY

Figure 8. Use of web-based autonomous learning in machine learning

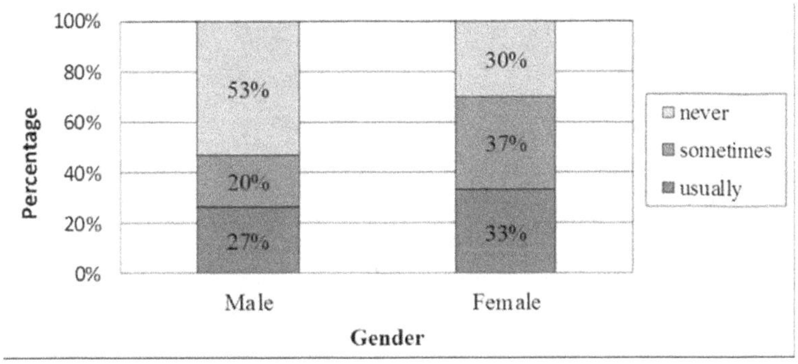

The second piece of the poll is to know the understudy's circumstance of utilizing web after class. Because of the quantity of male and female is unique, so it will be sensible to pick 30 guys and 30 females for the examination. From Figure 8, it is shown that over half guys don't think about the online learning and never utilize the organization for their investigation; almost 20% guys now and then utilize the organization to counsel data; the rest guys for the most part utilize the organization to help their examination. Interestingly, it is discovered that generally 30% female understudies frequently utilize the organization for their self-ruling learning; roughly 37% female understudies know electronic learning and at times use it; about 33% female understudies likewise never know the online learning. In view of the investigation gave, the male understudies and female understudies have a few contrasts in self-governing learning capacity.

CLUSTERING TOPIC MODELLING OUTPUT IN MACHINE LEARNING

Client interest by the strategy for point model is grouped utilizing straightforward K-implies bunching. Different bunch shaped are envisioned utilizing Gephi representation instrument. Figure 9 shows different bunches with its group and hub marks alongside the closeness measurements. The yield of subject displaying is gathered into three significant bunches where sports and games are assembled into one group, music, film, and TV-show are assembled into another group and travel, book and Apps are assembled into another bunch which mirror the truth.

Figure 9. User-interest clusters

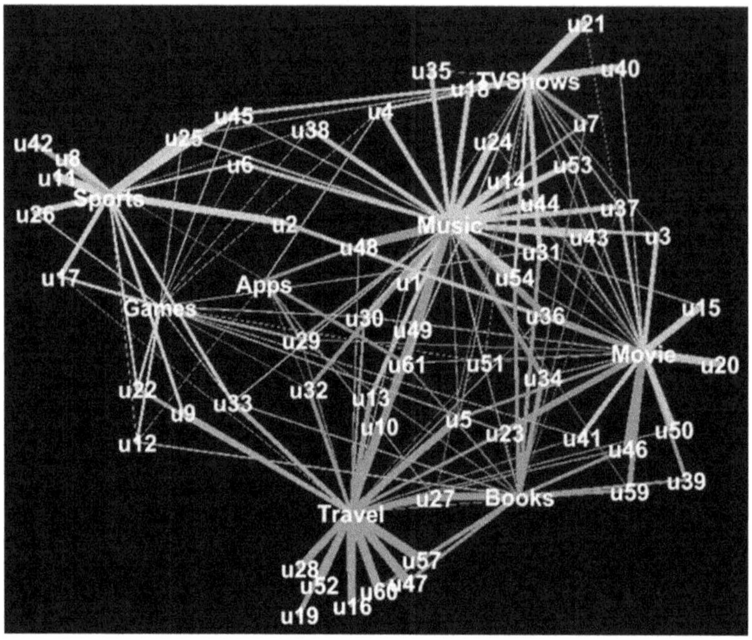

EVALUATION OF SEMANTIC MODEL IN MACHINE LEARNING

The consequence of any metaphysics is relative to the strength of the philosophy. Regardless of whether the corpus based thorough cosmology is constructed, new words will consistently prosper there by decreasing the force of results. In this manner ongoing semantic planning is fundamental for the fruitful client interest metaphysics. In this manner the proposed cosmology is improved by Wikipedia for new words. However, the words not in Wikipedia thus not a piece of the cosmology consequently decrease the strength of the philosophy. And furthermore, continuously frameworks new client with new astounding words are inclined to happen. Hence solo methodologies for planning client interest are relied upon to give great execution. Along these lines the semantic information working by theme displaying will be an effective strategy to follow the powerful idea of client premium as it registers the recurrence of word expression and furthermore the corpus is constructing each time during calculation among the given arrangement of records.

Along these lines the point displaying utilizing allocation is an option factual methodology which assesses the likelihood of the word w.r.t the subject and the corpus dependent on the recurrence of expression of the word. So, theme displaying demonstrates the subjects of client premium as well as the degree of premium in every point. Theme demonstrating likewise beats the issue of new client with new words as the corpus for the allocation is constructed recently at whatever point the application runs and furthermore the new client goes to the local area. The client space likelihood dissemination is grouped for the clients of comparable interests and is displayed in Figure 8 as bunch perception and in Figure 9 as warmth map.

Figure 10. User-interest mapping

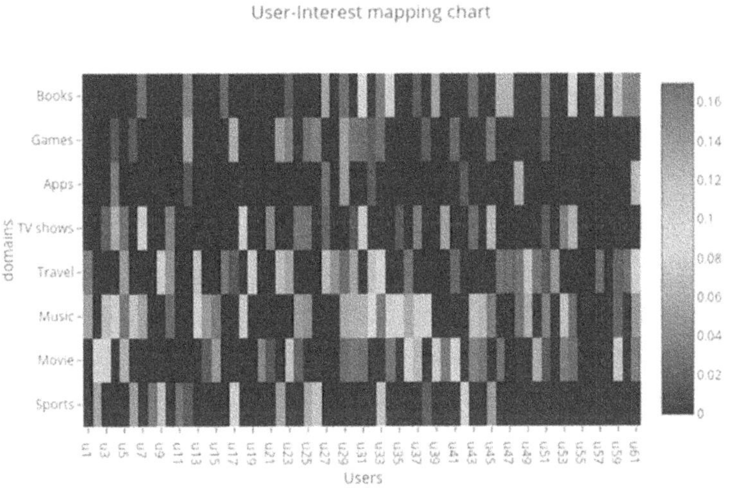

The second piece of the survey is to know the understudy's circumstance of utilizing web after class. Because of the quantity of male and female is unique, so it will be sensible to pick 30 guys and 30 females for the examination. From Figure 1, it is shown that over half guys don't think about the online learning and never utilize the organization for their investigation; almost 20% guys in some cases utilize the organization to counsel data; the rest guys typically utilize the organization to help their examination. Conversely, it is discovered that generally 30% female understudies regularly utilize the organization for their independent learning; roughly 37% female understudies know electronic learning and at times use it; about 33% female understudies additionally never know the online learning. In view of the investigation gave, the male understudies and female understudies have a few contrasts in self-governing learning capacity. The consequence of examination demonstrates that the female understudies self-sufficient learning capacity is fundamentally better compared to that of male understudy.

Figure 11. College students' satisfaction degree of the situation of autonomous learning

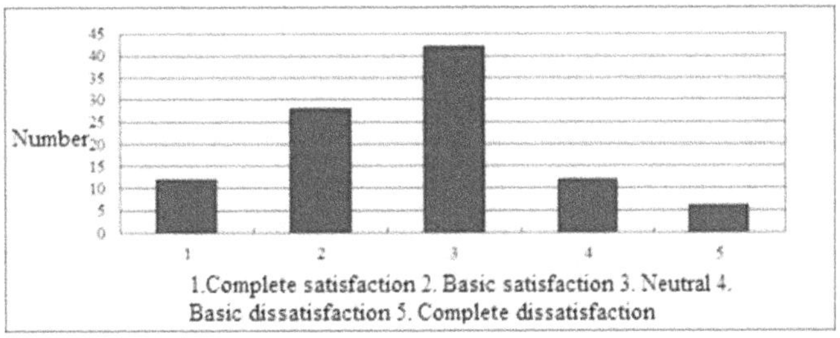

Mentalities are perhaps the most significant impacting elements of student self-rule. Uplifting perspectives can expand the inspiration, while negative mentalities have the contrary impact. The fourth piece of the poll is to study whether the electronic independent learning can help their learning. Because of the quantity of expressions major and science major isn't something very similar, so it will be sensible to pick 32 expressions understudies and 32 science understudies for the examination. As is displayed we could see that most of the two expressions and science significant understudies have the inspirational perspective towards independent learning and concur its significance. They think the organization is gainful to their learning and it likewise can further develop their learning effectiveness. However, in the interim there are some undergrads that are in lack of bias. They hold a conviction that organization could help the investigation yet couldn't have an impact in further developing learning proficiency. Also, it is tracked down that a couple of understudies have the latent disposition towards the self-sufficient learning and differ its utilization.

Figure 12. Comparative study

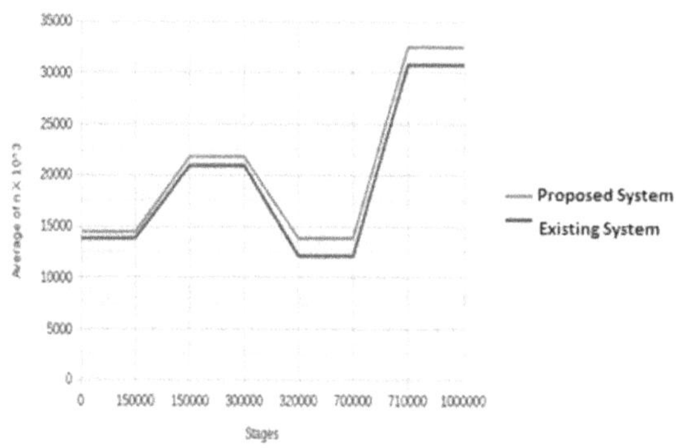

The current conventions burn-through more energy than the proposed plans. The goal of the proposed convention is to bargain forestalling jammer in CR. It considered energy metric of PU and SU in proposed plan to build the organization lifetime.

Figure 13. Average delay vs speed

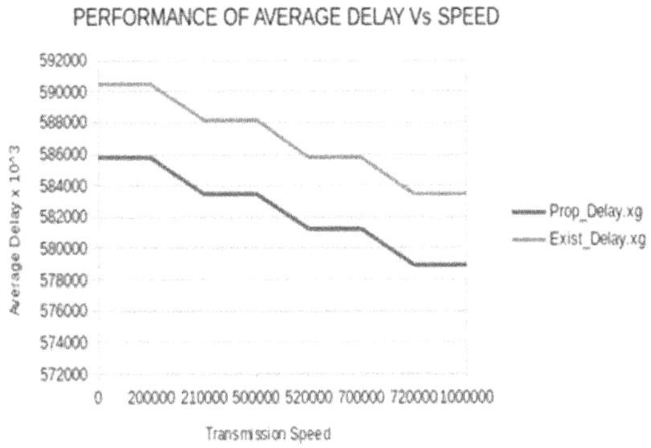

COMPARISON WITH EXISTING MODEL

It is obvious that the current model will fall short of the demands of the suggested system. We should aim for at least 10 frames per second in order to achieve object detection that is even somewhat close to real-time. Given this, the current model falls short of the 10 fps goal. However, the second iteration of this gadget, which is substantially more potent, is worth attempting, (Perez et al., 2010) (Ruta, Scioscia, & Di Sciascio, 2012). However, in the case of edge processing, the P2P model appears to be a workable option, as illustrated in figure 6. This model allows for a trade-off between inference time and average accuracy to attain the desired goal with 80% accuracy.

Figure 14. Comparison of Existing model with P2P model

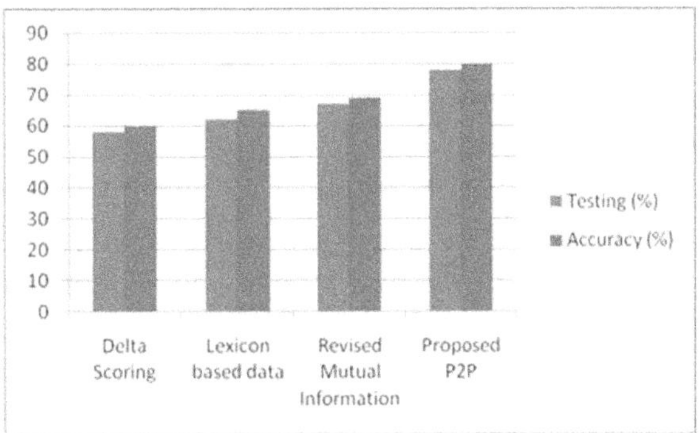

Initially, there is a need to track the object embedded on the client server using the P2P model on any one of the devices. Further, there arises a need for a classifier to process human profiling (i.e., gender, age classification). Later it is needed to compare the edge implementation of the system along with the client-server versions. It is worth investigating the two hybrid version of the above. Once the computer vision pipeline is ready with the required algorithms, there is a need to focus on the GUI applications to create an interface that allows users to easily collect and manipulate the captured data.

CONCLUSION

IoT is the emerging technology which includes all smart devices connected to each other through internet having the computation and communication capability, and possessing the ability of transmitting large amounts of data. The smart organization is one of the fortunate applications of Internet of Things containing the services across various domains including mobility, scheduling, power and many more. These services can be optimized and enhanced by making proper analysis of the smart data collected from all application areas. Many novel data analysis algorithms can be applied on this collected data to extract the meaningful information called as knowledge. In this paper a web browsing-based search engine for the agile semantic Web of Things is proposed and a scalable and convenient way to find their semantic data worldwide using real-time web- connected embedded devices. A thriving semantic search engine that can find data endpoints connected to search engines and search through P2P enabled devices and their services is proposed.

REFERENCES

Ahad, A., Kashyap, S., & Verghese, M. G. (2022, April). The Substructure for Estimation of Miscellaneous Data Failures Using Distributed Clustering Techniques. In Proceedings of International Conference on Information Technology and Applications: ICITA 2021 (pp. 539-546). Singapore: Springer Nature Singapore.

Ambhika, C., Gayathri, S., Anish, T. P., & Sheena, B. G. (2024, August). Enhancing Predictive Modeling in High Dimensional Data Using Hybrid Feature Selection. In 2024 5th International Conference on Electronics and Sustainable Communication Systems (ICESC) (pp. 873-879). IEEE.

Compton, M., Barnaghi, P., Bermudez, L., Garcia-Castro, R., Corcho, O., Cox, S., Graybeal, J., Hauswirth, M., Henson, C., Herzog, A., Huang, V., Janowicz, K., Kelsey, W. D., Le Phuoc, D., Lefort, L., Leggieri, M., Neuhaus, H., Nikolov, A., Page, K., & Taylor, K. (2012). The SSN ontology of the W3C semantic sensor network incubator group. *Journal of Web Semantics*, 17, 25–32. DOI: 10.1016/j.websem.2012.05.003

Davoodi, E., Kianmehr, K., & Afsharchi, M. (2013). A semantic social network-based expert recommender system. *Applied Intelligence*, 39(1), 1–13. DOI: 10.1007/s10489-012-0389-1

Garg, N., & Gupta, R. K. (2018). Performance evaluation of new text mining method based on GA and K-means clustering algorithm. In Advanced Computing and Communication Technologies: Proceedings of the 10th ICACCT, 2016 (pp. 23-30). Springer Singapore.

Guinard, D., Trifa, V. M., & Wilde, E. (2010). Architecting a mashable open world wide web of things. Technical Report/ETH Zurich, Department of Computer Science, 663.

Gulnashin, F., Sharma, I., & Sharma, H. (2019). A new deterministic method of initializing spherical K-means for document clustering. In Progress in Advanced Computing and Intelligent Engineering: Proceedings of ICACIE 2017, Volume 1 (pp. 149-155). Springer Singapore.

Janani, R., & Vijayarani, S. (2019). Text document clustering using spectral clustering algorithm with particle swarm optimization. *Expert Systems with Applications*, 134, 192–200. DOI: 10.1016/j.eswa.2019.05.030

Jara, A. J., Olivieri, A. C., Bocchi, Y., Jung, M., Kastner, W., & Skarmeta, A. F. (2014). Semantic web of things: An analysis of the application semantics for the iot moving towards the iot convergence. *International Journal of Web and Grid Services*, 10(2-3), 244–272. DOI: 10.1504/IJWGS.2014.060260

Kamilaris, A., Pitsillides, A., & Trifa, V. (2011). The smart home meets the web of things. *International Journal of Ad Hoc and Ubiquitous Computing*, 7(3), 145–154. DOI: 10.1504/IJAHUC.2011.040115

Karaa, W. B. A., Ashour, A. S., Sassi, D. B., Roy, P., Kausar, N., & Dey, N. (2016). Medline text mining: an enhancement genetic algorithm based approach for document clustering. Applications of intelligent optimization in biology and medicine: current trends and open problems, 267-287.

Kushwaha, N., & Pant, M. (2018). Link based BPSO for feature selection in big data text clustering. *Future Generation Computer Systems*, 82, 190–199. DOI: 10.1016/j.future.2017.12.005

Lakumarapu, S., Nithyanandhan, R., Bhargavi, V. S., Anish, T. P., & Nalini, M. (2024, August). Machine Learning Approaches for Liver Disease Prediction: A Comparative Analysis. In 2024 5th International Conference on Electronics and Sustainable Communication Systems (ICESC) (pp. 159-164). IEEE.

Lin, H., Sun, B., Wu, J., & Xiong, H. (2016, June). Topic detection from short text: A term-based consensus clustering method. In 2016 13th International Conference on Service Systems and Service Management (ICSSSM) (pp. 1-6). IEEE.

Madhu, G., Govardhan, D. A., & Rajinikanth, D. T. (2011). Intelligent semantic web search engines: a brief survey. arXiv preprint arXiv:1102.0831.

Maheshwaran, T., Muthumarilakshmi, S., Vinoth, N. A. S., Suganya, K., Maheswari, B., & Girija, P. (2024). Securing E-Commerce Strategies With Cloud, Blockchain, AI, and ML. In *Strategies for E-Commerce Data Security: Cloud, Blockchain, AI, and Machine Learning* (pp. 470–500). IGI Global. DOI: 10.4018/979-8-3693-6557-1.ch019

Maithili, K., Ponmalar, A., Yamini, B., Karthikeyan, M., Anish, T. P., Maheswari, B., & Siva Subramanian, R. (2024). Advances in AI and Machine Learning for Healthcare Informatics. In *Machine Learning and Generative AI in Smart Healthcare* (pp. 1–22). IGI Global. DOI: 10.4018/979-8-3693-3719-6.ch001

Perez, A. J., Labrador, M. A., & Barbeau, S. J. (2010). G-sense: A scalable architecture for global sensing and monitoring. *IEEE Network*, 24(4), 57–64. DOI: 10.1109/MNET.2010.5510920

Pfisterer, D., Romer, K., Bimschas, D., Kleine, O., Mietz, R., Truong, C., Hasemann, H., Kröller, A., Pagel, M., Hauswirth, M., Karnstedt, M., Leggieri, M., Passant, A., & Richardson, R. (2011). SPITFIRE: Toward a semantic web of things. *IEEE Communications Magazine*, 49(11), 40–48. DOI: 10.1109/MCOM.2011.6069708

Pschorr, J., Henson, C. A., Patni, H. K., & Sheth, A. P. (2010). Sensor discovery on linked data.

Ruta, M., Scioscia, F., & Di Sciascio, E. (2012, September). Enabling the Semantic Web of Things: framework and architecture. In *2012 IEEE Sixth International Conference on Semantic Computing* (pp. 345-347). IEEE.

Sailaja, M., Ahad, A., Sivaramakrishna, K., & Hussain, A. (2021, November). Machine Learning Medical Resource Allocation. [). IOP Publishing.]. *Journal of Physics: Conference Series*, 2089(1), 012082.

Subha, S., Balakrishnan, C., & Anish, T. P. (2024, August). Optimizing Machine Learning Algorithms for Heart Disease Prediction in Healthcare: A Comparative Study. In 2024 5th International Conference on Electronics and Sustainable Communication Systems (ICESC) (pp. 866-872). IEEE.

Sudha, K., Nithyanandhan, R., Anish, T. P., Girija, P., & Nalini, M. (2024, July). Enhancing Healthcare Data Security in the Cloud: Integrating ML-Based Intrusion Detection Systems. In 2024 2nd World Conference on Communication & Computing (WCONF) (pp. 1-7). IEEE.

Thakran, Y., & Toshniwal, D. (2014). A novel agglomerative hierarchical approach for clustering in medical databases. In Recent Advances in Intelligent Informatics: Proceedings of the Second International Symposium on Intelligent Informatics (ISI'13), August 23-24 2013, Mysore, India (pp. 245-252). Cham: Springer International Publishing.

Venketbabu, T., Aswathy, M. P., Sangeetha, J., Anish, T. P., Nalini, M., & Subramanian, R. S. (2024, October). Revolutionizing Image Processing: Innovations Impacts and Future Trends. In 2024 2nd International Conference on Self Sustainable Artificial Intelligence Systems (ICSSAS) (pp. 901-907). IEEE.

Zhou, Y., De, S., Wang, W., & Moessner, K. (2016). Search techniques for the web of things: A taxonomy and survey. *Sensors (Basel)*, 16(5), 600. DOI: 10.3390/s16050600 PMID: 27128918

Zhu, F., Patumcharoenpol, P., Zhang, C., Yang, Y., Chan, J., Meechai, A., Vongsangnak, W., & Shen, B. (2013). Biomedical text mining and its applications in cancer research. *Journal of Biomedical Informatics*, 46(2), 200–211. DOI: 10.1016/j.jbi.2012.10.007 PMID: 23159498

Chapter 10

Ethical Issues in Cyber-Security for Autonomous Vehicles (AV) and Automated Driving: A Comprehensive Review

Qais Al-Na'amneh
https://orcid.org/0009-0008-3034-7693
Applied Science Private University, Jordan

Mahmoud Aljawarneh
https://orcid.org/0000-0003-2003-6310
Applied Science Private University, Jordan

Rahaf Hazaymih
Jordan University of Science and Technology, Jordan

Rabia Emhamed Al Mamlook
Trine University, Libya

ABSTRACT

Autonomous Vehicles (AVs) revolutionize the transportation landscape, they also introduce a profound set of ethical dilemmas. The convergence of complex networks, sensors, software, and AI creates an unprecedented cybersecurity risk, imperiling not only user privacy and data security but also safety. This study shines a light on the critical ethical concerns surrounding liability, responsibility, and decision-making algorithms, posing fundamental questions about how we allocate blame in the event of cyber breaches and ensure fairness in AV decision-making during life-or-death scenarios. In this groundbreaking research, we delve into the depths of these ethical challenges, offering comprehensive solutions and expert recommendations for fortifying cybersecurity in AVs. By exploring the intricate interplay between ethics, technology, and society, we can create a safer, more trustworthy, and equitable future for autonomous vehicles.

DOI: 10.4018/979-8-3693-9919-4.ch010

I. INTRODUCTION

The automobile industry has undergone a significant transformation in recent years, driven by technological advancements. From traditional petrol-powered engines to Electric Vehicles (EVs), the industry has been revolutionized by the tech-world. The latest development is the emergence of AVs (AVs), which are no longer just a concept but a rapidly evolving reality, that enables AVs to navigate and drive without human interaction or intervention. This advancement in the industry has revolutionized and enhanced the vehicles' performance, and improved vehicles' design, manufacturing, and operational services. AVs have become capable of navigating and driving without human interaction or intervention, thanks to the integration of computer vision, AI & machine learning, and sensor fusion (Lowe & Kuru, 2024).

The Society of Automotive Engineers (SAE) has established a framework for classifying the level of automation in vehicles. The SAE's six-level classification system provides a clear understanding of the progression from human-driven vehicles to fully autonomous ones. Table 1 illustrates this categorization, highlighting the varying degrees of autonomy, from Level 0, where the driver is in full control, to Level 5, where the vehicle operates independently (WARRENDALE, 2021):

Table 1. Six levels of AV

Levels	Description
Level 0 – No automation	The driver remains fully in control at all times, with no automation or assistance.
Level 1 – Driver Assistance	The vehicle assists the driver through automated features such as braking or steering, but the driver maintains full control and responsibility for the vehicle's operation.
Level 2 – Partial Automation	The driver must still monitor the environment and be prepared to take over at all times. However, the vehicle can perform specific tasks autonomously, such as parking or executing automated lateral and longitudinal maneuvers during overtaking, within predetermined limits.
Level 3 – Conditional Automation	The vehicle can operate independently under certain conditions, including braking, steering, changing lanes, and overtaking. The driver must be prepared to take control at any time if needed, allowing for temporary diversion of attention. (This level is our reality today, where drivers must be ready to take back the wheel if required by the system.)
Level 4 – High Automation	If implemented correctly, the vehicle can perform all tasks from previous levels (Levels 1-3) without human oversight or monitoring.
Level 5 – Full Automation	The vehicle operates independently and is fully responsible for driving tasks, with humans acting only as passengers who do not need to be engaged. Note that this level of technology is currently unavailable but is being developed and refined.

As AVs become more prevalent, they have the potential to improve traffic flow and safety (Rana Hassam Ahmed, 2024). However, they also represent a new target for cyber criminality. The reliance on complex networks of software and hardware systems makes AVs vulnerable to various cyber threats, including remote hacking, vehicle spoofing, data breaches, and more.

In 2005, two security researchers demonstrated a dangerous vulnerability in an AV system, allowing them to control the key features of a self-driving Jeep remotely. Although this was an early experiment, it highlighted the potential risks associated with AVs. With advancements in technology, the threats have become even more serious and complex, posing significant disruptions to individuals' lives. In addition to technical challenges, AVs also raise moral and ethical concerns. The increasing dependence on AI-powered systems has led to a growing awareness of the need for ethical frameworks that guide the development and deployment of AVs. In this study, we draw upon the list of 21 AI ethical issues proposed by (Hagendorff, 2020) to identify the ethical challenges that arise in the AV industry.

Figure 1 illustrates the top ethical issues in the AV industry, with safety and cybersecurity concerns being the highest priorities due to the potential for extreme traffic situations. As industry continues to evolve, it is essential to address these ethical concerns and develop strategies to mitigate the risks associated with AVs.

Figure 1. Ethical issues in AV industry

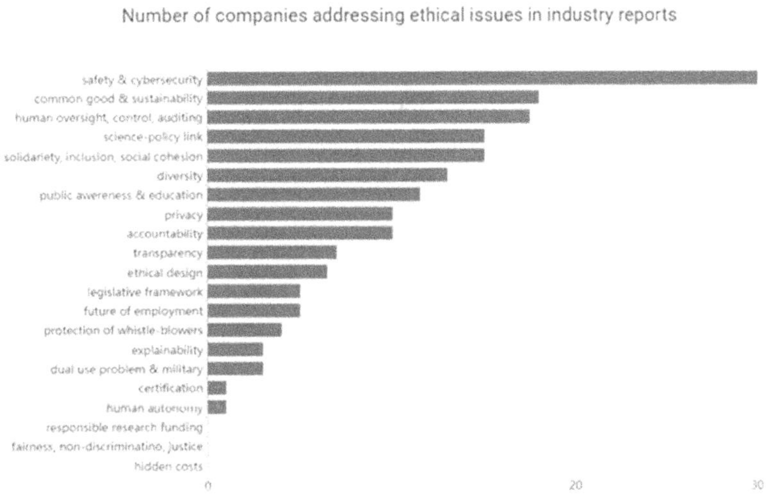

In this chapter, we reviewed the types of cyber-threats that occurs in AVs with the focus on those types where human factor is important, what are the potential consequences of cyber-attacks, we will also focus on suggesting way on how we can use cybersecurity to help reduce potential risks and threats in AVs.

II. LITERATURE REVIEW

The advent of AVs (AVs) has revolutionized the transportation landscape, promising enhanced convenience, efficiency, and safety for passengers and drivers alike. However, the integration of autonomous technologies into public and private transportation networks has also raised a plethora of complex ethical concerns, particularly regarding cybersecurity. The proliferation of sensors, software, and networked devices in AVs creates a vulnerability-rich environment, exposing these vehicles to an array of cyber threats that can compromise their integrity, safety, and security (Ibrahum et al., 2025).

As AVs increasingly rely on interconnected systems to operate autonomously, the potential consequences of successful cyber-attacks become increasingly dire. The ethical implications of these threats are far-reaching, impacting liability, safety, and privacy in profound ways. For instance, a compromised AV could potentially cause harm to passengers or other road users, raising questions about responsibility and accountability.

This literature review seeks to investigate the historical and present perspectives on the ethical and regulatory aspects of AVs, with a focus on major developments and comparative examinations of various regulatory approaches in different countries. By exploring the intersection of ethics, cybersecurity, liability, safety, and privacy, this study aims to provide a comprehensive understanding of the complex challenges posed by AVs and inform future research and policy-making efforts.

The advent of AVs (AVs) has raised a plethora of ethical concerns, particularly with regards to privacy, safety, security, liability, accountability, and decision-making. As AVs collect vast amounts of data on their users' behavior, including location, speed, and destination, the potential risks to personal privacy are significant. The introduction of new laws, such as the SPY Car Act in the US, aim to safeguard driving data, but more needs to be done to ensure that AVs are designed with privacy considerations at their core.

Moreover, the security risks associated with AV systems are a major concern. Cyber-attacks on these vehicles could have catastrophic consequences, such as loss of control or manipulation of vehicle functions. The complexity of AVs also raises questions about identifying and eliminating potential cyber threats, which may pose unsuspected safety concerns.

Another critical ethical issue is liability and accountability in the event of a cybersecurity breach. Who should be held responsible for the harm caused by an autonomous vehicle's malfunction? Should it be the software developers, hardware manufacturers, or users themselves? The existing legal frameworks are unclear on how to address these questions, leaving a moral void that needs to be filled.

Furthermore, AVs sometimes must make quick decisions with ethical impact, especially in situations where accidents are unavoidable. These decision-making processes need to be secure and reliable, as any manipulation or malfunction could be harmful. Also raises more general ethical concerns about biased data and results.

Considering these challenges, it is essential to establish reliable ethical and regulatory frameworks that address the unique difficulties presented by AVs. Collaboration between teams of experts from various fields, including ethics, engineering, and law, is crucial for creating a framework that balances technological innovation with societal expectations. The European Union's efforts to create an ecosystem for automation technologies are a step in the right direction, but more needs to be done to ensure that AVs are designed with ethical considerations at their core.

Ultimately, the development of AVs requires a nuanced understanding of the complex ethical issues involved. By acknowledging these challenges and working together to address them, we can create a safer, more responsible, and more equitable future for all.

1- Privacy Issues: The collection of personal data by AVs poses significant privacy risks, including unauthorized access or data breaches. This could lead to misuse of personal information, such as marketing and advertising exploitation, profiling, and identity theft. According to(Goodall, 2014) he asserts that there is very dangerous privacy concerns associated with the gathering and use of data by AVs. The potential for misuse of personal data whether through unauthorized access or data breaches, presents a serious ethical issue, especially when weighing an individual's right to privacy against the advantages of data-driven advancements in vehicle safety. Finding the exact root of cause of accidents with ERDs presents another problem since this information may be sold to third parties like insurance companies and used against drivers (Glancy, 2012). According to Glancy, the potential for exploiting this data to harass AV users through marketing and advertising to steal user identities, to profile users and forecast their behavior, and to predict their actions(Petit & Shladover, 2014). New privacy legislation has been passed by the governments of the US and

South Korea which are applicable to all cars including AVs. The NHTSA now has the power to safeguard the use and access to driving data in all vehicles manufactured for sale in the US due to the recently introduced SPY Car Act (Dhar, 2016).

2- Safety and Security Risks: Autonomous vehicle cybersecurity flaws can have catastrophic consequences, including loss of control or manipulation of vehicle functions, which can result in accidents. The complexity of AVs makes it difficult to identify and eliminate potential cyber threats, posing unsuspected safety concerns. The risks of cyber attacks on AV systems are emphasized by (Petit & Shladover, 2014), such attacks could allow hackers to take control of the vehicles' wheel to be in control and cause accidents. These flaws have significant legal consequences since they call into question the obligation of software developers, regulators, and manufacturers to guarantee that AVs are safe from online attacks. In addition, as (Lin, 2016) points out, it can be difficult to identify and eliminate every potential cyber threat due to the complexity of AVs, which may pose unsuspected safety concerns. According to (Dhar, 2016) vehicle accidents to the result of human are estimated by at least 90% so AVs can potentially reduce most of the car accidents while also outstand human driving skills especially in perception and execution. However, (Collingwood, 2017) mentioned that passengers might reduce the use of seatbelts being less cautious thinking that AVs will make them feel safer.

3- Liability and Accountability: In the event of a cybersecurity breach, assigning blame and determining liability becomes complex, involving software developers, hardware manufacturers, and users (Marchant & Lindor, 2012). This raises moral concerns regarding accountability and the suitability of existing legal frameworks. Autonomous systems raise doubt on conventional concepts of blame, which usually place the blame on human drivers. (Hevelke & Nida-Rümelin, 2015) believe that assigning blame in situations where AVs' cybersecurity is breached is a complex process what involves software developers, hardware manufacturers, and even the users. This raises moral concerns regarding the allocation of accountability and the suitability of the existing legal frameworks to address the difficulties presented by autonomous cars resulting in no clear legal framework to outline how liability is handled between third parties that are responsible for creating the AVs (Nyholm & Smids, 2016). The question of whether algorithms' decision-making standards during accidents should be standardized has not yet been addressed by governments. In (Zarsky, 2016) For example, should choices be made based on the quantity of injuries or on the type of how serious the injury is? So far, the only country that adopted a toleration-oriented strategy and risk insurances is the UK. In July 2016 ("Pathway to Driverless Cars: Proposals to Support Advanced Driver Assistance Systems and Automated Vehicle Technologies," 2016), the Center for Connected and AVs (CCAV) proposed to make changes to primary legislation to ensure insurance liability.

4- Ethical Decision-Making in AVs: AVs sometimes must make quick decisions with ethical impact (Tan, 2024), especially in situations where accidents are unavoidable. These decision-making processes need to be secure and reliable, as any manipulation or malfunction could be harmful. (Nyholm & Smids, 2016) assert that a major difficulty in AV decision-making in cyber threats is the careful examination of the data algorithms implemented by these systems. The involvement of human judgement in the creation and management of AV technology also brings up more general ethical concerns. When an AV is trained with data from a single country, it may learn localized patterns and become inaccurate in modeling driving behaviors that are applicable in other nations. Therefore, erroneous data and biased results may occur from the under or overrepresentation of groups in the data. (Fleetwood, 2017) The UK government and the Alan Turing Institute will work together to create an AI talented and auditing tools in order to reduce the "social inequalities" brought forth by algorithmic decision-making (Government Response, 2018).

5- Regulatory and Ethical Frameworks: The development of reliable ethical and regulatory frameworks is crucial to address the severe ethical issues facing cybersecurity in autonomous cars. Collaboration between experts from various fields, including ethics, engineering, and law, is essential for creating a framework that balances technological innovation with societal expectations. Like (Marchant & Lindor, 2012) pointed out, the difficulties presented by AVs may not be sufficiently addressed by the regulatory framework as it now. They push for the creation of new frameworks that consider the ethical effects of cybersecurity vulnerabilities, guaranteeing that AVs are both reliable technology and as well as compatible with the expectations of society. When creating these frameworks, collaborations between teams of ethical researchers, engineers, and legal experts are essential. Since the start of the 21st century, European policy makers have shown an interest in making an ecosystem for automation technologies, viewing it as the primary means of transforming the EU into "the most dynamic and competitive knowledge-based economy in the world" (Department for Transport, 2016).

Table 2 summarizes the key ethical concerns and their comparisons across privacy, safety, liability, decision-making, and regulatory aspects related to AVs and cybersecurity.

Table 2. Summarization

Aspect	Privacy Issues	Safety & Security Risks	Liability & Accountability	Ethical Decision-Making	Regulatory & Ethical Framework
Key Focus	Protecting personal data from unauthorized access, misuse, and potential identity theft through secure data handling and robust cybersecurity measures.	Ensuring AVs are secure against hacking attempts that could lead to accidents or safety risks by implementing robust cybersecurity measures and proactive risk management.	Establishing clear accountability and liability procedures for autonomous vehicle accidents or cyber breaches, which can be complex due to the unique complexities of autonomous systems.	Developing frameworks for making ethical decisions in case of accidents, ensuring that algorithms are fair, unbiased, and accountable for their actions, and prioritizing human safety and well-being.	Addressing the need for updated regulatory frameworks that address the unique challenges posed by AVs, while also ensuring that regulations prioritize safety, security, and accountability.
Main Concerns	Misuse of personal data, potential for identity theft and profiling, and need for secure data handling to protect travelers' sensitive information.	Cybersecurity threats and vulnerabilities that could lead to accidents or safety risks due to hacking attempts, emphasizing the need for robust cybersecurity measures to prevent such incidents.	Assigning blame in cases of cyber breaches or accidents, which can be complex due to autonomous system complexities, highlighting the need for clear accountability procedures.	Ensuring that decision-making algorithms are accurate, unbiased, and accountable for their actions, prioritizing human safety and well-being, particularly in situations where AVs make life-or-death decisions.	Updating regulatory frameworks to address the unique challenges posed by AVs, ensuring that regulations prioritize safety, security, and accountability to protect both humans and technology.
Technological Implications	The need for secure data handling and privacy measures to prevent misuse of personal data, including identity theft and profiling.	Ensuring robust cybersecurity measures to prevent hacking attempts that could lead to accidents or safety risks, and the need for proactive risk management to mitigate such threats.	The impact of autonomous systems on traditional notions of accountability, requiring new approaches to assign blame in cases of cyber breaches or accidents.	The importance of developing decision-making algorithms that are accurate, unbiased, and accountable for their actions, particularly in situations where AVs make life-or-death decisions.	The need for updated regulatory frameworks to address the unique technological challenges posed by AVs, including cybersecurity risks and accountability concerns.

This study examines the significant advancements in autonomous vehicle (AV) technology from its early theoretical stages to current real-world implementations. Over time, the need for updated ethical and regulatory frameworks has grown, driven by major research and trends (Ibrahum et al., 2025)in areas such as:

- Privacy: Protecting sensitive information
- Safety: Preventing accidents and harm
- Liability: Assigning responsibility for accidents or cyber breaches
- Ethical decision-making: Ensuring algorithms prioritize human safety and well-being
- Regulatory frameworks: Developing guidelines to govern the development and deployment of AVs

The study focuses on the evolution of these considerations between 1950 and 2024, highlighting key research and trends that have shaped our understanding of the complex ethical and regulatory challenges posed by autonomous vehicle technology.

Table 3. Comparative approaches taken by nations

Aspect	United States	European Union	China	Japan	Middle East
Regulatory Approach	Market-driven, innovation-friendly	Precautionary, safety-first	Government-led, with strict oversight	Collaborative, industry-government	Emerging, with focus on safety
Ethical Considerations	Focus on innovation, individual rights	Emphasis on safety, data protection	State control, societal harmony	Balance between innovation and safety	Mixed, with focus on cultural values
Data Privacy	Strong but industry-influenced	Strict GDPR compliance	Government-controlled, limited rights	Privacy respected within regulatory bounds	Varies by country, generally less strict
AI Bias and Fairness	Growing concern, industry-led solutions	Strong focus on algorithmic fairness	Less emphasis, focus on efficiency	Ethical AI development emphasized	Early stages of development
Public Trust	Moderate, influenced by tech companies	High, due to stringent regulations	High, driven by government narratives	High, due to collaborative efforts	Growing, but varied by region
Global Standards Influence	Strong advocate for flexible standards	Pushes for strict global regulations	Increasing influence in Asia	Supports international collaboration	Emerging voice in global discussions

Comparative evaluations of the approaches taken by various nations and areas to the ethical governance and regulation of AVs have been made possible by recent studies. These contrasts show notable variations in implementation techniques, values, and priorities as shown in Table 3.

III. METHODOLOGY

The study focuses on locating and evaluating moral issues with data privacy, algorithms used in decision-making, and security flaws that may affect people's safety. The process of gathering information on ethical dilemmas and suggesting solutions involves the use of security standards, forensics standards, addressing the problems and solutions as well.

1. Security Standards in AVs

The increase in connected devices is leading to a rise in vulnerable points for hackers, posing significant threats to the automotive industry as they directly impact driver safety and data privacy.

A. **ISO/SAE 213424**: The ISO/SAE 21434 standard plays a crucial role in establishing a process to ensure that cybersecurity is integrated into the design of road vehicles, component software, and connections to external devices or networks. This standard emphasizes the fundamental aspects of cybersecurity, encompassing requirements, processes, and objective in various area disciplines such as product development, construction, operations, and maintenance. ("SAE and ISO Publish Joint Automotive Cybersecurity Standard," 2021b)The standard promotes Security and Design approaches and encompasses phases ranging from engineering, design, specification, implementation, testing, operation, and security. Due to the encompassing nature of the phases included in ISO/SAE 21434, it is acknowledged as one of the most comprehensive strategies for connected vehicle cybersecurity (Staff, 2024).

B. **The World Forum for Harmonization of Vehicles Regulations (WP.29):** The adoption of the WP.29 standard in June 2020 introduces a fresh international automotive cybersecurity regulation that focuses on enabling connected vehicles and addressing cybersecurity threats to passenger vehicles. It establishes the criteria for cybersecurity performance and review requirements, as well as software update management for new passenger vehicles. Comprising development, production, and post-production phases, the standard involves monitoring, detecting, and responding to cyber-attacks (QNX, 2020).

A framework for discussions, research, or policy formulation in areas like AI ethics, cybersecurity, or digital transformation summarized in Table 4 with focus on critical aspects and concerns related to technology, ethics, and societal impacts.

Table 4. Aspects in AVs and cybersecurity and their ethical concerns

Aspect	AVs key considerations	Cybersecurity	Ethical Concern
Data Privacy	Ensure secure data handling and storage for sensitive information Implement robust cybersecurity measures to prevent unauthorized access Obtain informed consent from passengers before collecting and using their data	Implement robust data encryption and secure storage solutions Establish clear policies for data collection, usage, and sharing Ensure compliance with relevant data protection regulations (e.g., GDPR, CCPA (Seun Solomon Bakare et al., 2024)) Regularly conduct data breach assessments and risk evaluations	Ensure secure and transparent data collection and storage practices Implement robust access controls to prevent unauthorized access to sensitive information Develop guidelines for informed consent from individuals involved in CAV testing or deployment
Decision-Making Algorithms	Develop algorithms that are transparent, explainable, and fair Ensure algorithms prioritize human safety and well-being Address potential biases in algorithmic decision-making	Develop algorithms that are transparent, explainable, and auditable Implement robust testing and validation procedures to detect biases or errors Establish protocols for regular algorithm updates and maintenance Address potential challenges around algorithmic decision-making and accountability	Prioritize fairness, transparency, and explainability in decision-making algorithms Conduct regular testing and validation procedures to detect biases or errors Establish protocols for auditing and monitoring discriminatory practices
Security Vulnerabilities	Implement robust cybersecurity measures to prevent hacking attempts Regularly update and patch software to address vulnerabilities Conduct regular security audits and penetration testing	Regularly conduct vulnerability assessments and penetration testing Implement robust security measures to prevent hacking attempts (e.g., firewalls, intrusion detection systems) Develop incident response plans to address potential security breaches Establish protocols for continuous monitoring and threat intelligence	Implement robust security measures to prevent exploitation of vulnerabilities Regularly update software and firmware to ensure the security of CAV systems Develop guidelines for incident response and emergency management

continued on following page

Table 4. Continued

Aspect	AVs key considerations	Cybersecurity	Ethical Concern
Responsibility & Accountability	Establish clear accountability procedures for accidents or cyber breaches Define liability and responsibility in the event of an accident or incident Ensure that regulations prioritize safety, security, and accountability	Establish clear guidelines for liability and accountability in CAV-related incidents Define roles and responsibilities for different stakeholders (e.g., vehicle manufacturer, regulatory agencies, operators) Implement robust auditing and compliance mechanisms to ensure adherence to standards Regularly review and update policies to ensure alignment with evolving regulations	Assign clear responsibility and accountability for CAV operations, maintenance, and updates Establish protocols for transparency and reporting in case of accidents or incidents Develop guidelines for human oversight and review of autonomous decisions
Surveillance & Tracking	Implement tracking systems that prioritize passenger consent and data protection Ensure transparency around surveillance and tracking practices Address potential concerns around mass surveillance and data collection	Implement transparent and secure systems for tracking and monitoring CAVs Establish clear guidelines for data collection, usage, and sharing Ensure compliance with relevant regulations (e.g., GDPR, CCPA) Regularly conduct risk assessments and evaluate the impact of surveillance and tracking on passenger privacy	Implement robust security measures to prevent unauthorized tracking or surveillance Ensure transparent and informed consent from individuals involved in CAV testing or deployment Conduct regular assessments to ensure compliance with relevant regulations (e.g., GDPR, CCPA)
Human Dignity & Autonomy	Respect passengers' autonomy and dignity in the design of AVs Prioritize human well-being and safety in algorithmic decision-making Address potential risks to human dignity, such as data exploitation or manipulation	Design systems that prioritize human dignity and autonomy in CAV decision-making Implement measures to prevent exploitation or manipulation of passengers Establish clear guidelines for transparency and explainability in CAV decision-making Regularly review and update policies to ensure alignment with evolving standards	Prioritize human dignity and autonomy in CAV design and operation Develop guidelines for ensuring equal access and opportunities for all individuals Establish protocols for protecting vulnerable populations from exploitation
Job Displacement	Implement measures to support workers displaced by automation, such as retraining programs Address concerns around job displacement and the impact on local economies Encourage responsible innovation that prioritizes worker well-being	Develop strategies for re-skilling and up-skilling workers impacted by automation and AI in the CAV industry Implement measures to mitigate potential negative impacts on employment and social stability Establish clear guidelines for workforce development and training programs Regularly review and update policies to ensure alignment with evolving societal needs	Consider the potential impact of automation on jobs and develop strategies to mitigate negative effects Invest in retraining and upskilling programs to support workers affected by CAV deployment Develop guidelines for fair compensation and benefits for workers in the CAV industry

continued on following page

Table 4. Continued

Aspect	AVs key considerations	Cybersecurity	Ethical Concern
Safety and Security	Implement robust safety features to prevent accidents or incidents Regularly test and validate AV systems for safety and security Ensure transparency around safety and security protocols	Prioritize safety and security above all else in CAV design and operation Implement robust testing and validation procedures to detect potential safety and security risks Establish clear guidelines for emergency response and incident management Regularly review and update policies to ensure alignment with evolving regulations and standards	Prioritize safety and security in CAV design, testing, and operation Implement robust security measures to prevent accidents or incidents Conduct regular assessments to ensure compliance with relevant regulations (e.g., FMCSA)
Malicious Use of Technology	Implement measures to prevent malicious use of AV technology, such as hacking attempts Regularly update and patch software to address vulnerabilities Conduct regular security audits and penetration testing	Develop strategies for mitigating the impact of malicious attacks on CAVs Implement robust security measures to prevent hacking attempts (e.g., firewalls, intrusion detection systems) Establish incident response plans to address potential security breaches Regularly review and update policies to ensure alignment with evolving threat landscapes	Develop guidelines for the responsible use of technology in CAV systems Establish protocols for detecting and responding to malicious activities Invest in cybersecurity research and development to stay ahead of emerging threats
Bias and Fairness	Develop algorithms that prioritize fairness and non-discrimination Address potential biases in algorithmic decision-making Implement measures to prevent biased outcomes or decisions	Develop algorithms that prioritize fairness and non-discrimination Implement robust testing and validation procedures to detect biases or errors Establish protocols for regular algorithm updates and maintenance Address potential challenges around bias, fairness, and accountability in CAV decision-making	Prioritize fairness and non-discrimination in decision-making algorithms Conduct regular testing and validation procedures to detect biases or errors Establish protocols for auditing and monitoring discriminatory practices
Aspect	AVs	Cybersecurity	Ethical Concern
Informed Consent	Obtain explicit consent from passengers before collecting and using their data Clearly communicate how data will be used, stored, and protected Provide options for passengers to opt-out of data collection or sharing Establish protocols for updating and revoking consent	Obtain explicit consent from passengers before collecting and using their data Clearly communicate how data will be used, stored, and protected Provide options for passengers to opt-out of data collection or sharing Establish protocols for updating and revoking consent	Develop guidelines for informed consent from individuals involved in CAV testing or deployment Ensure transparent and clear communication about CAV risks, benefits, and limitations Implement robust security measures to protect sensitive information
Ethical Hacking	Implement robust security measures to prevent hacking attempts Regularly conduct penetration testing and vulnerability assessments Collaborate with cybersecurity experts to stay up-to-date on emerging threats Develop incident response plans to address potential security breaches	Implement robust security measures to prevent hacking attempts (e.g., firewalls, intrusion detection systems) Regularly conduct penetration testing and vulnerability assessments Collaborate with cybersecurity experts to stay up-to-date on emerging threats Develop incident response plans to address potential security breaches	Invest in cybersecurity research and development to stay ahead of emerging threats Establish protocols for responsible vulnerability disclosure and patching Develop guidelines for ethical hacking practices in CAV testing and deployment

continued on following page

Table 4. Continued

Aspect	AVs key considerations	Cybersecurity	Ethical Concern
Cross-Border Jurisdictions	Establish clear regulations and guidelines for AVs operating across international borders Ensure compliance with local laws and regulations regarding data protection, safety, and liability Collaborate with regulatory agencies to develop harmonized standards Address potential challenges around jurisdictional disputes and liability	Establish clear regulations and guidelines for CAVs operating across international borders Ensure compliance with local laws and regulations regarding data protection, safety, and liability Collaborate with regulatory agencies to develop harmonized standards Address potential challenges around jurisdictional disputes and liability	Ensure compliance with relevant regulations and laws across multiple jurisdictions Develop guidelines for international cooperation and collaboration on CAV standards and best practices Conduct regular assessments to ensure alignment with evolving regulations
Machine Learning Bias	Develop algorithms that prioritize fairness and non-discrimination Regularly audit and test for biases in decision-making models Implement measures to detect and mitigate biased outcomes or decisions Establish protocols for transparency and explainability	Develop algorithms that prioritize fairness and non-discrimination Implement robust testing and validation procedures to detect biases or errors Establish protocols for regular algorithm updates and maintenance Address potential challenges around bias, fairness, and accountability in CAV decision-making	Prioritize fairness, transparency, and explainability in machine learning algorithms Conduct regular testing and validation procedures to detect biases or errors Establish protocols for auditing and monitoring discriminatory practices
Accessibility and Inclusion	Design AVs to be accessible to passengers with disabilities Ensure equal access to safety features, services, and information Address potential barriers to inclusion, such as language or cultural differences Develop strategies for improving accessibility in emerging markets or regions	Design systems that are accessible to passengers with disabilities Ensure equal access to safety features, services, and information Implement measures to mitigate potential barriers to inclusion (e.g., language, cultural differences) Establish clear guidelines for transparency and explainability in CAV decision-making	Develop guidelines for ensuring equal access and opportunities for all individuals with disabilities Implement robust security measures to protect sensitive information and prevent unauthorized access Ensure transparent and clear communication about CAV risks, benefits, and limitations
Human Oversight	Implement human oversight systems to review and validate autonomous decision-making Establish protocols for emergency response and intervention Regularly conduct safety audits and risk assessments to identify potential risks Ensure that human operators are properly trained and equipped to respond to emergencies	Implement human oversight systems to review and validate autonomous decision-making Establish protocols for emergency response and incident management Regularly conduct safety audits and risk assessments to identify potential risks Ensure that human operators are properly trained and equipped to respond to emergencies	Prioritize human oversight and review of autonomous decisions Establish protocols for transparency and reporting in case of accidents or incidents Develop guidelines for ensuring accountability and responsibility in CAV operations

continued on following page

Table 4. Continued

Aspect	AVs key considerations	Cybersecurity	Ethical Concern
Dependence on Technology	Develop redundant and backup systems to ensure continued operation in the event of a failure Implement measures to mitigate the impact of technological failures or downtime Regularly test and validate AV systems for reliability and performance Address potential risks associated with over-reliance on technology, such as cybersecurity vulnerabilities	Implement robust cybersecurity measures to prevent exploitation of vulnerabilities Develop strategies for reducing dependence on technology and enhancing resilience Establish clear guidelines for incident response and emergency management Regularly review and update policies to ensure alignment with evolving regulations	Implement robust security measures to prevent exploitation of vulnerabilities Develop strategies to reduce dependence on technology and enhance resilience Ensure transparent and clear communication about CAV risks, benefits, and limitations
Discriminatory Practices	Develop algorithms that prioritize fairness and non-discrimination Regularly audit and test for biases in decision-making models Implement measures to detect and mitigate discriminatory outcomes or decisions Establish protocols for transparency and explainability	Implement algorithms that prioritize fairness and non-discrimination Conduct regular testing and validation procedures to detect biases or errors Establish protocols for auditing and monitoring discriminatory practices Develop guidelines for transparency and accountability in decision-making	Prioritize fairness, transparency, and explainability in decision-making algorithms Conduct regular testing and validation procedures to detect biases or errors Establish protocols for auditing and monitoring discriminatory practices
Energy and Environmental Impact	Design AVs with energy efficiency and environmental sustainability in mind Develop strategies for reducing carbon emissions and promoting sustainable transportation options Regularly assess and report on the environmental impact of AV operations Address potential challenges around charging infrastructure, resource extraction, and waste management	Prioritize energy efficiency and minimize environmental impact through cybersecurity measures Implement robust security measures to prevent cyber-attacks that could compromise energy systems Consider the environmental implications of cybersecurity measures, such as the use of renewable energy sources Regularly review and update policies to ensure alignment with evolving regulations	Prioritize energy efficiency and minimize environmental impact through cybersecurity measures Implement robust security measures to prevent cyber-attacks that could compromise energy systems Develop guidelines for responsible use of technology in CAV systems
Ethics of Warfare and Defense	Avoid development or deployment of AVs with military or defense applications Establish clear guidelines for the use of AVs in emergency response situations Regularly review and update policies to ensure alignment with international humanitarian law Address potential challenges around accountability, liability, and transparency	Ensure that CAVs do not participate in warfare or defense-related activities without explicit permission from authorized authorities Implement robust security measures to prevent unauthorized access to sensitive information Establish clear guidelines for transparency and accountability in decision-making related to warfare and defense Regularly review and update policies to ensure alignment with evolving regulations	Ensure that CAVs are not used for military purposes or warfare Develop guidelines for using CAVs in defense scenarios, prioritizing civilian safety and minimizing harm to non-combatants Establish protocols for accountability and transparency in CAV use in defense contexts

continued on following page

Table 4. Continued

Aspect	AVs key considerations	Cybersecurity	Ethical Concern
Children's Safety and Security	Develop strategies for protecting children from cyberbullying, data exploitation, or other online risks Establish protocols for age-restricted access to certain features or services Regularly monitor and update policies to ensure protection of minors' safety and well-being Address potential challenges around child online safety, parental consent, and education	Prioritize children's safety and security through robust cybersecurity measures, such as secure authentication and authorization protocols Implement age-restricted access controls to prevent unauthorized access to sensitive information or systems Establish clear guidelines for transparency and accountability in decision-making related to children's safety and security Regularly review and update policies to ensure alignment with evolving regulations	Implement robust security measures to prevent unauthorized access to CAV systems by children or others with malicious intent Develop guidelines for ensuring the safe deployment of CAVs near schools, playgrounds, or other areas where children frequent Establish protocols for emergency response in case of CAV-related accidents involving children
Transparency and Explainability	Develop algorithms that are transparent and explainable Establish protocols for transparency in decision-making processes Regularly provide clear and concise information about AV systems, data collection, and use Address potential challenges around complex technical issues or nuanced regulatory requirements	Implement transparent and explainable decision-making algorithms that prioritize fairness and non-discrimination Conduct regular testing and validation procedures to detect biases or errors Establish protocols for auditing and monitoring discriminatory practices Develop guidelines for transparency and accountability in decision-making	Ensure that CAV decision-making processes are transparent, explainable, and auditable Develop guidelines for providing clear and concise information about CAV capabilities, limitations, and potential risks to users and the public Establish protocols for ongoing evaluation and improvement of CAV systems to ensure they remain transparent and explainable
Ethical Use of Data	Develop policies and guidelines for the responsible use of passenger data Ensure transparent communication about data collection, storage, and use Regularly review and update policies to ensure alignment with evolving data protection standards Address potential challenges around consent, opt-out, and control	Ensure that data collected from CAVs is used ethically and in accordance with relevant regulations (e.g., GDPR, CCPA) Implement robust security measures to protect sensitive information and prevent unauthorized access Establish clear guidelines for transparency and accountability in data collection and usage Regularly review and update policies to ensure alignment with evolving regulations	Prioritize transparent and secure data collection, storage, and sharing practices Ensure informed consent from individuals involved in CAV testing or deployment Implement robust security measures to protect sensitive information
Vulnerability of Infrastructure	Regularly assess and evaluate infrastructure for vulnerabilities or weaknesses Develop strategies for mitigating risks associated with infrastructure failure or compromise Collaborate with regulatory agencies and industry partners to develop harmonized security standards Establish protocols for incident response and emergency preparedness	Prioritize the vulnerability of infrastructure by implementing robust cybersecurity measures, such as secure authentication and authorization protocols Conduct regular risk assessments and evaluate the impact of various CAV systems on passenger safety and security Establish clear guidelines for incident response and emergency management Regularly review and update policies to ensure alignment with evolving regulations	Implement robust security measures to prevent exploitation of vulnerabilities Conduct regular assessments to ensure compliance with relevant regulations (e.g., FMCSA) Develop guidelines for responsible use of technology in CAV systems

2. Forensic Standards

Currently, there is no established forensic investigation framework or standard for AVs which is important for addressing issues such as investigating attacks and ensuring compliance with AVs driving safety guidelines. The National Institute of Standards and Technology (NIST) has not yet issued any specific standards or guidelines involving AVs. However, the only standard available for handling digital data is ISO/IEC 27037, it provides regulations on handling digital evidence, which includes the identification, collection, acquisition, and preservation of potential digital evidence that can be helpful in court (Schlenoff, 2024).

Forensics can in theory be carried out using two methods: Reactive and Proactive as discussed in Table 5. The proactive forensics approach aims to collect data proactively, safeguard it, identify suspicious events, collect evidence, perform investigations, and construct a case against any potential crime *(Ieong, 2006)*. The evidence obtained through this approach comprises data relating to a specific event or occurrence.

As demonstrated in Figure 2 (Alharbi et al., 2011), the traditional method of directing digital crime investigations after an incident has taken place is known as the reactive approach. This includes locating, preserving, gathering, examining, and producing a final report.

Table 6 presents a comparison of proactive and reactive forensics.

Figure 2. Functional process for proactive & reactive digital forensics investigation system

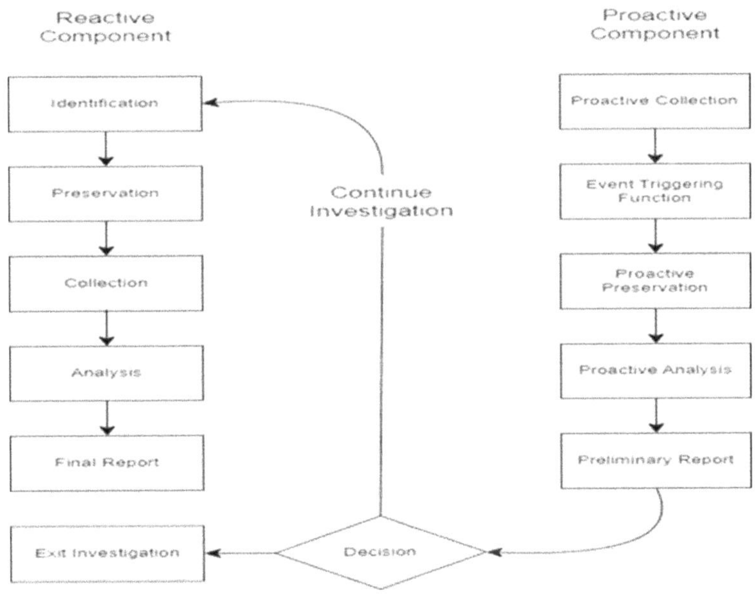

Table 5. Comparison of proactive and reactive forensics: Objectives, strategies, and considerations

Aspect	Proactive Forensics	Reactive Forensics
Objective	Prevent incidents by continuous monitoring and early detection.	Responding to a security incident or breach in a timely and effective manner.
Data Collection	Collecting data proactively, safeguarding it, identifying suspicious events, and collecting evidence.	Collecting data after an incident has occurred, with the goal of understanding what happened and how to prevent similar incidents in the future.
Incident Detection	Identifying potential threats or incidents before they occur or during their initial stages.	Detecting security incidents or breaches after they have already occurred.
System Response	Responding to detected incidents in a timely and effective manner.	Responding to detected incidents in a timely and effective manner, often with limited prior knowledge of the incident.
Forensic Analysis	Analyzing collected data to construct a case against potential crimes.	Analyzing collected data to understand what happened during the incident and how to prevent similar incidents in the future.
Preservation of Evidence	Preserving the integrity and authenticity of collected evidence.	Preserving the integrity and authenticity of evidence after an incident has occurred, as it may be compromised or destroyed.
Tools and Technologies	Utilizing specialized tools and technologies to support proactive forensics efforts.	Utilizing tools and technologies to aid in responding to security incidents, such as incident response software.
Stakeholder Involvement	Collaborating with stakeholders, such as law enforcement and incident responders, to ensure effective proactive forensics.	Collaborating with stakeholders, including incident responders, law enforcement, and other relevant parties, after an incident has occurred.
Latency in Response	Minimizing response latency to enable swift action against detected incidents.	Prioritizing speed over timeliness, often due to the need for rapid action to mitigate damage or prevent further compromise.
Outcome	Minimize the likelihood of incidents through preventive measures.	Containing and mitigating the impact of a security incident, while also learning from the incident to improve future incident response efforts.
Challenges	Identifying and addressing potential challenges in proactive forensics, such as ensuring data quality and integrity.	Responding to security incidents in a timely and effective manner, while ensuring data integrity and preservation
Time of Action	Minimizing latency and responding quickly to detected incidents to prevent further damage or compromise.	Prioritizing speed over timeliness when responding to security incidents, as delayed response can exacerbate damage or compromise further.
Primary Goal	Achieving the primary goal of proactive forensics, which is to identify and mitigate potential security threats before they materialize.	Containing and mitigating the impact of a security incident, while also learning from the incident to improve future incident response efforts.
Type of Monitoring	Implementing monitoring systems that can detect anomalies and alert investigators to potential incidents.	Conducting retrospective monitoring to identify potential security threats after they have occurred, rather than proactive monitoring to detect them before they happen.
Nature of Data Analyzed	Analyzing data in real-time or near-real-time to enable swift action against detected incidents.	Analyzing data collected during and after a security incident to understand what happened and how to prevent similar incidents in the future.
Examples of Threats Addressed	Identifying and addressing a wide range of cyber threats, including but not limited to malware, system malfunctions, abnormal sensor behavior, or unusual communication patterns.	Responding to various types of security including Crashes, cyber-attacks, component failure as well as responding to breaches and system compromises.
Incident Reporting	Establishing incident reporting processes that allow for quick and effective communication with stakeholders and incident responders.	Communicating incident reports to stakeholders, including incident responders, law enforcement, and other relevant parties, in a timely and transparent manner.

continued on following page

Table 5. Continued

Aspect	Proactive Forensics	Reactive Forensics
Chain of Custody	Ensuring the integrity and authenticity of collected evidence by maintaining a secure chain of custody.	Ensuring that evidence collected during an incident is properly preserved and handled, following established protocols for chain of custody.
Legal Considerations	Complying with relevant laws and regulations, such as data protection and privacy laws, when collecting and analyzing digital evidence.	Adhering to legal requirements and regulations when responding to security incidents, such as gathering and preserving evidence, notifying affected parties, and cooperating with law enforcement.
System Overhead	Minimizing system overhead to ensure that proactive forensics can be performed efficiently and effectively.	Optimizing system performance and resources during incident response, while minimizing downtime and disruption to critical systems.
Data Volume	Managing large volumes of data to ensure that proactive forensics efforts are not overwhelmed by the sheer amount of data being collected.	Managing the volume of data generated during an incident, including log data, network traffic, and other relevant information, to support effective incident analysis.
Security Implementation	Implementing robust security measures to prevent unauthorized access to collected evidence or systems.	Implementing security measures to prevent similar incidents from occurring in the future, such as updating software, patching vulnerabilities, and enhancing access controls.
Use of AI/ML	Utilizing artificial intelligence and machine learning techniques to enhance the effectiveness of proactive forensics efforts.	Leveraging artificial intelligence (AI) and machine learning (ML) techniques to improve incident response efforts, such as automating threat analysis or predicting potential threats.
Forensic Reporting	Presenting findings in a clear and concise manner, using standardized reporting formats and protocols.	Providing detailed and accurate reports on security incidents, including incident analysis, root cause identification, and recommendations for prevention and mitigation.
Cost Efficiency	Ensuring that proactive forensics efforts are cost-effective and meet business objectives while minimizing waste and inefficiency.	Prioritizing cost-effectiveness when allocating resources for incident response, while ensuring that adequate resources are available to respond effectively to security incidents.
Availability of Data	Ensuring that data is readily available when needed to enable swift action against detected incidents.	Ensuring that data is readily available and accessible during an incident response effort, to support effective analysis and decision-making.
System Downtime	Minimizing system downtime to ensure that proactive forensics can be performed continuously without interruption.	Minimizing system downtime and disruption during incident response efforts, by prioritizing rapid containment and resolution of the incident.
Recovery Time	Achieving rapid recovery from system or network failures to minimize the impact of a potential security breach.	Prioritizing recovery time and minimizing the duration of downtime during incident response efforts, while ensuring that data integrity is preserved.
Collaboration Requirements	Establishing clear collaboration requirements with stakeholders and incident responders to ensure effective information sharing and coordination.	Collaborating with stakeholders, including incident responders, law enforcement, and other relevant parties, to ensure effective incident response and communication.
Impact on Safety	Minimizing the impact of proactive forensics on safety, by ensuring that system downtime is minimized and data integrity is preserved.	Ensuring that security incidents do not compromise the safety and security of individuals or organizations, by prioritizing containment and mitigation efforts.

- Proactive Forensics

Proactive forensics focuses on identifying potential threats before they materialize, collecting data proactively, and analyzing it to construct a case against potential crimes. The primary goal is to identify and mitigate potential security threats before they occur or during their initial stages. This approach requires ongoing monitoring and analysis of data to detect anomalies and suspicious activity. Proactive forensics also involves collaborating with stakeholders, such as law enforcement and incident responders, to ensure effective proactive forensics efforts (Brown et al., 2024; Heba Abd El-Aziz, 2024).

- Reactive Forensics

Reactive forensics, on the other hand, responds to security incidents or breaches after they have already occurred. The primary goal is to contain and mitigate the impact of a security incident, while also learning from the incident to improve future incident response efforts. This approach prioritizes speed over timeliness, as delayed response can exacerbate damage or compromise further. Reactive forensics involves analyzing data collected during and after an incident to understand what happened and how to prevent similar incidents in the future. It also requires ensuring data integrity and preservation, managing system overhead, and minimizing downtime(Atakishiyev et al., 2024; Battel & Pearl, 2024; Neupane et al., 2024; Prinzel, n.d.).

While proactive forensics focuses on prevention and early detection, reactive forensics is focused on response and mitigation. Proactive forensics relies on ongoing monitoring and analysis of data to identify potential threats, whereas reactive forensics responds to incidents after they have occurred. However, both approaches are crucial in ensuring the overall effectiveness of forensic analysis and incident response efforts.

In terms of challenges, proactive forensics requires a high level of expertise and resources to continuously monitor and analyze data, while reactive forensics must respond quickly and effectively to minimize the impact of an incident. Proactive forensics also involves managing large volumes of data, while reactive forensics requires prioritizing speed over timeliness.

Despite these differences, both proactive and reactive forensics share common goals, such as containing and mitigating the impact of security incidents, learning from incidents to improve future incident response efforts, and ensuring the overall effectiveness of forensic analysis and incident response. Ultimately, a combination of both proactive and reactive forensics approaches is likely the most effective way to ensure comprehensive security and forensic analysis.

3. Security Challenges

AVs that are connected rely on sensors to understand their environments and make driving decisions. However, sensor technology is still developing and is at risk of cyberattacks that can disrupt, disable, or maliciously control the vehicle or its surroundings, as well as compromise data veracity (Petit et al., 2015).

The main threats include:

- **Spoofing Attacks:** Attackers can introduce false sensor data, manipulate distances, or create fake road signals using sensors such as GPS, LiDAR, and cameras.
- **Tampering Attacks:** Attackers can alter sensor data either remotely or physically.
- **Denial of Service Attacks:** Attackers can overwhelm sensors by injecting excessive fake objects, destabilizing the system and creating potential safety risks. *(Stottelaar, 2015)*

4. Existing Solutions to Cyberattacks

In this part, we will talk about the current cybersecurity approaches for AVs (Le-Khac et al., 2020), we will focus on solutions based on conventional (traditional) and AI-based solutions and compare between them as shown in Table 3:

- Conventional Approach: These refer to rule-based schemes that depend on predefined sets of rules coded into the software. These approaches are designed with evidently outlined rules and logic, ensuring specific system functionality and performance under specific conditions. However, they have limited flexibility in adapting to new or evolving threats.
- AI-Driven Approach: AI techniques particularly Machine Learning, are increasingly being applied to manage the large volumes of data generated by AVs. Unlike traditional methods, AI-powered solutions empower AVs to make autonomous decisions based on data analysis rather than explicit programming. Machine learning methods can identify differences in sensor data, recognize malicious activities, and enhance threat detection by analyzing logs and patterns. *(Liu et al., 2021)* discussed when combined with data from the Intelligent Transportation System, these algorithms can forestall vehicle movements and effectively respond to cybersecurity risks.

Table 6 discusses the two approaches' advantages and limitations while the different aspects consideration in the two approaches is shown in Table 7.

Table 6. Comparison of approaches of cyberattacks

Approach	Description	Advantages	Limitations
Traditional Solutions	Follows predefined coding logic that is rule-based	Gives predictable and consistent results	Adaptability is limited and there is no self-improvement
AI-Driven Solutions	Detect and improve detection by using ML algorithms to analyze and log data.	Adapts to new threats and is capable of self-learning	Complexity due to large amount of data

Table 7. Conventional vs AI solutions for cyberattacks

Aspect	Conventional Solutions	AI-based Solutions
Detection Capabilities	Relies on pre-existing knowledge and signatures, often falling short against emerging threats.	Employs advanced algorithms to detect novel and evolving threats in real-time.
Operational Efficiency	Requires manual intervention, leading to slower response times and increased workload.	Automates threat mitigation, freeing up resources for more critical tasks.
Scalability and Adaptability	Struggles with intricate systems, often requiring frequent updates and patches.	Dynamically adapts to emerging threats, minimizing the need for manual intervention.
Response Time	Responds slowly, often requiring manual intervention and increasing response times.	Responds rapidly, automating threat mitigation and minimizing downtime.
False Positives	Prone to false positives, necessitating manual verification and increased workload.	Reduces false positives over time, improving overall accuracy and reducing unnecessary responses.

continued on following page

Table 7. Continued

Aspect	Conventional Solutions	AI-based Solutions
Maintenance Requirements	Requires frequent manual updates and patches, increasing maintenance costs.	Employs autonomous learning and evolution, minimizing the need for manual intervention and reducing maintenance costs.
Initial Investment	Generally, less expensive upfront, requiring lower computational power.	Involves higher initial costs, necessitating advanced computing power to realize long-term savings.
Resource Usage	Lower resource usage; easier to deploy on systems with limited power.	Higher computational resources required (GPUs, cloud infrastructure).
Explainability	Easily understandable and explainable	Less transparent, often a "black box" decision-making

IV. CONCLUSION & FUTURE WORK

The use of self-driving vehicles offers many benefits in terms of suitability, effectiveness, and safety. However, the ethical issues related to cybersecurity in AVs present significant obstacles that need to be dealt with. The need for connected systems and data-driven algorithms exposes AVs to cyber threats that jeopardize user safety, privacy, and decision-making integrity. Given these difficulties, it's crucial to establish strong ethical and legal frameworks that protect both the technology and its users. It's important for future research to concentrate on enhancing the cybersecurity systems in AVs through the advancement of more AI-Driven solutions that can identify and prevent cyber threats in real time. It will also be vital to establish comprehensive forensic standards specifically personalized to AVs to address issues related to cyberattacks and accidents. Furthermore, there is a need for investigation into the ethical suggestions of decision-making algorithms. Essential efforts should be dedicated to researching and establishing global regulatory frameworks that can effectively block the unique challenges posed by AV Cybersecurity.

The integration of AI in AVs has shown promising results in enhancing cybersecurity measures, improving threat detection capabilities, and optimizing system performance. The conventional approach to cybersecurity has limitations in terms of adaptability and self-improvement, whereas the AI-driven solutions have demonstrated better detection capabilities, operational efficiency, scalability, and response time.

Future work directions for this research include:

1. Evaluating the effectiveness of machine learning algorithms in detecting novel threats against AVs.
2. Investigating the impact of edge cases on autonomous vehicle performance and cybersecurity.
3. Exploring the integration of other AI techniques, such as reinforcement learning or transfer learning, to further enhance autonomous vehicle security.
4. Developing more comprehensive testing frameworks for AVs, including simulation-based and real-world testing scenarios.

Overall, this research aims to contribute to the development of more secure and efficient AVs by leveraging the power of AI in cybersecurity.

REFERENCES

Alharbi, S., Weber-Jahnke, J., & Traore, I. (2011). The proactive and reactive digital forensics investigation process: A systematic literature review. *Information Security and Assurance:International Conference, ISA 2011,* Brno, Czech Republic, August 15-17, 2011. *Proceedings*, 87–100.

Atakishiyev, S., Salameh, M., & Goebel, R. (2024). *Incorporating Explanations into Human-Machine Interfaces for Trust and Situation Awareness in AVs.* http://arxiv.org/abs/2404.07383

Bakare, S. S., Adeniyi, A. O., Akpuokwe, C. U., & Eneh, N. E. (2024). DATA PRIVACY LAWS AND COMPLIANCE: A COMPARATIVE REVIEW OF THE EU GDPR AND USA REGULATIONS. *Computer Science & IT Research Journal*, 5(3), 528–543. DOI: 10.51594/csitrj.v5i3.859

Battel, K., & Pearl, D. (2024). A critical juncture: Promoting responsible innovation in the self-driving automobile sector while improving human factors. *Frontiers in Industrial Engineering*, 2, 1409748. Advance online publication. DOI: 10.3389/fieng.2024.1409748

Brown, A., Johnson, S. D., & Tuptuk, N. (2024). *A Scoping Study: Crime and Connected and AVs.* OSF.

Collingwood, L. (2017). Privacy implications and liability issues of AVs. *Information & Communications Technology Law*, 26(1), 32–45. DOI: 10.1080/13600834.2017.1269871

Department for Transport. (2016). Pathway to driverless cars: Proposals to support advanced driver assistance systems and automated vehicle technologies. In www.gov.uk/dft. Department for Transport. https://assets.publishing.service.gov.uk/government/uploads/system/uploads/attachment_data/file/581577/pathway-to-driverless-cars-consultation-response.pdf

Dhar, V. (2016). Equity, safety, and privacy in the autonomous vehicle era. *Computer*, 49(11), 80–83. DOI: 10.1109/MC.2016.326

Fleetwood, J. (2017). Public health, ethics, and AVs. *American Journal of Public Health*, 107(4), 532–537. DOI: 10.2105/AJPH.2016.303628 PMID: 28207327

Glancy, D. J. (2012). Privacy in AVs. *Santa Clara Law Review*, 52, 1171.

Goodall, N. J. (2014). Machine ethics and automated vehicles. *Road Vehicle Automation*, 93–102.

Government Response. (2018). *Government response to House of Lords Artificial Intelligence Select Committee's Report on AI in the UK: Ready, Willing and Able?* parliament.uk. https://www.parliament.uk/globalassets/documents/lords-committees/Artificial-Intelligence/AI-Government-Response.pdf

Hagendorff, T. (2020). The Ethics of AI Ethics: An Evaluation of Guidelines. *Minds and Machines*, 30(1), 99–120. DOI: 10.1007/s11023-020-09517-8

Heba Abd El-Aziz, B. (2024). Distributed Learning and Broad Applications in Scientific Research Threat Intelligence Fusion Techniques for Enhanced Cybersecurity in Autonomous Vehicle Networks. In *Distributed Learning and Broad Applications in Scientific Research Annual* (Vol. 10).

Hevelke, A., & Nida-Rümelin, J. (2015). Responsibility for crashes of AVs: An ethical analysis. *Science and Engineering Ethics*, 21(3), 619–630. DOI: 10.1007/s11948-014-9565-5 PMID: 25027859

Ibrahum, A. D. M., Hussain, M., & Hong, J. E. (2025). Deep learning adversarial attacks and defenses in AVs: A systematic literature review from a safety perspective. *Artificial Intelligence Review*, 58(1), 28. Advance online publication. DOI: 10.1007/s10462-024-11014-8

Ieong, R. S. C. (2006). FORZA–Digital forensics investigation framework that incorporate legal issues. *Digital Investigation*, 3, 29–36. DOI: 10.1016/j.diin.2006.06.004

Le-Khac, N.-A., Jacobs, D., Nijhoff, J., Bertens, K., & Choo, K.-K. R. (2020). Smart vehicle forensics: Challenges and case study. *Future Generation Computer Systems*, 109, 500–510. DOI: 10.1016/j.future.2018.05.081

Lin, P. (2016). Why ethics matters for autonomous cars. *Autonomous Driving: Technical, Legal and Social Aspects*, 69–85.

Liu, H., Zhang, S., Zhang, P., Zhou, X., Shao, X., Pu, G., & Zhang, Y. (2021). Blockchain and federated learning for collaborative intrusion detection in vehicular edge computing. *IEEE Transactions on Vehicular Technology*, 70(6), 6073–6084. DOI: 10.1109/TVT.2021.3076780

Lowe, J., & Kuru, K. (2024). Development of Machine Intelligence for Self-Driving Vehicles Through Video Capturing. *MESA 2024 - 20th International Conference on Mechatronic, Embedded Systems and Applications, Proceedings*. DOI: 10.1109/MESA61532.2024.10704876

Marchant, G. E., & Lindor, R. A. (2012). The coming collision between AVs and the liability system. *Santa Clara Law Review*, 52, 1321.

Neupane, S., Mitra, S., Fernandez, I. A., Saha, S., Mittal, S., Chen, J., Pillai, N., & Rahimi, S. (2024). Security Considerations in AI-Robotics: A Survey of Current Methods, Challenges, and Opportunities. *IEEE Access : Practical Innovations, Open Solutions*, 12, 22072–22097. DOI: 10.1109/ACCESS.2024.3363657

Nyholm, S., & Smids, J. (2016). The ethics of accident-algorithms for self-driving cars: An applied trolley problem? *Ethical Theory and Moral Practice*, 19(5), 1275–1289. DOI: 10.1007/s10677-016-9745-2

Petit, J., & Shladover, S. E. (2014). Potential cyberattacks on automated vehicles. *IEEE Transactions on Intelligent Transportation Systems*, 16(2), 546–556.

Petit, J., Stottelaar, B., Feiri, M., & Kargl, F. (2015). Remote attacks on automated vehicles sensors: Experiments on camera and lidar. *Black Hat Europe*, 11, 995.

Prinzel, L. J., Krois, P., Ellis, K. K., Vincent, M., Stephens, C., Oza, N., . . . Matthews, B. L. (2024). The Adaptable and Resilient Safety System: The Human Factor in Future In-Time Aviation Safety Management Systems. In AIAA SCITECH 2024 Forum (p. 1603).

QNX. B. (2020). WP.29 Cybersecurity Vehicle Regulation Compliance: Ultimate guides: Blackberry QNX. In *Ultimate Guides | BlackBerry QNX*. Blackberry. https://blackberry.qnx.com/en/ultimate-guides/wp-29-vehicle-cybersecurity

Rana Hassam Ahmed, M. H. H. A. S. Z. M. H. T. (2024). ENHANCING AUTONOMOUS VEHICLE SECURITY THROUGH ADVANCED ARTIFICIAL INTELLIGENCE TECHNIQUES. *Journal of Computer Science and Electrical Engineering*, 6(4). Advance online publication. DOI: 10.61784/jcsee3017

Schlenoff, C. I., Kootbally, Z., Rachakonda, P., Lightman, S., Vassilev, A., Wollman, D. A., & Griffor, E. (2024). Standards and Performance Metrics for On-Road Automated Vehicles.

Staff, F. (2024). A Beginner's Guide to the ISO/SAE 21434 Cybersecurity Standard for Road Vehicles. In *Beyond Security*. https://www.beyondsecurity.com/blog/iso-sae-21434-standard-road-vehicles

Stottelaar, B. G. B. (2015). *Practical cyber-attacks on AVs*. University of Twente.

Tan, S. (2024). Bridging the Gap: Machine Learning and Vision Neural Networks in AVs for the Aging Population. *International Journal of Advanced Computer Science and Applications*, 15(10). Advance online publication. DOI: 10.14569/IJACSA.2024.0151030

Warrendale, P. (2021). SAE and ISO Publish Joint Automotive Cybersecurity Standard. In *SAE International*. https://www.sae.org/news/press-room/2021/09/sae-and-iso-publish-joint-automotive-cybersecurity-standard

Zarsky, T. (2016). The trouble with algorithmic decisions: An analytic road map to examine efficiency and fairness in automated and opaque decision making. *Science, Technology & Human Values*, 41(1), 118–132. DOI: 10.1177/0162243915605575

Chapter 11
Post-Quantum Cryptography in the Age of Quantum Computing

Silvio Andrae
https://orcid.org/0000-0002-8586-7812
Independent Researcher, Germany

ABSTRACT

The ongoing development of powerful quantum computers poses a significant threat to the security of conventional encryption methods such as Rivest Shamir Adleman (RSA) and Elliptic Curve Cryptography (ECC). With algorithms such as Shor's Algorithm, quantum computers can solve the mathematical problems on which these methods are based and thus break them within a few hours. This work highlights this development's challenges and examines post-quantum cryptography (PQC) as a solution. PQC offers quantum-safe encryption based on mathematical problems that are difficult to solve, even for quantum computers. The text analyzes lattice, hash, and isogeny-based approaches and introduces the new NIST standards, including Kyber, Dilithium, and Sphinx+. It also discusses practical challenges in implementing quantum-safe systems, including performance degradation and cryptographic agility. It concludes with recommendations for migrating to PQC to ensure long-term security in an era increasingly characterized by quantum computing.

1. INTRODUCTION

It is time to prepare for theoretical mathematics and quantum computing risks. More 'store now, decrypt later' attacks will be expected in the coming years. In these attacks, encrypted data is intercepted today but only decrypted when the opportunity arises. These attacks can cause the availability of everyday services to collapse and undermine the security of the digital infrastructure. There is a great danger that future quantum computers could be able to undermine current public key cryptography methods such as Rivest Shamir Adleman (RSA) or Elliptic Curve Cryptography (ECC), which are based on discrete logarithms. It could cause data networks around the world to collapse. This concern is due to the ongoing development of large-scale, fault-tolerant quantum computers with a capacity of millions of qubits that can crack RSA or ECC because they use the Shor algorithm. This quantum algorithm was developed by Peter Shor in 1994 and is now one of the best-known algorithms in quantum computing, as it extends the possibilities of quantum computing. Researchers from China have recently been able to carry out

DOI: 10.4018/979-8-3693-9919-4.ch011

hacker attacks on highly encrypted systems using quantum computers. Blockchains were compromised for this purpose. It shows how quickly the development of quantum computers is progressing. For this reason, it is essential to move on to post-quantum cryptography (PQC)

Post-quantum cryptography is a subfield of cryptography that deals with developing and standardizing secure encryption methods that cannot be broken even when using quantum computers. Post-quantum cryptography is based on mathematical methods and not, like quantum cryptography (QC), on quantum physics. PQC can be implemented on classical computer hardware (Shaller et al., 2023; Chawla & Mehra, 2023; Li et al., 2023). This paper examines the threat scenarios from using quantum computers for cryptography and presents PQC as a promising response to these risks. The focus is on theoretical foundations and the practical implementation and standardization of quantum-safe procedures. The aim is to comprehensively understand the challenges and opportunities associated with the transition to quantum-resistant encryption technologies.

This work adopts an interdisciplinary approach, combining theoretical analysis with the evaluation of practical applications. The text is structured as follows: It begins with a presentation of the threat of 'store now, decrypt later' attacks and describes how quantum computers could jeopardize existing encryption methods. This is followed by a detailed analysis of classical methods such as RSA and ECC, including their strengths, weaknesses, and the impact quantum algorithms have on them (Section 2). The central part is devoted to post-quantum cryptography, particularly lattice-based, multivariate, and hash-based approaches. These are compared in terms of their security, efficiency, and implementability. Leading algorithms such as Kyber, Dilithium, and Sphinx+, standardized by the US American authority National Institute of Standards and Technology (NIST), are discussed (Section 3). The paper highlights the difficulties in implementing these methods, including issues of infrastructure, performance, and cryptographic agility. In addition, current standardization efforts by organizations such as NIST and the European Telecommunications Standards Institute (ETSI) are presented (Section 4). Finally, a systematic approach to introducing quantum-safe technologies is outlined, which includes the identification of quantum vulnerabilities, prioritizing critical systems, and the gradual transition to PQC (Section 5). This structured approach allows for an informed discussion of the key issues of post-quantum cryptography and offers practical recommendations for organizations preparing for the quantum age.

2. CURRENT PUBLIC-KEY CRYPTOGRAPHY METHODS

Public key cryptography is the foundation of securing many services that are part of our daily lives: Money transfers, the digital signing of contracts, and the control of smart home devices or communication services. However, the potential threat of quantum computers breaking the current public key systems is a matter of urgency. If this were to happen, it would have drastic consequences for the public digital infrastructure. Experts believe that this could become a reality in the 2030s (Shaller et al., 2023).

Common asymmetric encryption methods such as Rivest Shamir Adleman (RSA) or Elliptic Curve Cryptography (ECC) are particularly vulnerable to the threat of quantum computers. These methods, which are used for encrypting emails, securing internet connections (HTTPS), and digital signatures, are based on the assumption that certain mathematical problems, such as the factorization of large numbers or the calculation of discrete logarithms, are unsolvable for conventional computers. However, quantum computers could potentially solve these problems, rendering these methods ineffective.

Let's delve into the main asymmetric encryption methods and their potential vulnerabilities. This will provide a comprehensive understanding of the topic and help us prepare for the upcoming discussion.

2.1 Rivest Shamir Adleman

The Rivest-Shamir-Adleman (RSA) asymmetric encryption method, a cornerstone of modern cryptography, is among the best-known and most widely used public key cryptosystems. Its significance lies in the mathematical complexity of the prime factorization of large numbers (Federal Office for Information Security, 2024).

The key is generated as follows: Two large prime numbers p and q are randomly chosen. The product of these prime numbers is called the modulus. This modulus, along with other parameters, forms the public and private keys used in the RSA encryption and decryption processes:

$$n = p \bullet q \quad [1]$$

The Euler function φ -function is calculated:

$$\varphi(n) = (p-1)(q-1) \quad [2]$$

where the number of positive integers is less than n, which are not related to n

A public exponent e is selected, which is external to the divisor $\varphi(n)$

The private exponent d is determined so that$d \bullet e = 1 \pmod{\varphi(n)}$. This is the modular inverse of e modulo $\varphi(n)$.

The public key consists of(n, e), the private key of (n, d).

Encryption is performed as follows: A message M (as a number in the range ($0 \leq M < n$) is encrypted by exponentiating it with the public key and reducing *modulo n*.

$$C = M^e \bmod n \quad [3]$$

where C is the ciphertext.

During decryption, the recipient uses the private key to restore the original message.

$$M = C^d \bmod n \quad [4]$$

The security of RSA is based on the difficulty of prime factorization: The private key d can only be determined if $\varphi(n)$ is known, and $\varphi(n)$ can only be calculated if the prime factors p and q of n are known.

The strengths of RSA lie in its asymmetric encryption, i.e., no secure exchange of a key is necessary as the public key is freely available. The method has been used since the 1970s and has been well-researched. The mathematical basis is that the difficulty of prime factorization increases exponentially with the size of the prime numbers.

Despite its widespread use and mathematical elegance, RSA has several weaknesses that are relevant from both a technical and practical perspective. One of the main challenges is the need for long keys: to ensure sufficient security, key lengths of at least 2048 to 4096 bits are required. These large key sizes mean that RSA works significantly slower than symmetric encryption methods such as AES, especially when encrypting and decrypting large amounts of data.

In addition, RSA is vulnerable to various types of attacks. On a mathematical level, improved algorithms such as the General Number Field Sieve (GNFS) make it possible to perform the prime factorization of large numbers more efficiently, which could undermine the security of RSA. In addition, so-called timing attacks can be exploited, in which an attacker measures the runtime of specific calculations in order to conclude the secret key

Another weakness lies in the implementation of the method. The security of RSA depends crucially on the prime numbers being chosen correctly and randomly. However, faulty random number generators can make it easier to factorize, jeopardizing the system's overall security. These weaknesses make it clear that RSA must be carefully implemented in practice and regularly checked for possible security risks. This ongoing vigilance is crucial to ensure security even with increasing computing power and new attack vectors.

RSA is secure if the attackers cannot access quantum computers and sufficiently large keys are used (at least 2048 bits). However, the threat posed by quantum computers makes it necessary to switch to post-quantum cryptography, as quantum computers can factorize RSA.

2.2 Elliptic Curve Cryptography

Elliptic Curve Cryptography (ECC) is an asymmetric encryption method based on the mathematical properties of elliptic curves. It offers similar levels of security to other asymmetric methods, such as RSA, and surpasses them in some aspects. ECC's shorter keys result in more efficient and resource-saving implementations, making it particularly beneficial in today's fast-paced and resource-constrained environments. The method is explained in detail below, including its weaknesses in quantum computers.

An elliptic curve is a set of points that form an equation of the form:

$$y^2 = x^3 + ax + b$$

[4]

where$a$ and b are constants and the equation fulfills the condition $4a^3 + 27b^2 \neq 0$ (to avoid singularities). Over a finite body $\mathbb{F}_p$ (where p is a prime number), this equation forms a finite number of points.

Points on the elliptic curve form an abelian group where a special operation, the point addition, is defined. This operation makes it possible to calculate a new point by repeatedly adding a point P, which is known as scalar multiplication:

$$Q = kP$$

[5]

Here, k is a scaling factor (an integer) and Q is the resulting point. The difficulty of calculating k from P and Q is the basis of the security of ECC.

Similar to RSA, encryption is performed first. A private number$k$ is chosen at random (private key). The corresponding public key is calculated by multiplying k by a fixed base point G of the curve:

$$Q = kG$$

[6]

A sender encrypts a message M (which is mapped to a point on the curve) using the recipient's public key and the base point G . To do this, the sender generates a random integer$r$ and forms the encrypted text from two points:

$$C = (rG, M + rQ)$$

[7]

Here Q is the recipient's public key.

The recipient uses his private key k to recover the message M from the encrypted text C

$$M = (rM + rQ) - k(rG)$$

[8]

Since, $rQ = r(kG)M$ can be clearly reconstructed.

The safety of ECC is based on the Elliptic Curve Discrete Logarithm Problem (ECDLP):

Given P and $Q = kP$, it is extremely difficult to determine k. The calculation time increases exponentially with the size of the curve used.

Therefore, elliptic curve cryptography offers strong security with shorter key lengths. For example, an ECC key length of 256 bits offers similar security to a 3072-bit RSA key.

The weaknesses of ECC in the context of quantum computers are based on the efficiency of the Shor algorithm. This algorithm, specially developed for quantum computers, can solve the ECDLP in polynomial time. While the ECDLP is exponentially expensive to compute on classical computers, the Shor algorithm drastically reduces the computation time by efficiently exploiting the periodicity of the elliptic curve operations. It poses a serious threat to the security of ECC.

The shorter key sizes of ECC also amplify the threat from quantum computers, as fewer resources are required to break ECC keys than RSA keys. For example, a 256-bit ECC key could be cracked by a quantum computer that requires about 3000 error-corrected qubits. Although quantum computers with such a capacity do not currently exist, they are expected to be developed within the next few decades.

2.3 Signcryption

Signcryption is an important cryptographic process used for confidentiality and unforgeability. The process combines digital signature and encryption tasks in a single, integrated step. In contrast to traditional approaches, where these two functions are performed separately, signcryption offers a more efficient and compact alternative. The approach not only reduces computational costs but also minimizes the amount of data that needs to be transmitted, thereby reducing communication overhead. By combining the two operations, fewer computing resources are required. It is a decisive advantage, especially for resource-limited systems like IoT or mobile end devices. The idea behind signcryption was introduced by Yuliang Zheng in 1997 and has since gained importance in cryptography. Many interesting practical applications work with signcryption, such as in email encryption, blockchain, smart contracts, and cloud storage (Dey et al., 2022).

3. POST-QUANTUM CRYPTOGRAPHY

The advancing development of large-scale, fault-tolerant quantum computers can crack RSA or ECC due to the Shor algorithm. This quantum algorithm was developed by Peter Shor in 1994 and is now one of the best-known algorithms in quantum computing, as it extends the possibilities of quantum computing. However, the security of modern encryption methods such as RSA and ECC is based on these mathematical problems. What initially seems contradictory makes sense because it is easy to perform encryption but tough to undo without a key.

Companies such as Quantinuum, Quera, Microsoft, and IBM are working on such quantum computers. It can be assumed that cybercriminals are also developing quantum computers or have access to them. Moreover, cybercriminals are already storing encrypted data in order to decrypt it in the future using quantum computers. It is the 'store now, decrypt later' attack scenario. This poses a real threat to data that must remain protected for decades, such as medical records, industrial secrets, or diplomatic communications. As IT professionals, cybersecurity experts, and decision-makers in technology companies, this is a threat that directly impacts your work. Due to this attack scenario, sensitive content must be securely encrypted today.

3.1 Methods

Post-quantum cryptography (PQC) represents a significant leap in cryptographic research. It can be implemented on conventional computer hardware, unlike quantum cryptography, which is based on quantum physics. PQC is dedicated to developing and standardizing methods that are resistant to quantum computer attacks and can be used on today's computer hardware. In contrast, quantum cryptography relies on quantum mechanical effects such as coherence and entanglement, and requires new hardware and protocols (Yalamuri et al., 2022).

Post-quantum cryptography (PQC) is built on mathematical problems that are extremely difficult or even impossible to solve, even for quantum algorithms. This fundamental difference from classical cryptography, such as RSA and ECC, which relies on the difficulty of factorization problems or discrete logarithms, makes PQC a future-proof solution. By using alternative mathematical structures and problems that are resistant to known quantum attacks, PQC is preparing a secure foundation for cryptographic systems in the face of the anticipated availability of powerful quantum computers in the near future (Kumar, 2022).

Numerous methods and algorithms are being developed, researched, and standardized for quantum computer secure cryptography (Shaller et al., 2023; Chawla & Mehra, 2023; Kumar, 2022).

Lattice-based cryptosystems

Lattice-based cryptography, a leading approach in post-quantum cryptography, is based on mathematical problems that are difficult to solve in high-dimensional lattices. The two key challenges in this area, the shortest vector problem (SVP) and the closest vector problem (CVP), are considered highly complex in computer mathematics and are ideal for cryptographic applications. These problems are computationally expensive for both classical and quantum computers, making them a robust basis for cryptographic methods (Wang et al., 2024).

The Learning with Errors (LWE) algorithm and its optimized variant, Ring-LWE, is a well-known example of applying these concepts. These approaches utilize the inherent difficulty of problems in lattice structures to develop secure methods for encryption, digital signatures, and key exchange. Due to their efficiency and security compared to known quantum algorithms, lattice-based methods are considered a key technology in post-quantum cryptography. Algorithms like NTRU and CRYSTALS-Kyber are leading candidates for post-quantum encryption (Song, 2023). They offer protection against future quantum attacks and are comparatively easy to integrate into existing cryptographic systems, making them an important component of future cryptography.

Multivariate-based cryptosystems

Cryptography based on multivariate polynomials uses the difficulty of solving systems of equations with multivariate polynomials over finite fields as the basis for its security. These mathematical problems are considered highly complex for classical and quantum computers, making them a robust basis for cryptographic methods. A prominent example of the application of this method is the rainbow signature, a method for creating secure digital signatures.

Multivariate polynomial-based systems offer the advantage of being able to create and verify signatures very quickly and efficiently. This makes them particularly suitable for applications where high speed and low computing power are required, such as in embedded systems or mobile devices. However, challenges, such as the potential vulnerability to specific attacks on the underlying equation systems, require careful implementation and analysis. Nevertheless, cryptography based on multivariate polynomials remains a promising approach in PQC, especially in digital signatures.

Hash-based cryptosystem

Hash-based cryptography is an approach to PQC that bases its security entirely on cryptographically secure hash functions. These functions are difficult to reverse for both classical and quantum computers and thus provide a robust basis for cryptographic applications. One of the best-known examples of hash-based methods is Merkle tree signatures. These signatures use the structure of Merkle trees to manage a large number of one-time keys efficiently and thus create secure digital signatures.

Its simplicity and strong theoretical security characterize hash-based cryptography. Since it is based exclusively on hash functions with well-researched security, it offers a clear and comprehensible basis for cryptographic systems. Applications are mainly found in digital signatures, where they represent a quantum-safe alternative to traditional methods such as RSA or ECC.

However, hash-based cryptography also presents challenges. For example, the signature sizes can be significantly larger than those of other methods, and the number of possible signatures is limited for some methods. Nevertheless, it remains a promising approach, especially in scenarios where high security and transparency of the underlying methods are required. Hash-based methods could play an important role in post-quantum cryptography, especially in combination with other quantum-safe methods.

Isogeny-based cryptography

The isogeny-based cryptography (IBC) approach is one of the newer and most promising methods of PQC. It is based on isogenies, i.e., unique mathematical mappings between elliptic curves. These mappings preserve the basic properties of the curves but are extremely difficult to compute, especially when finding an isogeny between two given curves (Dey et al., 2022).

The underlying security of this method results from the complexity of this problem, which is challenging to solve for both classical and quantum computers. Isogeny-based cryptography thus provides a robust basis for quantum-safe key exchange methods. A well-known example is Supersingular Isogeny Key Exchange (SIKE), a method developed specifically for secure key exchange in resource-constrained environments such as the Internet of Things (IoT).

A significant advantage of isogeny-based cryptography is its efficiency. Compared to other post-quantum methods, isogeny-based methods require relatively small key sizes, making them particularly attractive for applications with limited storage space and data transfer rates. Nevertheless, there are challenges, especially in terms of implementation and protection against specific attacks that could rely on the mathematical properties of isogenies.

Despite the challenges, isogeny-based cryptography is considered promising, especially in scenarios requiring compact keys and strong security against quantum attacks. It could play a crucial role in hybrid cryptosystems that combine classical methods with quantum-safe approaches. These hybrid systems offer a promising path for a smooth transition into the post-quantum era, providing a sense of hope and optimism for the future of cryptography.

Code-based cryptosystem

Code-based cryptography is a method of post-quantum cryptography that bases its security on the difficulty of efficiently decoding specific error-correcting codes. This problem, which has long been studied in computer science and communications engineering, is considered highly complex, both for classical and quantum computers. As a result, the method provides a robust basis for secure encryption and key exchange procedures.

One prominent example is the McEliece cryptosystem, developed in the 1970s and now considered one of the most promising methods in post-quantum cryptography. The system uses linear block codes, such as Goppa codes, and uses their inherent complexity to encrypt data securely. The McEliece method is desirable due to its high resistance to known quantum attacks, including the Shor and Grover algorithms (Wang et al., 2024).

However, one disadvantage of code-based cryptography is the size of the public keys, which can be very large compared to other cryptographic methods. It poses a challenge, especially for applications with limited storage space or transmission bandwidth. Nevertheless, the method is still being intensively researched due to its efficiency and security.

Code-based cryptography plays an important role in the development of quantum-safe systems. It offers a proven and reliable alternative to traditional asymmetrical methods such as RSA and ECC. It could be used in hybrid cryptosystems to ensure security when transitioning to the post-quantum era.

The method relies on the complexity of decoding specific error correction codes and offers an alternative method for encryption and key exchange.

Symmetric algorithms with long keys

Symmetric methods with long keys are also considered part of PQC as they resist known quantum algorithms, especially the Grover algorithm. Although the Grover algorithm poses a comparatively minor threat to symmetric encryption, it speeds up the key search and thus creates potential vulnerabilities. Symmetric cryptography is based on sharing a secret key between sender and receiver and uses algorithms such as the Advanced Encryption Standard (AES) or hash functions such as SHA-3.

The Grover algorithm, a quantum mechanical search algorithm, enables quantum computers to reduce the adequate search space of a symmetric key by the root of the possible combinations. For a key with$n$ bits, the security level is therefore reduced to around n /2 bits. Longer keys can compensate for this weakening, whereby the security remains at a similar level as in classical cryptography. For example, 256-bit keys in symmetric algorithms offer sufficient security even in the quantum age.

Symmetric methods are characterized by their efficiency and simplicity. They are less computationally intensive and require smaller key sizes compared to some quantum-safe asymmetric methods. Symmetric methods are ideal for applications where large amounts of data need to be securely encrypted, such as VPNs or cloud storage services.

In the context of post-quantum cryptography, symmetric methods play an important role, especially in hybrid cryptosystems. Here, they are combined with quantum-safe asymmetric methods to ensure efficiency and security during the transition period. Despite the threat of quantum computers, symmetric cryptography with appropriately adapted key sizes remains a proven and secure component of modern cryptosystems. If PQC is supplemented by Quantum Key Distribution (QKD) networks, for example, the solution against cryptographic attacks by quantum computers is improved. QKD provides Information Theoretically Secure (IST), while PQC enables scalable authentication (Velasco et al., 2024).

These approaches use complex mathematical structures that should be difficult to crack, even for quantum computers. The challenge is to develop methods that are both secure and practical.

3.2 Standards

The publication of the first finalized standards for post-quantum cryptography by the US National Institute of Standards and Technology (NIST) on 13 August 2024 is a significant and decisive milestone. As a US federal agency, NIST is responsible for standardization processes and the development and promotion of standards and technologies. The release of these standards marks a crucial advancement in the field of cryptography.

The NIST standards, selected after a rigorous multi-year evaluation process involving cryptographers and security experts worldwide, represent a significant step forward. They provide industry with the necessary security and guidance to invest in implementing quantum-resistant processes. These standards cover algorithms for key exchange and digital signatures, offering practical solutions for various cryptographic tasks.

The NIST includes three published standards (Thanalakshmi et al., 2023; Li et al., 2023).

1. ML-KEM (also known as 'Kyber')—Key exchange

Kyber, also known as ML-KEM (Key Encapsulation Mechanism), is an innovative key exchange algorithm based on lattice-based cryptography. This type of cryptography relies on the difficulty of mathematical problems associated with lattices to ensure security

Kyber uses the Learning with Errors (LWE) problem, a complex mathematical problem that is extremely difficult to solve even for powerful quantum computers. By exploiting the properties of lattices, Kyber enables efficient and secure key exchange. Kyber is characterized by high speed and low resource requirements. It makes it ideal for applications with limited computing resources or bandwidth. The keys and encrypted data used with Kyber are relatively small. It is a great advantage, especially for devices with limited storage space. Kyber can be easily integrated into existing systems as it is compatible with common cryptography standards. Compared to other approaches, such as code-based cryptography, Kyber offers more compact data structures but remains similarly secure against quantum attacks.

Kyber is also well suited for integrating existing systems and balances security, speed, and memory requirements. Compared to approaches such as isogeny-based cryptography, which is also used for key exchange, Kyber is significantly faster and less complex to implement (Li et al., 2023).

2. ML-DSA (also known as 'Dilithium')—Signature

Dilithium is an algorithm for digital signatures based on lattice-based cryptography, specifically on the Learning with Errors (LWE) and Short Integer Solution (SIS) problems. It offers a combination of high security and efficiency, whereby the signature sizes and the computing resources required for verification are moderate (Wang et al., 2024).

Dilithium's security is based on SVP and Learning with Errors (LWE), a double dependency that strengthens resilience against classical and quantum adversaries. Studies show that Dilithium maintains a robust security margin against various attack vectors, including those arising from advanced quantum algorithms such as the Grover and Shor algorithms. Continued refinement of Dilithium's security parameters is essential to ensure its resilience against evolving threats in the quantum computing landscape (Wang et al., 2024).

The latest version of Dilithium is a testament to the continuous improvement in post-quantum cryptography. It can create signatures in about 15 ms and verify them within 2-3 ms, making it not only competitive in theoretical frameworks but also highly practical for applications such as blockchain technology and digital identity verification.

Compared to other signature solutions, such as those based on hash-based cryptography (e.g., Merkle tree signatures), Dilithium offers a more practical solution for general applications. There is no limit to the number of signatures, and the key size remains manageable. The public key structure of Crystals-Dilithium enables bidirectional authentication of both the certificate authority and the user (Alam et al., 2024). Dilithium is particularly suitable for high-speed applications like IoT environments or real-time secure communication.

Despite its remarkable potential, the signature size of Dilithium remains a concern, especially in scenarios that require compact signatures, such as mobile devices and embedded systems. Overcoming this challenge is crucial for the broader adoption of Dilithium in various applications (Wang et al., 2024).

3. SLH-DSA (also known as 'Sphinx+')—Signature

Sphinx+ is a signature system based on hash-based cryptography. Its security relies on the robustness of cryptographic hash functions. It is particularly suitable for scenarios in which long-term security is required, such as archiving systems or digital certificates. Compared to Dilithium, the signatures and keys in Sphinx+ are more extensive, but it offers a proven and highly transparent security basis, as hash functions are well-researched.

Sphinx+ is particularly valuable for applications that prioritize transparency and provable security. However, compared to lattice-based approaches such as Dilithium, it is less flexible and less efficient for applications that require high speed or low data volumes.

Two of the standards (ML-KEM and ML-DSA) were co-developed by cryptography researchers from IBM Research in Zurich. The third specification (SLH-DSA) was developed by a scientist who has since moved to IBM Research.

Compared to the six PQC approaches presented in Section 3.2, the three NIST standards are categorized as follows (Thanalakshmi et al., 2023):

- Lattice-based cryptography: Kyber and Dilithium belong to this category and exploit the inherent difficulty of problems in high-dimensional lattices. They are remarkably versatile and efficient and currently dominate the PQC landscape.
- Code-based cryptography: Although robust and proven, the larger key sizes are a disadvantage compared to Kyber.
- Hash-based cryptography: Sphinx+ represents this category and offers high security but suffers from larger signatures and limited flexibility.
- Isogeny-based cryptography: This approach offers compact keys and is attractive for key exchange but remains more complex to implement and slower than Kyber.
- Multivariate polynomials: These methods are well suited for digital signatures but are less versatile than lattice-based approaches.
- Symmetric methods with long keys: These can be used universally but usually in combination with quantum-safe asymmetric methods such as Kyber or Dilithium.

To standardize PQC algorithms, NIST announced open calls for developing quantum-resistant public key cryptography assets such as digital signatures and certificates.

While computer scientists believe that classical computers are practically incapable of factorizing numbers more significant than 2048 bits, researchers have shown that a cryptographically relevant quantum computer could crack RSA-2048 within a few hours by applying the Shor algorithm. The PQC standards are based on the complex mathematics of polynomial lattices and hash functions. Cracking them would be daunting even for the most potent cryptographically relevant quantum computer of the future. An additional advantage of PQC algorithms is their efficiency. Algorithms based on lattices, if properly designed, are more efficient than the algorithms used today. They are larger than classical cryptography, but their runtime is faster than classical algorithms based on discrete, larger RSA or elliptic curves.

Nevertheless, PQCs are exposed to mathematical attacks and so-called side-channel attacks (SCA). Shaller et al. (2023) provides a comprehensive overview of SCAs' threats in PQC algorithms. Such SCAs can be power, timing, fault injection, and electromagnetic attacks. All PQC algorithms are potentially vulnerable to SCAs, as these attacks exploit physical characteristics such as power consumption or runtime. Timing attacks and fault injections are particularly critical, as they can be carried out with little effort. Finally, the authors discuss approaches to minimize these security risks, such as masking, obfuscation, and randomization. Masking and randomization strategies are effective against many SCAs but often lead to increased computational and memory requirements. This line of research is particularly relevant as SCA attacks the implementations of cryptographic algorithms and can be successful regardless of their mathematical foundations.

Kim et al. (2024) introduce an efficient quantum-safe blockchain that integrates new consensus algorithms. They integrate the Falcon signature scheme into the blockchain's transaction signing and verification processes to increase resilience against quantum attacks. Although integrating the post-quantum signature scheme reduces the transactions per second (TPS) of the blockchain (TPSs), they recommend efficient approaches to mitigate this performance degradation. Our proposed Post-Quantum-Delegated-Proof-of-Luck (PQ-DPoL) combines a Proof-of-Luck (PoL) mechanism with a delegated approach that ensures quantum resilience, energy efficiency, and fairness in block generation. The PQ-DPoL algorithm effectively balances security and performance. It provides a viable solution for secure blockchain operations in a post-quantum era.

The biggest challenge is to put the developed quantum-safe methods into practice and test their suitability for everyday use (Section 5). Developers such as Google, Cloudflare, and Genoa have tested their quantum-safe methods in detail, such as experiments in the laboratory and on the Internet under realistic conditions. The first PQC procedures, such as Genua's quantum-safe product updates, have already been implemented. However, many procedures are still not beyond the experimental stage. It is, therefore, still completely unclear what will happen when all parties in a network or the entire Internet suddenly exchange, store, and process their data using quantum-safe methods. However, IT decision-makers will have to take this risk.

4. CHALLENGES

In anticipation of the new PQC standards, organizations and governments worldwide have adopted a proactive approach, establishing timelines and guidelines for quantum-safe migration. For instance, the White House issued a National Security Memorandum (NSM-10) in May 2022, outlining how US authorities will transition to the new standards. Shortly after, Congress passed the Quantum Computing Cybersecurity Preparedness Act, mandating federal agencies to create an inventory of quantum-vulnerable cryptosystems for the transition. The Commercial National Security Algorithm Suite 2.0, a recommendation provided by the US National Security Agency in response to these agencies, has set a deadline of 2035 for national security systems to complete the quantum-safe migration.

The European Telecommunications Standards Institute (ETSI) and the European Union Agency for Cyber Security (ENISA) have played a pivotal role in promoting PQC. Their collaborative efforts have encouraged European organizations to consider adopting and implementing the standards. Several European countries, including France, Germany, Austria, and the UK, are planning to adopt or use the NIST standards, further demonstrating the unity and shared responsibility in this global transition.

NIST has encouraged organizations to plan and prepare for the quantum-safe transition in advance. However, the formal publication of the standards gives organizations the certainty and guidance they need to transition to post-quantum cryptography. In addition, previous cryptographic migrations have taken nearly 20 years, and the quantum-safe cryptographic migration is more complex than previous migrations, as many security protocols need to be redeveloped and infrastructure updated. To manage the migration to minimize business disruption and associated costs, organizations need to develop a strategy for quantum-safe transformation now and begin a gradual transition to the new standards.

Despite all the progress, companies and organizations face considerable challenges when switching to quantum-resistant cryptography. Many new post-quantum algorithms require more computing power or longer key lengths than traditional methods. It can lead to performance losses and may require adjustments to the existing infrastructure. In addition, the new algorithms must be extensively tested and analyzed to identify and rule out potential vulnerabilities.

The Keysight Inspector test platform can be used to test devices to test implementations of the Dilithium algorithm, one of the PQC algorithms selected by NIST. Developers using this algorithm in hardware could use it to verify that their products are secure against these threats. The test solution is also required for government institutions and security test laboratories that want to check the security of third-party products. In addition, the Keysight Inspector can test the chips and analyze the design before implementation by simulating the hardware code before semiconductor manufacturing. Riscure has collaborated with PQShield, a PQC solutions developer, to perform pre-and post-silicon analysis of their products.

The cryptography community must ensure that new methods are robust against classical and quantum-based attacks. This is not just a goal, but a necessity in the face of evolving cyber threats. Cryptographic protocols must also be adapted for different use cases, including advanced protocols such as secure multi-party computation or zero-knowledge proofs, to ensure comprehensive protection.

Some security experts temporarily advocate using hybrid solutions that combine traditional and quantum-resistant methods. These hybrid approaches are intended to ensure systems are armed against current and future threats. For example, the quantum-safe hybrid encryption protocol TutaCrypt is combined with a post-quantum key encapsulation mechanism (CRYSTALS-Kyber) and an elliptic-curve Diffie-Hellmann key exchange (x25519). However, implementing such hybrid systems brings challenges, especially regarding compatibility and the management of different cryptographic primitives. These challenges include the need for additional resources to manage and maintain multiple cryptographic systems, potential interoperability issues, and the complexity of ensuring that all components of the hybrid system are secure against both classical and quantum-based attacks.

DigiCert and the Ponemon Institute (2023) surveyed 1,426 IT and IT security professionals in the US (605), EMEA (428), and Asia-Pacific (393) who are concerned with the impact of post-quantum cryptography on their organizations. 61 percent of respondents say their organizations have not addressed the security implications of PQC. Almost half of respondents (49%) also stated that their organization's executives are only slightly (26%) or not at all (23%) aware of the security implications of quantum computing. Only 30 percent of respondents state that their companies allocate budgets for PQC readiness. Fifty-two percent of respondents state that their companies are currently conducting an inventory of the cryptographic methods and processes used.

One of the study's key findings is that IT security teams must balance proactively defending their organizations against cyberattacks and preparing for a post-quantum computing future. However, only 50 percent of respondents say their organizations effectively mitigate risks, vulnerabilities, and attacks across the enterprise. Ransomware and credential theft are two of the most common cyberattacks.

In the study, 41 percent of participants stated that their company had less than five years to implement PQC successfully but lacked the time, money, and expertise to do so. Accordingly, only 30 percent of respondents had separate budgets for PQC readiness (DigiCert & Ponemon Institute, 2023).

Many companies are unaware of their cryptographic keys' characteristics and storage locations. Only half of those surveyed (52 percent) confirmed that their company keeps an inventory of the types of cryptographic keys used and their properties. Only 39 percent of respondents say they prioritize cryptographic resources, and only 36 percent know whether this data is stored locally or in the cloud.

Few companies have a centralized crypto management strategy consistently applied across the entire company. A centralized crypto management strategy is crucial for ensuring that cryptographic resources are used effectively and securely across the organization. Sixty-one percent of respondents said their organizations had only a limited crypto management strategy, restricted to specific applications or use cases (36 percent). Twenty-five percent of the organizations surveyed lacked one altogether (DigiCert & Ponemon Institute, 2023). This highlights the need for organizations to develop and implement comprehensive crypto management strategies that cover all aspects of cryptographic security, from key management to algorithm selection and implementation.

Companies must implement cryptographic solutions and methods to protect information resources and IT infrastructures more effectively. However, most respondents admit that their organizations cannot enforce best practices and policies across the enterprise or detect and respond to certificate/key misuse. Furthermore, algorithm errors, security breaches, and unwanted certificates cannot be corrected.

Companies recognize that they lack the expertise to meet post-quantum requirements actively. The recruitment and retention of qualified personnel is a top strategic priority for digital security, according to 55 percent of the study participants. For 51 percent of respondents, achieving crypto-agility - the ability to efficiently update cryptographic algorithms, parameters, processes, and technologies - is a key requirement to better respond to new protocols, standards, and security threats, including the use of quantum computing methods (DigiCert & Ponemon Institute, 2023).

To prepare for the quantum computing era, companies need a comprehensive strategy ranging from management support and transparency in using cryptographic keys and IT assets to centralized crypto management strategies. This approach must be applied consistently throughout the company with clear responsibilities and accountabilities.

Despite all the challenges, companies must take immediate action to prepare for the quantum age. A systematic approach is crucial. The suggestions presented here are based on the technical guidelines of the German Federal Office for Information Security (2024).

- Inventory: A thorough inventory of all potentially vulnerable systems and data is the first step. Every organization should review its processes to determine how quantum computing will affect the key public cryptography systems in use
- Criticality: After taking stock, organizations should be sorted according to their criticality level to be upgraded or replaced accordingly. It raises some crucial questions: Who issued the certificates? When do they expire? Which domains do they protect, and which algorithms are used? With this knowledge, IT managers can decide which encryption algorithms to replace. It makes sense to start updating the cryptographic infrastructure with the most important sub-areas for long-term trust. These include, for example, internal certification authorities or long-lasting devices.
- Risk assessment: Based on the inventory, a detailed risk assessment should be carried out to analyze the potential impact of a quantum attack on critical business processes and sensitive data. This analysis should also take into account regulatory requirements and potential reputational damage.
- Develop a migration strategy: Based on the risk assessment, companies should develop a comprehensive plan for the gradual transition to quantum-resistant processes. This strategy should set clear priorities, allocate resources, and set realistic timelines.
- Skills development: In parallel to technical planning, companies must invest in building specialist knowledge. Training in post-quantum cryptography and the associated technologies is essential to overcome the transition's challenges.
- Technology monitoring: Continuous monitoring of technological developments is essential. Companies should allocate resources to track advances in quantum computing technology and quantum-resistant processes and adapt their strategies accordingly.
- Cryptographic agility: Companies are well advised to focus on cryptographic agility—the ability to efficiently update cryptographic algorithms, parameters, processes, and technologies—and implement flexible security architectures that enable rapid switching between different algorithms. This facilitates the transition to post-quantum methods and makes systems more resistant to future cryptographic threats.
- Collaboration and exchange: The transition to quantum-resistant cryptography is a cross-industry challenge. Ideally, companies should actively seek exchange with other organizations, research institutions, and standardization bodies to benefit from experience and develop best practices.

The transition to quantum-resistant cryptography is not just a technical challenge but a task of importance to society. Close cooperation between companies, research institutions, standardization bodies, and political decision-makers is required to develop robust and practical solutions and implement them broadly.

5. CONCLUSION

The recent cyberattacks on encrypted systems using quantum computers show that new developments in quantum computing research must be taken seriously. Especially in security-critical sectors, such as banking or military facilities, measures are needed to address future threats from quantum computers. Security researchers have been investigating the possibility of quantum computers cracking traditional encryption methods for some time. However, the recent breakthrough demonstrates the potential of this technology worryingly. The challenges posed by the development of quantum computers affect not only cryptography but many other IT security areas. Researching and implementing post-quantum cryptography is becoming increasingly important, i.e., cryptographic methods resistant to quantum computers. These new encryption methods must be designed in such a way that they can withstand attacks by quantum computers (Chawla & Mehra, 2023).

However, the development and implementation of post-quantum encryption requires time and resources. Many companies and government organizations still rely on traditional cryptographic systems, the security of which will be questioned in the coming years by advances in quantum computing. However, NIST experts predict that RSA algorithms used for secrecy will be insecure by 2030. The US and Europe, in particular, are already investing in post-quantum encryption technologies to ensure the integrity of their security-critical infrastructures

PQC, in turn, refers to a subfield of cryptography that deals with cryptographic primitives that are practically impossible to decrypt even using quantum computers. As standardization progresses, dozens of new security algorithms are expected to become available for various applications and industries. Ultimately, these algorithms will require verifiable implementations.

The NIST standards ML-KEM (Kyber), ML-DSA (Dilithium), and SLH-DSA (Sphinx+) cover a wide range of cryptographic applications and rely on proven robust mathematical problems. They provide a solid foundation for implementing quantum secure systems and are superior to other PQC approaches, especially regarding efficiency, flexibility, and practical applicability. Research is still needed to optimize the security and efficiency of PQC algorithms and adapt them for different use cases.

The PQC methods highlight the crucial importance of resilience to quantum attacks and operational efficiency. As researchers continue to work on these systems' theoretical foundations and practical implementations, the future of secure digital communications will increasingly hinge on integrating post-quantum solutions into everyday technologies. The shift to quantum-resistant cryptography is not just important, it is inevitable. This transition will require the development of new algorithms and a comprehensive understanding of their impact in real-world scenarios to ensure they can meet society's evolving security needs in a post-quantum world. Organizations must act now to protect their digital infrastructure and prepare for a new era of cybersecurity.

However, many organizations today are not in a position to say where keys or security certificates are used in the company. Around 30 percent are undetected or not on the screen. In any case, replacing existing procedures is time-consuming and expensive and cannot be done at the touch of a button. However, 'forgetting' cryptographic security mechanisms is fatal in the case of quantum computers, which are used to attack secrets.

Depending on the threat, a combination of continuous asset visibility, efficient methods for deploying cryptographic technologies, and rapid responsiveness to security issues is required. According to the NIST recommendation, the focus should inevitably be on maintaining cryptographic agility because no replacement for the standardized public key algorithms is yet available.

For this reason, implementing quantum-safe processes cannot be accomplished in a short rush. Above all, organizations should start thinking about the quantum migration of their IT now. The longer they wait, the greater the potential for damage. Therefore, the following should be done:

- The starting point for this process is the thorough mapping of quantum vulnerabilities of deployed certificates across the data ecosystem. Organizations can deploy scalable and automated certificate lifecycle management tools with this knowledge base.

- The quantum migration-related need for change in the IT landscape must then be examined and analyzed.
- Also, the relevant PQC solutions from experienced manufacturers will be examined, and their suitability for everyday use is theoretically scrutinized.
- Finally, these must be implemented successively and checked for possible impairments to the use and performance of the IT landscape.
- The PQC changeover is facilitated by automated workflows that reduce both the error rate and operating costs. This step is the prerequisite for fast and uninterrupted provision of quantum-safe certificates.

IT decision-makers are playing a crucial role in the quantum migration process. They are not just behind schedule, but they are also the ones who must keep abreast of developments, analyze their situation, and finally plan and implement their transition—without exposing ongoing business operations to significant risks. PQC algorithms and crypto-agility are the keys to ensuring that assets such as data remain permanently protected.

REFERENCES

Alam, M., Hoffstein, J., & Cambou, B. (2024). Privately generated key pairs for post quantum cryptography in a distributed network. *Applied Sciences (Basel, Switzerland)*, 14(19), 8863. DOI: 10.3390/app14198863

Chawla, D., & Mehra, P. S. (2023). A roadmap from classical cryptography to post-quantum resistant cryptography for 5G-enabled IoT: Challenges, opportunities and solutions. *Internet of Things : Engineering Cyber Physical Human Systems*, 24, 100950. DOI: 10.1016/j.iot.2023.100950

Dey, K., Debnath, S. K., Stănică, P., & Srivastava, V. (2022). A post-quantum signcryption scheme using isogeny-based cryptography. *Journal of Information Security and Applications*, 69, 103280. DOI: 10.1016/j.jisa.2022.103280

DigiCert & Ponemon Institute. (2023). Preparing for a safe post quantum computing future. https://www.digicert.com/content/dam/digicert/pdfs/report/ponemon-preparing-safe-post-quantum-future-report-en-v1.pdf

European Commission. (2024). Commission recommendation of 11.4.2024 on a coordinated implementation roadmap for the transition to post-quantum cryptography. https://ec.europa.eu/newsroom/dae/redirection/document/104249

Federal Office for Information Security. (2024). Technical guideline TR-02102-2: Cryptographic mechanisms recommendations and key lengths. https://www.bsi.bund.de/SharedDocs/Downloads/EN/BSI/Publications/TechGuidelines/TG02102/BSI-TR-02102-2.pdf

Kim, H., Kim, W., Kang, Y., Kim, H., & Seo, H. (2024). Post-quantum delegated proof of luck for blockchain consensus algorithm. *Applied Sciences (Basel, Switzerland)*, 14(18), 8394. DOI: 10.3390/app14188394

Kumar, M. (2022). Post-quantum cryptography Algorithm's standardization and performance analysis. *Array (New York, N.Y.)*, 15, 100242. DOI: 10.1016/j.array.2022.100242

Li, S., Chen, Y., Chen, L., Liao, J., Kuang, C., Li, K., Liang, W., & Xiong, N. (2023). Post-quantum security: Opportunities and challenges. *Sensors (Basel)*, 23(21), 8744. DOI: 10.3390/s23218744 PMID: 37960442

National Institute of Standards and Technology (NIST). (2024). Announcing Issuance of Federal Information Processing Standards (FIPS) FIPS 203, Module-Lattice-Based Key-Encapsulation Mechanism Standard, FIPS 204, Module-Lattice-Based Digital Signature Standard, and FIPS 205, Stateless Hash-Based Digital Signature Standard. https://www.govinfo.gov/content/pkg/FR-2024-08-14/pdf/2024-17956.pdf

Shaller, A., Zamir, L., & Nojoumian, M. (2023). Roadmap of post-quantum cryptography standardization: Side-channel attacks and countermeasures. *Information and Computation, 295. Information and Computation*, 105112, 105112. Advance online publication. DOI: 10.1016/j.ic.2023.105112

Song, G., Jang, K., Eum, S., Sim, M., & Seo, H. (2023). NTT and inverse NTT Quantum circuits in CRYSTALS-Kyber for post-quantum security evaluation. *Applied Sciences (Basel, Switzerland)*, 13(18), 10373. DOI: 10.3390/app131810373

Thanalakshmi, P., Rishikhesh, A., Marion Marceline, J., Joshi, G. P., & Cho, W. (2023). A quantum-resistant blockchain system: A comparative analysis. *Mathematics*, 11(18), 3947. DOI: 10.3390/math11183947

Velasco, L., Ahmadian, M., Ortiz, L., Brito, J. P., Pastor, A., Rivas, J. M., Barzegar, S., Comellas, J., Martin, V., & Ruiz, M. (2024). Scenarios for optical encryption using quantum keys. *Sensors (Basel)*, 24(20), 6631. DOI: 10.3390/s24206631 PMID: 39460111

Wang, Y., Li, L., Zhou, Y., & Zhang, H. (2024). A comprehensive review of MI-HFE and IPHFE cryptosystems: Advances in internal perturbations for post-quantum security. *Axioms*, 13(11), 741. DOI: 10.3390/axioms13110741

Yalamuri, G., Honnavalli, P., & Eswaran, S. (2022). A review of the present cryptographic arsenal to deal with post-quantum threats. *Procedia Computer Science*, 215, 834–845. DOI: 10.1016/j.procs.2022.12.086

Chapter 12
Data Security With Replication for Cloud Computing

Cigdem Bakir
https://orcid.org/0000-0001-8482-2412
Dumlupinar University, Turkey

Mecit Yüzkat
Presidency of Turkish Health Institutes, Turkey

ABSTRACT

Cloud computing is an advanced technology that provides access to different services via the internet. These services include applications such as servers, networking, data storage, databases, and software. Instead of storing files on local storage device, cloud-based storage makes it possible to store files in a secure database. As long as an electronic device has access to the web, it has access to data and the software programs to run it. For this reason, this technology is very popular for institutions and individuals for many reasons such as cost, production, efficiency and speed. However, with the advantages of cloud computing, some security risks also arise. At the beginning of these security risks are data breaches and data losses caused by malicious software applications. In this study, data replication is discussed in order to solve security breaches in cloud computing technologies.

INTRODUCTION

Nowadays, the size and variety of data produced is increasing rapidly. People prefer platforms where they can access online rather than physical storage devices, so that the access to this increasing data is more efficient and secure. Cloud computing, which enables storage, backup and data control-management via remote internet, meets these needs of people. When the cloud is mentioned, it can be briefly called the transfer of computer resources to virtual networks and platforms. The content of data and applications that can be stored in the cloud may contain information that may have low security concerns, as well as very sensitive data (social security numbers, medical records, private personal information or government data). It is important to know the methods to be used to ensure the security of these data and applications, (Al Hachemi, 2022). In this study, it is mentioned how to ensure the confidentiality, integrity and availability of the cloud with data replication. In order to help the content of the study,

DOI: 10.4018/979-8-3693-9919-4.ch012

other articles on the subject were examined and data replication on platforms with cloud features and the protection of individuals or companies' shares, private information, applications and the benefits it provides to the user are shown.

Data replication is the backup of the data accumulated in the environment during the process, or a certain part of it, in more than one location, (Mansouri, Javidi, & Zade, 2021). It is the process of transferring all the transactions made by all users in the system to another source without causing any inconsistency. In this system, data moves according to the wishes of the person and two different users can perform their duties without interfering with each other's work. In short, data replication is the ability of data to move freely without creating confusion in the internet environment. In this way, all transactions are replicated and the update is performed simultaneously on all the replicated data.

Data replication is not a static backup of data. It ensures replication of transactions, such that backups are in a consistently updated state and synchronized with the source, (Miloudi, Yagoubi, & Bellounar, 2021). There are different methods of performing replication operations, depending on the specific availability requirements for the data. Problems with data replication can result from data transfer delays or service interruptions. Commercial data replication products attempt to mitigate business risk due to replication errors or failures.

There are various data replication tools used today. For example; Oracle GoldenGate is a comprehensive tool that enables data replication between both Oracle and non-Oracle data stores. Another example of real-time data replication, DBMoto, provides fast data transfer between databases.

Data replication ensures that data is securely protected in different environments. It provides a fast and accurate return on queries performed on the database. It allows authorized users to access the data. This increases usability in all transactions. High performance is provided. However, despite all these positive aspects, data replication can create complex structures by requiring additional storage areas because it copies a lot of data. For this reason, it may require more cost.

Rapidly increasing data and applications have increased the usage rate of cloud platforms a lot compared to previous years. The security of data stored in the cloud is important for many people. In this study, the importance of data replication for data security in cloud computing is emphasized. It also demonstrates how the three key elements of cloud security (availability, integrity and confidentiality) are ensured by data replication. In this study, data security methods have been shown with some definitions and examples, and it has been concluded that it would be beneficial for the individual or corporate environment to use cloud platforms to use these methods. Emphasizing that businesses providing cloud computing services and customers using this service should pay great attention to security for both parties, some methods are included.

RELATED WORKS

Within the scope of this study, different scientific publications on data replication in cloud computing in recent years have been examined and the results of these studies are given in detail below:

Based on the rapid development of big data and cloud technology in recent years, there has been an increasing demand to process and analyze data produced and stored in geographically dispersed data centers. However, collecting data and performing calculations in a single data center is becoming increasingly inefficient due to the limited network bandwidth between data centers and the data volume spread over different areas. Convolbo et al., with the DRASH (Data Replication Awake Timer) method they developed in their work, used data replication to prevent unnecessary data transfer in a job planning and increase overall system performance, (Convolbo *et al.*, 2016). As a result of the evaluations using simulations with realistic workloads, they found that the DRASH method outperforms other existing approaches. DRASH performed significantly better in average job completion time than other available methods. They also achieved further improvement under high data duplication factors.

Reliable access to data is the foundation of most information technology services. High availability, low operating cost and data consistency creates major problems in almost every data replication research. Usman et al. referred to a data replication strategy called semantic data replication (SDR) in their study. SDR aims at low cost high processing capabilities built on data semantics, coding schemes and efficient search algorithms, (Usman, Schadek, & Theel, 2017). SDR primarily takes advantage of the finite state space introduced by the encoding scheme for replicated objects. It also makes the replication strategy more efficient by using the previous information obtained from the finite state space. Leveraging the data encoding sketch has made a significant contribution to SDR as the encoding sketch runs fast in reads and writes. It also provides consistent access to the state of the replicated object for read operations.

When outsourcing data in the cloud information system, high security measures are required as it can be modified by illegal users or attackers. This can affect the performance of the cloud due to the longer data acquisition time. The time of data acquisition should be taken into account when implementing security measures. Salunkhe et al. sought to solve both problems by deploying them on cloud nodes. Cloud nodes only store a portion of the file that is split into multiple parts. In the study, cloud nodes are set at a certain distance that the attacker cannot follow the next node using the concept of T-coloring, (. File fragments are replicated onto cloud nodes to improve the retrieval time of file fragments. To increase the security standard, the fragmented file is encrypted before it is placed on the cloud node. An audit scheme is used that constantly monitors cloud nodes. In case of any damage, the control system regenerates the data. This system provides security and control of cloud data.

The traditional way to achieve high data availability in a structured P2P network is to replicate data items held in one node to neighboring nodes. However, in some heterogeneous structural P2P networks, neighboring nodes are always close to each other in location. Therefore, permanent loss of some data may be inevitable in case of some local disasters. Moreover, this traditional data replication strategy entails moving data when there are node ingress and egress in a complex Distributed Hash Tables (DHT) network. Wang et al. proposed a new data replication strategy for heterogeneous structural P2P networks. This has greatly reduced the complexity of not only maintaining large-scale local disaster data items, but also data migration whenever nodes enter and exit the network, that is, when new nodes are added to the system or when nodes leave the system, (Wang *et al.,* 2009).

Data duplication and synchronization techniques have recently attracted the attention of researchers working in this field. Data transferred during replication must be secure. The protocol is one of the ways to ensure security before sending information to an external copy site. When comparing the two existing protocol types, TCP and UDP, the UDP protocol type is claimed to be faster during data transfer than TCP. The main reason for this is that UDP does not use excessive confirmation messages. UDP is the preferred option when bandwidth is limited. In their study, Soyjaudah et al. discussed the reliability of the UDP protocol when measuring packets in sending packets of different lengths. It is desired to determine whether the UDP protocol can be used as a transfer mode during data replication. A series of tests have been performed and the Maximum Transmission Unit (CPU) size has been adjusted to have minimal packet loss. As a result, the authors have obtained the information that the UDP protocol with the size of 1150 bytes can be used as a transport mode for data centers, (Soyjaudah, Catherine, & Coonjah, 2016).

Mansouri developed an adaptive replication strategy model in cloud computing in order to increase data availability, provide fast data processing time and reliability, (Mansouri, 2016). In the author's work, if all the replicated data and requests are correct and distributed, the replication process realizes the successful processing time in cloud computing. This convenient processing time is however much more complex for large-scale, dynamic and virtualized data centers. For this reason, in the study, cost-effective replication process and adaptive data replication strategy that will minimize application and work times has been proposed for very large data centers. The proposed model consists of five stages such as average service time, calculation of failure probability, load variance, delay and storage usage. In the study, data replication has been done in a logical way and a recommendation model has been presented that will enable the replacement of newly created copies depending on the use of the files. Using this model CloudSim simulator, the number of accesses is evaluated according to the replication size and the results are presented. This proposed model was compared with the ARS, DRSP, CIR and CDRM algorithms used in the literature in the simulation environment, and the results were interpreted according to the criteria of average response time, effective network usage, storage usage, replication frequency and load variance.

Data replication algorithms are divided into static and dynamic. In static replication, replication is predetermined and well defined. In dynamic replication, on the other hand, the replication process is automatically identified and duplicates are automatically deleted according to changing access patterns. Both of these data replication algorithms are classified by grouping them into distributed and centralized algorithms. Sun et al. developed a dynamic data replication model in order to ensure data security and data availability among users in cloud computing environments. By increasing the usability, this model reduces the false copying process and error rate that occurs during data replication, thus ensuring a highly effective and efficient interaction between users. In the study, it was aimed to reduce the waiting time of the users and to increase the data access speed with data replication, (Sun *et al.,* 2012). Duplications created on data centers with dynamic data replication are mathematically formulated. Execution time and cloud computing bandwidth are minimized. The trigger times of missing copies and duplication processes were calculated. Copies are conveniently placed within the data nodes, and when a certain threshold value is passed, data replication operations are triggered. In addition, the applicability of this study is presented with an experimental study and the obtained data are shown comparatively.

Lin et al. have proposed a QoS (different quality of service) based data replication model and minimum-cost maximum-flow (MCMF) models in order to scale the increasing data in cloud computing and to prevent changes in the errors that occur in the data. The main idea behind this model is intuitive QoS-based replication. In addition, this study has been developed to solve the flow problem in networks for systems with very dense data. With this proposed greedy algorithm, data replication cost is reduced and QoS-based data replication is performed securely without causing data loss. With the MCMF algorithm used in this study, the polynomial analysis time and the computation time of data replication are reduced. In addition, since cloud computing systems contain many nodes, node aggregation techniques have been proposed to reduce these nodes and increase performance, (Lin, Chen, & Chang, 2013). QoS has increased the heterogeneity of devices in cloud computing for secure and accurate data replication. Data replication compatible with QoS has been taken into account. The MCMF algorithm is proposed to best solve the QADR problem. The computational complexity that occurs during data replication is tried to be solved. Node combinations are used for very large data.

CLOUD COMPUTING

Cloud computing is explained as a service model used for information technologies and services, which requires low-scale management and can be accessed flexibly when needed, (Tamimi, Dawood, & Sadaqa, 2019) (Information Week, 2013). To make a general definition on the basis of this definition, cloud computing is based on the principle of using the required storage areas and processing unit power as much as needed, as well as allowing remote access of data in a controlled manner, where infrastructure and applications are processed independently from each other, and capacity usage is flexible. It is a type of informatics where, thanks to its structure, it can be increased or decreased rapidly, the use of resources can be easily controlled and reported. Cloud computing resources are shown in Figure 1. Access is provided from many devices and applications such as computers, laptops, smartphones, servers, etc. with internet connection.

Figure 1. Cloud computing source

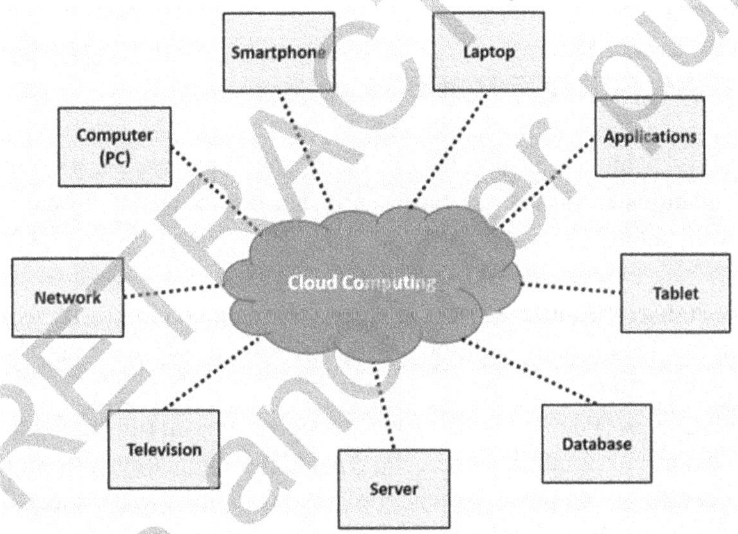

In order to conserve resources, reduce costs and maintain efficiency, cloud service providers often store the data of multiple customers on the same server without separating them, (Haghighat, Zonouz, & Abdel-Mottaleb, 2015). A user's private data may be viewed by other users. Therefore, to handle such vulnerabilities, cloud service providers must provide appropriate data isolation and logical storage separation, (Srivastava & Khan, 2018).

In order to ensure the security of data in cloud computing, it is important to note that the effective security measure in the data security part of the study covers some or all of the three categories (accessibility, integrity and confidentiality). For example, encryption prevents unauthorized access and ultimately ensures the confidentiality, availability and integrity of data. Similarly, backups mostly define data integrity and firewalls used only cover privacy and access controllability, (Tahirkheli *et al.*, 2021) (Yu *et al.*, 2010).

Security concerns associated with cloud computing; It can be classified as security problems that cloud service providers, customers using cloud platforms, organizations that host applications or store data in the cloud may encounter, (Shirgaonkar *et al.,* 2022). The cloud service provider must be able to assure the customer that its infrastructure is secure and that its customers' stored data and applications are protected. Customers, on the other hand, need to use strong passwords and authentication, taking measures to strengthen their data and applications, (Cai *et al.*, 2019).

When an organization or individual chooses to store data or store applications in the public cloud, they lose physical access to the servers that host their information. For these reasons, sensitive data may be at risk from attacks. According to the Cloud Security Alliance (2010) report, insider attacks are one of the biggest threats in cloud computing, (NIST, 2013). Therefore, cloud service providers must ensure that extensive background checks are performed for employees who have physical access to servers in the data center. In addition, frequent monitoring of data centers is recommended to prevent suspicious activity.

Data replication has been proposed to minimize the loss of important data of users as a result of possible attacks in cloud computing. Thus, in case of data invasion, users' access to their original data is provided by data replication.

CLOUD COMPUTING SERVICE MODELS

Cloud computing service models are divided into three groups: software as a service (SaaS), platform as a service (PaaS), and infrastructure as a service (IaaS). The definitions of these three different service models are briefly given below:

- **Software As A Services (SaaS)**: Users can access the data and applications they want over the internet without the need for any additional application or software. Examples of this are e-mail services, ERP applications.
- **Platform As A Services (PaaS):** In this service model, users can run applications they create. By renting a Java platform on Windows, users can create Java applications. In short, with this service model, many users can develop and present applications on the same project. This service model includes the entire technological infrastructure.
- **Infrastructure As A Services (IaaS):** Users provide their own network equipment, processors and applications through physical servers that are available. Users rent these physical servers according to their wishes and make the payment as much as they want. Users can use this service model in applications that require huge processor performance, such as big data applications. Users retain the right to access the applications and operating system on these physical servers. All updates are the responsibility of the user.

Cloud computing service models are the combination of some services by service providers according to the needs of the customers. Suggesting a suitable cloud service model for that user is of great importance for the success of the services of the people who will use the cloud. When the traditional information technology (Traditional IT) concept and cloud technology service models are compared, they all have different authorizations and shares. Figure 2 shows which services are managed by whom.

Figure 2. Cloud computing service models

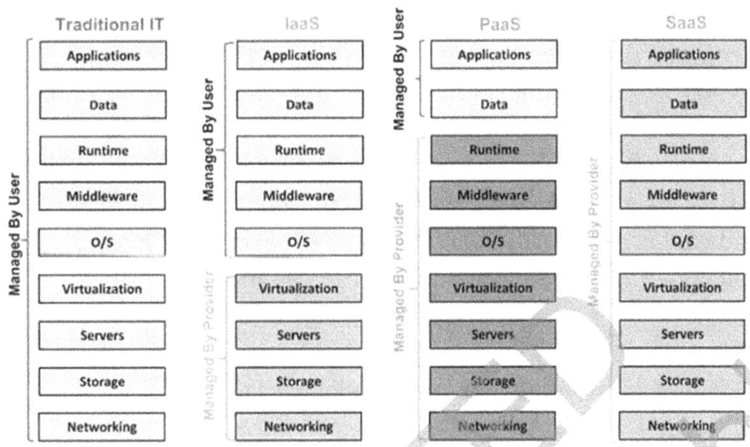

CLOUD COMPUTING INSTALLATION MODELS

Cloud services during the installation of cloud platforms; It can be classified into four groups as Public Cloud, Private Cloud, Hybrid Cloud and Community Cloud.

Public Cloud: This cloud deployment model is delivered and managed to customers through servers in internet networks. In addition, this installation model includes the basic structure of the cloud system. It is for all users and users pay as much as they use. Cloud services are provided by resources or services connected to a data center. Although institutions and organizations do not transfer their applications to the public cloud due to security vulnerabilities, users can make their applications more usable thanks to the public cloud. For example, institutions and organizations can adapt applications such as data that cannot be kept confidential, web, e-mail, virtual document sharing in the public cloud more easily. For such reasons, public cloud has advantages such as ease of use, flexibility, scalability, cost and reliability.

Private Cloud: This cloud model is built on data centers housed within the scope of a business or organization. It is a very old and frequently used classic model. Institutions undertake all operations, from infrastructure to software, to maintenance and management of systems. Private cloud provides more control, flexibility and energy efficiency than other cloud models. But aside from these benefits, it doesn't scale as well as the public cloud model.

Hybrid Cloud: Hybrid Cloud; It uses public and private cloud options together. In order for this model to be successful, the transfer of applications must have a management strategy. Examples of this cloud type are configuration management, budgeting, security, change display, and error catching. The advantages of hybrid clouds are flexibility, scalability, security and cost efficiency. The disadvantages are networking problems and security compatibility.

Community Cloud: The community cloud is the cloud model that caters to users with common needs, and customers and organizations jointly use their data sources, goals, and policies. It includes two or more installation models. It also shares IT resources among users and makes them available for common use. For example, the E-Government application is built on the community cloud.

CLOUD COMPUTING AND VIRTUALIZATION

When it comes to cloud computing, the first concept that comes to mind is the concept of virtualization. Virtualization concept; It is called leaving the physical structure to virtual machines. In other words, creating a virtual system with the simulation method in the hypervisor or Linux phase of a physical structure is called virtualization.

The name of the software used to create a virtual system and to increase the functionality of the hardware is called Hypervisor. The hypervisor enables the aggregation of multiple virtual machines on a single piece of hardware in terms of task. IBM first developed native hypervisors in the 1960s.

Virtualization categories can be listed as six items as follows:

1. Network Virtualization: It allows working with less hardware and more virtual network setup. It enables the creation of virtual networks by establishing bridges between systems. Such networks can provide end-to-end service.
2. Server Virtualization: It is the most commonly used virtualization method. It is intended to aggregate multiple servers on only one physical server.
3. Desktop Virtualization: It enables computers to be virtualized so that users can connect with remote access. The computer is virtualized and the user can access this server via a network.
4. Application Virtualization: Application virtualization allows applications to run as if they were installed on the device by running them through the server layer without the need to install them on devices.
5. Memory Virtualization: Memory virtualization allows networked and therefore distributed servers to share a memory pool to overcome physical memory limitations, a common bottleneck in software performance.
6. Storage Virtualization: Storage virtualization is performed by combining multiple data storage devices and managing them from a common management interface. Thanks to this common interface, the management factor is facilitated and system complexity is reduced. Thus, special powers are given to individuals.

DATA REPLICATION

Companies have to ensure the security of customer data in order to determine the customer portfolio and to meet the needs of the customers. In particular, the inappropriate use of data, the ignorance of individuals about information security threats, the weakness of risk taking and the emergence of information security risks that can be considered difficult to compensate. Confidentiality, integrity and accessibility are the basic concepts that need to be emphasized in order to ensure security in cloud computing, (Alimjon, 2022).

There are too many security threats associated with data services to be stored and backed up in the cloud. This includes traditional threats and non-traditional threats. Traditional threats include: network eavesdropping, illegal invasion and denial of service attacks, as well as specific cloud computing threats such as side-channel attacks, virtualization vulnerabilities, and abuse of cloud services. The most widely used technique to ensure data security in cloud technologies is data replication, (Mealha *et al.,* 2019).

Data replication, which can be defined as the process of copying data from a central database, means keeping data in more than one location. In this system, data is stored the same in all locations without any inconsistency. In data replication, different systems are preferred according to the needs of the institutions. For example, a system that many people want to access may not be able to handle this load. In this case, the data copied by data replication is shared on different servers, thus increasing both speed and data accessibility, (Boru *et al.,* 2015). Data in one center can be copied or reproduced in another database. All users see data the same way. Or, the user who updates the data in one center sees the data in the other center in the same way. There is no inconsistency in the data. Operations such as editing and deletion performed on records in a replicated database are also reflected in other databases. For this reason, solutions such as temporary deletion are used in database replication applications. Soft deletion means marking data as deleted so that it can be restored if needed. Such data is not truly deleted and continues to be left in the database. Only administrators can see the temporarily deleted data. Since all deleted data will continue to be stored in the database in this method, the system in question may create a serious data load in the long run and therefore server costs due to the need for additional storage unit. Data replication operations performed in databases are shown in Figure 3. The data owned by more than one user is saved through a single server and then duplicated and stored in multiple databases. Thus, in case of data loss that users may experience in the future, a solution is produced for their problems thanks to the copied databases.

Figure 3. Data replication

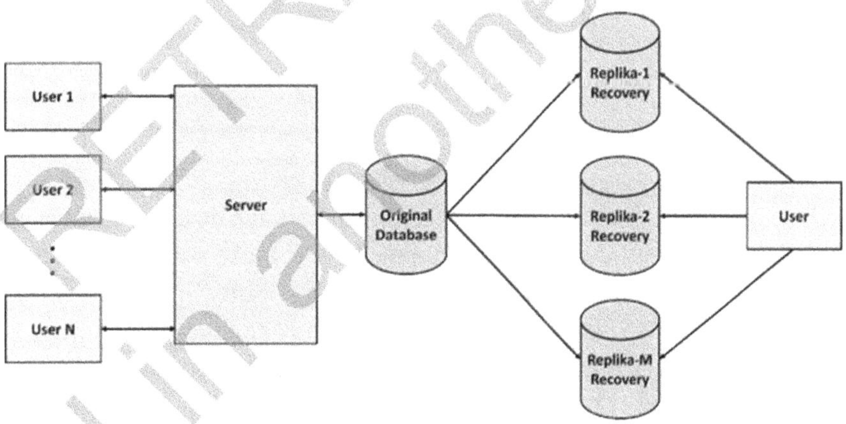

Data is kept in multiple sources, copied. A failure in the central database does not cause data loss. Multiple users can operate on the same data. With database replication, multiple users can work with the same data over databases. Thus, it becomes possible to carry out the work of a change to be made in the central database in other databases. The data on which the transaction is made is seen in an updated form in the database. Thus, secure data sharing is ensured, (Silva, Holanda, & Araujo, 2016).

CLOUD COMPUTING SECURITY MODELS

Data security elements in cloud computing are shown in Figure 4. These security elements include: Data protection, privacy, accessibility and access control, integrity, identity management, physical security, personnel security, cloud application/network layer, and penetration testing and penetration testing.

Figure 4. Cloud computing security

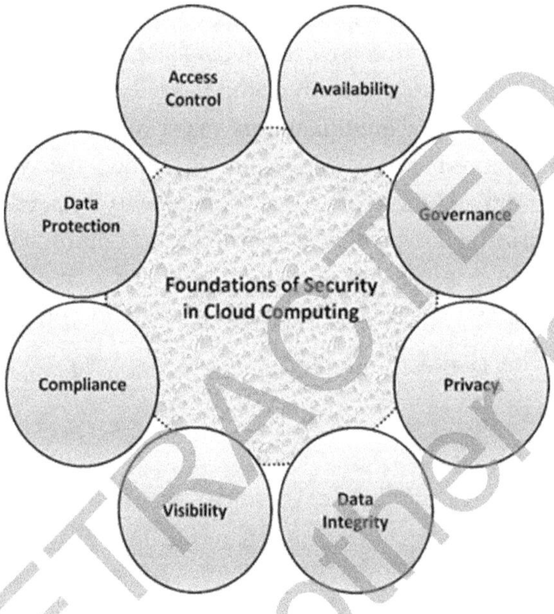

Data Protection: The processing of data has accelerated with the developments in application software and internet. Inappropriate use of these developments that make people's life easier, the fact that individuals do not have enough information about information security threats, etc. have brought about problems related to data security. The security of digital data is gaining importance today in order to protect data in electronic environment such as copyrights and ethics, privacy, security and encryption. Information security was defined as three different concepts by ISACA in 2009; It is shown as ensuring the confidentiality, integrity and accessibility of information at any time. These defined privacy, integrity and accessibility issues are the basic concepts that should be emphasized in order to ensure security in cloud computing. In addition to network eavesdropping, illegal invasion and denial of service attacks, there are certain cloud computing threats such as side-channel attacks, virtualization vulnerabilities, and abuse of cloud services. To mitigate these threats, security controls are generally followed by the confidentiality, integrity and availability specified by ISACA above.

Privacy

Data privacy defines the property that data content is not made available or disclosed to undesired users. The concept of privacy means that sensitive and confidential data should be kept confidential to users who are not authorized to access. Data from an external source is stored in a cloud and beyond the direct control of its owners. Only authorized users can access sensitive data, while others, including CSPs (Cloud Solution Providers), should not obtain any information about the data. However, data owners expect to take full advantage of cloud data services, such as data searching, data computing, and data sharing, without leaking data content to CSPs or other unauthorized users. An example of a security audit involving privacy is encryption so that only authorized users can access data, (Younis, Kifayat, & Merabti, 2014).

Providers are required to ensure that all critical data (eg citizenship information, military information, card information, etc.) is masked or encrypted and that only authorized users can access all of the data. In addition, digital identity information must be protected, such as any data that the cloud provider collects or generates about the customer calendar in the cloud.

Accessibility and Access Control

Accessibility means that a data owner can restrict access to their data as they wish, in order to externally participate in the cloud system. Accessibility can also be referred to as usability. Availability and access control ensure that the right people are given the appropriate amount of permissions. While legitimate users can be authorized by the data owner to access the data, other people cannot gain unauthorized access to the data as they are not authorized to access them. However, applying granular access control to external data is often requested by individuals, ie different users need to be offered different access privileges according to different pieces of data. The access authorization phase only needs to be controlled by the original owner of the data in untrusted cloud environments. Unauthorized access should be strictly prohibited, but in some cases, access for users' use should be allowed and monitored at the same time by providing administrative savings, (Younis, Kifayat, & Merabti, 2014).

Integrity

Data integrity requires ensuring the accuracy and completeness of data. Owners of data or applications always want their data to be stored accurately and reliably in a cloud. This means that data should not be accessed, altered, intentionally deleted, or maliciously generated. If any undesired operation corrupts or deletes data, the cloud service owner should be able to detect it. If some of the external data is corrupted or lost, the data should still be retrieved by the users. Effective integrity security controls go beyond malicious intent and also protect data from unintentional changes. An example of an integrity-encompassing security audit is the automatic backup of data.

Identity Management

Every organization needs to have its own identity management system to control access to information and computing resources. In identity management, cloud providers integrate the customer's identity management system into their infrastructure or provide their own identity management system using unified identity, SSO (Single Sign-On) technology or a biometric-based identification system, (Charaya & Aramudhan, 2016). SSO refers to a user's ability to log in with a single user ID and password to access more than one system they need. Cloud identity provides the user with cloud-based and inter-enterprise biometric identification that protects their privacy. It matches the confidential information given by the users with their biometric data and then stores it in an encrypted manner. By using a searchable encryption technique, biometric identification is performed in the encrypted area to ensure that the cloud service provider or potential data attackers do not access any sensitive data or even the content of individual queries, (Kılıç, 2017).

Physical Security

Cloud service providers (Amazon, Azure, Oracle, IBM etc.) protect IT hardware (servers, routers, cables, etc.) from unauthorized access, interference, theft, fires, flooding, etc. and ensures that essential supplies (such as electricity) are robust enough to minimize the possibility of outages. This is normally achieved by servicing cloud applications from professionally designated, designed, built, managed, monitored and maintained data centers, (Mell & Grance, 2011).

Personnel Security

Various data security concerns regarding information technology and other employees associated with cloud services are addressed through pre- and post-employment activities such as the security screening process, potential recruits, security awareness, training programs, and proactive methods.

Cloud Application/Network Layer and Penetration Testing

In short, penetration testing is to attack the system in order to understand the existence of any problem in the system. This is also called a penetration test. What is important when performing penetration testing is the difference between application and network layer testing. It is very important to understand what is being asked when performing the test. Network layer testing refers to tests involving interconnected systems throughout the local network, as well as internal or external connections. Often the vulnerable party is the employee and social engineering attacks are carried out.

Penetration Test

Penetration testing is the stage of performing attacker security tests to find security weaknesses in a system, service or computer network. Because the cloud platform is a shared environment with multiple businesses leasing services, step-by-step penetration test participation rules must be followed. Scanning and penetration testing from inside or outside the cloud must be authorized by the cloud provider. If the aforementioned usage policies are violated, this will result in the complete termination of the cloud service, (Meghanathan, 2013).

CONCLUSION

As a result of the widespread use of the Internet and the rapid increase in information, the importance of information technologies has increased. The basis of the concept of cloud computing, which is one of the information technology concepts that has been heard a lot recently, is based on the internet. One of the biggest advantages of using the cloud is that the device performance and features of the users who will access the cloud are not important. The person can connect to the cloud platform at any time he wants and from any location, provided that he has internet access. At the beginning of its advantages is to connect to the internet from anywhere, but integration with the internet also brings a disadvantage. If the user does not have internet access, they will not be able to access the cloud platform.

It is necessary to take some security measures to protect the data and applications transferred to the cloud platform and to prevent unwanted situations. Since cloud platforms work with a system open to internet access, they are open to attacks that may come from the internet. While ensuring the security of transferred and stored data, the important point is not only to protect the data and applications against external attacks, but also to ensure the integrity of the data, to prevent unwanted data loss, and to reach the desired response in the system in terms of data security.

Institutions and companies have turned to cloud technologies in order to increase business continuity and obtain reliable and efficient resources and have grown rapidly. However, in proportion to this growth, some problems such as data breaches and data leakage have arisen due to the continuous use of cloud technologies. In order to prevent these possible disaster scenarios, replication services have emerged, which have made significant progress in establishing the systemic infrastructure. This replication process is performed by storing data on remote virtual servers at certain time intervals. Replication services, which are an ideal solution for institutions, also reduce the need for hardware and labor and improve the performance of institutions. The fact that the replication service can be performed at short intervals, fast action in recovery scenarios and other features make cloud replication services an important cloud computing service in the digital age.

REFERENCES

Al_Hachemi, S. A. G. A. (2022). Cloud Computing Services with Minimal Redundancy, Storage, and Effective Processing Capabilities. Texas Journal of Engineering and Technology, 9, 143-149.

Alimjon, D. (2022). Problems of data replication in distribution systems. *ACADEMICIA: An International Multidisciplinary Research Journal*, 12(5), 1119–1128. DOI: 10.5958/2249-7137.2022.00585.7

Boru, D., Kliazovich, D., Granelli, F., Bouvry, P., & Zomaya, A. Y. (2015). Energy-efficient data replication in cloud computing datacenters. *Cluster Computing*, 18(1), 385–402. DOI: 10.1007/s10586-014-0404-x

Cai, F., Zhu, N., He, J., Mu, P., Li, W., & Yu, Y. (2019). Survey of access control models and technologies for cloud computing. *Cluster Computing*, 22(3), 6111–6122. DOI: 10.1007/s10586-018-1850-7

Charanya, R., & Aramudhan, M. (2016, February). Survey on access control issues in cloud computing. In *2016 International Conference on Emerging Trends in Engineering, Technology and Science (ICETETS)* (pp. 1-4). IEEE. DOI: 10.1109/ICETETS.2016.7603014

Convolbo, M. W., Chou, J., Lu, S., & Chung, Y. C. (2016, December). DRASH: A data replication-aware scheduler in geo-distributed data centers. In *2016 IEEE International Conference on Cloud Computing Technology and Science (CloudCom)* (pp. 302-309). IEEE.

Haghighat, M., Zonouz, S., & Abdel-Mottaleb, M. (2015, November). CloudID: Trustworthy cloud-based and cross-enterprise biometric identification. *Expert Systems with Applications*, 42(21), 7905–7916. DOI: 10.1016/j.eswa.2015.06.025

Kılıç, H. (2017). *Kamuda Bulut Bilişim Kullanımına Yönelik Risk Analizi ve Yönetimi, Uzmanlık Tezi, (yayımlanmamış)*. Çevre ve Şehircilik Bakanlığı.

Lin, J. W., Chen, C. H., & Chang, J. M. (2013). QoS-aware data replication for data-intensive applications in cloud computing systems. *IEEE Transactions on Cloud Computing*, 1(1), 101–115. DOI: 10.1109/TCC.2013.1

Mansouri, N. (2016). Adaptive data replication strategy in cloud computing for performance improvement. *Frontiers of Computer Science*, 10(5), 925–935. DOI: 10.1007/s11704-016-5182-6

Mansouri, N., Javidi, M. M., & Zade, B. M. H. (2021). Hierarchical data replication strategy to improve performance in cloud computing. *Frontiers of Computer Science*, 15(2), 1–17. DOI: 10.1007/s11704-019-9099-8

Mealha, D., Preguiça, N., Gomes, M. C., & Leitão, J. (2019, March). Data replication on the cloud/edge. In *Proceedings of the 6th Workshop on Principles and Practice of Consistency for Distributed Data* (pp. 1-7).

Meghanathan, N. (2013). Review of access control models for cloud computing. *Computer Science & Information Science*, 3(1), 77–85. DOI: 10.5121/csit.2013.3508

Miloudi, I. E., Yagoubi, B., & Bellounar, F. Z. (2021, October). A Survey of Dynamic Replication Strategies in Cloud Computing Systems. In *2021 International Conference on Networking and Advanced Systems (ICNAS)* (pp. 1-6). IEEE. DOI: 10.1109/ICNAS53565.2021.9628963

NIST. (2013). *Cloud Computing Standards Roadmap*. National Institue of Standards and Tecnology Special Publication.

Salunkhe, S. D., & Patil, D. (2016, August). Division and replication for data with public auditing scheme for cloud storage. In *2016 International Conference on Computing Communication Control and automation (ICCUBEA)* (pp. 1-5). IEEE.

Shirgaonkar, M., Shinde, A., Sankpal, P., & Gutte, V. (2022, March). Cloud Computing Security using Cryptographic Algorithms. In *2022 6th International Conference on Computing Methodologies and Communication (ICCMC)* (pp. 31-37). IEEE. DOI: 10.1109/ICCMC53470.2022.9753711

Silva, G. H. G., Holanda, M., & Araujo, A. (2016, June). Data replication policy in a cloud computing environment. In *2016 11th Iberian conference on information systems and technologies (CISTI)* (pp. 1-6). IEEE.

Soyjaudah, K. M. S., Catherine, P. C., & Coonjah, I. (2016, April). Evaluation of UDP tunnel for data replication in data centers and cloud environment. In 2016 international conference on computing, communication and automation (ICCCA) (pp. 1217-1221). IEEE.

Srivastava, P., & Khan, R. (2018). A review paper on cloud computing. *International Journal of Advanced Research in Computer Science and Software Engineering*, 8(6), 17–20. DOI: 10.23956/ijarcsse.v8i6.711

Sun, D. W., Chang, G. R., Gao, S., Jin, L. Z., & Wang, X. W. (2012). Modeling a dynamic data replication strategy to increase system availability in cloud computing environments. *Journal of Computer Science and Technology*, 27(2), 256–272. DOI: 10.1007/s11390-012-1221-4

Tahirkheli, A. I., Shiraz, M., Hayat, B., Idrees, M., Sajid, A., Ullah, R., Ayub, N., & Kim, K. I. (2021). A survey on modern cloud computing security over smart city networks: Threats, vulnerabilities, consequences, countermeasures, and challenges. *Electronics (Basel)*, 10(15), 1811. DOI: 10.3390/electronics10151811

Tamimi, A. A., Dawood, R., & Sadaqa, L. (2019, April). Disaster recovery techniques in cloud computing. In *2019 IEEE Jordan International Joint Conference on Electrical Engineering and Information Technology (JEEIT)* (pp. 845-850). IEEE. DOI: 10.1109/JEEIT.2019.8717450

Usman, A., Schadek, R., & Theel, O. (2017, January). A Novel Highly Available Data Replication Strategy exploiting Data Semantics, Coding Techniques and Prior At-Hand Knowledge. In 2017 IEEE 22nd Pacific Rim International Symposium on Dependable Computing (PRDC) (pp. 301-310). IEEE.

Wang, Y., Qiu, X., Zhang, C., Mi, W., Li, L., & Ji, Y. (2009, September). Effective data replication in heterogeneous structured P2P networks. In 2009 5th International Conference on Wireless Communications, Networking and Mobile Computing (pp. 1-4). IEEE.

Younis, Y. A., Kifayat, K., & Merabti, M. (2014). An access control model for cloud computing. *Journal of Information Security and Applications*, 19(1), 45–60. DOI: 10.1016/j.jisa.2014.04.003

Yu, S., Wang, C., Ren, K., & Lou, W. (2010, March). *Achieving secure, scalable, and fine-grained data access control in cloud computing. In 2010 Proceedings IEEE INFOCOM*. Ieee.

Chapter 13
Trust Evaluation Enhancing Security in the Cloud Market Based on Trust Framework Using Metric Parameter Selection

Qais Al-Na'amneh
https://orcid.org/0009-0008-3034-7693
Applied Science Private University, Jordan

Mahmoud Aljawarneh
https://orcid.org/0000-0003-2003-6310
Applied Science Private University, Jordan

Rahaf Hazaymih
Jordan University of Science and Technology, Jordan

Laith Alzboon
https://orcid.org/0000-0002-7715-9306
Applied Science Private University, Jordan

Dena Abu Laila
Zarqa University, Jordan

Sahel Albawaneh
Yarmouk University, Jordan

ABSTRACT

Cloud services have become popular in global technology because they let users rent computers, networks, and storage infrastructure resources that are specific to their needs., trust in the cloud relationship is essential before interaction takes place between cloud providers and consumers. The concept of trust encompasses multiple elements. The usability, security, scalability, and availability characteristics of IaaS, PaaS, SaaS, and DaaS are among these dimensions. Fuzzy characteristics and linguistic terminology characterize each of these dimensions. This chapter applies fuzzy-set theory to create models for each dimension of IaaS services. The Mamdani fuzzy-inference approach is used to assess the trustworthiness of cloud providers generally. Evaluating cloud metrics across multiple domains can be challenging. In this work, we propose a trust framework. We consider level trust; the node's level trust Score uses a fuzzy model to evaluate trust in cloud computing. The proposed model is evaluated for its efficacy and resilience through tests and findings.

DOI: 10.4018/979-8-3693-9919-4.ch013

INTRODUCTION

Trust is a state of mind when individuals are willing to be vulnerable to others due to favorable expectations of their future behavior (Alkadi et al., 2020). Trust is especially important in situations with high uncertainty, vulnerability, long-term relationships, and high risks of failure (Arif et al., 2024). Cloud service customers and suppliers typically have all four traits. Consumers often rely on service providers for long-term assistance for critical company operations. This service operates on a distributed network, with limited consumer understanding of its security and functionality (Yuan & Wu, 2021). Trust in Cloud services involves three stages: consumer views of providers, the decision to trust, and adoption behavior (e.g., purchasing) (Saba et al., 2022). In this scenario, trust can refer to the Cloud provider, the Cloud service, or the Cloud itself. Trust in a cloud provider depends on their ability to fulfill agreed-upon quality obligations, such as uptime. Trust in a Cloud service depends on its capacity to achieve its intended aims (Li et al., 2020). This can be assessed based on user satisfaction and usage history. Making users use Cloud technology is the most challenging aspect of establishing trust.

Distinguishing between trust referents is crucial for developing trust in technology interactions (Arif et al., 2024; Yaseen, 2023). In Cloud computing, the focus is on calculus-based trust, which involves weighing the costs and advantages of adopting new technologies. However, it is intentionally suspicious, bureaucratic, and transactional (Camacho, 2024).

Cloud computing allows users to access highly available computing resources from a remote location on demand. The lack of quantitative criteria for evaluating the tradeoffs (features, challenges, and economics) of security has hindered the migration of important industry applications to the Cloud (Akinbowale et al., 2023), despite its obvious economic and technological benefits. Metrics are useful for evaluating tradeoffs in many settings but establishing a formal and standard-based method for security metrics in the cloud remains a challenge (Olaniyi & Omubo, 2023).

Since the start of Amazon's EC2 in 2006, the phrase "cloud computing" has been relatively new in the mainstream of IT. it originated from commercial requirements and applications. Software as a Service (SaaS) Platform as a Service (PaaS), and Infrastructure as a Service (IaaS) are the three primary categories of cloud provision according to NIST . For cloud users who want maximum control over their resources, IaaS offers the most flexibility. In contrast, SaaS offers the most focused option, appropriate for designs in which cloud providers maintain complete power over virtual resources. Users may include, for instance, corporations with an established enterprise infrastructure or non-technical end users' who may be interested in outsourcing some of their operations (Al-Harrasi et al., 2023). Building trust in the cloud should consider the needs of various user types by offering them various models. Each approach ought to offer appropriate degrees of openness given the technical difficulties and the building of confidence. Designing secure and trusted Cloud services raises the dilemma of how to scientifically and quantitatively assess a provider's security (Nasir et al., 2021).

In other IT ecosystems, such as critical infrastructures, well-designed security metrics can help understand a system's security guarantees, raise awareness about vulnerabilities, and assess the effectiveness of implemented security mechanisms. Due to the unique properties of the Cloud, there are limited efforts to establish a framework and quantitative security metrics.

To provide security in cloud environment, a systematic approach is necessary. This involves relying on trusted third parties for protection. In recent years, researchers have focused on trust-related challenges. Trust management systems generally consider all comments to be accurate. Trust management structures rely on feedback from trading partners, making them vulnerable to strategic manipulation and attacks. Identifying and addressing fake input is a significant challenge in the trust management area (Alsowail & Al-Shehari, 2021).

The essential criteria and standards for e-commerce trust frameworks to follow remain unclear. There are two issues to resolve. First, the model must reliably estimate the trust significance of successful interactions. The trust model must remain accurate under dynamic conditions and react to changes introduced by others. Second, the trust system for management itself may be attacked and corrupted. Improving trust management is crucial for e-commerce. Essential security services include identity validation, secure storage, privacy assistance, and an effective trust determination tool (Sun et al., 2021).

Today's cloud computing platforms allow users to collaborate in multi-cloud environments, with collaborators, clouds, and compute nodes from other universities or companies. Different groups may have their own policies. Security remains a major concern in cloud computing. To support cloud companies and customers in detecting and preventing such attacks (Yuan et al., 2020).

In cloud computing, three delivery modes are typically defined (Al-Mhiqani et al., 2020):

i. Software as a Service (SaaS): Cloud Service Providers (CSPs) use a single location to host, update, and administer demand-based software, or SaaS. SaaS suppliers include companies like Salesforce.com, Google Docs, and Zoho (Denney et al., 2020). When using SaaS, the cloud service is frequently accessed through a client interface, such as a web browser or mobile app.
ii. Platform as a Service (PaaS): When CSPs offer a platform as a service, clients can utilize it to develop and launch their applications utilizing a range of auxiliary libraries and programming languages, application technology, and a development environment (M. Singh et al., 2020). PaaS can be helpful when multiple clients use the same development environment. Integration with databases and internet services through a variety of standards is another benefit of PaaS. PaaS allows programmers to easily automate testing and development.
iii. IaaS, or infrastructure as a service: The client is granted control over installed programs, operating systems, and middleware in addition to a collection of virtual computing resources, including storage and network components when CSPs provide infrastructure as a service. IaaS must have protocols that offer confidentiality, integrity, availability, and non-repudiation—all security elements necessary in the cloud market. In cloud computing, Infrastructure as a Service (IaaS) controls how hardware is used and is essential to system security (Alhajjar & Bradley, 2021).

Some of the advantages of e-commerce for providers and consumers are shown in Table 1:

Table 1. Advantages of e-commerce

No	e-commerce for customers (Alsowail & Al-Shehari, 2020)	e-commerce for CSPs (Boakye-Gyan, 2021)
1	Reduces transaction charges for the cloud market.	Increased income for the CSPs.
2	It does not need any actual interaction with any dealer or seller, transactions can be done online.	Less cost of operation and maintenance.
3	They are saving a lot of time by using the internet to sell or purchase anything at any time they want.	Manage and reduce the cost of purchasing goods.
4	Customers may simply search and check whatever information they want.	Customer satisfaction could be increased.

continued on following page

Table 1. Continued

No	e-commerce for customers (Alsowail & Al-Shehari, 2020)	e-commerce for CSPs (Boakye-Gyan, 2021)
5	If a customer believes that a company's service is not great, they can switch to another company at any time.	It saves money by online tracking and monitoring instead of physical heading which requires transportation.
6	A customer can purchase a product that isn't available at a physical store. This gives consumers a wide selection of items to pick from and purchase.	Improve customer and supplier relationships.
7	Help customers by enabling product reviews to allow them to read about products before purchasing.	Increase the selling frequency and improve both internal and external communication.

This chapter aims to identify crucial characteristics of the trust relationship between cloud providers and their clients. Furthermore, a fuzzy framework will be used to represent each trust dimension and construct corresponding metrics. Additionally, a total trust value for cloud providers will be calculated.

The remainder of the chapter is structured as follows. Section 2 discusses the related work. Section 3 presents the research methodology, details the proposed trust assessment framework of cloud services, and elaborates on the proposed trust assessment methods. Section 4 presents results and discussion, and finally, Section 6 presents this chapter's conclusions and outlines directions for future work.

Related work

Some commonly used trust evaluation techniques have been put out from various angles to gauge how trustworthy cloud services are. Among them is the QoS-driven trust evaluation approach for cloud services. A proposed compliance-based multi-dimensional trust evaluation method in (Wei et al., 2020) It allowed Cloud Service Consumer (CSCs) to assess a CSP's level of trustworthiness. This approach assists CSC in selecting a CSP from among candidate CSPs that meet its targeted quality of service standards. A trust-centric method based on hypergraph-binary fruit fly optimization was introduced by Somu et al. (Al-Na'amneh, Almomani, et al., 2024) to identify appropriate and reliable CSPs.

A unique approach and trust mechanism based on cloud model theory were developed by (Al-Na'amneh, Nasayreh, et al., 2024). This technique uses the analytic hierarchy process method to help CSCs choose the right cloud service while accounting for trust, costs, and time. A framework for evaluating trust was presented in (Aljaidi et al., 2023); it makes use of the compliance monitoring mechanism to assess the reliability of CSPs. On the other hand, it is frequently difficult to obtain complete QoS statistics for cloud services. Furthermore, cloud service QoS metrics may not be accurate. As a result, using the QoS value alone to assess the accuracy and reliability of CSPs is not feasible. It is also typical practice to evaluate cloud service reliability using CSCs' experiences and opinions (i.e., feedback ratings). A big data processing approach was promoted by (Laila et al., 2024) as a means of assessing the reliability of cloud services. The MapReduce framework is included in a cloud broker to pre-process the feedback ratings of CSCs. A novel approach to evaluating trust was presented in (Jaradat et al., 2023), wherein the Bayesian game model and the feedback assessment component were integrated to identify malicious CSCs and their feedback ratings. While the latter is used to find malevolent users and their feedback, the former is used to investigate and identify false identities. A framework for managing trust based on reputation was created and put into place by (Al-Na'amneh et al., 2023). Using this concept, cloud services can be safeguarded from malevolent CSCs by gauging the reliability of feedback ratings.

A cloud model-based lightweight reputation measuring method for cloud services was presented by (Akbar et al., 2024). This approach makes use of fuzzy set theory to determine cloud service reputation rankings based on CSC feedback ratings. However, in the actual cloud world, there are unscrupulous users and biased feedback ratings, which have a big impact on CSPs' reputations. In a similar vein, one cannot determine a CSP's genuine trustworthiness solely by looking at user feedback scores. Many research also integrated subjective and objective assessment techniques. A reliable selection paradigm for cloud service selection was put forth by (Dubey & Mishra, 2024). This methodology introduced an integrated approach to evaluating trust, which blends a subjective trust assessment (feedback ratings) with an objective trust assessment (QoS monitoring). However, trustworthy individuals and their actual feedback ratings may be inadvertently excluded by the one-size-fits-all algorithm designed to identify untrustworthy people. A unique framework that integrates customer satisfaction estimates and QoS forecasts was presented in (A. Singh & Chatterjee, 2024) for evaluating cloud service trust. This system was designed to estimate customer happiness for a target cloud service and improve the accuracy of QoS value predictions of quantitative trustworthy qualities. It did not, however, consider how the time factor. In addition to the trust evaluation techniques previously described, there are additional approaches to guarantee the reliability of the market environment. To safeguard user data and computation integrity and secrecy, (Krishna & Mangalampalli, 2024) presented an improved trustworthy cloud computing platform. To prevent eavesdropping and tampering during transmission and to ensure the security of the virtual machine against inside attackers, this reliable platform offers effective and safe virtual machine management procedures. In (Hussain et al., 2024), writers enumerated several elements that must be considered when calculating trust, including ownership, control, transparency, and more. Consequently, we can observe that cloud vendors must be able to give their clients trustworthy information for cloud computing platforms to function properly.

The trust issues posed by the advent of cloud computing are comparable to those highlighted by the Internet as a whole. Cloud computing users, like Internet users, rely on providers to supply quality service, securely store data, and respect privacy (Vangoor et al., 2024). confidence markings, defined as any third-party logo, picture, or symbol, are used on the internet to alleviate customer concerns about risk and boost confidence (Narayanan & Kannan, 2024). Trustmark recipients undergo human verification and certification, which varies by sector and is not apparent to consumers. Critics argue that the approach lacks accuracy, consistency, timeliness, and transparency, and is easy to exploit (Ahmadi, 2024).

Cloud computing, a digital corporate environment based on service chains, can pose trust and dependability challenges. These factors include data provenance, transparency in technology development and operations, and predictability of technology behavior to meet expectations (Kolevski & Michael, 2024). To address dependability issues in Cloud computing, strategies may include constructing dependability arguments, evaluating Cloud infrastructures and configurations, self-aware systems that provide information about operation and failure, and highlighting trustworthy service providers through regulatory and social mechanisms (Prakash et al., 2024). However, these solutions require formal definition and implementation.

However, other works also concentrate on evaluating risk or trust in distributed systems. The idea of fuzzy belief was employed by the authors in (Patel, 2024) to describe risk to address the uncertainty aspect of risk. The authors of (Velmurugan et al., 2024) created a network of connected hosts. Additionally, they investigated page rank and Hypertext Induced Topic Search (HITS) algorithms in their research.

Methodology

Cloud computing platforms are increasingly popular in several industries such as e-commerce, web applications, storage of data, healthcare, gaming, and mobile social networks. Cloud computing allows clients to access Internet-based services without purchasing hardware. Cloud computing applications and platforms continue to face serious security and privacy problems. Cloud companies must prioritize data confidentiality and auditability when convincing consumers to store sensitive information in the cloud. Cloud vendors must ensure continuity of operations and service availability for their customers.

This methodology introduced a new security metric trust (trust-Security) and a new algorithm to calculate it. Our trust management architecture helps administrators and customers make informed decisions.

The algorithm provides a holistic view of system trustworthiness by stressing performance, sustainability, and dependability. This is critical for decision-making and future optimization attempts. The process for assessing a node's confidence in the Cloud is predicated on the computation and contrast of trust metrics in various contexts. In this framework, performance (P), sustainability (ST), and reliability (R) are the main criteria used to assess trustworthiness in the Cloud environment. Through the examination of multiple facets of the system's behavior, these metrics offer a comprehensive understanding of trust. Every measure is computed for a range of predetermined scenarios to compare the degrees of reliability in every situation. The following is the methodology:

1. Reliability (R): Indicates how well a system will function over time. A dependable system is one that consistently produces the desired results. The following equation 1 is used to determine reliability:

$$R = \frac{T}{D} \tag{1}$$

where T indicates the number of successful transactions and D indicates the total of transactions in the cloud market.

2. Sustainability (ST): Evaluate the system's capacity to remain reliable over the long haul. It considers variables including adaptation, long-term availability, and resource usage. To assess sustainability, a time-dependent metric equation 2 is used to determine Sustainability:

$$ST = \frac{A}{O} \tag{2}$$

where A indicates the availability system and O indicates the Overall period of observation in the cloud market.

3. Performance (P): Indicates the rate at which the system can produce outcomes within reasonable time constraints. The following formula can be used equation 3 is used to determine Sustainability:

$$P = \frac{T}{E} \tag{3}$$

where T indicates the Task Completion Time and E indicates the Expected Completion Time in the cloud market.

4. Trust (TS): The composite Trust Score (TS), which measures each scenario's level of trustworthiness, is produced by adding the weighted totals of the three main metrics: Performance (P), Sustainability (ST), and Reliability (R). The following formula can be used equation 4 is used to determine (TS):

$$TS = (W_R * R) + (W_{ST} * ST) + (W_P * P) \tag{4}$$

where $W_R(0<W_R<1)$, $W_{ST}(0<W_{ST}<1)$ and $W_P(0<W_P<1)$ indicates are weighted according to how important they are in the context. To make sure that the total equals 1, the weights are adjusted.

The algorithm as shown in Algorithm 1 offers a methodical way to assess cloud service providers in a market for cloud computing, giving priority to those who exhibit the highest degrees of reliability, sustainability, and performance.

Algorithm 1 Pseudo-code of the Trust Score in Cloud Market Algorithm

1. **Initialize** Weight for Trust Score:
   W_R // Reliability Weight
   W_{ST} // Sustainability Weight
   W_P // Performance Weight

2. **cloud_Service_provider in** the cloud market
   I in Cloud_Providers FOR EVERY PROVIDER
   .
3. Check the trust metric for provider i:
   R_i = GET_Reliability
   ST_i = GET_Sustainability
   P_i = GET_Performance
4. **Trust score** TS **for provider Compute:**

$$TS = (W_R * R) + (W_{ST} * ST) + (W_P * P)$$

   Return trust score **for provider**

5. **Calculated** Trust Score for provider i:
   STORE Trust_Score (provider_i, TS):
   Return is_malicious, reason
   END FOR

6. **Ranking** cloud_providers based on the proposed framework
   Evaluate the trust score for each Cloud_Provider
7. **Return** the list of cloud providers **Ranking**
   Return Ranking

   End

RESULTS AND DISCUSSION

Five scenarios are outlined based on the results. Our approach may be used to filter out misbehaving clients with low trust, and CSP promptly notifies all clients in the marketplace of any warnings. Python will be used to implement the suggested model. The following four scenarios have been used to assess the effectiveness of the trust model:

Scenario-1: the nodes with a moderate level of trust are identified by their trust score. The suggested trust model was used to describe and carry out the first scenario. Based on equations (1) through (4), we computed each node's trust score using the suggested model.

Assuming the input parameter values listed in Table 2 below, we have the following scenario:

Table 2. Scenario-1 input parameters values

Parameter	value
W_R	0.4
W_{ST}	0.3
W_P	0.3
R	0.75
ST	0.70
P	0.80

Now, the Trust Score is calculated according to equation (4) as follows:

TS= (0.4*0.75) + (0.3*0.70) + (0.3*0.80), then TS=0.75

Finally, the first scenario using the suggested trust model and calculating the node's trust score returns a moderate trust score.

Scenario 2: the nodes with the highest level of trust are identified by their trust score. The suggested trust model was used to describe and carry out the first scenario. Based on equations (1) through (4), we computed each node's trust score using the suggested model.

Assuming the input parameter values listed in Table 3 below, we have the following scenario:

Table 3. Scenario-2 input parameters values

Parameter	value
W_R	0.4
W_{ST}	0.3
W_P	0.3
R	0.90
ST	0.85
P	0.95

Now, the Trust Score is calculated according to equation (4) as follows:

TS= (0.4*0.90) + (0.3*0.85) + (0.3*0.95), then TS=0.90

Finally, the second scenario using the suggested trust model and calculating the node's trust score returns the highest trust score.

Scenario 3: the nodes with the lowest level of trust are identified by their trust score. The suggested trust model was used to describe and carry out the first scenario. Based on equations (1) through (4), we computed each node's trust score using the suggested model.

Assuming the input parameter values listed in Table 4 below, we have the following scenario:

Table 4. Scenario-3 input parameters values

Parameter	value
W_R	0.4
W_{ST}	0.3
W_P	0.3
R	0.50
ST	0.40
P	0.45

Now, the Trust Score is calculated according to equation (4) as follows:

TS= (0.4*0.50) + (0.3*0.40) + (0.3*0.45), then TS=0.45

Finally, the second scenario using the suggested trust model and calculating the node's trust score returns the lowest trust score.

Scenario 4: the nodes with a moderate level of trust are identified by their trust score. The suggested trust model was used to describe and carry out the first scenario. Based on equations (1) through (4), we computed each node's trust score using the suggested model.

Assuming the input parameter values listed in Table 5 below, we have the following scenario:

Table 5. Scenario-4 input parameters values

Parameter	value
W_R	0.4
W_{ST}	0.3
W_P	0.3
R	0.60
ST	0.55
P	0.65

Now, the Trust Score is calculated according to equation (4) as follows:

TS= (0.4*0.60) + (0.3*0.55) + (0.3*0.65), then TS=0.60

Finally, the second scenario using the suggested trust model and calculating the node's trust score returns a moderate trust score.

Figure 1 compares the Trust Scores for the four situations. The visualization shows that Scenario 2 has the greatest trust score, indicating trustworthy conditions.

Scenario 3 has the lowest trust score, making it the least trustworthy scenario.

Scenarios 1 and 4 show a modest trust score.

Figure 1. Trust score comparison across scenarios

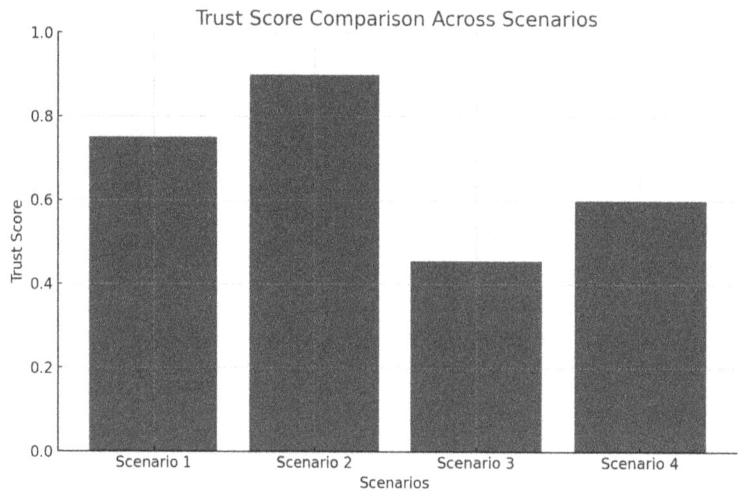

Figure 2 shows how each statistic affects the overall trust score in each scenario

Figure 2. Metrict trust for each scenario

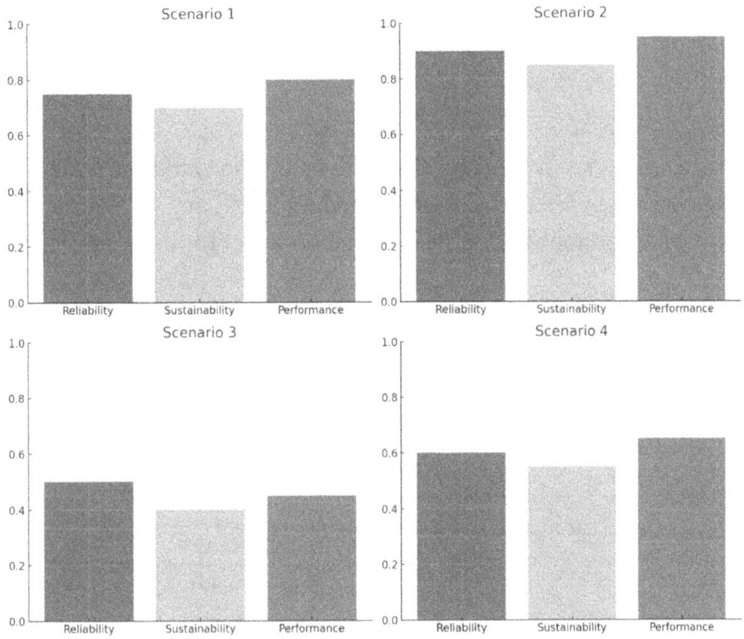

To help clients make decisions, the fuzziness model in Figure 3 converts factors like performance (P), sustainability (ST), and reliability (R) into fuzzy variables using inputs, a knowledge base, and an inference engine. The following steps make up Figure 3's fuzzy logic process:

Figure 3. Fuzzy logic process

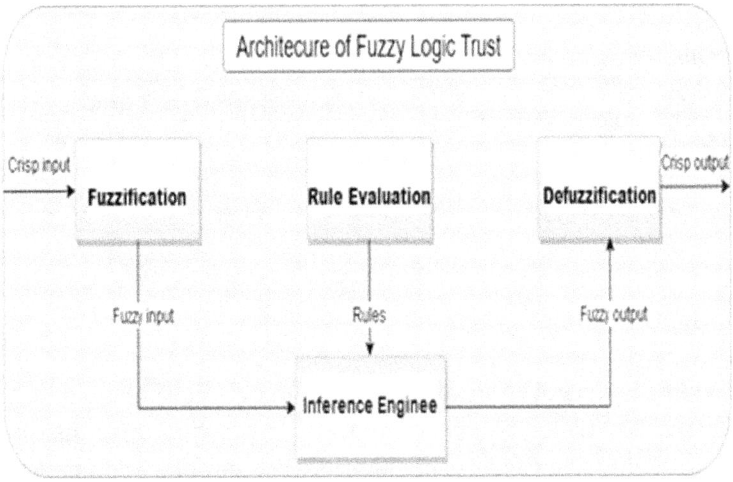

Now to describe and clarify the component of the fuzzy logic According to our proposed Trust Model clients in the cloud marketplace help clients choose the best Cloud provider in the marketplace based on many factors:

1. Input Variable:

The cloud trust level exploration has been calculated using the values provided as statistical criteria. This chapter examines the cloud marketplace's trust model by utilizing three distinct sorts of input variables. Table 6 displays these parameters and their varying ranges for the input variables.

Table 6. Trust model input variables

No#	Input parameters	Range values on the cloud marketplace	Class Level
1	Performance (P)	< 0.5 0.4-0.7 >0.6	L M H
2	Sustainability (ST)	< 0.5 0.4-0.7 >0.6	L M H
3	Reliability (R)	< 0.5 0.4-0.7 >0.6	L M H

2. Output Variables

A single-layered cloud market environment serves as the current location for testing the cloud trust model's parameters. The output parameters of this suggested model are listed in Table 7.

Table 7. Trust model output variables

No#	Output parameter	Range values on the cloud marketplace	Class level
1	Trust Score (TS)	< 0 . 5 0.4-0.7 >0.6	L M H

3. Membership Function

In addition to providing the curve value excluding accuracy values, this suggested trust framework for the cloud marketplace automation System's membership functions also distributes a meticulously designed fuzzy logic procedure that suggests mathematical values of equal input and output variables. Table 8 displays the suggested automated trust model membership function.

Table 8. Automated trust membership

No#	I/O Variables	Graphical representations of MF
1	Performance (P)	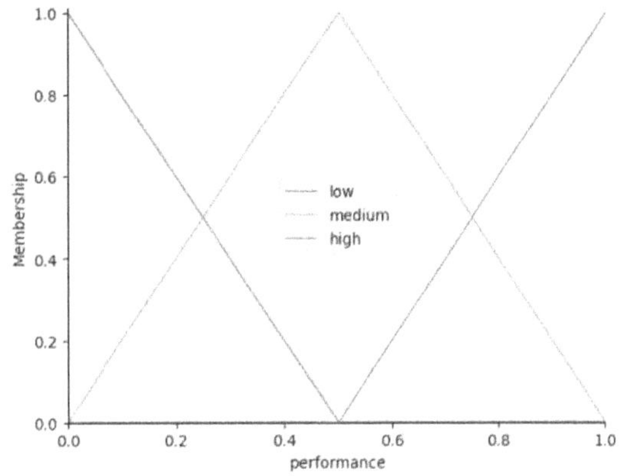
2	Sustainability (ST)	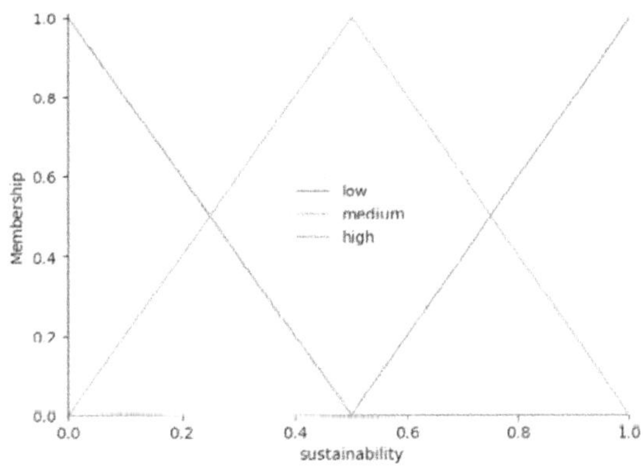

continued on following page

Table 8. Continued

<table>
<tr><td>3</td><td>Reliability (R)</td><td>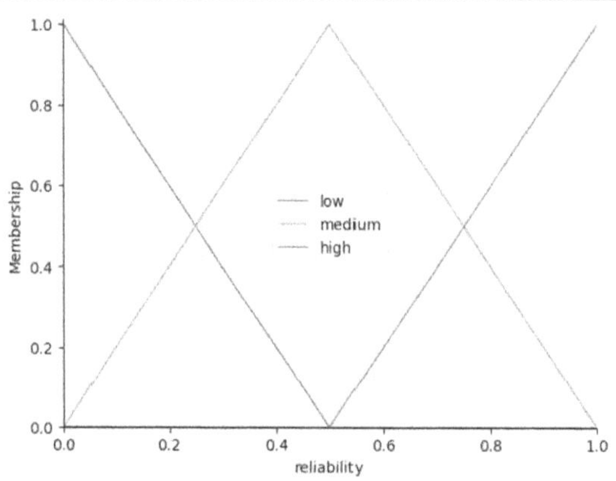
</td></tr>
<tr><td>4</td><td>Trust Score (TS)</td><td>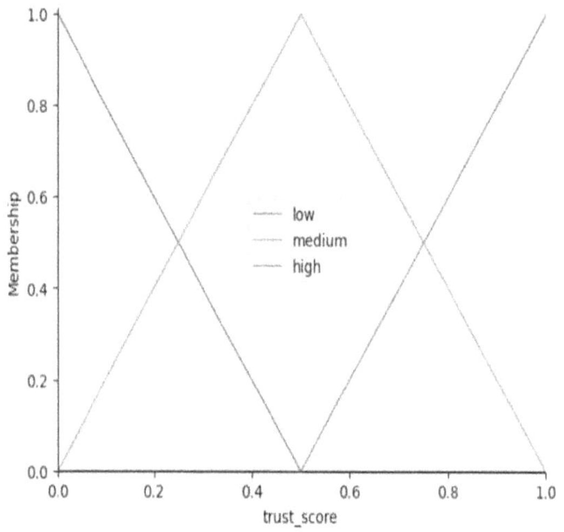
</td></tr>
</table>

4. Lookup Table

Input and output rules are included in the proposed collection of rules table, which commonly relies on the cloud marketplace following the suggested trust model. Table 9 displays a list of these input and output rules. To calculate the Trust Score for cloud providers or any other similar evaluation situation, these 25 criteria make sure that different combinations of the three inputs are sufficiently covered.

Table 9. Lookup table rules according to the cloud trust model

Rule	Reliability (R)	Sustainability (ST)	Performance (P)	Trust Score (TS)
1	H	H	H	H
2	M	M	M	M
3	L	L	L	L
4	H	M	H	H
5	M	H	M	M
6	L	H	H	M
7	H	L	H	M
8	M	M	H	M
9	L	L	H	L
10	H	H	L	M
11	M	L	M	L
12	H	M	M	H
13	M	H	L	M
14	L	M	M	L
15	H	H	M	H
16	M	L	H	M
17	L	H	L	L
18	H	M	L	M
19	M	M	L	L
20	L	M	H	M
21	H	L	L	M
22	M	H	H	H
23	L	L	M	L
24	H	L	M	M
25	M	L	L	L

5. Rule Base

Rules for input and output variables are necessary. A set of guidelines determines a cloud marketplace's level of success.

6. Inference Engine

Another essential element of any trustworthy model for the cloud marketplace is the Inference Engine. Any fuzzy-based trust system that incorporates judgment capacity, like the one presented here, must have a fuzzy inference system. By using a few sets of rules, also known as inference rules, it transforms the fuzzy set values into crisp values.

7. Defuzzification

The Trust Score is represented by a crisp value that is created from the final fuzzy set.

Figure 4, 5, 6 and 7 shows the surface viewer (SV) of the trust score Fuzzy Inference system, and the influence of trust parameters on the trust score, the change of the input variables also subsequently changes in the output variables and automatically influences the trust score. The sustainability input variable has a high impact on the trust score as the less sustainability value the less the trust score. That is how it proposes a very optimized way to predict the trustworthiness of a CSP.

Figure 4. Trust score surface for fixed sustainability (0.7)

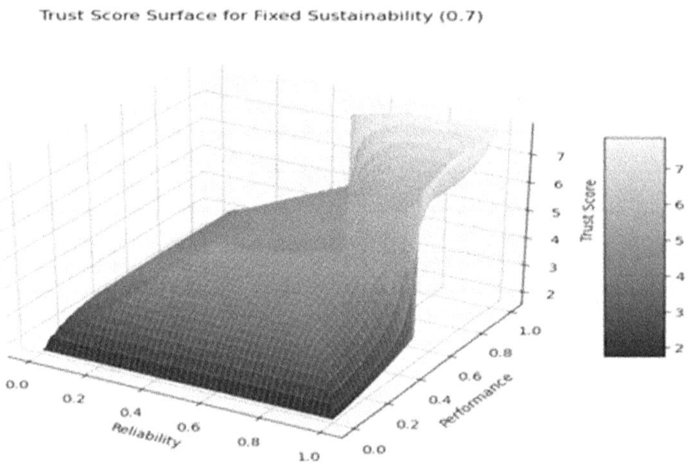

Figure 5. Trust score surface for fixed sustainability (0.7)

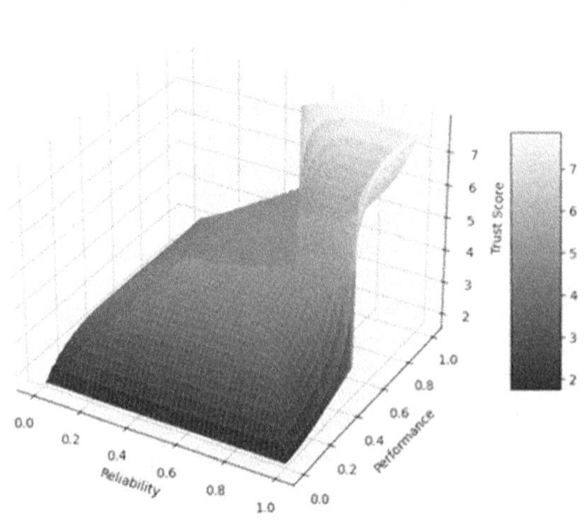

Figure 6. Trust score surface for fixed sustainability (0.3)

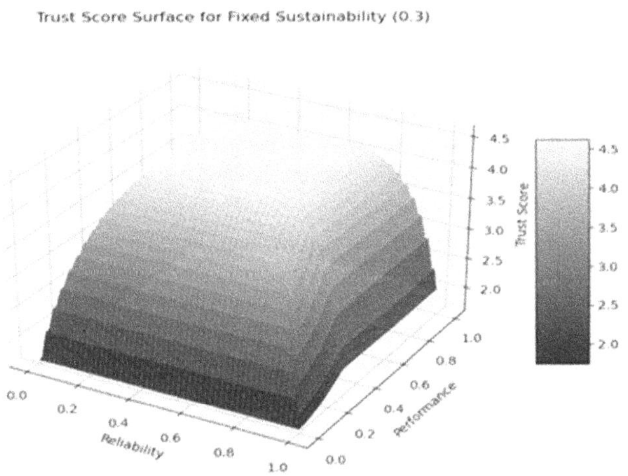

Figure 7. Trust score for fixed sustainability (1.0)

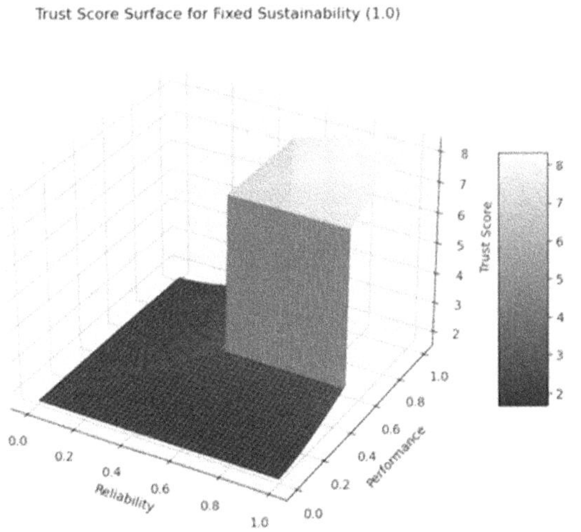

CONCLUSION AND FUTURE WORK

This study describes a fuzzy logic-based approach for evaluating trust. The suggested plan gives cloud users the ability to assess the reliability of cloud service providers before building or migrating their distributed systems to cloud data centers. Our evaluation technique employs the cloud-based e-commerce system as an example of a cloud-based service, considering specific issues like performance (P), sustainability (ST), and reliability (R) are the main criteria. Since the experiment results produced using the real data sets are near the model output, we feel the suggested model offers a valid strategy. It is possible to expand the use of this fuzzy-based model by including more input factors. Additionally, our approach may be expanded to include a range of web-based applications, including e-learning apps.

REFERENCES

Ahmadi, S. (2024). Zero trust architecture in cloud networks: application, challenges, and future opportunities. Ahmadi, S.(2024). Zero Trust Architecture in Cloud Networks: Application, Challenges and Future Opportunities. *Journal of Engineering Research and Reports*, 26(2), 215–228. DOI: 10.9734/jerr/2024/v26i21083

Akbar, M., Waseem, M. M., Mehanoor, S. H., & Barmavatu, P. (2024). Blockchain-based cyber-security trust model with multi-risk protection scheme for secure data transmission in cloud computing. *Cluster Computing*, 27(7), 1–15. DOI: 10.1007/s10586-024-04481-9

Akinbowale, O. E., Mashigo, P., & Zerihun, M. F. (2023). The integration of forensic accounting and big data technology frameworks for internal fraud mitigation in the banking industry. *Cogent Business & Management*, 10(1), 2163560. DOI: 10.1080/23311975.2022.2163560

Al-Harrasi, A., Shaikh, A. K., & Al-Badi, A. (2023). Towards protecting organisations' data by preventing data theft by malicious insiders. *The International Journal of Organizational Analysis*, 31(3), 875–888. DOI: 10.1108/IJOA-01-2021-2598

Al-Mhiqani, M. N., Ahmad, R., Zainal Abidin, Z., Yassin, W., Hassan, A., Abdulkareem, K. H., Ali, N. S., & Yunos, Z. (2020). A review of insider threat detection: Classification, machine learning techniques, datasets, open challenges, and recommendations. *Applied Sciences (Basel, Switzerland)*, 10(15), 5208. DOI: 10.3390/app10155208

Al-Na'amneh, Q., Aljaidi, M., Gharaibeh, H., Nasayreh, A., Al Mamlook, R. E., & Almatarneh, S. others, & Husien, A. S. (2023). Feature Selection for Robust Spoofing Detection: A Chi-Square-based Machine Learning Approach. *2023 2nd International Engineering Conference on Electrical, Energy, and Artificial Intelligence (EICEEAI)*, 1–7.

Al-Na'amneh, Q., Almomani, A., Nasayreh, A., Nahar, K. M., Gharaibeh, H., Al Mamlook, R. E., & Alauthman, M. (2024). Next Generation Image Watermarking via Combined DWT-SVD Technique. *2024 2nd International Conference on Cyber Resilience (ICCR)*, 1–10.

Al-Na'amneh, Q., Nasayreh, A. N., Al Mamlook, R., Gharaibeh, H., Alsheyab, A. M., & Almaiah, M. (2024). Improving Memory Malware Detection in Machine Learning With Random Forest-Based Feature Selection. In *Risk Assessment and Countermeasures for Cybersecurit* (pp. 96–114). IGI Global. DOI: 10.4018/979-8-3693-2691-6.ch006

Alhajjar, E., & Bradley, T. (2021). Survival analysis for insider threat: Detecting insider threat incidents using survival analysis techniques. *Computational & Mathematical Organization Theory*, •••, 1–17.

Aljaidi, M., Alsarhan, A., Al-Fraihat, D., Al-Arjan, A., Igried, B., & El-Salhi, S. M. others, & Al-Na'amneh, Q. (2023). Cybersecurity Threats in the Era of AI: Detection of Phishing Domains Through Classification Rules. *2023 2nd International Engineering Conference on Electrical, Energy, and Artificial Intelligence (EICEEAI)*, 1–6.

Alkadi, O., Moustafa, N., Turnbull, B., & Choo, K. K. R. (2020). A deep blockchain framework-enabled collaborative intrusion detection for protecting IoT and cloud networks. *IEEE Internet of Things Journal*, 8(12), 9463–9472. DOI: 10.1109/JIOT.2020.2996590

Alsowail, R. A., & Al-Shehari, T. (2020). Empirical detection techniques of insider threat incidents. *IEEE Access : Practical Innovations, Open Solutions*, 8, 78385–78402. DOI: 10.1109/ACCESS.2020.2989739

Alsowail, R. A., & Al-Shehari, T. (2021). A multi-tiered framework for insider threat prevention. *Electronics (Basel)*, 10(9), 1005. DOI: 10.3390/electronics10091005

Arif, H., Kumar, A., Fahad, M., & Hussain, H. K. (2024). Future Horizons: AI-Enhanced Threat Detection in Cloud Environments: Unveiling Opportunities for Research. *International Journal of Multidisciplinary Sciences and Arts*, 3(1), 242–251. DOI: 10.47709/ijmdsa.v2i2.3452

Boakye-Gyan, K. (2021). *An Approach to a Comprehensive Framework for Insider Threat*. Capitol Technology University.

Camacho, N. G. (2024). The Role of AI in Cybersecurity: Addressing Threats in the Digital Age. [JAIGS]. *Journal of Artificial Intelligence General Science*, 3(1), 143–154. DOI: 10.60087/jaigs.v3i1.75

Denney, K., Babun, L., & Uluagac, A. S. (2020). USB-watch: A generalized hardware-assisted insider threat detection framework. *Journal of Hardware and Systems Security*, 4(2), 136–149. DOI: 10.1007/s41635-020-00092-z

Dubey, A. K., & Mishra, V. (2024). Analysis of performance and trust in load balancing algorithm in cloud computing environment. *International Journal of Advanced Intelligence Paradigms*, 27(2), 91–103. DOI: 10.1504/IJAIP.2024.137185

Hussain, M., Pal, S., Jadidi, Z., Foo, E., & Kanhere, S. (2024). Federated Zero Trust Architecture using Artificial Intelligence. *IEEE Wireless Communications*, 31(2), 30–35. DOI: 10.1109/MWC.001.2300405

Jaradat, A. S., Nasayreh, A., Al-Na'amneh, Q., Gharaibeh, H., & Al Mamlook, R. E. (2023). Genetic optimization techniques for enhancing web attacks classification in machine learning. *2023 IEEE Intl Conf on Dependable, Autonomic and Secure Computing, Intl Conf on Pervasive Intelligence and Computing, Intl Conf on Cloud and Big Data Computing, Intl Conf on Cyber Science and Technology Congress (DASC/PiCom/CBDCom/CyberSciTech)*, 130–136. DOI: 10.1109/DASC/PiCom/CBDCom/Cy59711.2023.10361399

Kafi, M. A., & Akter, N. (2023). Securing financial information in the digital realm: Case studies in cybersecurity for accounting data protection. *American Journal of Trade and Policy*, 10(1), 15–26. DOI: 10.18034/ajtp.v10i1.659

Kolevski, D., & Michael, K. (2024). Edge Computing and IoT Data Breaches: Security, Privacy, Trust, and Regulation. *IEEE Technology and Society Magazine*, 43(1), 22–32. DOI: 10.1109/MTS.2024.3372605

Krishna, M. S. R., & Mangalampalli, S. (2024). A Systematic Review on Various Task Scheduling Algorithms in Cloud Computing. *EAI Endorsed Transactions on Internet of Things, 10.*

Laila, D. A., Al-Na'amneh, Q., Aljaidi, M., Nasayreh, A. N., Gharaibeh, H., Al Mamlook, R., & Alshammari, M. (2024). Simulation of Routing Protocols for Jamming Attacks in Mobile Ad-Hoc Network. In *Risk Assessment and Countermeasures for Cybersecurit* (pp. 235–252). IGI Global. DOI: 10.4018/979-8-3693-2691-6.ch013

Li, B., Wu, Y., Song, J., Lu, R., Li, T., & Zhao, L. (2020). DeepFed: Federated deep learning for intrusion detection in industrial cyber–physical systems. *IEEE Transactions on Industrial Informatics*, 17(8), 5615–5624. DOI: 10.1109/TII.2020.3023430

Narayanan, G., & Kannan, S. (2024). Enhancing security in cloud-based VM migration: A trust-centric hybrid optimization approach. *The International Arab Journal of Information Technology*, 21(1), 166–177. DOI: 10.34028/iajit/21/1/15

Nasir, R., Afzal, M., Latif, R., & Iqbal, W. (2021). Behavioral based insider threat detection using deep learning. *IEEE Access : Practical Innovations, Open Solutions*, 9(1), 14327–43266. DOI: 10.1109/ACCESS.2021.3118297

Olaniyi, O. O., & Omubo, D. S. (2023). The importance of COSO framework compliance in information technology auditing and enterprise resource management. *International Journal of Innovative Research and Development*, 12(4).

Patel, N. (2024). SECURE ACCESS SERVICE EDGE (SASE): EVALUATING THE IMPACT OF CONVEREGED NETWORK SECURITY ARCHITECTURES IN CLOUD COMPUTING. *Journal of Emerging Technologies and Innovative Research*, 11(3), 12.

Prakash, N., Vignesh, J., Ashwin, M., Ramadass, S., Veeranjaneyulu, N., Athawale, S. V., Ravuri, A., & Subramanian, B. (2024). Enabling secure and efficient industry 4.0 transformation through trust-authorized anomaly detection in cloud environments with a hybrid AI approach. *Optical and Quantum Electronics*, 56(2), 251. DOI: 10.1007/s11082-023-05781-x

Saba, T., Rehman, A., Sadad, T., Kolivand, H., & Bahaj, S. A. (2022). Anomaly-based intrusion detection system for IoT networks through deep learning model. *Computers & Electrical Engineering*, 99, 107810. DOI: 10.1016/j.compeleceng.2022.107810

Singh, A., & Chatterjee, K. (2024). Trust management in online computing environment: A complete review. *Journal of Ambient Intelligence and Humanized Computing*, 15(1), 491–545. DOI: 10.1007/s12652-023-04676-9

Singh, M., Mehtre, B. M., & Sangeetha, S. (2020). Insider threat detection based on user behaviour analysis. *Machine Learning, Image Processing, Network Security and Data Sciences: Second International Conference, MIND 2020, Silchar, India, July 30-31, 2020. Proceedings*, 2(Part II), 559–574.

Sun, D., Liu, M., Li, M., Shi, Z., Liu, P., & Wang, X. (2021). DeepMIT: a novel malicious insider threat detection framework based on recurrent neural network. *2021 IEEE 24th International Conference on Computer Supported Cooperative Work in Design (CSCWD)*, 335–341.

Vangoor, V. K. R., Yellepeddi, S. M., Ravi, C. S., Venkata, A. K. P., & Katari, P. (2024). Zero Trust Architecture: Implementing Microsegmentation in Enterprise Networks. *Journal of Artificial Intelligence Research and Applications*, 4(1), 512–538.

Velmurugan, S., Prakash, M., Neelakandan, S., & Radhakrishnan, A. (2024). Provably secure data selective sharing scheme with cloud-based decentralized trust management systems. *Journal of Cloud Computing (Heidelberg, Germany)*, 13(1), 86. DOI: 10.1186/s13677-024-00634-8

Wei, Y., Chow, K. P., & Yiu, S. M. (2020). Insider threat detection using multi-autoencoder filtering and unsupervised learning. *Advances in Digital Forensics XVI: 16th IFIP WG 11.9 International Conference, New Delhi, India, January 6–8, 2020, Revised Selected Papers 16. Springer International Publishing.*, 273–290.

Yaseen, A. (2023). AI-driven threat detection and response: A paradigm shift in cybersecurity. *International Journal of Information and Cybersecurity*, 7(12), 25–43.

Yuan, S., & Wu, X. (2021). Deep learning for insider threat detection: Review, challenges and opportunities. *Computers & Security*, 104, 102221. DOI: 10.1016/j.cose.2021.102221

Yuan, S., Zheng, P., Wu, X., & Tong, H. (2020). Few-shot insider threat detection. *Proceedings of the 29th ACM International Conference on Information & Knowledge Management*, 2289–2292.

Chapter 14
Secure Cloud-Marketplaces: A Trust Framework for Evaluating Security for Client Service Providers

Qais Al-Na'amneh
https://orcid.org/0009-0008-3034-7693
Applied Science Private University, Jordan

Rahaf Hazaymih
Jordan University of Science and Technology, Jordan

Mohammed Almaiah
https://orcid.org/0009-0008-9785-485X
University of Jordan, Jordan

Laith Alzboon
https://orcid.org/0000-0002-7715-9306
Applied Science Private University, Jordan

ABSTRACT

Trustworthy cloud service selection is a major concern in growing marketplaces. The Cloud Security Alliance (CSA) has developed a framework for cloud providers to self-assess their security policies and capabilities. This framework allows users to choose a cloud service based on the capabilities and controls published by providers. Cloud services improve efficiency in managing IT resources and operations. Cloud services are gaining popularity in on-demand and information and communication technology industries, leading to significant market expansion both locally and globally. In this paper, the trust-based framework is proposed to determine trustworthiness in Intercloud computing environments using many scenarios based on different parameters and contextual parameters (e.g., privacy, security, reliability, reputation, support, transparency, and compliance) which are important means to evaluate the Client Service Providers in cloud Marketplaces

DOI: 10.4018/979-8-3693-9919-4.ch014

I. INTRODUCTION

By allocating a score based on their interactions and conduct, a reputation-based approach could assist in the detection of rogue nodes in cloud markets. Reputation-poor nodes would be marked as possibly malicious and removed from the network. Additionally, the system might use machine learning algorithms to examine behavioral patterns and more effectively identify possible dangers. This could assist cloud service providers in locating and removing rogue nodes before they have a big impact. All users can benefit from increased network security and integrity by implementing a reputation-based system, which makes cloud computing safer and more dependable overall.

An early method of identifying malicious nodes in networks is anomaly detection. Network traffic and behavior patterns are analyzed to find anomalous or suspicious activity. Machine learning algorithms are used in the collection and analysis of data, including system logs, network traffic, and user activity. A baseline of typical network activity is created, and possibly anomalous activity is reported as malicious. Taking a proactive stance can quickly identify and address possible threats, improving network and data security against malevolent actors (Ficco, (2015).).

With key competitors like AWS, Microsoft Azure, Google Cloud Platform, IBM Cloud, and Oracle Cloud offering a range of services like Infrastructure as a Service (IaaS), Platform as a Service (PaaS), and Software as a Service (SaaS) (Alkhalidy, (2022).), the cloud market is a competitive and fast increasing sector as shown figure 1. These suppliers provide pay-as-you-go networking, storage, and virtualized computing resources. PaaS providers give developers a platform to create, launch, and maintain apps without having to deal with the hassles of complicated infrastructure administration. Smaller suppliers serve niche markets or sectors. There is a lot of rivalry in the industry, and suppliers are always coming up with new products and making deals (Kumar, (2023)). The cloud industry is expected to keep growing and changing as more companies shift to cloud for its scalability, flexibility, and cost-savings (Al-Sit, (2022, October).2022).

Figure 1. Data center cloud environment

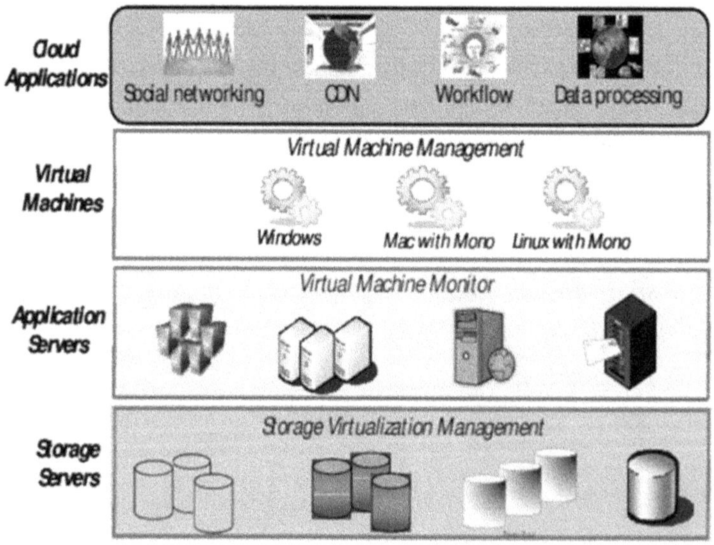

Participants' confidence in the cloud is growing, particularly in public clouds where users are exposed to other customers. The prospect of their data being moved to distant service providers or other third parties is being contested by cloud users, making the cloud environment less user-friendly (Alsarhan, (2022)).

Cloud markets necessitate robust security since customer data is so sensitive. Since attackers frequently have access to client information and may be aware of its intended purpose, internal attacks are more difficult to stop and identify. They might also sell other clients' confidential information. Wireless networks are used to deliver numerous services (Alhamad, (2011).).

To improve user trustworthiness and estimate trust levels in the cloud services environment, the fuzzy logic technique is developed to resolve ambiguity in trust evaluation for cloud providers. Using mathematical structures to support wise decision-making, the research attempts to alleviate uncertainty in trust evaluation for cloud providers by applying fuzzy logic theory to the cloud services environment (Li, (2024)).

In machine learning for cloud marketplaces, bad nodes could be identified by a reputation-based approach. Based on previous interactions and conduct, a score is assigned to each node. Nodes with malevolent behavior or inaccurate predictions receive lower scores, whereas high-performing nodes receive higher points. By proactively separating malevolent actors, the system's security and dependability can be enhanced by the identification and flagging of questionable nodes through ongoing monitoring and updating of these scores (Al-Na'amneh Q. A., (2023))

Cloud marketplaces are transforming IT management by allowing people and businesses to buy and sell computer resources over the Internet. Fuzzy logic technology helps optimize resource allocation, increase efficiency, and improve decision-making capabilities by representing inaccurate or uncertain data. These markets allow companies to better manage their IT requirements by providing flexibility, scalability, affordability, etc. (Al-Na'amneh Q., (2024).).

A framework is intended to clarify and construct tools that combine data from today's closed systems and enable the development of e-commerce applications, as well as security and tracing problems.

Six levels of functionality or services make up the electronic commerce application architecture (Al-Na'amneh, (2024)):

Primarily real transferring data, the first four levels commonly referred to lower layers.

That last three layers are referred to as the higher layers because they are primarily concerned with the message handling of the data packets delivered, the data connection and network layers can run in either of two nodes.

The first mode, connection-oriented, sends the full message as a data stream, then the connection is created, the data is transmitted, error checks are performed, data reception is confirmed, and the connection is closed (Alangari, (2024).)

The second method, connectionless, divides the message into packets or datagrams and delivers them to the destination on an intermittent basis.

The datagrams are gathered and reassembled at the destination, and any missing packets are recognized the transport layer essentially conceals the underlying transport method and is in charge of data dependability and integrity checks (Alzoubi, (2024)).

As a result, the OSI model serves as a reference model for understanding the underlying data transport mechanisms used by the protocols as shown in Table 1:

Table 1. E-commerce architecture

Layer No	OSI Model	E-commerce Architecture	CONCEPTUAL FRAMEWORK
1	Application	Application services	Business-to-business (B2B). Business-to-Consumer (B2C). Consumer-to-Business (C2B). Consumer-to-Consumer (C2C).
2	Presentation	Broker and data management	Order process mail order Payment schemes electronic cash Clearing or virtual mail
3	Session	Interface Layer	Interactive catalogs Directory support functions Software agents
4	Transport	Secure messaging	Secure hypertext transfer protocol Encrypted e-mail, EDI Remote programming (RFC)
5	Network	Middleware service	Structured documents (SGML, HTML) Compound documents (OLE, OPEN DOC)
6	Data link	Network infrastructure	Wireless cellular, radio, PCS Wire line-POTS, coaxial, fiber optic
7	Physical		

Businesses and people all over the world are becoming more easily susceptible to cybercrime and financial fraud as they transition more of daily services online.

There are various security services necessary for E-commerce to ensure the security of data that is electronically transferred over the internet (Xu, (2024)):

1) Confidentiality: transactions passing from source to destination may be intercepted easily by the attacker. To hide this message from all relay nodes, it's important for E-commerce to securely transmit message End-to-End. Device storage may be equally usable as well. The encryption/decryption mechanism is a simple solution for this.
2) Integrity: The transactions passing from source to destination should not change; the transactions should be received on the same sender side, on the receiver side. While passing or on your device, no intermediary should modify content (Omrany, (2024).).
3) Availability: It is also important that services provided by the E-commerce apps are always available and continuously in work mode for the continuous operation of E-commerce and access to data where necessary. Therefore, to ensure availability, it is important to detect intrusion and prevent intrusion (Rahman, (2020).).
4) Authenticity: End user should able to identify each other's identity to ensure that they are interacting with same entities that who they claim (Rizvi, (2020).).
5) Non-repudiation: it means someone cannot deny the data of the message. Additionally, it also defines a service, we can prove the integrity and author of the data (Al-Shargabi, (2020).)
6) Privacy: how to protect (sensitive information) privacy of the company involved in trading through e-commerce ([18] Mehraj, 2020)
7) Transparency: indicates that consumers should be completely unaware that they are interacting with various systems.

Transparency is critical for dealing with higher-level concerns like as physical media and connectivity, which are managed by the underlying network architecture transparency is achieved using middleware, which helps the distributed computing environment (Narang, (2021).).

The Main contribution of this study can be indicated as follows:

- A novel Trust Framework for Evaluating Security for Client Service Providers in Cloud-Marketplaces
- A trust-based framework is proposed to determine trustworthiness in Intercloud computing environments using many scenarios
- Many contextual and parameter-based factors (such as privacy, security, dependability, reputation, support, transparency, and compliance), which are crucial methods for assessing the Client Service Providers in cloud marketplaces
- The evaluation framework is trustworthy to prevent manipulation by malevolent providers.
- Proposed a more secure and trustworthy e-commerce cloud computing architecture.
- Provide a MFIS fuzzy logic-based trust model.

This is how the remainder of the paper is structured. Section II evaluates related works, and Section III explains the architecture framework to compute trust models. Section IV presents the experimental results and their discussion. Finally, Section VI presents the conclusion and future work.

ii. RELATED WORK

Because fuzzy logic techniques can handle imprecision and uncertainty, they are frequently utilized in decision-making processes. Finding rogue nodes is essential for security and confidence in cloud markets. This section examines similar works that use fuzzy logic to identify rogue nodes, offering insights into the state of the art now and suggesting future directions for research.

The use of game theoretical models to security concerns in cloud computing settings is investigated in this work. It highlights how crucial cloud computing's scalability, affordability, and accessibility are. The study makes the case that although game theory may provide security solutions, more investigation is necessary to handle real-world cloud computing constraints (Bamakan, (2021).).

The Internet of Things, or IoT, is a network of electronically connected things that facilitates easy data sharing and communication. It includes parking management systems, embedded sensors in the road, and smart cars to build a "smart city" with less traffic and energy usage. Wireless communication requires the convergence of cloud computing and Internet of Things. To enhance academic knowledge of IoT applications, this paper offers an overview of the functions of IoT and the security dangers that are linked with it (Habbal, (2024).).

In this study, IoT-based sensor systems are essential for threat detection, environmental monitoring, and smart home automation. However, there are network reliability issues as well as expensive production and maintenance costs. Predictive modeling and information description can be enhanced through machine learning. Security flaws in Mobile Ad hoc Networks (MANET) include Blackhole and Gray hole attacks. Unsupervised machine learning is used by Advanced Hybrid Optimization (AHGFFA) to protect IoT sensors (Ranathunga, 2020).

The paper examines 26 fog computing consensus mechanisms, such as capability-based, voting-based, and work-proof-based techniques. Work evidence is the most common. Only current databases are included in the study; future iterations of the database and fresh literature may be added. To comprehend their special qualities and uses, more study is required (Awaysheh, (2021).). In (Hizam, (2020).)Fuzzy logic was used to evaluate the trust value of CSPs based on their performance, assisting users in selecting a CSP. Trust in a CSP is mostly evaluated based on physical factors such as processor count, speed, and memory size. They did not provide additional trust-related measures. In contrast, according to (Rahmani, (2022).), the trust value of each CSP is determined by four key parameters: security, availability, cost, and performance. However, evaluating the metrics separately does not ensure that the trust values accurately reflect the CSP's exact status, unlike when assessed combined. Using fuzzy logic, (Groen, (2024).)evaluated trust based on performance, reliability, security, price, and reputation. In (Al-Na'amneh Q. N., (2024).), the Seguno fuzzy technique is used to evaluate the trustworthiness of cloud providers based on four criteria: scalability, availability, security, and usability.

The essay addresses vulnerabilities and hackers by examining how big data computing might be used to enhance software security. It suggests a large data Spark platform design strategy for intelligent software protection systems. After the system's performance was assessed, it was found that identification speed, accuracy, and data loss rate had all improved by 2.14%. The paper highlights how network security technology must advance in the future to fulfill demands for societal development and offer complete services (Abou-Nassar, (2020).). Trust and reputation models are effective for decision-making in various service environments, including e-commerce, peer-to-peer networks, and product evaluations (Wang, (2021).).

The techniques have been used for grid computing (Al-Na'amneh Q. A., (2024, February).), cloud computing (Al-Na'amneh Q. N., (2024).)and selecting online services (Jaradat, (2023, November).). TR-based decision-making in varied environments sometimes fails to consider multiple aspects, including security, compliance, and data governance. In (Aljaidi, (2023, December).)offered ways for evaluating trust based on numerous qualities in grid computing, web services, and cloud computing contexts, however, these are exceptions. In the context of a cloud-specific project (Al-Na'amneh Q. A., 2023), a trust model (Laila, Enhancing 2D Logistic Chaotic Map for Gray Image Encryption. In Risk Assessment and Countermeasures for Cybersecurity (pp. 170-188)., (2024).)that addresses SLA compliance has recently been proposed. The suggested methodology aims to assess the reliability of cloud infrastructure providers by gauging their compliance with performance requirements that are mutually agreed upon through service level agreements (SLAs). Unlike (Laila, Simulation of Routing Protocols for Jamming Attacks in Mobile Ad-Hoc Network. In Risk Assessment and Countermeasures for Cybersecurit, (2024).), the trust model in (Nivethitha, (2019).)considers two more factors: I) Customer behavior, such as choosing to use a cloud provider's service regardless of the rating they have given the provider; ii) Customer satisfaction ratings, such as when a customer rates the provider.

It has previously been demonstrated that considering customer satisfaction scores in addition to professional evaluations, self-evaluations, and certificate-based assessments is necessary and useful in determining credibility. In (Somu, (2017).), the authors focus on the most important factors to consider while selecting a trustworthy CSP. The established trust model prioritizes data security, identity management, authorization, authentication, and virtualization to ensure efficient security for CSPs.

The suggested trust model uses a cloud consumer's security characteristics as input and a point-based system to calculate trust value, based on the ratio of user-gained points to total points. Users can choose a cloud service that meets their specific demands. (Cruz, (2019, June).) suggest a model to create a CSP's trust score by utilizing the fuzzy inference system and comparing the policies of service brokers and load balancing. This method calculates a CSP's trust score by considering three Service Broker Policies and three Load Balancing Policies. To compare services individually and choose the best option for the user, the trust model architecture incorporates User Bundles and Data Centers of the service providers. Applications, storage, networks, and IP are among the data center sectors that are considered by the load balancing and service broker policies. After receiving input from the user, such as their geography, the regulations determine how many data centers are in that specific area. Like (Afzali, (2022).) suggests a trust based on fuzzy logic; nevertheless, the maintenance of trust is the primary focus.

An equation that determines the distinction between direct and indirect trust is the basis of the trust assessment. with interaction weight and trust weight. The drawback of this approach is that figuring out trust in a fuzzy environment includes many kinds of cloud networks, Trust scores, and agreement kinds are not covered by the writers. A trust model like (Hasnain, (2020).) was proposed in (Ghosh N, (2015)), in which the consumer's trust percentage is determined by the trust metric stage. But Reputation, customer satisfaction, majority agreement, and cloud service users' capabilities are among the factors that vary from (Ding S, (2014)). Using methods like Particle Swarm Optimization, Multiple Regression, Analytic Hierarchical Process, and Particle Swarm Optimization-Multiple Regression, the trust metric stage determines each consumer's trust percentage. Nevertheless, despite the apparent accuracy of these methods, there is a percentage of average deviation that can only be eliminated by creating a scheduling procedure that allows customers to test the model according to their trust levels.

III. METHODOLOGY

Trust has sparked widespread commitment from scholars from disparate domains such as psychology, sociology, economics, computer science, and management science, however with a minor compromise. There is no general definition of trust, and explanations are often manner specific. In general, trust is an act of confidence, assurance, and belief that is predictable to execute or distribute as assured. Cloud computing classifies many techniques in an environment as open or secretive. It offers an amazing structure for bidding and data storage. Because of its extremely exposed environment to outer users, confidence in the cloud is gradually gaining traction among all parties, particularly in public clouds.

This section describes how to calculate the "Trust in the Cloud Marketplace" directly, a set of trust criteria, and then aggregate them into a single trust score. Also organized and evaluated the direct trust cloud model using MFIS to estimate the trust value of a specific source of cloud shown in figure 2.

First, determine the important trust metrics and criteria. For this example, we will use the following measurements such as:

- **Security:** There is no doubt about data security's importance in online markets. Sensitive data, such as financial records, confidential company information, and personal identifiable information (PII), is stored on these platforms. A data security breach can have serious repercussions, including monetary loss, harm to one's reputation, and legal problems. It is imperative that cloud-based marketplaces continuously invest in data security as cyber threats continue to change and become more sophisticated. This entails working with cybersecurity specialists, exchanging threat intelligence, and monitoring proactively. These steps are crucial to a comprehensive data security plan because they guarantee the safety of sensitive data and the integrity of the market.

- **Compliance:** rules, guidelines, and benchmarks are being adopted to address a variety of challenges related to the exponential expansion of data acquired by companies, which is causing a rapid change in the compliance landscape. These laws cover a wide range of topics, including cybersecurity, financial reporting, environmental standards, and data protection and privacy. As businesses move from on-premises data centers to cloud-based infrastructure, information technology is also changing. This presents new opportunities and problems for ensuring compliance across a variety of operational domains. As a result, a lot of businesses struggle to define cloud compliance and understand their compliance responsibilities. But whether data is hosted in the public cloud or on-premises,
- **Reliability:** Platforms such as utility computing, grid computing, distributed computing, and autonomic computing are all part of cloud computing, which is a vast platform that falls under three main service models: platform as a service (PaaS), software as a service (Saas), and infrastructure as a service (Iaas) (Al-Na'amneh Q. A., (2023)). Because of the massive architecture of the Cloud, it is extremely complex to consistently provide services under a wide range of conditions and scenarios. In the context of the cloud, there is always a chance of various failures, including those involving missing resources, networks, databases, overflows, timeouts, software, and hardware. (Ficco, (2015).) (Alsarhan, (2022)), (Al-Na'amneh Q., (2024).). According to dependability analysis, the cloud comprises many equally important components. Specifically, consumers should ensure that their data is recoverable by replicating it across accounts; this should be done by building a highly dependable storage system.
- **Support and Transparency:** Effective service comparisons are made possible by automating data collection about cloud services with software APIs. This strategy is still in its early phase, though. New industry analysis methodologies are emerging to comprehend the cloud service supply chain as cloud computing continues to grow in popularity and expand in the enterprise IT deployment market.

Including software automation in the list of cloud services will shield internal organizational capabilities from a public view. For businesses and cloud service providers, this can be an excellent place to start when aiming for transparency.

- **Privacy:** security and privacy concerns in cloud systems. Researchers used a variety of criteria to provide a complete picture of these challenges and their links. In (Tang M, (2016)) propose modeling the security ecosystem around three cloud system participants: service users, service instances, and cloud providers. The authors divide the attack into six sections (user to service, service to user, cloud to user, service to cloud, and cloud to service).
- **Reputation and Trust:** Trust and reputation play crucial roles in decision-making across several industries, including historic fish markets and eCommerce. According to trust is an individual's subjective anticipation of another in a certain situation. In contrast, reputation refers to an entity's perceived status in the community (Kawser Wazed Nafi, 2012). This belief may be based on past contacts between entities, either directly or indirectly. Trust and reputation can impact each other (Kim, 2013.). Our goal is to investigate methods based on reputation and trust that can assist clients in choosing cloud service providers. Models of reputation and trust are helpful in decision-making in online service environments (Lin, 2014.). The ideas have also been used for wireless sensors and ad-hoc networks to address issues with relay node selection for packet forwarding and

beacon node location acceptance, for example (Rajendran, 2015.). Moreover, there has previously been discussion about the integration of trust management systems with Grid computing (Pathan, 2015.).

Figure 2. Proposed compute trust score

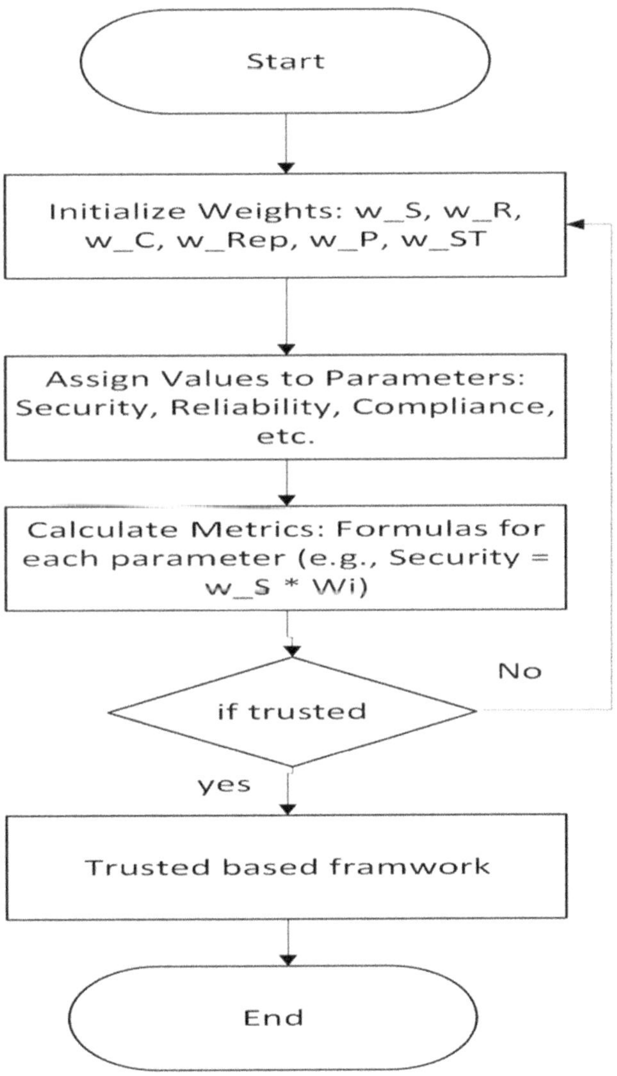

Let w_i be the weight for each metric i, where i corresponds to Security, Reliability, Privacy, Compliance, Reputation, and Support & Transparency.

First: The summation of all weights $w_S+w_p+w_C+w_{Rep}+w_{ST}$ should be equal to 1.

Second: Give each cloud provider a score based on a predetermined range of 0 to 10 or 0 to 100. Let S_i be the score for metric i for a given provider.
Third: Use the following equation to determine each metric's weighted score $WS_i = w_i * S_i$
Fourth: The total trust score (T) for each cloud provider is calculated by adding the weighted scores $T = \sum_i (w_i * S_i)$ where i represent S, R, P, C, Rep, and ST.

Algorithm 1 Pseudo-code of the Calculate Trust in Cloud Market Algorithm

1. **Initialize** Weight for Metrics:
   w_S
   w_R
   w_C
   w_{Rep}
   w_{ST}
   w_P

$w_S + w_p + w_C + w_{Rep} + w_{ST} = 1$

2. **Assign a value to each parameter in** the cloud market
   w_S: value for Security
   w_R: value for Reliability
   w_C: value for Compliance
   w_{Rep}: value for Reputation
   w_P: value for Privacy
   w_{ST}: value for Support & Transparency
3. Calculated the metric
   Security= $w_S * Wi$
   Reliability= $w_R * wi$
   Compliance= $w_C * wi$
   Reputation= $w_{Rep} * wi$
   Privacy= $w_P * wi$
   Support & Transparency= $w_{ST} * wi$
4. Calculated Trust:

TS= $w_S + w_R + w_P + w_C + w_{Rep} + w_{ST}$

Return trust score

5. **Calculated** Trust Score for provide:

$T = \sum_i (w_i * S_i)$

END FOR

6. **Ranking** Trust proposed framework
7. **Return** the total trust score

End

I. RESULTS ANALYSIS

The results are presented in four scenarios. Our model may be used to compute trust. The proposed model will be implemented in Python. Four scenarios have been developed to assess the impact of the trust model:

Scenarios 1 and 2: Determine the trust value that has the highest value of trustworthiness, the first two scenario possibilities were discussed and implemented following the proposed trust model. We used the proposed approach to calculate trust using equations.

1. **Scenario-1:** In a scenario, we suppose the following values for input parameters as given in Table 1:

Table 2. Metric and weight parameter

Metric parameter	Value	Weight parameter	value
S	8	w_S	0.25
R	9	w_R	0.20
P	7	w_P	0.15
C	8	w_C	0.15
Rep	6	w_{Rep}	0.10
ST	7	w_{ST}	0.15

Table 2 describes how to calculate the weighted score $WS_i = w_i * S_i$

Table 2. Weighted score

S	0.25*8 = 2.00
R	0.20*9 = 1.80
P	0.15*7 = 1.05
C	0.15*8 = 1.20
Rep	0.10*6 = 0.60
ST	0.15*7 = 1.05

Table 3 describes how to calculate the trust $T = \sum_i (w_i * S_i)$

Table 3. Trust score

T	2.00+1.80+1.05+1.20+0.60+1.05 = 7.70

2. **Scenario-2:** In a scenario, we suppose the following values for input parameters as given in Table 4:

Table 4. Metric and weight parameter

Metric parameter	Value	Weight parameter	value
S	10	w_S	0.4
R	7	w_R	0.1
P	8	w_P	0.15
C	6	w_C	0.1
Rep	8	w_{Rep}	0.2
ST	9	w_{ST}	0.15

Table 5 calculates the weighted score $WS_i = w_i*S_i$

Table 5. Weighted scorer

S	10*0.4 = 4
R	7*0.1 = 0.7
P	8*0.15 = 1.2
C	6*0.1 = 0.6
Rep	8*0.2 = 1.6
ST	9*0.15 = 1.35

Table 6 calculates the trust $T = \sum_i (w_i * S_i)$

Table 6. Trust scorer

T	4+0.7+1.2+0.6+1.6+1.35 = 9.45

Scenario 2 is more trustworthy based on its higher trust score. This is because each metric has a different set of weights and values. For example, Scenario 2 has a larger value for “S” (10 compared to 8) and gives “S” more weight (0.4 compared to 0.25) resulting in a significantly higher weighted score for this metric. The overall trust score is further raised in Scenario 2 by “Rep” having a larger weight (0.2) and a higher value (8 compared to 6). This illustrates how altering trust measures' values and weights can have a big impact on the outcome of trustworthiness. With a higher trust score and a better balance between metrics, Scenario 2 is more likely to be approved when it comes to service requests.

Figure 3. Comparison of weighted score in two scenarios

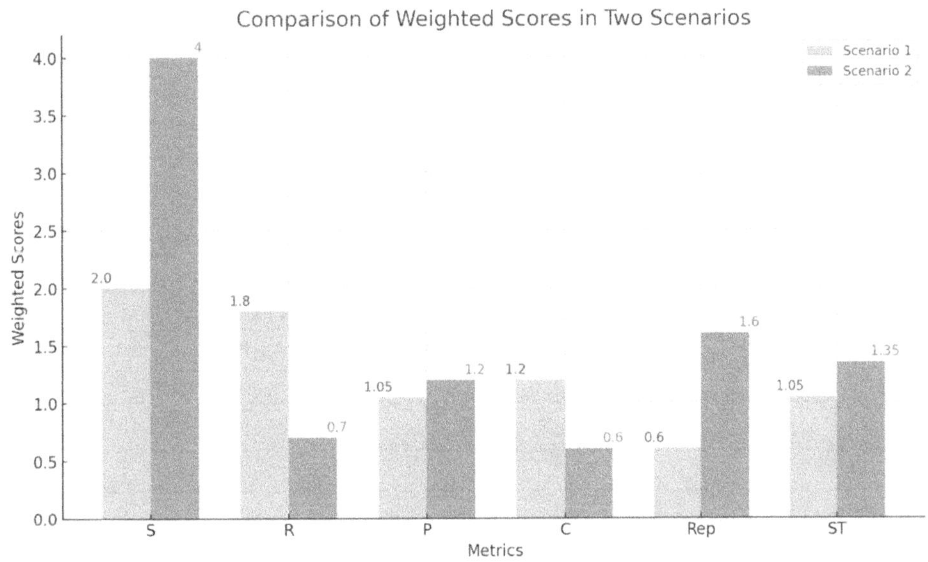

Figure 3 and 4 shows the trust value that was determined by using the suggested trust model for two distinct scenarios. Compared to Scenario 1 (7.70), Scenario 2 has a higher trust score (9.45). This suggests that Scenario 2 is more trustworthy than Scenario 1 based on the suggested trust model. Different weightings and values supplied to the trust indicators account for the difference in trust scores between the two scenarios, highlighting how crucial it is to choose these parameters appropriately to accurately assess trustworthiness. In each case, the trust scores can be utilized to determine whether to approve service requests. Both scenarios in this instance point to a perhaps acceptable degree of reliability, with Scenario 2 being the more dependable choice.

Figure 4. Trust value in scenario 1 and 2

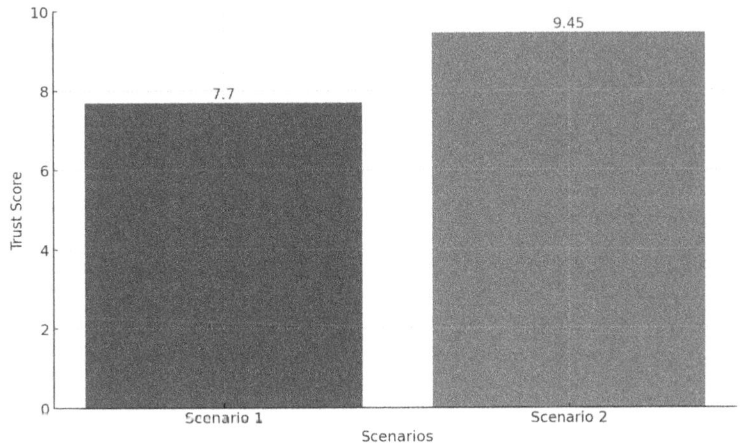

In scenarios 3 and 4 determine the trust value for the lowest level of untrustworthiness. The third and fourth possibilities were presented and implemented using the proposed trust model. We used the proposed approach to calculate trust through equations.

3. **Scenario-3:** In a scenario, we suppose the following values for input parameters as given in Table 7:

Table 7. Metric and weight parameter

Metric parameter	Value	Weight parameter	value
S	2	w_S	0.1
R	3	w_R	0.01
P	1	w_P	0.1
C	2	w_C	0.02
Rep	4	w_{Rep}	0.05
ST	3	w_{ST}	0.2

In Table 8 calculate the weighted score $WS_i = w_i{*}S_i$

Table 8. Weighted scorer

S	2*0.1 = 0.2
R	3*0.01 = 0.03
P	1*0.1 = 0.1
C	2*0.02 = 0.04
Rep	4*0.05 = 0.2
ST	3*0.2 = 0.6

Table 9 calculates the trust $T = \sum_i (w_i{*}\, S_i)$

Table 9. Trust scorer

T	0.2+0.03+0.1+0.04+0.2+0.6 = 1.17

4. **Scenario-4:** In a scenario, we suppose the following values for input parameters as given in Table 10:

Table 10. Metric and weight parameter

Metric parameter	Value	Weight parameter	value
S	3	w_S	0.1
R	4	w_R	0.2
P	3	w_P	0.15
C	3	w_C	0.12
Rep	4	w_{Rep}	0.01
ST	5	w_{ST}	0.3

In Table 11 calculate the weighted score $WS_i = w_i{*}S_i$

Table 11. Weighted score

S	3*0.1 = 0.3
R	4*0.2 = 0.8
P	3*0.15 = 0.45
C	3*0.12 =0.36
Rep	4*0.01 = 0.04
ST	5*0.3 = 1.5

Table 12 calculates the trust $T = \sum_i (w_i {*} S_i)$

Table 12. Trust score

T	0.3+0.8+0.45+0.36+0.04+1.5 = 3.45

The proposed trust model in cloud marketplace automated System's membership functions provide the curve value excluding accuracy values and also distribute a carefully worked-out fuzzy logic procedure that proposes mathematical values of equally input and output variables. The proposed automated trust model membership function is shown in Table 13.

Table 13. I/O variables proposed automated according to cloud trust model

No#	I/O Variables	Graphical representations of MF
1	Security	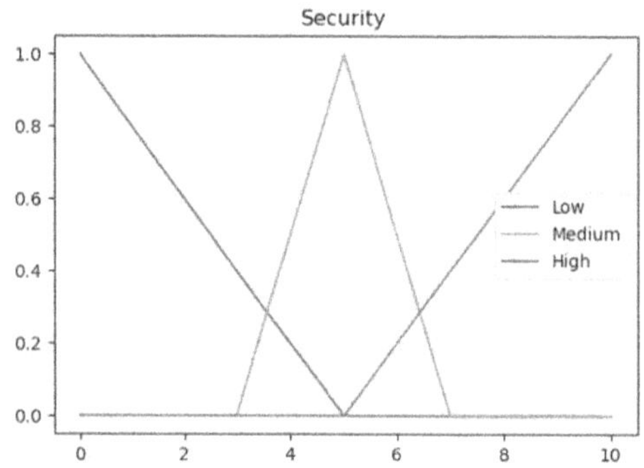
2	Reliability	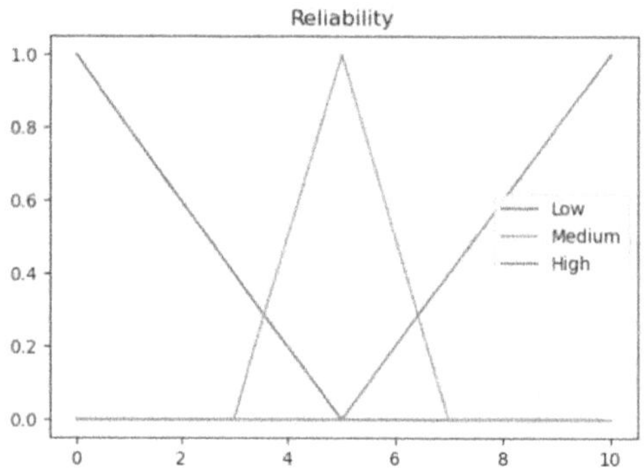

continued on following page

Table 13. Continued

3	Privacy	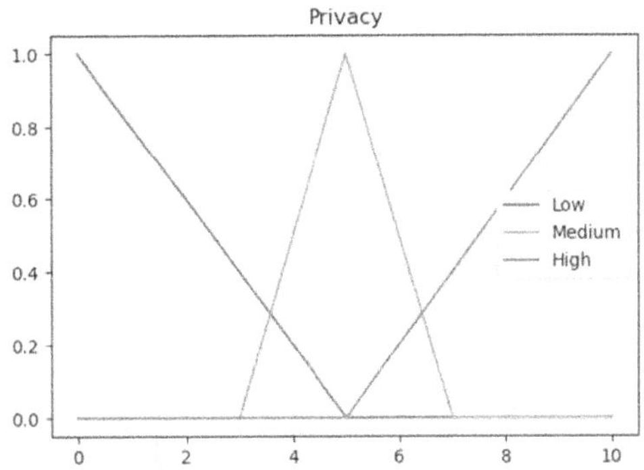
4	Compliance	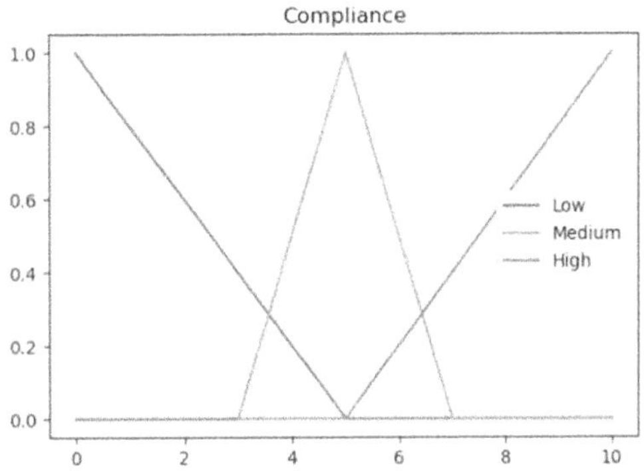
5	Reputation	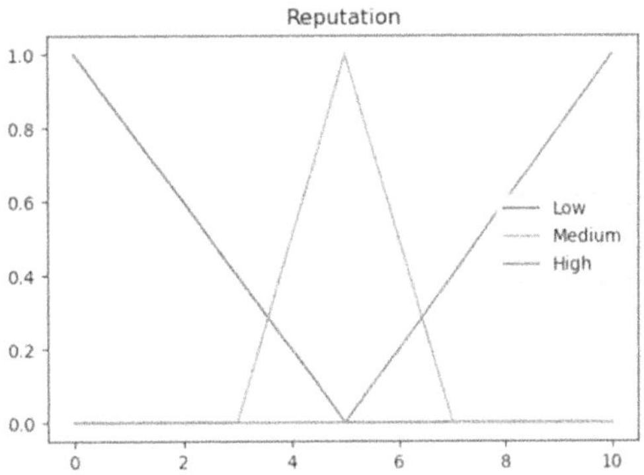

continued on following page

Table 13. Continued

6	Support and Transparency	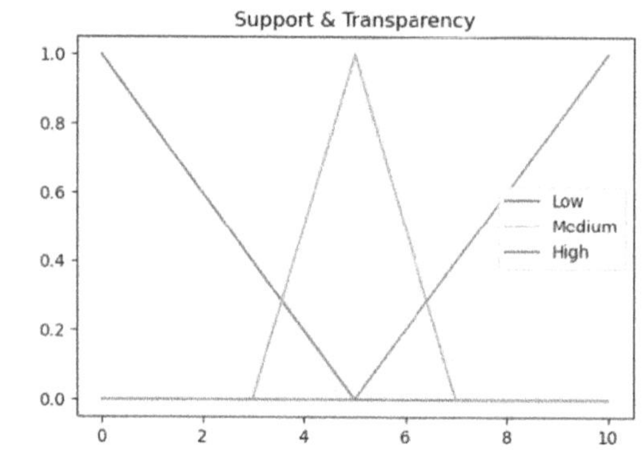
7	Trust Score	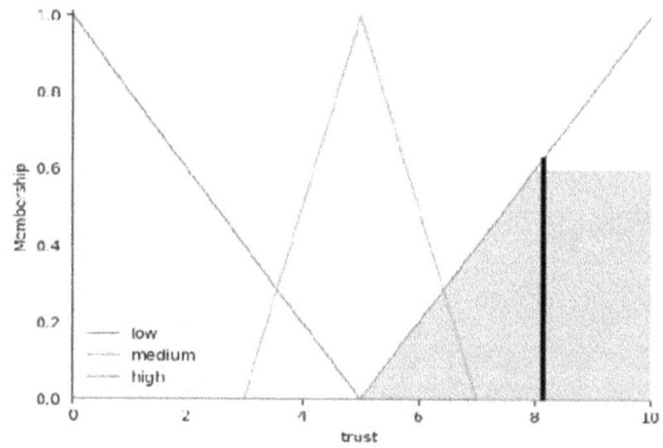

Figure 5 shows a measured score between Scenarios 3 and 4 across a range of measures shown in the above visual comparison. Reliability (R), Sustainability (ST), and Performance (P) have much higher scores in Scenario 4 than they do in Scenario 3. Scenario 4 (3.45) has an overall greater trust score than Scenario 3 (1.17) because of the higher weighting.

Figure 5. Comparison of weighted score in two scenarios

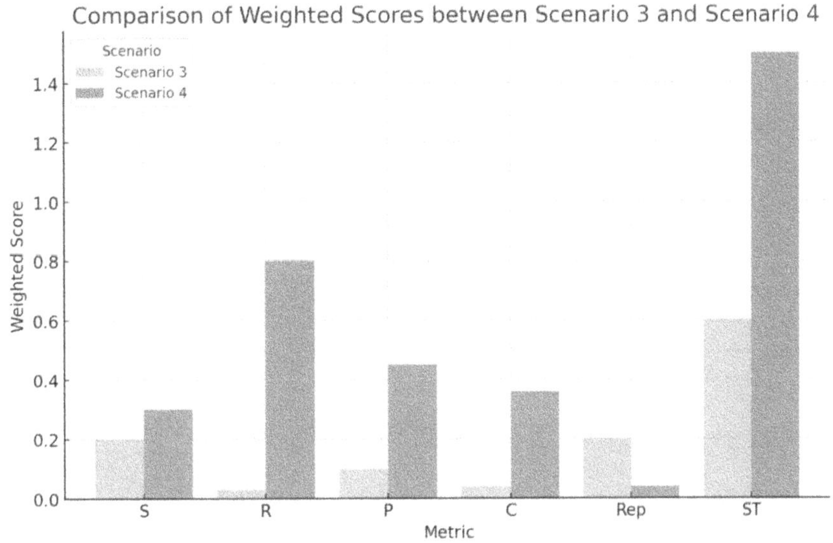

Figure 6 shows the trust value that was determined using the suggested trust model for two distinct scenarios. With a trust score of 1.17, Scenario 3 is the least trustworthy, suggesting the largest degree of unreliability. This implies that among the two scenarios, this one is the least dependable. Although Scenario 4's trust score (3.45) is higher than Scenario 3's, it is still untrustworthy when compared to earlier scenarios. Different weightings and values supplied to the trust indicators account for the difference in trust scores between the two scenarios, highlighting how crucial it is to choose these parameters appropriately to accurately assess trustworthiness. In each case, the trust scores can be utilized to determine whether to approve service requests. Both scenarios in this instance point to an unacceptable degree of reliability,

Figure 6. Trust value in scenario 3 and 4

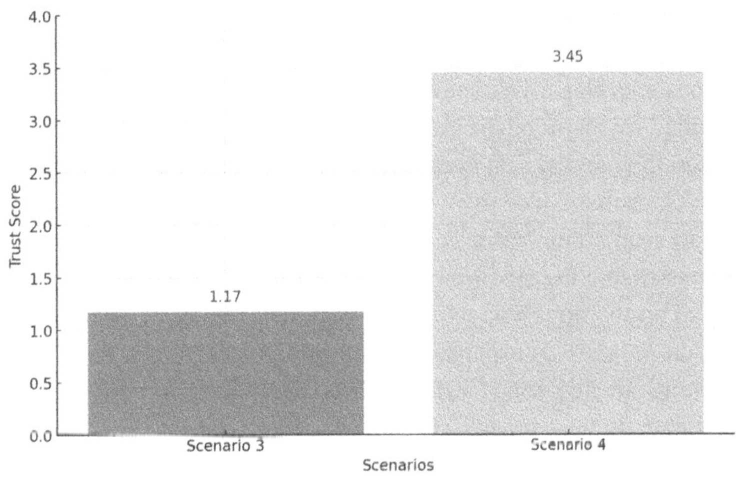

Figure 6 and 7 shows weighted scores for each of the four scenarios are shown in the graph above. The findings show the main variations in the contributions of each measure (S, R, P, C, Rep, and ST) to the total trust score for every scenario. The goal of scenarios 1 and 2 is to determine who is the most trustworthy. As a result of its constant higher "S" and "Rep" numbers, Scenario 2 has a higher overall trust score of 9.45 than 1's Scenario 7.70.

Scenarios 3 and 4 investigate the least amount of unreliability. In comparison to Scenario 3, Scenario 4 has substantially higher scores for "R" and "ST". As a result, Scenario 4 has the highest trust score is 3.45 while Scenario 3 has the lowest— 1.17.

Figure 7. Comparison of weighted score in two scenarios

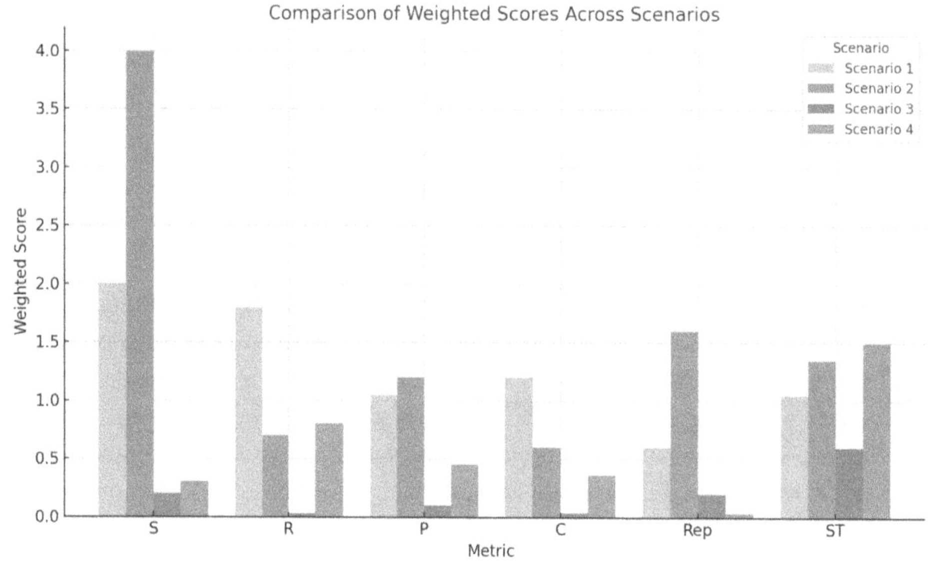

IV. CONCLUSIONS AND FUTURE WORK

Nowadays, Cloud consumers have the issue of selecting trustworthy services in growing marketplaces. The markets are controlled by major businesses (Amazon, Microsoft, Google) and newcomers (Vodafone, NEC, Fujitsu) from the networks and telecommunications industry. Many providers offer similar services and functions. Consumers face the issue of identifying trustworthy cloud providers based on their unique needs before using their services. The trust-based framework is presented in this paper as an efficient method for assessing the credibility of Client Service Providers in cloud marketplaces. It is based on many scenarios and various contextual and parameter-based factors, including privacy, security, reliability, reputation, support, transparency, and compliance. Moreover, Future work. Our present project involves integrating our suggested trust-aware verification framework with actual cloud provider datasets into the cloud environment-based Trust Management system. As a result, user-specified and confirmed claims can be included in the process of evaluating the trustworthiness of the cloud provider using actual datasets. Also, we aim to provide a secure connection between users and the system. We want to develop a more secure and lightweight encryption solution to protect file information.

REFERENCES

Abou-Nassar, E. M.-K.-L., Iliyasu, A. M., El-Kafrawy, P. M., Song, O.-Y., Bashir, A. K., & El-Latif, A. A. A. (2020). DITrust chain: Towards blockchain-based trust models for sustainable healthcare IoT systems. *IEEE Access : Practical Innovations, Open Solutions*, 8, 111223–111238. DOI: 10.1109/ACCESS.2020.2999468

Afzali, M. P., Pourmohammadi, H., & Mohammad Vali Samani, A. (2022). An efficient framework for trust evaluation of secure service selection in fog computing based on QoS, reputation, and social criteria. *Computing*, 104(7), 1643–1675. DOI: 10.1007/s00607-022-01053-w

Al-Na'amneh, Q. ((2024).). Next Generation Image Watermarking via Combined DWT-SVD Technique. (pp. 1-34.). In 2024 2nd International Conference on Cyber Resilience (IC. Al-Na'amneh, Q. A. ((2023)). Feature Selection for Robust Spoofing Detection: A Chi-Square-based Machine Learning Approach. *Jordan.* In 2023 2nd International E.

Al-Na'amneh, Q. A. (2023). Feature Selection for Robust Spoofing Detection: A Chi-Square-based Machine Learning Approach. In . *2nd Internation.*

Al-Na'amneh, Q. A. ((2024, February).). Next Generation Image Watermarking via Combined DWT-SVD Technique. In 2024 2nd International Conference on Cyber Resilience. DOI: 10.1109/ICCR61006.2024.10532782

Al-Na'amneh, Q. A., Aljaidi, M., Nasayreh, A., Gharaibeh, H., Al Mamlook, R. E., Jaradat, A. S., Alsarhan, A., & Samara, G. (2024). Enhancing IoT device security: CNN-SVM hybrid approach for real-time detection of DoS and DDoS attacks. *Journal of Intelligent Systems*, 33(1), 20230150. DOI: 10.1515/jisys-2023-0150

Al-Na'amneh, Q. N. ((2024).). Improving Memory Malware Detection in Machine Learning With Random Forest-Based Feature Selection. In Risk Assessment and Countermeasures for Cybe. DOI: 10.4018/979-8-3693-2691-6.ch006

Al-Shargabi, B. A.-J. (2020). A cloudlet based security and trust model for e-government web services. *Journal of Theoretical and Applied Information Technology*, 98(1), 27–37.

Al-Sit, W. T. ((2022, October).2022). Direct Trust in Cloud Computing Based on Fuzzy Logic. In. *International Conference on Cyber Resilience (ICCR)*, (pp. 1-6). IEEE.

Alangari, S. (2024). An Unsupervised Machine Learning Algorithm for Attack and Anomaly Detection in IoT Sensors. *Wireless Personal Communications*, •••, 1–25. DOI: 10.1007/s11277-023-10811-8

Alhamad, M. (2011). SLA-based trust model for secure cloud computing. *(Doctoral dissertation, Curtin University).*

Aljaidi, M. A.-F.-A.-S.-N. ((2023, December).). Cybersecurity Threats in the Era of AI: Detection of Phishing Domains Through Classification Rules. In 2023 2nd Internationa.

Alkhalidy, M. A.-S., Al-Serhan, A. F., Alsarhan, A., & Igried, B. (2022). A new scheme for detecting malicious nodes in vehicular ad hoc networks based on monitoring node behavior. *Future Internet*, 14(8), 223. DOI: 10.3390/fi14080223

Alsarhan, A. A.-G. (2022). A novel scheme for malicious nodes detection in cloud markets based on fuzzy logic technique. *Int. J. Interact. Mob.Technol.*, 16(3), 136–150.

Alzoubi, Y. I., & Mishra, A. (2024). Blockchain consensus mechanisms comparison in fog computing: A systematic review. *ICT Express*, 10(2), 342–373. DOI: 10.1016/j.icte.2024.02.008

Awaysheh, F. M., Aladwan, M. N., Alazab, M., Alawadi, S., Cabaleiro, J. C., & Pena, T. F. (2021). Security by design for big data frameworks over cloud computing. *IEEE Transactions on Engineering Management*, 69(6), 3676–3693. DOI: 10.1109/TEM.2020.3045661

Bamakan, S. M., Faregh, N., & ZareRavasan, A. (2021). Di-ANFIS: An integrated blockchain–IoT–big data-enabled framework for evaluating service supply chain performance. *Journal of Computational Design and Engineering*, 8(2), 676–690. DOI: 10.1093/jcde/qwab007

Cruz, J. M. ((2019, June).). The metric matters: The art of measuring trust in electronics. In *Proceedings of the 56th Annual Design Automation Conference 2019* (pp. 1-4). DOI: 10.1145/3316781.3323488

Ding, S., Xia, C.-Y., Zhou, K.-L., Yang, S.-L., & Shang, J. S. (2014, June 27). X. C. ((2014)). Decision support for personalized cloud service selection through multi-attribute trustworthiness evaluation. *PLoS One*, 9(6), e97762. Advance online publication. DOI: 10.1371/journal.pone.0097762 PMID: 24972237

Ficco, M., & Palmieri, F. (2015). Introducing fraudulent energy consumption in cloud infrastructures: A new generation of denial-of-service attacks. *IEEE Systems Journal*, 11(2), 460–470. DOI: 10.1109/JSYST.2015.2414822

Ghosh N, G. S. ((2015)). A framework to facilitate selection of cloud service providers. IEEE Trans Cloud 3(1):66–79. .DOI: 10.1109/TCC.2014.2328578

Groen, J. D. (2024). Implementing and evaluating security in O-RAN: Interfaces, intelligence, and platforms. *IEEE Network*.

Habbal, A. A., Ali, M. K., & Abuzaraida, M. A. (2024). Artificial Intelligence Trust, risk and security management (AI trism): Frameworks, applications, challenges and future research directions. *Expert Systems with Applications*, 240, 122442. DOI: 10.1016/j.eswa.2023.122442

Hasnain, M. P., Pasha, M. F., Ghani, I., Imran, M., Alzahrani, M. Y., & Budiarto, R. (2020). Evaluating trust prediction and confusion matrix measures for web services ranking. *IEEE Access : Practical Innovations, Open Solutions*, 8, 90847–90861. DOI: 10.1109/ACCESS.2020.2994222

Hizam, S. M. ((2020).). A conceptual paper on SERVQUAL-framework for assessing quality of Internet of Things (IoT) services. arXiv preprint arXiv. 2001.01840.

Jaradat, A. S.-N. ((2023, November).). Genetic optimization techniques for enhancing web attacks classification in machine learning. In 2023 IEEE Intl Conf on Dependable, Autonomic and Secu.

Kawser Wazed Nafi, T. S. (2012). An Advanced Certain Trust Model Using Fuzzy Logic andProbabilistic Logic theory". *IJACSA, Vol 3, No 12.*

Kim, M. P., & Park, S. O. (2013). Trust management on user behavioral patterns for a mobile cloud computing. *Cluster Computing*, 16(4), 725–731. DOI: 10.1007/s10586-013-0248-9

Kumar, V. S., Shaheen, , Rajani, D., & Medikondu, N. R. (2023). Secure Deep Learning Framework for Cloud to Protect the Virtual Machine from Malicious Events. *Wireless Personal Communications*, 131(3), 1859–1879. DOI: 10.1007/s11277-023-10524-y

Laila, D. A., Al-Na'amneh, Q., Aljaidi, M., Nasayreh, A. N., Gharaibeh, H., Al Mamlook, R., & Alshammari, M. (2024). Enhancing 2D Logistic Chaotic Map for Gray Image Encryption. In Risk Assessment and Countermeasures for Cybersecurity (pp. 170-188). (n.d.).

Laila, D. A.-N. ((2024).). Enhancing 2D Logistic Chaotic Map for Gray Image Encryption. In Risk Assessment and Countermeasures for Cybersecurity (pp. 170-188).

Laila, D. A.-N. ((2024).). Simulation of Routing Protocols for Jamming Attacks in Mobile Ad-Hoc Network. In Risk Assessment and Countermeasures for Cybersecurit.

Li, H. W. (2024). Driving Intelligent IoT Monitoring and Control through Cloud Computing and Machine Learning. arXiv preprint arXiv:2403.18100.

Lin, G. B., Bie, Y., Lei, M., & Zheng, K. (2014). a behavior trust model in cloud computing environment. [ACO-BTM.]. *Int. J. Comput. Intell. Syst.*, 7(4), 785–795. DOI: 10.1080/18756891.2013.864479

Mehraj, S. &. (2020). *International Conference on Computer Communication and Informatics (ICCCI)* (pp. 1-6). IEEE.

Narang, N., & Kar, S. (2021). A hybrid trust management framework for a multi-service social IoT network. *Computer Communications*, 171, 61–79. DOI: 10.1016/j.comcom.2021.02.015

Nivethitha, S. G., Gauthama Raman, M. R., Gireesha, O., Kannan, K., & Shankar Sriram, V. S. (2019). An improved rough set approach for optimal trust measure parameter selection in cloud environments. *Soft Computing*, 23(22), 11979–11999. DOI: 10.1007/s00500-018-03753-y

Omrany, H. A.-O.-D., Al-Obaidi, K. M., Hossain, M., Alduais, N. A. M., Al-Duais, H. S., & Ghaffarianhoseini, A. (2024). IoT-enabled smart cities: A hybrid systematic analysis of key research areas, challenges, and recommendations for future direction. *Discover Cities*, 1(1), C. DOI: 10.1007/s44327-024-00002-w

Pathan, A.-S. M., & Mohammed, M. M. Z. E. (2015). Building Customer trust in cloud computing with an ICT-enabled global regulatory body. *Wireless Personal Communications*, 85(1), 77–99. DOI: 10.1007/s11277-015-2729-z

Rahman, F. H., Au, T.-W., Newaz, S. H. S., Suhaili, W. S., & Lee, G. M. (2020). Find my trustworthy fogs: A fuzzy-based trust evaluation framework. *Future Generation Computer Systems*, 109, 562–572. DOI: 10.1016/j.future.2018.05.061

Rahmani, M. K. (2022). *Blockchain-Based Trust Management Framework for Cloud Computing-Based Internet of Medical Things (IoMT): A Systematic Review*. Computatio. [Retracted] DOI: 10.1155/2022/9766844

Rajendran, V. S. (2015). Hybrid model for dynamic evaluation of trust in cloud services. *Wireless Networks*, ●●●, 1–12.

Ranathunga, T. M. (2020). A DLT-based trust framework for IoT ecosystems. In. *International Conference on Cyber Security and Protection of Digital Services (Cyber Security) (pp. 1-8). IEEE.*

Rizvi, S. M., Mitchell, J., Razaque, A., Rizvi, M. R., & Williams, I. (2020). A fuzzy inference system (FIS) to evaluate the security readiness of cloud service providers. *Journal of Cloud Computing (Heidelberg, Germany)*, 9(1), 1–17. DOI: 10.1186/s13677-020-00192-9

Somu, N. K., Kirthivasan, K., & Shankar Sriram, V. S. (2017). A rough set-based hypergraph trust measure parameter selection technique for cloud service selection. *The Journal of Supercomputing*, 73(10), 4535–4559. DOI: 10.1007/s11227-017-2032-8

Tang, M., Dai, X., Liu, J., & Chen, J. (2017, September). D. X. ((2016)). Towards a trust evaluation middleware for cloud service selection. *Future Generation Computer Systems*, 74, 302–312. Advance online publication. DOI: 10.1016/j.future.2016.01.009

Wang, B. W., Wang, P., & Tu, Y. (2021). Customer satisfaction service match and service quality-based blockchain cloud manufacturing. *International Journal of Production Economics*, 240, 108220. DOI: 10.1016/j.ijpe.2021.108220

Xu, C., & Li, J. (2024). Design of Intelligent Software Security System Based on Spark Big Data Computing. *Wireless Personal Communications*, ●●●, 1–21. DOI: 10.1007/s11277-024-11015-4

Chapter 15
Evolution of Data Security in E-Commerce

Deepak Varadam
https://orcid.org/0000-0002-6079-4805
M.S. Ramaiah University of Applied Sciences, India

Mummadi Shyam Kumar Reddy
https://orcid.org/0009-0000-2044-9620
M.S. Ramaiah University of Applied Sciences, India

Sahana P. Shankar
https://orcid.org/0000-0001-8977-9898
M.S. Ramaiah University of Applied Sciences, India

R. Mohan
M.S. Ramaiah University of Applied Sciences, India

J. Priyanka
https://orcid.org/0009-0009-9297-5713
M.S. Ramaiah University of Applied Sciences, India

Aditya Katare
https://orcid.org/0009-0004-2880-6564
M.S. Ramaiah University of Applied Sciences, India

ABSTRACT

The rise of consumerism and technology has accelerated the demands of the general public. With the growth of ecommerce platforms there has been an exponential growth in the rate of trade that takes place which was previously unimaginable. The need for data security and preventing fraudulent activities has now been at the highest level of scrutiny than ever and the need for more advanced systems that can handle increasing number of challenges has been discussed in our chapter. The debate on whether traditional methods of data security and detecting such vulnerabilities have been talked about for a while now. The need for today is a system that is robust, adaptive to new fraudulent trends and also be proactive in detecting and mitigating threats. Artificial Intelligence and Machine Learning are now pivotal technologies that help shape better robust systems. Their ability of identifying patterns and thus outliers that go hand in hand with what an anomaly or a fraudulent event is has been automating security services without the need of any human intervention.

DOI: 10.4018/979-8-3693-9919-4.ch015

INTRODUCTION

The rise of consumerism and technology has accelerated the demands of the general public. With the growth of ecommerce platforms there has been an exponential growth in the rate of trade that takes place which was previously unimaginable. However, with this sudden new advent of humankind there has also been challenges that come along with it. The need for data security and preventing fraudulent activities has now been at the highest level of scrutiny than ever and the need for more advanced systems that can handle increasing number of challenges has been discussed in our chapter. The debate on whether traditional methods of data security and detecting such vulnerabilities have been talked about for a while now. They are now considered to be slow, complex and have a high overhead cost as it relies on labelled data. The need for today is a system that is robust, adaptive to new fraudulent trends and also be proactive in detecting and mitigating threats. Artificial Intelligence and Machine Learning are now pivotal technologies that help shape better robust systems. Their ability of identifying patterns and thus outliers that go hand in hand with what an anomaly or a fraudulent event is has been automating security services without the need of any human intervention. The core theme of the work is to discuss about the possibilities of Artificial Intelligence and Machine Learning models that are used for e-commerce data security. This involves a comprehensive approach that integrates various AI mechanisms like Deep Learning and explainable AI to detect anomalies and create a secure e-commerce environment. This work also talks about the challenges faced in implementing these systems and the future scope of research in this aspect.

RELATED WORK

This paper talks about how the increase in number of devices that connect to the network and share large amount of data along with it has created a vast amount of vulnerabilities. Conventional methods of detecting vulnerabilities have been deemed to be slow, complex and higher overhead costs as it relies on the past data where the vulnerabilities have been detected. This data driven approach is not that effective in the present time as it requires continuous monitoring by cybersecurity professionals. Machine learning models are now being implemented by taking the vast amount of data already present and reduces the needed of human intervention thus making the whole process autonomous. This way each step that has been taken is documented and also reasoned as to why it was taken. The use of explainable Artificial Intelligence (XAI) also tries to interpret the decisions made by the ML model and has seen an increase in popularity and importance. The paper also discusses evaluation techniques such as Support Vector Machine, Random Forest and Precision Recall Curves in order to evaluate the trueness of the ML model, (Mahbooba, n.d.). The paper talks about how ecommerce platforms have integrated AIML to create applications on the banking operations such as risk management, customer retention, fraud detection. It deals with the legal aspects of using AIML tools in ecommerce while also giving insights into qualitative methods used to create models suitable for the banking sector. It also discussed the strategies used to create models based on previously discussed fields of the banking operations, (Prakash, Venkatasubbu, & Konidena, 2022).

The continuous progress of humanization and the availability of products has also made the methods of selling of products to evolve as well. Marketing has been developed along with the technologies present in the world. Its adaptability and ability to integrate newer technologies has resulted in the need of digitization. AI in digital marketing helps to automate tasks, customize experiences based on each customer and its superiority over traditional marketing analysis like using keywords, hashtags and Search Engine Marketing. It states that traditional methods do not really connect with the users and are only used to create a pattern of interest and not the person itself. The paper states that the ability of marketing to adapt overtime has created a better opportunity for AI applications to thrive in, (Dumitriu & Popescu, 2020).

Figure 1. The proposed four step sequential model

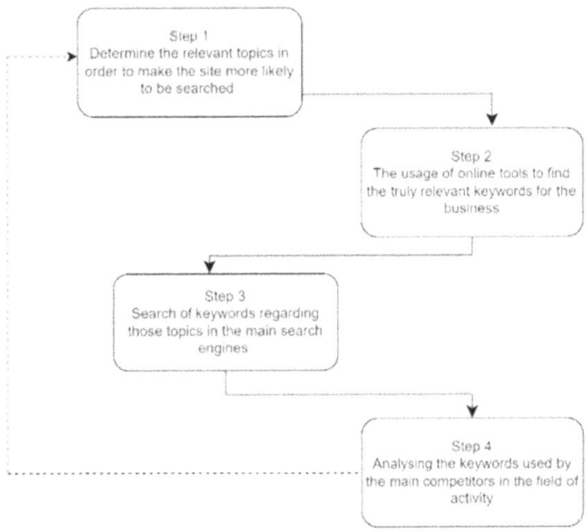

The paper talks about how electronic devices has boomed the ability to buy and sell products and services over the internet. It talks about the various ways in which ecommerce takes place. As its reliance on the usage of unmoderated devices such as personal computers and mobiles that eliminate the need of any physical proof, security becomes a crucial aspect in views of data security and safeguarding of assets. By reading the paper we are able to learn about the different strategies we can impose on not just the service itself but the whole system all together. By this we are able to keep the users and the servers out of the offender's reach. It also helps us to map the weak points of a given platform and the ability to overcome it, (Patro, Padhy, & Panigrahi, 2016). The paper discusses about the market value of ecommerce platforms and how the integration of machine learning can help to predict sales of a particular platform. The main purpose of this paper is to review other papers and understand the different models being used and selecting the best and suitable models that can be implemented to provide sales predictions, (Singh, Booma, & Eaganathan, 2020). The paper talks about different ways in which ecommerce takes place. The integration of third-party software onto a website also brings its level of complexity in terms of security. It talks about what actors are considered to be "weak connections" within the given system. The rising cyber threats results in the resources that were allocated to security goes into fixing what is already damaged and is insufficient for further enhancements, (Khan, 2019)

The paper talks about how machine learning is being used in wide variety of tasks such as computer vision, pattern recognition and cyber security. As security is a vulnerable aspect of any given system, it emphasizes on creating models that are resilient to such attacks. ML models have been categorized into four groups during testing that are security assessment mechanisms, countermeasures, data security and privacy. The different types of attacks are the attacks on the model itself, attacks on the data that the model is being trained on, attack so that the model leaks sensitive information, (Liu *et al.,* 2018)

Figure 2. The taxonomy of security threats towards machine learning

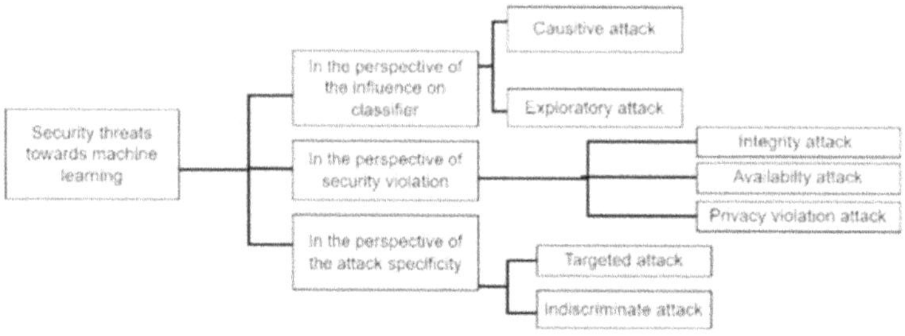

The paper talks about how the integration of machine learning and cybersecurity enhances security measures and improves detection of attacks. It explains how ML models work based on previously known or historical data to notice any patterns and create decision without the need of human intervention. The paper also talks about the ways we can overcome the challenges mentioned, (Wazid *et al.,* 2022). The paper firstly explains what a cyber physical system is, healthcare, transportation and commerce are such cyber physical system. ML models are used to defend against various threats and attacks that are being directed towards the cyber physical infrastructures. The paper discusses defence mechanisms used by ML models. The model is phased into training and deployment. It explains all the details of the processes taken in each phase. Furthermore, it discusses information security principles, such as confidentiality, integrity, and availability, and their relevance in ensuring data protection, (Singh *et al.,* 2022). This work provides an insight to the relationship between AI and cybersecurity and the possible prospects. In this current digital era, the rate of cybercrimes is also increasing hence the need for robust cybersecurity mechanisms have become a necessity.AI has emerged as a powerful tool for learning, detecting and responding to threats in real time. AI algorithms can analyze data patterns and also detect anomalies in data.ML algorithms like random forests neural networks are highly capable of detecting malicious activity by analyzing factors like traffic, user behavior and system logs. These models are capable of rapid threat detection and response. Cyber criminals are also using AI mechanisms to launch sophisticated cyber threats so research to counter their threats. Another con is the cost of implementation of such AI mechanisms which in the present market scenario may not be affordable by all scale companies. In conclusion the relationship between AI and cybersecurity is crucial and highlights human creativity and innovation. The collaboration of these 2 fields can be secure our digital future, (Shanmugam, Katari, & Thirunavukkarasu, 2024).

This work discusses about how blockchain alongside ML is capable of enhancing data privacy and security. This system ensures that data once recorded cannot be tampered. This is done using cryptographic hashing and consensus mechanisms, and this requires the agreement of most network participants before a transaction is added to blockchain. Ecommerce platforms deal with highly sensitive and large volume of customer data and financial data and thus are vulnerable to cyber threats. By introducing blockchain in ecommerce platforms, transaction records are safer.ML models can be deployed for fraud detection ensuring data security and fostering customer trust, (Arjunan, 2024). This work discusses the use and implementation of machine learning techniques required to enhance security in NoSQL databases like MongoDB, Cassandra and many more. Therefore, the implementation of ML algorithms to detect threats on these NoSQL databases enhances the security of these platforms by quickly identifying and mitigating fraudulent activities. This is critical for protecting financial transactions, customer data and other confidential data for these ecommerce websites, thereby maintaining customer trust, (Mutemi & Bacao, 2024).

The rise of COVID-19 pandemic gave a boost to the business of the ecommerce platforms like Amazon, Flipkart, E-bay etc. However, this also led to the alarming rise of digital frauds and data breaches. This work conducted a PRISMA approach analysis for identifying the deployment of various artificial neural networks and machine learning techniques in this aspect. [PRISMA-Preferred Reporting Items for Systematic Reviews and Meta-Analysis, an evidence-based study]. Customer data is highly confidential data for any of these E-commerce websites. However, another aspect of data security and the highest place of vulnerability is the frauds in terms of financial transactions on these platforms. This work describes the use of ANNs predominantly and also various other machine learning algorithms that can be deployed for detection of such frauds. The fraud types in case of credit cards and other payments methods keep evolving and therefore these ML models and ANNs must also be frequently retrained and updated to keep up with the fraud trends and detect them as accurately as possible for customer safety concerns and growth of these ecommerce platform, (Shukla, Raghuvanshi, & Sharan, 2024).

Figure 3. Proposed methodology

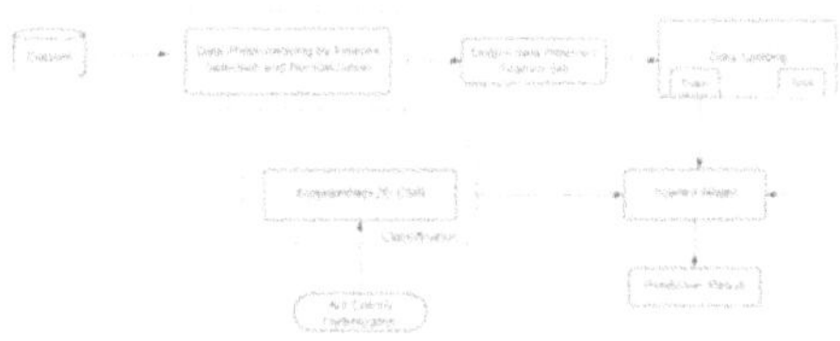

Ecommerce platforms are known for possessing large quantities of data which includes customer details, product details, retailer information, transaction details etc. Most of these data a highly confidential and still susceptible to intrusions and data breaches. This work uses the concept of Regression Analysis to build an intrusion detection system (IDS) to detect potential threats to such platforms. Results obtained show that the proposed IDS mechanism is effective and useful for ecommerce architecture. In conclusion, the work highlights the necessity to build robust ecommerce architectures for data security, (Abbas, 2024).

In today's retail business architecture cybersecurity is a very important aspect especially amidst the digitalization era. This work explores the integration of business analytics, ML and blockchain for security of data for the retail industry. ML is known for its ability to analyze and learn vast amounts of data, identify patterns and anomalies that pose potential data threats. This real-time threat detection is necessary for reducing response time to cyber-attacks. ML's ability to continuously adapt to new trends helps to detect the threats and malicious activities over time. Therefore, it is necessary for retailers to adapt this kind of framework in order to maintain the integrity of their data and their customer trust which is very essential in their future growth, (Aburbeian & Fernández-Veiga, 2024). Earlier works had given an overview of financial fraud detection systems. This work talks about securing financial transaction on ecommerce and various platforms. This massive and quick shift to digital shopping platforms and digital payment methods has made life comfortable but also at the same time increased the rate of cybercrimes across the globe. This, study proposes a framework of MFA (multifactor authentication) and ML to enhance and secure transactions. Two layers of security were implemented. The first layer being a 2FA and the second layer being machine learning algorithms when a potential fraud is detected. ML was used to incorporate facial recognition systems. The framework of MFA implemented addresses the usability, and adaptability to the dynamic nature of the ecommerce platforms. This work also develops a simple frontend to demonstrate the working of a successful transaction when the identity is verified and a failed transaction when the facial recognition system detects a potential fraud, (Gerdelius & Hugo, 2024). This work investigates the effectiveness of using ML models in identifying fraudulent users on an ecommerce platform. For this purpose, the authors have used Event and screen data collected over 4 weeks to distinguish between a genuine user and a fraudulent one. The key methodologies used were PCA to reduce the dimensionality of the screen data, feature extraction and a random forest model was deployed for classification task. Since there was an imbalance in number of genuine and fraudulent users 2 balancing techniques were used

1. Synthetic Minority Over-sampling for oversampling minority class.
2. Adjusting the Probability threshold to find proper balance for classification.

An optimal 80% accuracy was achieved. This approach helps detect fraudulent users and can be deployed by ecommerce platforms so that their data can be secure from potential threats. This work provides for a robust framework for improving security of data in ecommerce platforms, thereby providing a more safe and trustworthy shopping environment for genuine customers, (Raimundo & Rosário, 2021).

In this work the authors have conducted a bibliometric analysis of 77 articles from Scopus DB to understand the trends in the domain. AI techniques like ML, Neural Networks, and NLP are now being increasingly used to handle security breaches in various domains and more popularly in e-commerce which is a hub of large databases. AI algorithms have the ability to learn patterns in data and therefore detect anomalies to prevent cyber-attacks. Apart from that AI ML mechanisms are capable of adaptive existence i.e. they can evolve to detect new threats and keep up with the cyber threat trends. Therefore, we can say that integrating AI ML mechanisms into ecommerce architectures help them keep their database more secure, and more importantly helps build customer trust which is essential in this domain, (Kazemi, 2021). This work focuses on the enhancement of security measure on an e-commerce platform. The work proposes 2 mechanisms for this purpose, Adaptive Neuro-Fuzzy Inference System (ANFIS) and Firefly Optimization Algorithm (FOA). Therefore, these 2 mechanisms are integrated to form a robust mechanism to identify cyber-attacks like phishing, account takeovers and fraudulent transactions. ANFIS ensures that the model adapts itself to new trends in cyber threats and FOA ensures the system's efficiency so lesser false positive security threats are raised. The work's results show that the mechanism proposed is a highly reliable security architecture for e-commerce platforms. Therefore, incorporating this mechanism into the security architecture of e-commerce platforms will help such businesses keep their data safe from intruders and breaches. It also shows that AI ML systems can be reliable to an extent for detecting and mitigating cyber threats in real time, (Rawindaran, Jayal, & Prakash, 2021). This work has conducted a comprehensive analysis to gather data on the effectiveness and adoption of ML techniques for cyber security. The survey indicates that larger industries have more percentage of adoption of ML techniques for security as compared to small and medium industries. Even commerce platforms whether a large business or a small one is in need of security architecture that is robust to threats and is capable of securing the company's DB. Thus, these ML mechanisms will help in detecting and mitigating threats in real time and also adapt to new changes in the environment.ML can to a great extent help commerce platforms provide a secure and seamless experience to their customer, which is of utmost importance to such businesses, (Mohd, Bhatla, & Upadhyay, 2021).

Figure 4. IDS in ANN

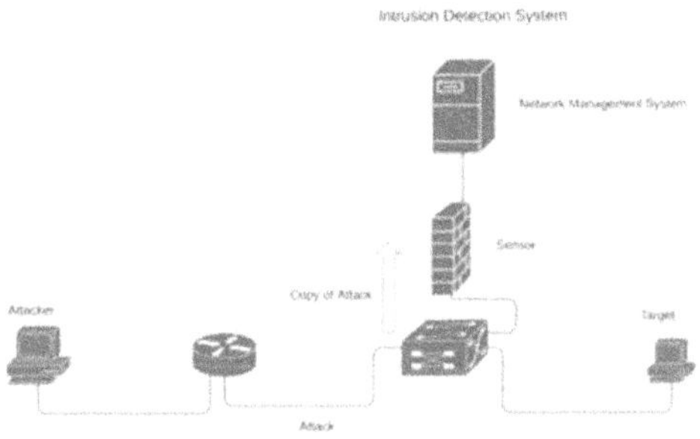

This work talks about the use of ML algorithms to detect and mitigate cyber threats. The work also talks about ML's capacity to predict future cyber-attacks and help the organisation build defence systems and response plans accordingly. ML systems improve threat detection accuracy and are also capable of adapting to new trends in cyber threats. Ecommerce platforms are primary targets of data breaches because they have vast quantities of customer information, product information and financial records which are highly confidential. This helps such business keep their data secure and also build customer trust, (Han *et al.,* 2021). This work introduces a concept called DeepRec. It is a framework that is designed to provide recommendation system on mobile devices without hindering the user privacy. Generally, the regular recommendation systems rely on cloud processing which is a sensitive approach and user data can be easily exposed on the internet thus breaching privacy. Lightweight neural networks are used for low computational complexity. Ecommerce platforms can adopt this technique to enhance data security and user privacy. By keeping the data localized i.e. on device will also minimize the risk of data breaches, (Wang *et al.*, 2021).

This work talks about the challenges and strategies for protecting customer privacy of AI Driven online shopping. The evolutionary game model helps the businesses understand user behaviour and build strategies over time. The results of this work indicate that robust privacy protection techniques can actually build a good customer DB. The AI ML techniques mentioned in the work show that they can be implemented by e-commerce platforms for security architecture. Balance of customer personalization and data security can benefit both the customer and the business helping them grow better, (Das & Sandhane, 2021). This work explores the applications of AI techniques in cyber security and their importance to detect and mitigate cyber threats in this time of continuous changes in trends of cyber-attacks. AI branches like ML, NLP are highly capable of identifying and responding to threats. AI Algorithms are also very good at anomaly detection i.e. some unusual trend in patterns which is helpful in detecting potential security breaches. AI systems are capable of continual learning, so it is easy for them to adapt to new changes and still identify new types of threats on periodic training. E-commerce platforms are businesses that possess large customer, product, financial and other DB that needs to be kept safe. This business can implement AI-powered mechanisms to keep fraudulent customers, transactions and data breaches at bay. Since introducing AI techniques will automate and fasten the security architecture it will also help these platforms provide a more secure and reliable experience for the customers, (Shachi *et al.,* 2021). This work highlights the attacks on DB queries and allowing attackers access to sensitive information. They provide a review about detection and prevention methods for injection attacks. A multi layered security system is needed wherein traditional methods of preventing injection attacks are combined with AI ML techniques for protecting the server of the applications from both DQL and NoSQL injection attacks. (An attackers attempt to send data to an application in a way that will change the meaning of commands being sent to an interpreter. These ML algorithms can learn data patterns from the company's DB and the DB queries and detect abnormal behaviours which maybe potential attackers or intruders. AI enabled input validation enhances security for the DB since they can automatically update validating rules based on anomalies or frauds detected, (Patil *et al.*, n.d.). This work explores the use of ML in data security which includes identifying, preventing, responding to various cyber threats. This work is concentrated on the use of supervised and unsupervised ML techniques for anomaly detection, intrusion detection and other potential data breach mechanisms. ML algorithms are capable of detecting anomalies in patterns, flag malicious activities before they pose a bigger threat.

Therefore, AIML techniques can be implemented to these online retail platforms to provide uninterrupted secure services that are also capable of adapting and modelling themselves o changes in the trends of techniques and cyber threats. It will help security analysts stay a step ahead of the intruders, (Osita *et al.*, 2022). This paper explores the emerging technologies for mitigation security challenges in the ecommerce domain. The study emphasizes the need for mitigating potential risks associated with online transactions like identity theft, data breaches etc. AI ML models can enhance data security mechanisms on the ecommerce platforms. The work highlights the capabilities of AI ML models to detect malicious activities and mitigate them as early as possible therefore ensuring the safety of customers and the company details. The use of blockchain also is discussed in this work. Blockchain technologies ensure the safety of monetary transactions which is also an important aspect in this domain. Various other techniques like fingerprint recognition and facial recognition also in order to increase security measures against fraudulent methods. Therefore, the AI ML technologies have proven to be a popular approach for data security in ecommerce platforms. ML techniques like random forests or ANNs are a popular choice for detecting and mitigating potential risks and safeguarding customer information and other confidential information, (Aghnihotri & Sharma, 2023).

NAAS (Neural Adaptive Authentication System) is an AI framework aimed at making the security of ecommerce transactions robust. NAAS is known for its sophisticated integration of AI ML techniques for detecting fraudulent real time activities. NAAS makes use of deep learning algorithms; these algorithms are known to excel at pattern recognition and anomaly detection. These algorithms enhance the security of e-commerce. NAAS also incorporates adaptive learning abilities. This is essential because the trend of fraudulent data breaches is constantly changing, so these algorithms must be adaptive to such trends at all times. Ecommerce platforms must deploy these techniques for a more secure data environment and building of customer trust, (Palllathadka *et al.,* 2023). This work explores the applications of AI in business management, e-commerce and finance. AI models can enhance user experience while shopping on any of the e-retail platforms. Use of AI in this domain ensures efficient operations and also, ensures the data security of these platforms. E-commerce is a hub of vast quantities of data and therefore they are also a prime target for data breaches and fraudulent activities. The use of this AI driven framework can provide for a robust mechanism for data security on ecommerce platforms and build customer trust on this basis, especially in this era of digitalization Vs high rates of cyber-crimes, (Ma & Wang, 2024).

This work emphasized the need for a robust security mechanism to protect sensitive data and ensure integrity in terms of financial transactions. This is a must for ensuring customer trust. The work highlights the role of AI ML on how they can automate these security mechanisms. The integration of AI ML models in the security infrastructure of these e-commerce platforms helps the business to keep their customer relations and other confidential data safe. AI ML models like ANNs and random forests are highly capable of learning large volumes of data and recognize anomalies in patterns which help these platforms mitigate risks to their databases. Therefore, the work provides an insight into how modern technologies like AI ML etc. can be integrated into e-commerce platforms in this digital era for improve their security architecture, (Kumar *et al.*, 2023). This study proposes a comprehensive framework that employs ML techniques to analyze patterns of transactions, usability, efficiency etc. For security analysis the authors have used e-commerce security tools to find potential vulnerabilities and ensure a strong security mechanism. The integration of static ML models (models trained offline) helps to detect and mitigate cyber threats more efficiently. In the sense of e-commerce these models prove to be useful since they are capable of continuously learning patterns and improving their ability to detect anomalies in patterns thereby enabling more efficient and secure e-commerce resource managements, (Wainaina *et al.,* n.d.a). This work addresses the growing concern about data breaches and privacy violations by implementing ML algorithms. ML techniques discussed here are anomaly detection, classification and clustering that are capable of detecting anomalies and improving data encryption mechanisms to ensure safety of user data. The effectiveness of ML in monitoring and analyzing user behavior can be achieved using algorithms like Support Vector machines (SVMs), Random Forests, Neural networks. These models help builds a robust security mechanism to preserve personal data on ecommerce platforms. Therefore, the integration of these ML mechanisms on ecommerce sites can help secure personal data from break and misuse, (Sasmal, 2021). Supervised learning, unsupervised learning, pattern recognition for anomaly detection are few ML techniques that can be used for improving the detection of fraudulent activities in terms of credit card scams.

AI models are capable of analysing transaction data and identify fraudulent transactions by their varied pattern. Neural networks, decision trees are all highly precise ML algorithms to detect fraudulent transactions in real-time. Integrating AI models in credit card payment systems reduces losses and also builds a secure payment environment. E-commerce are hubs of credit card transactions on a daily basis. Implementing AI ML models in payment gateways and credit card transaction mechanisms helps carry out safe transactions. This helps the companies build trust among customer community and also the user's money is safely transacted, (Srivastava, 2021). The use of e-commerce platforms has increased for shopping since the COVID pandemic. ML algorithms can detect breaches very well and help secure the business' DB. Implementing AI ML models to these platforms for security can be help the business keep their data safe and also build customer trust which a primary necessity, (Desamsetti, 2021). The paper talks about the nature of Advanced Persistent Threats (APT), these are complex cyber-attack mechanisms that are hard to detect and mitigate quickly. E-commerce platforms that are the core of vast data are needed to have a robust security mechanism against such threats. Firewalls, antivirus software's etc. may not be enough for security, there is a need to incorporate AI ML models into the cyber security architecture. These models are capable of learning vast amount of data and detect regular patterns and anomalies in case of fraudulent activities. AI based threat detection system for ecommerce platforms can be used to monitor user behaviour and transaction patterns in real time. They are also capable of adaptive learning i.e. learn new types of threats and detect them quickly. This will enable a secure shopping experience for the users, (Kilincer, Ertam, & Sengur, 2021).

This paper emphasises on the need for IDS in mitigating cyber threats. They have used a variety of datasets like KDD CUP 99, NSL-KDD and CICIDS2017 that have a variety of network traffic, data breach patterns. The work compares ML models like decision trees, SVM, k-NN, DL, CNN, RNN for detecting complex and sophisticated cyber threats. The results show that decision trees, SVM perform well, but DL techniques perform the best. E-commerce platforms can implement such ML empowered IDS for securing the vast Databases. These models are capable of quick response, adaptive learning and detecting anomalies in network traffic thus keeping the companies' DB safe and also building the customer trust, (Aldallal & Alisa, 2021). This paper talks about the integration of ML and cloud for IDS. ML algorithms like SVM, decision trees are capable of pattern learning and anomaly detection. Along with this cloud-based IDS will offer flexibility and scalability. This is needed for the dynamic nature of e-commerce platform operations. Building such security systems can help the companies protect their vast DB and also predict future vulnerabilities and help the workforce take action accordingly. Automated or ML enabled IDS systems are a great way to monitor and mitigate cyber threats thus safeguarding confidential information and also financial transactions. Adopting these mechanisms help e-commerce platforms enhance customer trust and that is needed for sustained growth of the platform, (Rajesh & Chintalapudi, 2021). This paper analyses the use of ML algorithms in various aspects of managing an e-commerce platform. Key areas of application are product recommendations, fraud detection, sentiment analysis etc.ML plays an important role in identifying unusual patterns in transaction data. ML models are capable of being robust security framework for the data related to ecommerce platforms. They can analyse vast amount of data and detect anomalies and threats in real time. This will prevent data breaches. By continuously learning from new data being added to ecommerce DB the models can mend themselves to respond to varying threats in the cyber-attack's domain. Adopting, this mechanism can help these businesses achieve long term success, (Paintal, 2021). This work emphasises on the need for AI ML in e-commerce security framework for developing a complex IDS system. These models monitor network traffic, user behaviour and such features to detect any unusual happenings. They are also adaptive in nature which helps them stay ahead of cyber criminals and up to date with the evolving cyber-attack tactics. By implementing AI ML models for data security, the e-commerce platforms will be able to keep their customer information, product related information and other confidential data safe. This will thereby help them to grow in the market and build customer trust which is of utmost importance in such businesses, (Kumain, Chaudhary, & Joshi, 2020).

E-commerce platform allows user to shop for various products from a single online location, eliminating the need to visit physical stores. This model depends heavily on network security, so it is a big concern. Besides selling products, e-commerce includes online banking, payment gateways, and online auctions. It reduces cost, saves time and boosts productivity, but the security remains as a critical concern. E-commerce systems face threats such as snooping, back-door attacks, man-in-the-middle attacks, denial-of-service attacks, interception and eavesdropping. These threats highlight the need of robust security measures. E-commerce faces several security issues like replay attacks involving intercepting and reusing keys to pretend to be original sender, preventable with timestamp method and session keys. Phishing and illegal access, where attackers steal user credentials, can be prevented using two-factor authentication and email filtering. Eavesdropping on private communication is another threat and this can be reduced by switching from HTTP to HTTPS. Integrating these technologies into e-commerce platforms is essential for improving security and operational efficiency, (Wainaina *et al.,* n.d.b). The surge in e-commerce demands robust security measures to safeguard user privacy and safety. Machine learning, including NLP, SVM-based algorithms, neural networks and text mining plays a vital role in cybersecurity. These algorithms detect anomalies, like fraud activities, ensuring secure user authentication and data protection. Encryption and privacy measures further shield sensitive data from cyber threats. Fraud detection is enhanced through machine learning algorithms, identifying suspicious activities and safeguarding personal data. NLP algorithms scan privacy agreements for vulnerabilities, ensuring data confidentiality. Fine-grained privacy settings allow users control over data sharing with third-party partners for logistics and payments. Support vector machine algorithms identify potential XSS attacks, while deep learning models create early warning system for the financial risk in e-commerce. Text mining and machine learning will analyze consumer satisfaction and extract relevant information from the reviews. Artificial Intelligence and Machine Learning offer robust solutions against data breaches in e-commerce platforms. Their adaptability to vast data volumes ensures continuous learning and adaptation to evolving threats. With AI and ML, the future of e-commerce promises enhanced security, personalized experiences and effectiveness in combating emerging risks, (Youssef & Hossam, 2023).

The integration of AI into e-commerce raises privacy concerns, including biases leading to incorrect assumptions and storage of sensitive customer conversations by automated customer services like chatbots. Cloud computing poses risks of data breach and ambiguity in data ownership. To address these, robust frameworks are needed to mitigate risks and safeguard customer data. E-commerce benefits both online and offline stores, expanding their customer base and offering flexible shopping experiences. Key advantage includes variety gains and convenience gains, allowing customers to find wide range of products in one place without visiting physical stores. AI integration enhances e-commerce with innovative solutions, personalize product suggestions and tailored experiences for customers, leading to increased order values. Chatbots are virtual assistants play essential roles in customer service, handling tasks like answering questions, assisting with website navigation and facilitating checkout processes. Visual recognition technologies aid customers in finding products by recognizing images. AI also improves fraud detection and security through real-time transaction analysis and multi-factor authentication processes, making unauthorized access difficult. Attackers target businesses with inadequate encryption measures and security loopholes to breach databases containing consumer financial information, (Ali, 2023). AI algorithms analyze transaction data to suggest personalized products, but biased recommendations may result from flawed data, potentially leading to unfair practices. Implementing robust data minimizing techniques and continuous monitoring of AI algorithms can mitigate privacy issues and build a more secure environment for e-commerce users. Regular audits can identify vulnerabilities or biases, enhancing the efficiency and trustworthiness of AI systems, (Cheng, Cohen, & Mou, 2023). AI driven threat detection by identifying patterns and anomalies. Machine learning models can also be trained on large number of datasets to identify and respond to new attack vectors quickly. AL algorithms can detect fraud activities by analyzing transaction patterns and user behaviors like login times and IP addresses. AI can be used to develop more advanced encryption algorithms that are harder for attackers to crack. AI can improve Identity and Access Management (IAM) systems by continuously learning and adapting to user behavior, ensuring only authorized users have access to sensitive data. AI systems can help e-commerce platforms meet industry standards and regulations by constantly checking and updating security measures. AI can make handling security breaches easier by quickly figuring out what happened and start actions to control and reduce the impact of attack. AI can help keep user data safe by making sure privacy rules are always followed. It can also hide data to prevent unauthorized access or use, (Saeed, 2023). Using AI driven technology innovations such as recommender system, risk management system, virtual assistants and customer relationship management, play a crucial role in e-commerce. These technological innovations improve the performance of e-commerce platforms.

AI makes e-commerce more personalized and enhances user experience. But gathering and using lot of data to personalize these experiences might put people's privacy and data security at risk. AI chat bots are the most significant application in e-commerce. They improve the service to assist efficiently, there might be some concerns regarding the security and privacy of data shared during interactions with these chat bots. The customer needs to be careful about what kind of data is being shared and how valuable the information shared contains. Fraud detection and risk management is another role of AI in e-commerce platform where the AI algorithms continuously work to analyze patterns and anomalies in data and also help in identifying potential security threats and measures to the same. To maintain ethical standards in e-commerce, it's important to address issues like data security and privacy. So, we need to focus on building trust between users and AI system so that technology is used responsibly and transparently, (Agnihotri & Sharma, 2023). Secure e-commerce applications are important for increasing customer base. This requires understanding of customer reservations and perceptions about security and privacy. This understanding includes factors such as customer's credit card usage, information security and trust on e-commerce site. All these factors impact customer's perception about security and trust in e-commerce platforms. All the above factors by customers about e-commerce is influenced by cultural factors, individual preferences and privacy concerns. Most of the hacking attacks happen to customers by factors such as age and gender. The Protection Motivation Theory (PMT) is utilized to comprehend customer perception of regarding security in e-commerce, focusing on vulnerability, risk, effectiveness and cost. A positive view of security and trust is required for safe behavior, and insights from studies can help create better policies and technology. These studies have limits like small sample sizes and not enough gender and location diversity, which will affect the result. Future research plans to test these models in diverse groups to see how well they work, (Ikhtiyorov, 2023).

The ethical considerations include getting permission from participants, making data available for transparency, and giving credit to those who help with the research. To enhance e-commerce security and trust among their customers, organizations and businesses must prioritize transparency, accountability and data privacy while also building trust between users and AI systems to ensure responsible and transparent use of the technology. Trust building efforts between users and AI systems are crucial for encouraging long-term relationships and ensuring responsible use of technology, particularly in context of e-commerce security. Based on the given data, if we use suitable neural networks, we can find the customer perception about security and privacy for each of the factors like credit card usage, trustworthiness, customer worries, etc. in the e-commerce store, (Ma & Wang, 2024). Data security is crucial for online transactions to protect against external threats which are more now a days. As online transactions are important for e-commerce usage, to address security challenges in these, robust measures are necessary. An AI based system called as NAAS is proposed to handle such data security by assessing the complexity and applying suitable security measures. For highly complex financial data, the system uses Enhanced K-anonymity (EK-A). For less complex simple data, the system uses Enhanced-Symmetric Key Cryptography Algorithm (E-SKA). This approach will improve the security efficiency, showing a 14,03% improvement over traditional manual methods. To build trust with their customers, e-commerce can use enhanced security solutions such as cryptography which are needed for secure online transaction. Symmetric encryption uses a secret key shared between the sender and receiver, while asymmetric encryption uses a pair of public and private keys. Symmetric encryption faces challenges with secure key distribution, and asymmetric encryption will need high computational power, this makes both methods complex to implement effectively. Anonymization is another method that transforms data to prevent interpretation by intruders, working along with cryptographic techniques, (Rangaraju, 2023). The proposed method integrates AI with enhanced Advanced Encryption Standard (AES) and K-anonymity. Using supervised learning technique in AI, we can classify complex data. Financial data is more complex, and general data is less complex. Depending on the complexity, wither of EK-A or E-AES is applied to secure the data. The model uses a method called K-Nearest Neighbours (KNN) to sort data based on complexity. If the data is not too complex, we can boost it by using lattice k-anonymity. For data that is more complex, we can use enhanced symmetric key cryptography for extra protection of data. For most complex data, we can use mix of both methods. Once the data is secured, we can give it to users or keep safe on a local system. The AI systems will carefully examine the complexity of data to determine the most appropriate security measures, which results in improved efficiency and reduces the memory usage. It looks into various factors like accuracy, precision, recall and the F-1 Score to ensure effectiveness. Compared to traditional methods, the new model demonstrates a significant 14.30% enhancement in execution time, making it a big improvement in how things are done. The AI-based models efficiently work on the safety of data transmitted through public channels by carefully selecting the most suitable security measures according to the complexity of the data. This not only improves the overall efficiency of operations but also reduces processing time and reduces the memory usage. We can also improve the potential of the system exploring the semi-supervised learning methods and implementing defences against potential threats from quantum computing attacks, (Shankar & Chaudhari, 2024).

Artificial Intelligence is changing how we shop online, gives more options in personalization, improved customer experiences, and optimizes decision making. Using advance algorithms and machine learning techniques, it can solve most of the human problems and can provide better solutions to all kinds of problems faced by users. AI in e-commerce enables personalized recommendations, search for items automatically, boots efficiency, optimizes pricing strategy and revenue. But using AI also brings legal, ethical and regulatory challenges. As online shopping is evolving, e-commerce companies are using AI more to keep up with competition. AI algorithms personalize customers experience, tailor product recommendations and optimize marketing strategy. They also improve supply chain management by predicting demand of product and making sure they have enough of it. But challenges like data privacy, algorithmic bias and transparency in decision making must be seen regularly to prevent reputational damage and legal problems, (Shankar & Chaudari, 2023).

Data privacy laws, like the General Data Protection Regulation (GDPR) in Europe and California Consumer Privacy Act (CCPA) in the US, play a crucial role in regulation AI adaption. These laws make it necessary for companies to ask people before using their information and give them control over it. Following these rules makes customers feel safe and helps businesses succeed for long time. Companies need to make sure that they do right things and use AI in a way that helps everyone. Transparency in AI decision making is very important, especially regarding customers data. AI algorithms should explain decisions transparently without any bias. The absence of clear legal framework will face challenges in ethical and privacy concerns. Developing unbiased AI algorithms and safeguarding customer data is really important so that there is no customer data leak, (Shankar *et al.*, 2023a). The rapid growth of the e-commerce market brings significant challenges to business operations and user trust. Issues such as security of consumer data, safeguarding payment transactions made by customers and protecting against cyber-attacks and fraud. Computer technology is essential to enhance the security of e-commerce platforms, protect user information and promote sustainable business models. As e-commerce grows, big data analytics play a crucial role in improving customer satisfaction, personalizing customer experience and increasing profits. By analyzing customer shopping behaviors and market trends, businesses can better target their advertising, develop products that address complaints and staff to deliver high-quality service consistently. Building effective e-commerce business models involves advanced electronic systems for data release and transaction processing. Key strategies include understanding how online trade works, creating new promotions and combining online and offline trade channels. Improving IT infrastructure is essential for success in today's digital world. The Big Data-assisted E-commerce Business Model (BD-ECBM) addresses slow e-commerce development and insecurity. By collecting and analyzing relevant data, businesses can make informed decisions and improve management practices. Big data analytics benefits various business areas, including customer service, cost reduction and resource optimization, (Shankar *et al.,* 2023b). Developing a business model architecture with data fusion technology on big data integrates the e-commerce background, system capabilities and supply-demand analytics into the information service layer, application-level layer and client session layer. This approach enhances customer satisfaction and brand visibility. Using an e-commerce dataset, the accuracy rate of the e-commerce platforms, based on the big data predictive analytics, ranges between 96% and 98%. High accuracy in order fulfilment boosts customer trust and loyalty, which is crucial for business success. Performance evaluation indicates that big data marketing has higher profits than traditional sales models. Big data enables businesses to reach the right audience, improve product management and increase earnings for small and medium-sized enterprises (SMEs). The precision rate of the decision-making system is approximately 98.34%, highlighting the effectiveness of the proposed approach in identifying and prioritizing the customer relationships. Customer satisfaction ranking highlights the importance of logistical service factors such as product safety, delivery timeliness and helpfulness of delivery staff. The proposed method surpasses alternative models in terms of customer satisfaction, demonstrating the effectiveness of big data analytics in e-commerce marketing. Profit analysis shows that the BD-ECBM approach is more profitable than traditional sales methods. Using big data, businesses can improve brand image, increase demand and boost revenue. Applying computer security technology in e-commerce platform construction boots user trust, safeguards data security, prevents payment risks, combats cyber-attacks and supports sustainable industry development, (Shankar *et al.,* 2023c).

In today's digital world, the constant evolution of cyber threats creates a significant challenge in safeguarding products and services. Traditional security measures often struggle to keep up with these advanced dangers, highlighting the need for innovative and adaptive approaches to cybersecurity. The concept of "Secure by Intelligence" emerges as game changing model, using advantage of the power of Artificial Intelligence (AI) to strengthen defences and actively reducing risks, (Shankar, Naresh, & Agrawal, 2022). By integrating AI-driven security measures, organizations can improve to recover of their digital assets across various industries. AI serves as a foundation in this new approach, using machine learning, deep learning, natural language processing and anomaly detection to predict, identify and respond to potential threats in real time. One important part of "Secure by Intelligence" is Dynamic Threat Detection and Prediction. With AI-based automation, systems can quickly respond to security incidents, reducing risks fast. Adaptive AI systems keep learning from each encounter, getting better at stopping future attacks. Behavioral Analysis and Anomaly Detection are key in strengthening defences against new threats. AI systems are great at spotting unusual patterns, helping to quickly find insider threats, unauthorized access or unusual activities that might be security risks. Privacy Preserving Solutions are key to keeping sensitive data safe and secure. By focusing on privacy, AI driven security measures provide strong protection and meet regulatory standards. AI driven security measures are flexible and effective in different fields, like finance, healthcare, IoT and critical infrastructure, offering tailored solutions for each. Using AI-driven security measures has many benefits. These include better threat detection, faster response times and greater adaptability to new threats. Automating security responses helps reduce human errors and improves overall security. Adopting AI-driven security measures is a proactive and adaptive way to protect products against ever-changing threats. By using AI-driven systems, organizations can predict, detect and respond to threats effectively, ensuring they stay strong and protected against changing cyber threats. AI driven security measures change the old reactive way of handling cybersecurity by providing a comprehensive approach to enhancing product security. With ongoing improvement and innovation, AI driven security measures lead to a safer and more secure digital world, (Shankar, Agrawal, & Naresh, 2022).

EVOLUTION OF DATA SECURITY IN E-COMMERCE

- **Traditional Security measures**

E-commerce platforms have historically relied on conventional security methods like:

1. **Firewalls:** Act as a barrier between trusted internal network and the external network. Monitors the incoming and outgoing traffic to infiltrate suspicious entities in the channel.
2. **Two-Factor Authentication(2FA):** Adds an extra layer of security requiring 2 forms of identification like a password followed by an OTP (one time password).
3. **Antivirus Software:** Detects and removes malicious software. Requires regular updates to detect and alert on malicious activity.

- **Need for advanced security**

Though, these conventional methods provide protection but still they have certain disadvantages like

1. **Static Defence mechanisms:** Conventional methods are usually static and not able to adapt to evolving threats. They cannot work beyond what threat they are designed to detect or mitigate. They cannot evolve with time and has to be handled manually.
2. **Manual Monitoring:** Requires significant human intervention, making it prone to inefficiency at times. Sometimes, unintentional human errors or intentional threats can be overlooked if security is being handled manually.
3. **Limited Scope:** These methods are not sophisticated to handle advanced persistent threats and zero-day delays.

Due to these limitations, there is a need for more advanced security mechanism to be implemented for the e-commerce platforms that will safeguard their sensitive information and also help build customer trust. AI ML techniques like Deep Learning, clustering, pattern recognition, anomaly detection and the use of algorithms like decision trees, random forests etc can be good for security deployment. These mechanisms are very good at learning patterns and also can detect any anomaly in patterns to find fraudulent activities. DL and ML techniques are highly adaptable to evolving cyber-attacks and this characteristic can be used to detect threats and mitigate them automatically as soon as detected.

APPLICATIONS OF AI ML IN E-COMMERCE DATA SECURITY

1. Fraud Detection

AI ML are highly effective in detecting fraudulent transactions. They can analyse large volumes of transactional data and identify unusual patterns or anomalies that can be potential frauds. Techniques like supervised learning can be deployed to classify transactions as fraudulent or not.

2. Behavioural Analytics

These algorithms can analyse user behaviour in real-time and detect anomalies. Behavioural analytics involves monitoring and analysing user interactions with e-commerce platforms to identify deviations from regular behaviour patterns.

3. Threat Intelligence

These technologies can learn from huge amount of data to detect new attack vectors and predict potential threats so appropriate security measures can be taken. This helps these, online business to keep intruders away from their sensitive information.

4. Access Control

ML algorithms can be used to dynamically adjust access controls based on user behaviour and risk assessments thereby ensuring that only authorized individuals can access sensitive data.

CASE STUDIES OF AI ML IN E-COMMERCE DATA SECURITY

1. Case Study 1: AI/ML in Fraud Detection: Real-world example of how AI/ML has improved fraud detection.

AI/ML algorithms are very good at leaning from patterns in data and predicting future patterns almost perfectly most often than not. This characteristic of ML algorithms can be used to do fraud detection on online websites. ML algorithms can learn patterns of genuine transactions well and they can detect anomalies in fraudulent ones. Deploying, these techniques give the companies a more robust security to the platform and data. PayPal founded in 1998, is a digital payments company that enables online payments and money transfers. It is one of the widely used online payment systems globally. PayPal implemented an AI powered fraud detection system that analyses transactions in real time using ML algorithms to identify patterns in transactional data, user behaviour and other contextual information and also detect anomalies in these patterns thereby indicating potential threats and frauds. By using this mechanism PayPal reduced its fraud rates by 50% and improved customer satisfaction by reducing false positives.

2. Case Study 2: Behavioural Analytics: Detail an instance where behavioural analytics secured e-commerce platforms.

Schneider Electric uses Behavioural analytics to enhance their cybersecurity framework. The company, has implemented a Systems Applications and Products (SAP) security platform from Security Bridge, thereby integrating behavioural analytics to monitor network behaviour in real-time. This has enabled the detection of unusual activities like unexpected configuration changes or network traffic spikes, which were quickly flagged to be potential threats. This proactive approach by Schneider Electric, has significantly strengthened their network defences, and also allowing them to swiftly respond to anomalous activities and prevent data breaches.

3. Case Study 3: Threat Intelligence: Example of AI/ ML in threat intelligence for e-commerce.

STU Inc., a firm that had faced severe phishing attack, in response to the breach occurred has deployed AI-Driven threat intelligence systems to monitor and analyse phishing patterns. These systems leveraged machine learning algorithms to identify suspicious emails and mitigate potential threats before reaching employees, thereby reducing future risk. The system analysed past attacks and phishing behaviour patterns to build these predictive models and improve overall security.

CHALLENGES OF AI ML DATA SECURITY SYSTEMS

1. Model Explainability

These deep learning models are often black box strategy and do not actually justify the decisions they make. E-commerce platforms could face customer dissatisfaction if legitimate transactions are blocked by these AI systems.

2. Adversarial Attacks

Fraudsters could exploit weaknesses in an e-commerce platform like by creating fake accounts with manipulated data. So, these AI systems require continuous training and updates.

3. Cost and Experience

Small players in the e-commerce space can be priced out of using advanced AI security solutions. This doesn't allow businesses of all scales to actually implement these automated security solutions.

4. System Integration

It can be technically hard to integrate these advanced technology models with existing systems. So, these businesses need to ensure compatibility and avoid security vulnerabilities.

5. Data quality and privacy regulations

E-commerce platforms need to find ways to collect sufficient customer data for training AI models while still anonymizing the sensitive information to ply with the security regulations. This balance is very important for robust security and customer data privacy.

FUTURE TRENDS

1. Explainable AI(XAI) for Security

Although presently, AI ML mechanisms are able to effectively detect the threats, it is still necessary to achieve transparency in the model's decision-making process.

XAI will help enable these online businesses to understand how AI technologies alert on malicious activities on the sites thereby improving the security mechanism.

2. Need for decentralized security

Most of these e-commerce platforms hold data across multiple servers.

The concept of federated leaning allows ML models to train on decentralized datasets without compromising on security and data privacy.

Each device would train the model on its local data ensuring that sensitive information doesn't leave the device.

3. Dynamic Access Controls

AI can enhance access controls by dynamically adjusting user permissions based on context and behaviour.

For example, an ML system might deny access to sensitive information if it detects unusual login time or location or if user behaviour is suspicious.

4. Blockchain Integration

Blockchain is a popular technology being used in domain like stock markets and bitcoins. However, integration of AI techniques with blockchain technologies can enhance data security.

AI can monitor blockchain transactions for anomalies and blockchain can provide decentralized nature for making transactions tamper proof.

5. Adversarial ML for Defence

Future research holds place for ML techniques wherein automated models able to withstand against manipulation by hackers and keep up with the trends of cyber-attacks.

CONCLUSION

AI and ML mechanisms offer advanced techniques to help enhance data security for e-commerce platforms by detecting anomalies in patterns of user behaviour, transactional patterns, mitigating cyber threats almost immediately when detected. However, there are few challenges like transparency, implementation cost, and integration of these intelligent systems with already existing security systems. But the AI models are being continuously refined so that they can be effectively deployed across various business models of the online sites and be more available to online businesses at all scales. These models are highly capable of adaptability and anomaly detection that significantly help in detecting and mitigating cyber threats. As AI ML techniques advance rapidly, the e-commerce platforms can look forward to enhanced automated security measures that will not only protect their data but also foster a sense of trust and confidence among their customers.

REFERENCES

Abbas, A. (2024). *Secure Retail: Harnessing Machine Learning*. Business Analytics, and Blockchain for Cybersecurity Excellence.

Aburbeian, A. M., & Fernández-Veiga, M. (2024). Secure Internet Financial Transactions: A Framework Integrating Multi-Factor Authentication and Machine Learning. *AI*, 5(1), 177–194. DOI: 10.3390/ai5010010

Agnihotri, N., & Sharma, A. K. (2023). NAAS: an ai-based amalgamated approach for securing e-commerce transactions.

Aldallal, A., & Alisa, F. (2021). Effective intrusion detection system to secure data in cloud using machine learning. *Symmetry*, 13(12), 2306. DOI: 10.3390/sym13122306

Ali, S. A. (2023). DESIGINING SECURE AND ROBUST E-COMMERCE PLAFORM FOR PUBLIC CLOUD. *The Asian Bulletin of Big Data Management*, 3(1), 164–189. DOI: 10.62019/abbdm.v3i1.56

. Arjunan, T. (2024). Fraud Detection in NoSQL Database Systems Using Advanced Machine Learning. *International Journal of Innovative Science and Research Technology(IJISRT), March, 13*, 248-53.

Cheng, X., Cohen, J., & Mou, J. (2023). AI-enabled technology innovation in e-commerce. *Journal of Electronic Commerce Research*, 24(1), 1–6.

Das, R., & Sandhane, R. (2021, July). Artificial intelligence in cyber security. [). IOP Publishing.]. *Journal of Physics: Conference Series*, 1964(4), 042072. DOI: 10.1088/1742-6596/1964/4/042072

Desamsetti, H. (2021). Crime and Cybersecurity as Advanced Persistent Threat: A Constant E-Commerce Challenges. *American Journal of Trade and Policy*, 8(3), 239–246. DOI: 10.18034/ajtp.v8i3.666

Dumitriu, D., & Popescu, M. A. M. (2020). Artificial intelligence solutions for digital marketing. *Procedia Manufacturing*, 46, 630–636. DOI: 10.1016/j.promfg.2020.03.090

. Gerdelius, P., & Hugo, S. (2024). Detecting Fraudulent User Behaviour: A Study of User Behaviour and Machine Learning in Fraud Detection.

Han, J., Ma, Y., Mei, Q., & Liu, X. (2021, April). Deeprec: On-device deep learning for privacy-preserving sequential recommendation in mobile commerce. In *Proceedings of the Web Conference 2021* (pp. 900-911). DOI: 10.1145/3442381.3449942

Ikhtiyorov, F. (2023). Navigating AI's Potential in E-Commerce: Legal Regulations, Challenges, and Key Considerations. *Agrobiotexnologiya Va Veterinariya Tibbiyoti Ilmiy Jurnali*, 2(5), 41–49.

. Kazemi, M. A. A. (2021). Detection of E-commerce Attacks and Anomalies using Adaptive Neuro-Fuzzy Inference System and Firefly Optimization Algorithm.

Khan, D. S. W. (2019). Cyber security issues and challenges in E-commerce. In *Proceedings of 10th international conference on digital strategies for organizational success*. DOI: 10.2139/ssrn.3323741

Kilincer, I. F., Ertam, F., & Sengur, A. (2021). Machine learning methods for cyber security intrusion detection: Datasets and comparative study. *Computer Networks*, 188, 107840. DOI: 10.1016/j.comnet.2021.107840

Kumain, K., Chaudhary, P., & Joshi, N. (2020). E-commerce security issues and role of AI: A review. *International Journal of Management*, 11(10).

Kumar, B., Roy, S., Singh, K. U., Pandey, S. K., Kumar, A., Sinha, A., Shukla, S., Shah, M. A., & Rasool, A. (2023). A static machine learning based evaluation method for usability and security analysis in e-commerce website. *IEEE Access : Practical Innovations, Open Solutions*, 11, 40488–40510. DOI: 10.1109/ACCESS.2023.3247003

Liu, Q., Li, P., Zhao, W., Cai, W., Yu, S., & Leung, V. C. (2018). A survey on security threats and defensive techniques of machine learning: A data driven view. *IEEE Access : Practical Innovations, Open Solutions*, 6, 12103–12117. DOI: 10.1109/ACCESS.2018.2805680

Ma, X., & Wang, Z. (2024). Computer security technology in E-commerce platform business model construction. *Heliyon*, 10(7), e28571. DOI: 10.1016/j.heliyon.2024.e28571 PMID: 38586367

Ma, X., & Wang, Z. (2024). Computer security technology in E-commerce platform business model construction. *Heliyon*, 10(7), e28571. DOI: 10.1016/j.heliyon.2024.e28571 PMID: 38586367

Mahbooba, B. *Enhancing Trust in Detecting Security Threats Using Machine Learning Approaches and its relevance in the Internet of Things Scenarios* (Doctoral dissertation, The Insight Centre for Data Analytics).

Mohd, N., Bhatla, S., & Upadhyay, D. (2021). Using machine learning for cyber security enhancement. *Webology*, 18(4), 2381–2386.

Mutemi, A., & Bacao, F. (2024). E-Commerce Fraud Detection Based on Machine Learning Techniques: Systematic Literature Review. *Big Data Mining and Analytics*, 7(2), 419–444. DOI: 10.26599/BDMA.2023.9020023

Osita, G. C., Chisom, C. D., Okoronkwo, M. C., Esther, U. N., & Vanessa, N. C. (2022). Application of Emerging Technologies in Mitigation of e-Commerce Security Challenges. *CCU J. Sci*, 2, 2734–3766.

Paintal, S. (2021). Ecommerce and online security. [IJM]. *International Journal of Management*, 12(1).

Pallathadka, H., Ramirez-Asis, E. H., Loli-Poma, T. P., Kaliyaperumal, K., Ventayen, R. J. M., & Naved, M. (2023). Applications of artificial intelligence in business management, e-commerce and finance. *Materials Today: Proceedings*, 80, 2610–2613. DOI: 10.1016/j.matpr.2021.06.419

. Patil, S., Amrutkar, R., Korde, P., & Kadam, P. THE ROLE OF MACHINE LEARNING IN DATA SECURITY.

Patro, S. P., Padhy, N., & Panigrahi, R. (2016). Security issues over E-commerce and their solutions. *International Journal of Advanced Research in Computer and Communication Engineering*, 5(12), 81–85. DOI: 10.17148/IJARCCE.2016.51216

Prakash, S., Venkatasubbu, S., & Konidena, B. K. (2022). Streamlining regulatory reporting in US banking: A deep dive into AI/ML solutions. *Journal of Knowledge Learning and Science Technology ISSN: 2959-6386 (online), 1*(1), 148-166.

Raimundo, R., & Rosário, A. (2021). The impact of artificial intelligence on data system security: A literature review. *Sensors (Basel)*, 21(21), 7029. DOI: 10.3390/s21217029 PMID: 34770336

Rajesh, M. V., & Chintalapudi, S. R. (2021). A Review on Applications of Machine Learning In E-Commerce. *Advances and Applications in Mathematical Sciences*, 20(11), 2831–2841.

Rangaraju, S. (2023). Secure by Intelligence: Enhancing Products with AI-Driven Security Measures. *EPH-International Journal of Science And Engineering*, 9(3), 36–41. DOI: 10.53555/ephijse.v9i3.212

Rawindaran, N., Jayal, A., & Prakash, E. (2021). Machine learning cybersecurity adoption in small and medium enterprises in developed countries. *Computers*, 10(11), 150. DOI: 10.3390/computers10110150

Saeed, S. (2023). A customer-centric view of E-commerce security and privacy. *Applied Sciences (Basel, Switzerland)*, 13(2), 1020. DOI: 10.3390/app13021020

. Sasmal, S. (2021). Preventing Card Fraud and Scam Using Artificial Intelligence.

Shachi, M., Shourav, N. S., Ahmed, A. S., Brishty, A. A., & Sakib, N. (2021). A survey on detection and prevention of SQL and NoSQL injection attack on server-side applications. *International Journal of Computer Applications*, 183(10), 1–7. DOI: 10.5120/ijca2021921396

Shankar, S. P., Agrawal, H., & Naresh, E. (2022). A Survey on Different Approaches to Automating the Design Phase in the Software Development Life Cycle. In Research Anthology on Agile Software, Software Development, and Testing (pp. 542-564). IGI Global. DOI: 10.4018/978-1-6684-3702-5.ch027

Shankar, S. P., & Chaudhari, S. S. (2023). Framework for the Automation of SDLC Phases using Artificial Intelligence and Machine Learning Techniques. *International Journal on Recent and Innovation Trends in Computing and Communication*, 11(6s), 379–390. DOI: 10.17762/ijritcc.v11i6s.6944

Shankar, S. P., & Chaudhari, S. S. (2024). Analysis of Bio Inspired Based Hybrid Learning Model for Software Defect Prediction. *SN Computer Science*, 5(7), 825. DOI: 10.1007/s42979-024-03171-y

Shankar, S. P., Naresh, E., & Agrawal, H. (2022). Optimization of association rules using hybrid data mining technique. *Innovations in Systems and Software Engineering*, 18(2), 251–261. DOI: 10.1007/s11334-021-00387-6

Shankar, S. P., Pushp, D., Makadia, N., Dubey, R., Nayak, A., & Chaudhari, S. S. (2023, September). Software Defect Predictor and Classifier Tool Using Machine Learning Techniques. In *2023 International Conference on Network, Multimedia and Information Technology (NMITCON)* (pp. 1-6). IEEE. DOI: 10.1109/NMITCON58196.2023.10275871

Shankar, S. P., Supriya, M. S., Varadam, D., Kumar, M., Gupta, H., & Saha, R. (2023). A Comprehensive Study on Algorithms and Applications of Artificial Intelligence in Diagnosis and Prognosis: AI for Healthcare. In Digital Twins and Healthcare: Trends, Techniques, and Challenges (pp. 35-54). IGI Global.

Shankar, S. P., Varadam, D., Bharadwaj, A., Saxena, T., Mohta, R., & Shankar, A. (2023). Artificial Intelligence for Defence: A Comprehensive Study on Applying AI for the Airforce, Navy, and Army. In Emerging Trends, Techniques, and Applications in Geospatial Data Science (pp. 244-262). IGI Global.

Shanmugam, L., Katari, M., & Thirunavukkarasu, K. (2024). Blockchain and Machine Learning Integration for Data Privacy and Security. *European Journal of Technology*, 8(3), 1–11. DOI: 10.47672/ejt.2006

Shukla, P. K., Raghuvanshi, C. S., & Sharan, H. O. (2024). Building an Intrusion Detection System on Ecommerce Data using Regression Analysis. *International Journal of Intelligent Systems and Applications in Engineering*, 12(4s), 731–743.

Singh, J., Wazid, M., Das, A. K., Chamola, V., & Guizani, M. (2022). Machine learning security attacks and defense approaches for emerging cyber physical applications: A comprehensive survey. *Computer Communications*, 192, 316–331. DOI: 10.1016/j.comcom.2022.06.012

Singh, K., Booma, P. M., & Eaganathan, U. (2020, December). E-commerce system for sale prediction using machine learning technique. [). IOP Publishing.]. *Journal of Physics: Conference Series*, 1712(1), 012042. DOI: 10.1088/1742-6596/1712/1/012042

Srivastava, A. (2021). The Application & Impact of Artificial Intelligence (AI) on E-Commerce. *Contemporary Issues in Commerce & Management*, 1(1), 165–175.

. Wainaina, G. N., Nakuru, K., Oginga, R., & Kiyeng, D. K. Investigating Potential Applications of Machine Learning Techniques for Personal Data Protection in E-commerce.

. Wainaina, G. N., Nakuru, K., Oginga, R., & Kiyeng, D. K. Investigating Potential Applications of Machine Learning Techniques for Personal Data Protection in E-commerce.

Wang, S., Chen, Z., Xiao, Y., & Lin, C. (2021). Consumer Privacy Protection With the Growth of AI-Empowered Online Shopping Based on the Evolutionary Game Model. *Frontiers in Public Health*, 9, 9. DOI: 10.3389/fpubh.2021.705777 PMID: 34307290

Wazid, M., Das, A. K., Chamola, V., & Park, Y. (2022). Uniting cyber security and machine learning: Advantages, challenges and future research. *ICT Express*, 8(3), 313–321. DOI: 10.1016/j.icte.2022.04.007

Youssef, H. A. H., & Hossam, A. T. A. (2023). Privacy issues in AI and cloud computing in e-commerce setting: A review. *International Journal of Responsible Artificial Intelligence*, 13(7), 37–46.

Compilation of References

Abbas, A. (2024). *Secure Retail: Harnessing Machine Learning*. Business Analytics, and Blockchain for Cybersecurity Excellence.

Abiodun, O. I., Jantan, A., Omolara, A. E., Dada, K. V., Mohamed, N. A., & Arshad, H. (2018). State-of-the-art in artificial neural network applications: A survey. *Heliyon*, 4(11), e00938. DOI: 10.1016/j.heliyon.2018.e00938 PMID: 30519653

Abou-Nassar, E. M.-K.-L., Iliyasu, A. M., El-Kafrawy, P. M., Song, O.-Y., Bashir, A. K., & El-Latif, A. A. A. (2020). DITrust chain: Towards blockchain-based trust models for sustainable healthcare IoT systems. *IEEE Access : Practical Innovations, Open Solutions*, 8, 111223–111238. DOI: 10.1109/ACCESS.2020.2999468

Abu Laila, D., Al-Na'amneh, Q., Aljaidi, M., Nasayreh, A. N., Gharaibeh, H., Al Mamlook, R., & Alshammari, M. (2024). *Simulation of Routing Protocols for Jamming Attacks in Mobile Ad-Hoc Network.*, DOI: 10.4018/979-8-3693-2691-6.ch013

Aburbeian, A. M., & Fernández-Veiga, M. (2024). Secure Internet Financial Transactions: A Framework Integrating Multi-Factor Authentication and Machine Learning. *AI*, 5(1), 177–194. DOI: 10.3390/ai5010010

Adil, M., Almaiah, M. A., Omar Alsayed, A., & Almomani, O. (2020, April 18). An anonymous channel categorization scheme of edge nodes to detect jamming attacks in wireless sensor networks. *Sensors (Basel)*, 20(8), 2311. DOI: 10.3390/s20082311 PMID: 32325646

Admass, W. S., Munaye, Y. Y., & Diro, A. A. (2024). Cyber security: State of the art, challenges, and future directions. *Cyber Security and Applications*, 2, 100031. DOI: 10.1016/j.csa.2023.100031

Afzali, M. P., Pourmohammadi, H., & Mohammad Vali Samani, A. (2022). An efficient framework for trust evaluation of secure service selection in fog computing based on QoS, reputation, and social criteria. *Computing*, 104(7), 1643–1675. DOI: 10.1007/s00607-022-01053-w

Agnihotri, N., & Sharma, A. K. (2023). NAAS: an ai-based amalgamated approach for securing e-commerce transactions.

Ahad, A., Kashyap, S., & Verghese, M. G. (2022, April). The Substructure for Estimation of Miscellaneous Data Failures Using Distributed Clustering Techniques. In Proceedings of International Conference on Information Technology and Applications: ICITA 2021 (pp. 539-546). Singapore: Springer Nature Singapore.

Ahmad, W., Almaiah, M. A., Ali, A., & Al-Shareeda, M. A. (2024, April). Deep Learning Based Network intrusion detection for unmanned aerial vehicle (UAV). In *2024 7th World Conference on Computing and Communication Technologies (WCCCT)* (pp. 31-36). IEEE.

Ahmadi, S. (2024). Zero trust architecture in cloud networks: application, challenges, and future opportunities. Ahmadi, S.(2024). Zero Trust Architecture in Cloud Networks: Application, Challenges and Future Opportunities. *Journal of Engineering Research and Reports*, 26(2), 215–228. DOI: 10.9734/jerr/2024/v26i21083

Ahsan, M., & Nygard, K. E. (2020, March; Vol. 69). Convolutional Neural Networks with LSTM for Intrusion Detection. In CATA.

Akbar, M., Waseem, M. M., Mehanoor, S. H., & Barmavatu, P. (2024). Blockchain-based cyber-security trust model with multi-risk protection scheme for secure data transmission in cloud computing. *Cluster Computing*, 27(7), 1–15. DOI: 10.1007/s10586-024-04481-9

Akinbowale, O. E., Mashigo, P., & Zerihun, M. F. (2023). The integration of forensic accounting and big data technology frameworks for internal fraud mitigation in the banking industry. *Cogent Business & Management*, 10(1), 2163560. DOI: 10.1080/23311975.2022.2163560

Akoglu, A. (2018). Natural Language Processing (NLP) Applications in Cyber security. *IEEE Security and Privacy*, 16(1), 70–75.

Al Mamlook, R. E., Nasayreh, A., Gharaibeh, H., Aljaidi, M., Al-Na'amneh, Q., & Alzu'bi, D. others, & Abdeltawab, A. (2023). Fine-Tuning Pre-Trained Models for Automated Analysis of Ophthalmic Imaging in Diagnosing Eye Diseases. *2023 24th International Arab Conference on Information Technology (ACIT)*, 1–6.

Al Sawafi, Y., Touzene, A., & Hedjam, R. (2023). Hybrid deep learning-based intrusion detection system for RPL IoT networks. *Journal of Sensor and Actuator Networks*, 12(2), 21.

Al_Hachemi, S. A. G. A. (2022). Cloud Computing Services with Minimal Redundancy, Storage, and Effective Processing Capabilities. Texas Journal of Engineering and Technology, 9, 143-149.

Alabadi, M., & Celik, Y. (2020, June). Anomaly detection for cyber-security based on convolution neural network: A survey. In *2020 International Congress on Human-Computer Interaction, Optimization and Robotic Applications (HORA)* (pp. 1-14). IEEE.

Alam, M., Hoffstein, J., & Cambou, B. (2024). Privately generated key pairs for post quantum cryptography in a distributed network. *Applied Sciences (Basel, Switzerland)*, 14(19), 8863. DOI: 10.3390/app14198863

Alangari, S. (2024). An Unsupervised Machine Learning Algorithm for Attack and Anomaly Detection in IoT Sensors. *Wireless Personal Communications*, •••, 1–25. DOI: 10.1007/s11277-023-10811-8

Aldallal, A., & Alisa, F. (2021). Effective intrusion detection system to secure data in cloud using machine learning. *Symmetry*, 13(12), 2306. DOI: 10.3390/sym13122306

Alhajjar, E., & Bradley, T. (2021). Survival analysis for insider threat: Detecting insider threat incidents using survival analysis techniques. *Computational & Mathematical Organization Theory*, •••, 1–17.

Alhamad, M. (2011). SLA-based trust model for secure cloud computing. *(Doctoral dissertation, Curtin University)*.

Alharbi, S., Weber-Jahnke, J., & Traore, I. (2011). The proactive and reactive digital forensics investigation process: A systematic literature review. *Information Security and Assurance:International Conference, ISA 2011,* Brno, Czech Republic, August 15-17, 2011. *Proceedings*, 87–100.

Al-Harrasi, A., Shaikh, A. K., & Al-Badi, A. (2023). Towards protecting organisations' data by preventing data theft by malicious insiders. *The International Journal of Organizational Analysis*, 31(3), 875–888. DOI: 10.1108/IJOA-01-2021-2598

Ali, S., Ali, A., Uzair, M., Amir, H., Bari, R. Z. A., Sharif, H., . . . Allaberdiev, S. (2024, July). Empowering Cybersecurity: CyberShield AI Advanced Integration of Machine Learning and Deep Learning for Dynamic Ransomware Detection. In *International Conference on Deep Learning Theory and Applications* (pp. 95-117). Cham: Springer Nature Switzerland. DOI: 10.1007/978-3-031-66705-3_7

Alimjon, D. (2022). Problems of data replication in distribution systems. *ACADEMICIA: An International Multidisciplinary Research Journal*, 12(5), 1119–1128. DOI: 10.5958/2249-7137.2022.00585.7

Ali, S. A. (2023). DESIGINING SECURE AND ROBUST E-COMMERCE PLAFORM FOR PUBLIC CLOUD. *The Asian Bulletin of Big Data Management*, 3(1), 164–189. DOI: 10.62019/abbdm.v3i1.56

Aljaidi, M. A.-F.-A.-S.-N. ((2023, December).). Cybersecurity Threats in the Era of AI: Detection of Phishing Domains Through Classification Rules. In 2023 2nd Internationa.

Aljaidi, M., Alsarhan, A., Al-Fraihat, D., Al-Arjan, A., Igried, B., & El-Salhi, S. M. others, & Al-Na'amneh, Q. (2023). Cybersecurity Threats in the Era of AI: Detection of Phishing Domains Through Classification Rules. *2023 2nd International Engineering Conference on Electrical, Energy, and Artificial Intelligence (EICEEAI)*, 1–6.

Aljaidi, M., Alsarhan, A., Al-Fraihat, D., Al-Arjan, A., Igried, B., El-Salhi, S. M., . . . Al-Na'amneh, Q. (2023, December). Cybersecurity Threats in the Era of AI: Detection of Phishing Domains Through Classification Rules. In *2023 2nd International Engineering Conference on Electrical, Energy, and Artificial Intelligence (EICEEAI)* (pp. 1-6). IEEE.

Aljaidi, M., Alsarhan, A., Al-Fraihat, D., Al-Arjan, A., Igried, B., El-Salhi, S. M., Khalid, M., & Al-Na'amneh, Q. (2023). Cybersecurity Threats in the Era of AI: Detection of Phishing Domains Through Classification Rules. *2023 2nd International Engineering Conference on Electrical, Energy, and Artificial Intelligence (EICEEAI)*, 1–6. https://doi.org/DOI: 10.1109/EICEEAI60672.2023.10590011

Alkadi, O., Moustafa, N., Turnbull, B., & Choo, K. K. R. (2020). A deep blockchain framework-enabled collaborative intrusion detection for protecting IoT and cloud networks. *IEEE Internet of Things Journal*, 8(12), 9463–9472. DOI: 10.1109/JIOT.2020.2996590

Alkhalidy, M. A.-S., Al-Serhan, A. F., Alsarhan, A., & Igried, B. (2022). A new scheme for detecting malicious nodes in vehicular ad hoc networks based on monitoring node behavior. *Future Internet*, 14(8), 223. DOI: 10.3390/fi14080223

Almaiah, A. M. I. N., & Almomani, O. M. A. R. (2020). An investigator digital forensics frequencies particle swarm optimization for dectection and classification of apt attack in fog computing enviroment (idf-fpso). *Journal of Theoretical and Applied Information Technology*, 15, 98.

Almaiah, A., & Almomani, O. (2020). An investigation of digital forensics for shamoon attack behaviour in FOG computing and threat intelligence for incident response. *Journal of Theoretical and Applied Information Technology*, 15, 98.

Almaiah, M. A., Almomani, O., Alsaaidah, A., Al-Otaibi, S., Bani-Hani, N., Hwaitat, A. K. A., Al-Zahrani, A., Lutfi, A., Awad, A. B., & Aldhyani, T. H. H. (2022). Performance investigation of principal component analysis for intrusion detection system using different support vector machine kernels. *Electronics (Basel)*, 11(21), 3571. DOI: 10.3390/electronics11213571

Almaiah, M. A., Al-Zahrani, A., Almomani, O., & Alhwaitat, A. K. (2021). Classification of cyber security threats on mobile devices and applications. In *Artificial intelligence and blockchain for future cybersecurity applications* (pp. 107–123). Springer International Publishing.

Almaiah, M. A., Dawahdeh, Z., Almomani, O., Alsaaidah, A., Al-Khasawneh, A., & Khawatreh, S. (2020). A new hybrid text encryption approach over mobile ad hoc network. [IJECE]. *International Journal of Electrical and Computer Engineering*, 10(6), 6461–6471.

Almaiah, M. A., Saqr, L. M., Al-Rawwash, L. A., Altellawi, L. A., Al-Ali, R., & Almomani, O. (2024). Classification of Cybersecurity Threats, Vulnerabilities and Countermeasures in Database Systems. *Computers, Materials & Continua*, 81(2).

Al-Mhiqani, M. N., Ahmad, R., Zainal Abidin, Z., Yassin, W., Hassan, A., Abdulkareem, K. H., Ali, N. S., & Yunos, Z. (2020). A review of insider threat detection: Classification, machine learning techniques, datasets, open challenges, and recommendations. *Applied Sciences (Basel, Switzerland)*, 10(15), 5208. DOI: 10.3390/app10155208

Almomani, O., Almaiah, M. A., Madi, M., Alsaaidah, A., Almomani, M. A., & Smadi, S. (2023, October). Reconnaissance attack detection via boosting machine learning classifiers. In *AIP Conference Proceedings* (Vol. 2979, No. 1). AIP Publishing. DOI: 10.1063/5.0174730

Almomani, O. (2020). A feature selection model for network intrusion detection system based on PSO, GWO, FFA and GA algorithms. *Symmetry*, 12(6), 1046. DOI: 10.3390/sym12061046

Almomani, O. (2021). A Hybrid Model Using Bio-Inspired Metaheuristic Algorithms for Network Intrusion Detection System. *Computers, Materials & Continua*, 68(1).

Almomani, O., Almaiah, M. A., Alsaaidah, A., Smadi, S., Mohammad, A. H., & Althunibat, A. (2021, July). Machine learning classifiers for network intrusion detection system: comparative study. In *2021 International Conference on Information Technology (ICIT)* (pp. 440-445). IEEE.

Almomani, O., Alsaaidah, A., Shareha, A. A. A., Alzaqebah, A., & Almomani, M. (2024). Performance Evaluation of Machine Learning Classifiers for Predicting Denial-of-Service Attack in Internet of Things. *International Journal of Advanced Computer Science and Applications*, 15(1).

Almusaylim, Z. A., Alhumam, A., Mansoor, W., Chatterjee, P., & Jhanjhi, N. Z. (2020). Detection and mitigation of rpl rank and version number attacks in smart internet of things.

Almusaylim, Z. A., Alhumam, A., Mansoor, W., Chatterjee, P., & Jhanjhi, N. Z. (2020). *Detection and Mitigation of RPL Rank and Version Number Attacks in Smart Internet of Things*. https://doi.org/DOI: 10.20944/preprints202007.0476.v1

Almusaylim, Z. A., & Zaman, N. (2019). A review on smart home present state and challenges: Linked to context-awareness internet of things (IoT). *Wireless Networks*, 25(6), 3193–3204. DOI: 10.1007/s11276-018-1712-5

Al-Na'amneh, Q. ((2024).). Next Generation Image Watermarking via Combined DWT-SVD Technique. (pp. 1-34.). In 2024 2nd International Conference on Cyber Resilience (IC. Al-Na'amneh, Q. A. ((2023)). Feature Selection for Robust Spoofing Detection: A Chi-Square-based Machine Learning Approach. *Jordan*. In 2023 2nd International E.

Al-Na'amneh, Q. A. ((2024, February).). Next Generation Image Watermarking via Combined DWT-SVD Technique. In 2024 2nd International Conference on Cyber Resilience. DOI: 10.1109/ICCR61006.2024.10532782

Al-Na'amneh, Q., Aljaidi, M., Gharaibeh, H., Nasayreh, A., Al Mamlook, R. E., & Almatarneh, S. others, & Husien, A. S. (2023). Feature Selection for Robust Spoofing Detection: A Chi-Square-based Machine Learning Approach. *2023 2nd International Engineering Conference on Electrical, Energy, and Artificial Intelligence (EICEEAI)*, 1–7.

Al-Na'amneh, Q., Aljaidi, M., Gharaibeh, H., Nasayreh, A., Al Mamlook, R. E., Almatarneh, S., . . . Husien, A. S. (2023, December). Feature Selection for Robust Spoofing Detection: A Chi-Square-based Machine Learning Approach. In *2023 2nd International Engineering Conference on Electrical, Energy, and Artificial Intelligence (EICEEAI)* (pp. 1-7). IEEE. DOI: 10.1109/EICEEAI60672.2023.10590243

Al-Na'amneh, Q., Almomani, A., Nasayreh, A., Nahar, K. M., Gharaibeh, H., Al Mamlook, R. E., & Alauthman, M. (2024). Next Generation Image Watermarking via Combined DWT-SVD Technique. *2024 2nd International Conference on Cyber Resilience (ICCR)*, 1–10.

Al-Na'amneh, Q., Nasayreh, A. N., Al Mamlook, R., Gharaibeh, H., Alsheyab, A. M., & Almaiah, M. (2024). Improving Memory Malware Detection in Machine Learning With Random Forest-Based Feature Selection. In R. Assessment & C. for Cybersecurit (Eds.), *IGI Global* (pp. 96–114). . DOI: 10.4018/979-8-3693-2691-6.ch006

Al-Na'amneh, Q. A., Aljaidi, M., Nasayreh, A., Gharaibeh, H., Al Mamlook, R. E., Jaradat, A. S., Alsarhan, A., & Samara, G. (2024). Enhancing IoT device security: CNN-SVM hybrid approach for real-time detection of DoS and DDoS attacks. *Journal of Intelligent Systems*, 33(1), 20230150. DOI: 10.1515/jisys-2023-0150

Al-Na'amneh, Q. A. (2023). Feature Selection for Robust Spoofing Detection: A Chi-Square-based Machine Learning Approach. In . *2nd Internation.*

AlQahtani, R., Farooq, H. M., & Khoraidly, A. (2024). Sentiment Clustering: A Hybrid Approach for Insider Threat Detection. *International Journal of Simulation–Systems, Science & Technology, 25*(1).

Alrawashdeh, K., & Purdy, C. (2016). Toward an online anomaly intrusion detection system based on deep learning. In: *Proceedings of the 15th IEEE international conference on machine learning and applications (ICMLA).* IEEE; p. 195–200. DOI: 10.1109/ICMLA.2016.0040

Alsarhan, A. A.-G. (2022). A novel scheme for malicious nodes detection in cloud markets based on fuzzy logic technique. *Int. J. Interact. Mob.Technol.*, 16(3), 136–150.

Alshamkhany, M., Alshamkhany, W., Mansour, M., Khan, M., Dhou, S., & Aloul, F. (2020, November). Botnet attack detection using machine learning. In 2020 14th International Conference on Innovations in Information Technology (IIT) (pp. 203-208). IEEE.

Al-Shargabi, B. A.-J. (2020). A cloudlet based security and trust model for e-government web services. *Journal of Theoretical and Applied Information Technology*, 98(1), 27–37.

Al-Shehari, T., Rosaci, D., Al-Razgan, M., Alfakih, T., Kadrie, M., Afzal, H., & Nawaz, R. (2024). Enhancing Insider Threat Detection in Imbalanced Cybersecurity Settings Using the Density-Based Local Outlier Factor Algorithm. *IEEE Access : Practical Innovations, Open Solutions*, 12, 34820–34834. DOI: 10.1109/ACCESS.2024.3373694

Al-Sit, W. T. ((2022, October).2022). Direct Trust in Cloud Computing Based on Fuzzy Logic. In. *International Conference on Cyber Resilience (ICCR)*, (pp. 1-6). IEEE.

AlSlaiman, M., Salman, M. I., Saleh, M. M., & Wang, B. (2023). Enhancing false negative and positive rates for efficient insider threat detection. *Computers & Security*, 126, 103066. DOI: 10.1016/j.cose.2022.103066

Alsowail, R. A., & Al-Shehari, T. (2020). Empirical detection techniques of insider threat incidents. *IEEE Access : Practical Innovations, Open Solutions*, 8, 78385–78402. DOI: 10.1109/ACCESS.2020.2989739

Alsowail, R. A., & Al-Shehari, T. (2021). A multi-tiered framework for insider threat prevention. *Electronics (Basel)*, 10(9), 1005. DOI: 10.3390/electronics10091005

Alsukayti, I. S., & Alreshoodi, M. (2023). RPL-Based IoT Networks under Simple and Complex Routing Security Attacks: An Experimental Study. *Applied Sciences (Basel, Switzerland)*, 13(8), 4878. DOI: 10.3390/app13084878

Alsuwayh, A. (2024). *Effectiveness of Artificial Intelligence (AI) Strategies Against Cyber Security Threats* (Doctoral dissertation, Marymount University).

Alzaabi, F. R., & Mehmood, A. (2024). A review of recent advances, challenges, and opportunities in malicious insider threat detection using machine learning methods. *IEEE Access, 12, .* , 30907–30927.

Alzoubi, Y. I., & Mishra, A. (2024). Blockchain consensus mechanisms comparison in fog computing: A systematic review. *ICT Express*, 10(2), 342–373. DOI: 10.1016/j.icte.2024.02.008

Amal, H. (2024, June 06). Sami, Alqurashi., Omar, Ben, Bahri., Mouna, Karmani., Hamzah, Faraj., Mohsen, Machhout. (2024). Performance Evaluation of Mobile RPL-Based IoT Networks under Hello Flood Attack. *Electronics (Basel)*, 13(11), 2226. Advance online publication. DOI: 10.3390/electronics13112226

Amanullah, M. A., Habeeb, R. A. A., Nasaruddin, F., Gani, A., Ahmed, E., Ninar, A. S. M., Akim, N. M., & Imran, M.. (2020). Deep learning and big data technologies for IoT security. *Computer Communications*, 151, 495–517. DOI: 10.1016/j.comcom.2020.01.016

Ambhika, C., Gayathri, S., Anish, T. P., & Sheena, B. G. (2024, August). Enhancing Predictive Modeling in High Dimensional Data Using Hybrid Feature Selection. In 2024 5th International Conference on Electronics and Sustainable Communication Systems (ICESC) (pp. 873-879). IEEE.

Amini, P., Azmi, R., & Araghizadeh, M. (2019). Analysis of Network Traffic Flows for Centralized Botnet Detection. *Journal of Telecommunication.*, 11, 7–17.

Andreoni, M., Lunardi, W. T., Lawton, G., & Thakkar, S. (2024). Enhancing autonomous system security and resilience with generative AI: A comprehensive survey. *IEEE Access : Practical Innovations, Open Solutions*, 12, 109470–109493. DOI: 10.1109/ACCESS.2024.3439363

Anitha, A. A. (2021). VeNADet: Version Number Attack Detection for RPL based Internet of Things. *Solid State Technology*, 64(February).

Arif, H., Kumar, A., Fahad, M., & Hussain, H. K. (2024). Future Horizons: AI-Enhanced Threat Detection in Cloud Environments: Unveiling Opportunities for Research. *International Journal of Multidisciplinary Sciences and Arts*, 3(1), 242–251. DOI: 10.47709/ijmdsa.v2i2.3452

Arora, M. K., Lal, S., Singh, B., & Olyaee, M. (2024). Through an Energy Lens: Examining SDGs From a Policy Perspective. In Riswandi, B., Singh, B., Kaunert, C., & Vig, K. (Eds.), *AI Applications for Clean Energy and Sustainability* (pp. 320–343). IGI Global., DOI: 10.4018/979-8-3693-6567-0.ch016

Asha, S., Shanmugapriya, D., & Padmavathi, G. (2023). Malicious insider threat detection using variation of sampling methods for anomaly detection in cloud environment. *Computers & Electrical Engineering*, 105, 108519. DOI: 10.1016/j.compeleceng.2022.108519

Atakishiyev, S., Salameh, M., & Goebel, R. (2024). *Incorporating Explanations into Human-Machine Interfaces for Trust and Situation Awareness in AVs*. http://arxiv.org/abs/2404.07383

Awaysheh, F. M., Aladwan, M. N., Alazab, M., Alawadi, S., Cabaleiro, J. C., & Pena, T. F. (2021). Security by design for big data frameworks over cloud computing. *IEEE Transactions on Engineering Management*, 69(6), 3676–3693. DOI: 10.1109/TEM.2020.3045661

Bakare, S. S., Adeniyi, A. O., Akpuokwe, C. U., & Eneh, N. E. (2024). DATA PRIVACY LAWS AND COMPLIANCE: A COMPARATIVE REVIEW OF THE EU GDPR AND USA REGULATIONS. *Computer Science & IT Research Journal*, 5(3), 528–543. DOI: 10.51594/csitrj.v5i3.859

Bamakan, S. M., Faregh, N., & ZareRavasan, A. (2021). Di-ANFIS: An integrated blockchain–IoT–big data-enabled framework for evaluating service supply chain performance. *Journal of Computational Design and Engineering*, 8(2), 676–690. DOI: 10.1093/jcde/qwab007

Battel, K., & Pearl, D. (2024). A critical juncture: Promoting responsible innovation in the self-driving automobile sector while improving human factors. *Frontiers in Industrial Engineering*, 2, 1409748. Advance online publication. DOI: 10.3389/fieng.2024.1409748

Belkhira, H. S. A., Belkheir, M., Rouissat, M., Mokaddem, A., Lorenz, P., Boukhobza, M. A., Salmi, A., & Kouar, A. (2024). Comprehensive Examination of Version Number Attacks in IoT Networks: Nodes Hyperactivity as Specific Criterion. *Open Information Science*, 8(1), 20220165. Advance online publication. DOI: 10.1515/opis-2022-0165

Biplob, M. B., Mong Marma, S., & Akther, M. (2024). Securing Tomorrow's Digital World: Key Trends in Cyber security for 2024.

Bishop, M. (2002). *Computer and Network Security*. Addison-Wesley.

Boakye-Gyan, K. (2021). *An Approach to a Comprehensive Framework for Insider Threat*. Capitol Technology University.

Boru, D., Kliazovich, D., Granelli, F., Bouvry, P., & Zomaya, A. Y. (2015). Energy-efficient data replication in cloud computing datacenters. *Cluster Computing*, 18(1), 385–402. DOI: 10.1007/s10586-014-0404-x

Boudouaia, M. A., Ali-Pacha, A., Abouaissa, A., & Lorenz, P. (2020). Security Against Rank Attack in RPL Protocol. *IEEE Network*, 34(4), 133–139. DOI: 10.1109/MNET.011.1900651

Brown, A., Johnson, S. D., & Tuptuk, N. (2024). *A Scoping Study: Crime and Connected and AVs*. OSF.

Cai, F., Zhu, N., He, J., Mu, P., Li, W., & Yu, Y. (2019). Survey of access control models and technologies for cloud computing. *Cluster Computing*, 22(3), 6111–6122. DOI: 10.1007/s10586-018-1850-7

Camacho, N. G. (2024). The Role of AI in Cybersecurity: Addressing Threats in the Digital Age. *Journal of Artificial Intelligence General science (JAIGS) ISSN: 3006-4023, 3*(1), 143-154.

Camacho, N. G. (2024). The Role of AI in Cybersecurity: Addressing Threats in the Digital Age. [JAIGS]. *Journal of Artificial Intelligence General Science*, 3(1), 143–154. DOI: 10.60087/jaigs.v3i1.75

Chandola, V., Kumar, V., & Banerjee, P. (2009). Anomaly Detection: A Survey. *ACM Computing Surveys*, 41(3), 1–58. DOI: 10.1145/1541880.1541882

Charanya, R., & Aramudhan, M. (2016, February). Survey on access control issues in cloud computing. In *2016 International Conference on Emerging Trends in Engineering, Technology and Science (ICETETS)* (pp. 1-4). IEEE. DOI: 10.1109/ICETETS.2016.7603014

Chawla, D., & Mehra, P. S. (2023). A roadmap from classical cryptography to post-quantum resistant cryptography for 5G-enabled IoT: Challenges, opportunities and solutions. *Internet of Things : Engineering Cyber Physical Human Systems*, 24, 100950. DOI: 10.1016/j.iot.2023.100950

Cheng, X., Cohen, J., & Mou, J. (2023). AI-enabled technology innovation in e-commerce. *Journal of Electronic Commerce Research*, 24(1), 1–6.

Cheng, Y., Liu, Y., Chen, T., & Yang, Q. (2020). Federated learning for privacy-preserving AI. *Communications of the ACM*, 63(12), 33–36. DOI: 10.1145/3387107

Chithaluru, P., Al-Turjman, F., Kumar, M., & Stephan, T. (2020). I-AREOR: An Energy-Balanced Clustering Protocol for Implementing Green IoT in Smart Cities. *Sustainable Cities and Society*, 61, 102254. DOI: 10.1016/j.scs.2020.102254

Choudhary, S. P., & Vidyarthi, M. D. (2015). A simple method for detection of metamorphic malware using dynamic analysis and text mining. *Procedia Computer Science*, 54, 265–270. DOI: 10.1016/j.procs.2015.06.031

Choukri, W., Lamaazi, H., & Benamar, N. (2020, December). RPL rank attack detection using Deep Learning. In *2020 International Conference on Innovation and Intelligence for Informatics, Computing and Technologies (3ICT)* (pp. 1-6). IEEE DOI: 10.1109/3ICT51146.2020.9311983

Collingwood, L. (2017). Privacy implications and liability issues of AVs. *Information & Communications Technology Law*, 26(1), 32–45. DOI: 10.1080/13600834.2017.1269871

Compton, M., Barnaghi, P., Bermudez, L., Garcia-Castro, R., Corcho, O., Cox, S., Graybeal, J., Hauswirth, M., Henson, C., Herzog, A., Huang, V., Janowicz, K., Kelsey, W. D., Le Phuoc, D., Lefort, L., Leggieri, M., Neuhaus, H., Nikolov, A., Page, K., & Taylor, K. (2012). The SSN ontology of the W3C semantic sensor network incubator group. *Journal of Web Semantics*, 17, 25–32. DOI: 10.1016/j.websem.2012.05.003

Convolbo, M. W., Chou, J., Lu, S., & Chung, Y. C. (2016, December). DRASH: A data replication-aware scheduler in geo-distributed data centers. In *2016 IEEE International Conference on Cloud Computing Technology and Science (CloudCom)* (pp. 302-309). IEEE.

Cordero, C. G., Hauke, S., Mühlhäuser, M., & Fischer, M. (2016, December). Analyzing flow-based anomaly intrusion detection using replicator neural networks. In 2016 14th Annual Conference on Privacy, Security and Trust (PST) (pp. 317-324). IEEE.

Cruz, J. M. ((2019, June).). The metric matters: The art of measuring trust in electronics. In *Proceedings of the 56th Annual Design Automation Conference 2019* (pp. 1-4). DOI: 10.1145/3316781.3323488

Dalai, A. K., & Jena, S. K. (2017). Neutralizing SQL Injection Attack Using Server Side Code Modification in Web Applications. *Security and Communication Networks*, 2017, 1–12. DOI: 10.1155/2017/3825373

Daniel, S. A., & Victor, S. S. (2024). Emerging Trends in Cybersecurity for Critical Infrastructure Protection: A Comprehensive Review. *Computer Science & IT Research Journal*, 5(3), 576–593. DOI: 10.51594/csitrj.v5i3.872

Das, P., Gupta, I., & Mishra, S. (2024). Artificial intelligence driven cybersecurity in digital healthcare frameworks. In *Securing Next-Generation Connected Healthcare Systems* (pp. 213–228). Academic Press. DOI: 10.1016/B978-0-443-13951-2.00002-7

Das, R., & Sandhane, R. (2021, July). Artificial intelligence in cyber security. []. IOP Publishing.]. *Journal of Physics: Conference Series*, 1964(4), 042072. DOI: 10.1088/1742-6596/1964/4/042072

Davoodi, E., Kianmehr, K., & Afsharchi, M. (2013). A semantic social network-based expert recommender system. *Applied Intelligence*, 39(1), 1–13. DOI: 10.1007/s10489-012-0389-1

Denney, K., Babun, L., & Uluagac, A. S. (2020). USB-watch: A generalized hardware-assisted insider threat detection framework. *Journal of Hardware and Systems Security*, 4(2), 136–149. DOI: 10.1007/s41635-020-00092-z

Department for Transport. (2016). Pathway to driverless cars: Proposals to support advanced driver assistance systems and automated vehicle technologies. In www.gov.uk/dft. Department for Transport. https://assets.publishing.service.gov.uk/government/uploads/system/uploads/attachment_data/file/581577/pathway-to-driverless-cars-consultation-response.pdf

Desamsetti, H. (2021). Crime and Cybersecurity as Advanced Persistent Threat: A Constant E-Commerce Challenges. *American Journal of Trade and Policy*, 8(3), 239–246. DOI: 10.18034/ajtp.v8i3.666

Devaraju, S., & Ramakrishnan, S. (2014). Performance comparison for intrusion detection system using neural network with kdd dataset. *ICTACT J Soft Comput*, 4(3), 743–752. DOI: 10.21917/ijsc.2014.0106

Dey, D., & Ghosh, N. (2024). *iTRPL: An Intelligent and Trusted RPL Protocol based on Multi-Agent Reinforcement Learning*.

Dey, K., Debnath, S. K., Stănică, P., & Srivastava, V. (2022). A post-quantum signcryption scheme using isogeny-based cryptography. *Journal of Information Security and Applications*, 69, 103280. DOI: 10.1016/j.jisa.2022.103280

Dhar, V. (2016). Equity, safety, and privacy in the autonomous vehicle era. *Computer*, 49(11), 80–83. DOI: 10.1109/MC.2016.326

DigiCert & Ponemon Institute. (2023). Preparing for a safe post quantum computing future. https://www.digicert.com/content/dam/digicert/pdfs/report/ponemon-preparing-safe-post-quantum-future-report-en-v1.pdf

Ding, S., Xia, C.-Y., Zhou, K.-L., Yang, S.-L., & Shang, J. S. (2014, June 27). X. C. ((2014)). Decision support for personalized cloud service selection through multi-attribute trustworthiness evaluation. *PLoS One*, 9(6), e97762. Advance online publication. DOI: 10.1371/journal.pone.0097762 PMID: 24972237

Ding, W., Bhagoji, A. N., Zhao, B. Y., & Zheng, H. (2024). Towards Scalable and Robust Model Versioning. *2024 IEEE Conference on Secure and Trustworthy Machine Learning (SaTML)*, 592–611. https://doi.org/DOI: 10.1109/SaTML59370.2024.00036

Dodiya, K. R., Jha, M., & Jha, S. (2024). Fortifying the Digital Forge: Unleashing Cybersecurity in the Interconnected World of Digital Manufacturing. In *Emerging Technologies in Digital Manufacturing and Smart Factories* (pp. 230-256). IGI Global.

Dong, B., & Wang, X. (2016). Comparison deep learning method to traditional methods used for network intrusion detection. In: *Proceedings of the 8th IEEE international conference on communication software and networks (ICCSN)*. IEEE; p. 581–5.

Duan, S. M., Yuan, J. T., & Wang, B. (2024). Contextual feature representation for image-based insider threat classification. *Computers & Security*, 140, 103779. DOI: 10.1016/j.cose.2024.103779

Dubey, A. K., & Mishra, V. (2024). Analysis of performance and trust in load balancing algorithm in cloud computing environment. *International Journal of Advanced Intelligence Paradigms*, 27(2), 91–103. DOI: 10.1504/IJAIP.2024.137185

Dumitriu, D., & Popescu, M. A. M. (2020). Artificial intelligence solutions for digital marketing. *Procedia Manufacturing*, 46, 630–636. DOI: 10.1016/j.promfg.2020.03.090

Dvir, A., Holczer, T., & Buttyan, L. (2011). VeRA - Version Number and Rank Authentication in RPL. *2011 IEEE Eighth International Conference on Mobile Ad-Hoc and Sensor Systems*, 709–714. https://doi.org/DOI: 10.1109/MASS.2011.76

Eddine Khalfoune, A., & Beghdad, R. (2024). Securing RPL-Based Networks Against Version Number and Rank Attacks. *Acta Informatica Pragensia*, 13(3), 340–358. DOI: 10.18267/j.aip.234

Elmrabit, N., Zhou, F., Li, F., & Zhou, H. (2020, June). Evaluation of machine learning algorithms for anomaly detection. In 2020 international conference on cyber security and protection of digital services (cyber security) (pp. 1-8). IEEE.

European Commission. (2024). Commission recommendation of 11.4.2024 on a coordinated implementation roadmap for the transition to post-quantum cryptography. https://ec.europa.eu/newsroom/dae/redirection/document/104249

Federal Office for Information Security. (2024). Technical guideline TR-02102-2: Cryptographic mechanisms recommendations and key lengths. https://www.bsi.bund.de/SharedDocs/Downloads/EN/BSI/Publications/TechGuidelines/TG02102/BSI-TR-02102-2.pdf

Ficco, M., & Palmieri, F. (2015). Introducing fraudulent energy consumption in cloud infrastructures: A new generation of denial-of-service attacks. *IEEE Systems Journal*, 11(2), 460–470. DOI: 10.1109/JSYST.2015.2414822

Finlayson, S. G., Bowers, J. D., Ito, J., Zittrain, J. L., Beam, A. L., & Kohane, I. S. (2019). Adversarial attacks on medical machine learning. *Science*, 363(6433), 1287–1289. DOI: 10.1126/science.aaw4399 PMID: 30898923

Fleetwood, J. (2017). Public health, ethics, and AVs. *American Journal of Public Health*, 107(4), 532–537. DOI: 10.2105/AJPH.2016.303628 PMID: 28207327

Gao, N., Gao, L., Gao, Q., & Wang, H. (2014). An intrusion detection model based on deep belief networks. In: *Proceedings of the international conference on advanced cloud and big data*. p. 247–52. DOI: 10.1109/CBD.2014.41

Garg, N., & Gupta, R. K. (2018). Performance evaluation of new text mining method based on GA and K-means clustering algorithm. In Advanced Computing and Communication Technologies: Proceedings of the 10th ICACCT, 2016 (pp. 23-30). Springer Singapore.

Ghaleb, B., Al-Dubai, A., Hussain, A., Ahmad, J., Romdhani, I., & Jaroucheh, Z. (2023). (POSTER) Resolving the Decreased Rank Attack in RPL's IoT Networks. *2023 19th International Conference on Distributed Computing in Smart Systems and the Internet of Things (DCOSS-IoT)*, 65–67. https://doi.org/DOI: 10.1109/DCOSS-IoT58021.2023.00018

Gharaibeh, H., Aljaidi, M., Nasayreh, A., Al-Na'amneh, Q., Jaradat, A. S., Samara, G., & Al Mamlook, R. E. (2023, December). Deep Feature Extraction Framework Based on DNN for Enhancing Mirai Attachment Classification in Machine Learning. In *2023 2nd International Engineering Conference on Electrical, Energy, and Artificial Intelligence (EICEEAI)* (pp. 1-5). IEEE. DOI: 10.1109/EICEEAI60672.2023.10590608

Ghorbani, A. (2014). Phishing Detection Using Machine Learning and Natural Language Processing. *IEEE Transactions on Information Forensics and Security*, 9(6), 969–980.

Ghosh N, G. S. ((2015)). A framework to facilitate selection of cloud service providers. IEEE Trans Cloud 3(1):66–79. .DOI: 10.1109/TCC.2014.2328578

Glancy, D. J. (2012). Privacy in AVs. *Santa Clara Law Review*, 52, 1171.

Goodall, N. J. (2014). Machine ethics and automated vehicles. *Road Vehicle Automation*, 93–102.

Government Response. (2018). *Government response to House of Lords Artificial Intelligence Select Committee's Report on AI in the UK: Ready, Willing and Able?* parliament.uk. https://www.parliament.uk/globalassets/documents/lords-committees/Artificial-Intelligence/AI-Government-Response.pdf

Groen, J. D. (2024). Implementing and evaluating security in O-RAN: Interfaces, intelligence, and platforms. *IEEE Network.*

Guan, Y., Noferesti, M., & Ezzati-Jivan, N. (2023). CNN-BiLSTM-Based Classification of RPL Attacks in IoT Smart Grid Networks (Industry Track). *Proceedings of the 24th International Middleware Conference: Industrial Track*, 29–34. https://doi.org/DOI: 10.1145/3626562.3626832

Guinard, D., Trifa, V. M., & Wilde, E. (2010). Architecting a mashable open world wide web of things. Technical Report/ETH Zurich, Department of Computer Science, 663.

Gulnashin, F., Sharma, I., & Sharma, H. (2019). A new deterministic method of initializing spherical K-means for document clustering. In Progress in Advanced Computing and Intelligent Engineering: Proceedings of ICACIE 2017, Volume 1 (pp. 149-155). Springer Singapore.

Habbal, A. A., Ali, M. K., & Abuzaraida, M. A. (2024). Artificial Intelligence Trust, risk and security management (AI trism): Frameworks, applications, challenges and future research directions. *Expert Systems with Applications*, 240, 122442. DOI: 10.1016/j.eswa.2023.122442

Habeeb, R. A. A., Nasaruddin, F., Gani, A., Hashem, I. A. T., Ahmed, E., & Imran, M.. (2019). Real-time big data processing for anomaly detection: A survey. *International Journal of Information Management*, 45(4), 289–307. DOI: 10.1016/j.ijinfomgt.2018.08.006

Hagendorff, T. (2020). The Ethics of AI Ethics: An Evaluation of Guidelines. *Minds and Machines*, 30(1), 99–120. DOI: 10.1007/s11023-020-09517-8

Haghighat, M., Zonouz, S., & Abdel-Mottaleb, M. (2015, November). CloudID: Trustworthy cloud-based and cross-enterprise biometric identification. *Expert Systems with Applications*, 42(21), 7905–7916. DOI: 10.1016/j.eswa.2015.06.025

Hammad, A., Saleh, H. M., & Alomari, M. (2024). Advancements in Cybersecurity: Novel Approaches to Protecting Against Emerging Threats and Vulnerabilities. *CyberSystem Journal*, 1(1), 9–22. DOI: 10.57238/r15e5074

Han, J., Ma, Y., Mei, Q., & Liu, X. (2021, April). Deeprec: On-device deep learning for privacy-preserving sequential recommendation in mobile commerce. In *Proceedings of the Web Conference 2021* (pp. 900-911). DOI: 10.1145/3442381.3449942

Haq, M. A., Khan, M. A. R., & Alshehri, M. (2022). Insider threat detection based on NLP word embedding and machine learning. *Intelligent Automation & Soft Computing*, 33(1), 619–635. DOI: 10.32604/iasc.2022.021430

Haq, S., & Singh, Y. (2018, December). Botnet detection using machine learning. In *2018 Fifth International Conference on Parallel, Distributed and Grid Computing (PDGC)* (pp. 240-245). IEEE.

Hasnain, M. P., Pasha, M. F., Ghani, I., Imran, M., Alzahrani, M. Y., & Budiarto, R. (2020). Evaluating trust prediction and confusion matrix measures for web services ranking. *IEEE Access : Practical Innovations, Open Solutions*, 8, 90847–90861. DOI: 10.1109/ACCESS.2020.2994222

Heba Abd El-Aziz, B. (2024). Distributed Learning and Broad Applications in Scientific Research Threat Intelligence Fusion Techniques for Enhanced Cybersecurity in Autonomous Vehicle Networks. In *Distributed Learning and Broad Applications in Scientific Research Annual* (Vol. 10).

Hebbaka Shivanajappa, M., Maidanahalli Seetharamaiah, R., Viswaraju Sai, B., Jakkanahally Siddegowda, A., & Kuppanna Rajuk, V. (2024). An Intrusion Detection System against RPL-based Routing Attacks for IoT Networks. *Indonesian Journal of Electrical Engineering and Computer Science*, 34(2), 1324. DOI: 10.11591/ijeecs.v34.i2.pp1324-1335

Hevelke, A., & Nida-Rümelin, J. (2015). Responsibility for crashes of AVs: An ethical analysis. *Science and Engineering Ethics*, 21(3), 619–630. DOI: 10.1007/s11948-014-9565-5 PMID: 25027859

Hinton, G. E., & Salakhutdinov, R. R. (2006). Reducing the dimensionality of data with neural networks. *Science*, 313(5786), 504–507. DOI: 10.1126/science.1127647 PMID: 16873662

Hizam, S. M. ((2020).). A conceptual paper on SERVQUAL-framework for assessing quality of Internet of Things (IoT) services. arXiv preprint arXiv. 2001.01840.

Hoang, X. D., & Nguyen, Q. C. (2018). Botnet Detection Based On Machine Learning Techniques Using DNS Query Data. *Future Internet*, 10(5), 43. DOI: 10.3390/fi10050043

Hong, W., Yin, J., You, M., Wang, H., Cao, J., Li, J., others, & Man, C. (2023). A graph empowered insider threat detection framework based on daily activities. *ISA Transactions, 141, .* , 84–92.

Hossain, M. T. (2024). *Privacy and Security for Trustworthy AI/ML in Multi-Agent Critical Infrastructures: An Analysis of Adversarial Dynamics and Protective Strategies* (Doctoral dissertation).

Huang, Y., Zhang, X., & Wang, X. (2016). A Deep Learning Approach to Network Intrusion Detection. *IEEE Transactions on Neural Networks and Learning Systems*, 58(5), 3481–3492.

Hussain, M., Pal, S., Jadidi, Z., Foo, E., & Kanhere, S. (2024). Federated Zero Trust Architecture using Artificial Intelligence. *IEEE Wireless Communications*, 31(2), 30–35. DOI: 10.1109/MWC.001.2300405

Huyen, N. T. M., & Bao, T. Q. (2024). Advancements in AI-Driven Cybersecurity and Comprehensive Threat Detection and Response. *Journal of Intelligent Connectivity and Emerging Technologies*, 9(1), 1–12.

Ibrahum, A. D. M., Hussain, M., & Hong, J. E. (2025). Deep learning adversarial attacks and defenses in AVs: A systematic literature review from a safety perspective. *Artificial Intelligence Review*, 58(1), 28. Advance online publication. DOI: 10.1007/s10462-024-11014-8

Ieong, R. S. C. (2006). FORZA–Digital forensics investigation framework that incorporate legal issues. *Digital Investigation*, 3, 29–36. DOI: 10.1016/j.diin.2006.06.004

Ikhtiyorov, F. (2023). Navigating AI's Potential in E-Commerce: Legal Regulations, Challenges, and Key Considerations. *Agrobiotexnologiya Va Veterinariya Tibbiyoti Ilmiy Jurnali*, 2(5), 41–49.

Ioulianou, P. P., Vassilakis, V. G., & Shahandashti, S. F. (2022). A trust-based intrusion detection system for RPL networks: Detecting a combination of rank and blackhole attacks. *Journal of Cybersecurity and Privacy*, 2(1), 124–153.

Jahani, M., & Rahmati, M. (2021). Malware Detection Using Deep Learning: A Survey. *Journal of Computer and System Sciences*, 116, 1–37.

Janani, R., & Vijayarani, S. (2019). Text document clustering using spectral clustering algorithm with particle swarm optimization. *Expert Systems with Applications*, 134, 192–200. DOI: 10.1016/j.eswa.2019.05.030

Jara, A. J., Olivieri, A. C., Bocchi, Y., Jung, M., Kastner, W., & Skarmeta, A. F. (2014). Semantic web of things: An analysis of the application semantics for the iot moving towards the iot convergence. *International Journal of Web and Grid Services*, 10(2-3), 244–272. DOI: 10.1504/IJWGS.2014.060260

Jaradat, A. S.-N. ((2023, November).). Genetic optimization techniques for enhancing web attacks classification in machine learning. In 2023 IEEE Intl Conf on Dependable, Autonomic and Secu.

Jaradat, A. S., Nasayreh, A., Al-Na'amneh, Q., Gharaibeh, H., & Al Mamlook, R. E. (2023). Genetic optimization techniques for enhancing web attacks classification in machine learning. *2023 IEEE Intl Conf on Dependable, Autonomic and Secure Computing, Intl Conf on Pervasive Intelligence and Computing, Intl Conf on Cloud and Big Data Computing, Intl Conf on Cyber Science and Technology Congress (DASC/PiCom/CBDCom/CyberSciTech)*, 130–136. DOI: 10.1109/DASC/PiCom/CBDCom/Cy59711.2023.10361399

Jaradat, A. S., Nasayreh, A., Al-Na'amneh, Q., Gharaibeh, H., & Al Mamlook, R. E. (2023, November). *Genetic optimization techniques for enhancing web attacks classification in machine learning. In 2023 IEEE Intl Conf on Dependable, Autonomic and Secure Computing, Intl Conf on Pervasive Intelligence and Computing, Intl Conf on Cloud and Big Data Computing, Intl Conf on Cyber Science and Technology Congress (DASC/PiCom/CBDCom/CyberSciTech) (pp. 0130-0136)*. IEEE.

Jimmy, F. N. U. (2024). Cyber security Vulnerabilities and Remediation Through Cloud Security Tools. *Journal of Artificial Intelligence General science (JAIGS) ISSN: 3006-4023, 2*(1), 129-171.

K., Kowsalyadevi., N.V., Balaji. (2023). IoBTSec-RPL: A Novel RPL Attack Detecting Mechanism Using Hybrid Deep Learning Over Battlefield IoT Environment. International journal of computer networks and applications, DOI: 10.22247/ijcna/2023/223317

Kafi, M. A., & Akter, N. (2023). Securing financial information in the digital realm: Case studies in cybersecurity for accounting data protection. *American Journal of Trade and Policy*, 10(1), 15–26. DOI: 10.18034/ajtp.v10i1.659

Kamilaris, A., Pitsillides, A., & Trifa, V. (2011). The smart home meets the web of things. *International Journal of Ad Hoc and Ubiquitous Computing*, 7(3), 145–154. DOI: 10.1504/IJAHUC.2011.040115

Kang, M. J., & Kang, J. W. (2016). Intrusion detection system using deep neural network for in-vehicle network security. *PLoS One*, 11(6), e0155781.

Karaa, W. B. A., Ashour, A. S., Sassi, D. B., Roy, P., Kausar, N., & Dey, N. (2016). Medline text mining: an enhancement genetic algorithm based approach for document clustering. Applications of intelligent optimization in biology and medicine: current trends and open problems, 267-287.

Kaufman, C., Perlman, R., & Speciner, M. (2002). Network Security: Private Communication in a Public World. Prentice Hall.

Kaur, J. (2019). An ultimate approach of mitigating attacks in RPL based low power lossy networks. arXiv preprint arXiv:1910.13435.

Kawser Wazed Nafi, T. S. (2012). An Advanced Certain Trust Model Using Fuzzy Logic andProbabilistic Logic theory". *IJACSA, Vol 3, No 12.*

Khan, A., Jhanjhi, N., Abdulhabeb, G. A. A., Ray, S. K., Ghazanfar, M. A., & Humayun, M. (2025). Securing IoT Devices Using Generative AI Techniques. In *Reshaping CyberSecurity With Generative AI Techniques* (pp. 219–264). IGI Global.

Khan, D. S. W. (2019). Cyber security issues and challenges in E-commerce. In *Proceedings of 10th international conference on digital strategies for organizational success*. DOI: 10.2139/ssrn.3323741

Khan, M. A., Rais, R. N., & Khalid, O. (2023). Collaborative Detection and Prevention of Sybil Attacks against RPL-Based Internet of Things. *Computers, Materials & Continua*, 77(1), 827–843. DOI: 10.32604/cmc.2023.040756

Khan, N. J., Houghton, R., & Sharples, S. (2022). Understanding factors that influence unintentional insider threat: A framework to counteract unintentional risks. *Cognition Technology and Work*, 24(3), 393–421. DOI: 10.1007/s10111-021-00690-z PMID: 34725543

Kılıç, H. (2017). *Kamuda Bulut Bilişim Kullanımına Yönelik Risk Analizi ve Yönetimi, Uzmanlık Tezi, (yayımlanmamış).* Çevre ve Şehircilik Bakanlığı.

Kilincer, I. F., Ertam, F., & Sengur, A. (2021). Machine learning methods for cyber security intrusion detection: Datasets and comparative study. *Computer Networks*, 188, 107840. DOI: 10.1016/j.comnet.2021.107840

Kim, A., Oh, J., Ryu, J., Lee, J., Kwon, K., & Lee, K. (2019). SoK: A Systematic Review of Insider Threat Detection. *Journal of Wireless Mobile Networks, Ubiquitous Computing and Dependable Applications*, 10(4), 46–67.

Kim, H., Kim, W., Kang, Y., Kim, H., & Seo, H. (2024). Post-quantum delegated proof of luck for blockchain consensus algorithm. *Applied Sciences (Basel, Switzerland)*, 14(18), 8394. DOI: 10.3390/app14188394

Kim, J., Kim, J., Thu, H. L. T., & Kim, H. (2016). Long short term memory recurrent neural network classifier for intrusion detection. In: *Proceedings of the international conference on platform technology and service (PlatCon).* IEEE; p. 1–5. DOI: 10.1109/PlatCon.2016.7456805

Kim, J., Shin, N., Jo, S. Y., & Kim, S. H. (2017). Method of intrusion detection using deep neural network. In: *Proceedings of the IEEE international conference on big data and smart computing (BigComp).* IEEE; p. 313–6.

Kim, M. P., & Park, S. O. (2013). Trust management on user behavioral patterns for a mobile cloud computing. *Cluster Computing*, 16(4), 725–731. DOI: 10.1007/s10586-013-0248-9

Kolevski, D., & Michael, K. (2024). Edge Computing and IoT Data Breaches: Security, Privacy, Trust, and Regulation. *IEEE Technology and Society Magazine*, 43(1), 22–32. DOI: 10.1109/MTS.2024.3372605

Kosugi, A., Teranishi, K., & Kogiso, K. (2024). Experimental Validation of the Attack-Detection Capability of Encrypted Control Systems Using Man-in-the-Middle Attacks. *IEEE Access : Practical Innovations, Open Solutions*, 12, 10535–10547. DOI: 10.1109/ACCESS.2024.3353289

Krishna, M. S. R., & Mangalampalli, S. (2024). A Systematic Review on Various Task Scheduling Algorithms in Cloud Computing. *EAI Endorsed Transactions on Internet of Things, 10.*

Kumain, K., Chaudhary, P., & Joshi, N. (2020). E-commerce security issues and role of AI: A review. *International Journal of Management*, 11(10).

Kumar, S., Yadav, S., & Singh, S. K. (2011). A Survey on Network Security: Techniques, Attacks, and Challenges. International Journal of Computer Applications, 29(10), 09-16.

Kumar, B., Roy, S., Singh, K. U., Pandey, S. K., Kumar, A., Sinha, A., Shukla, S., Shah, M. A., & Rasool, A. (2023). A static machine learning based evaluation method for usability and security analysis in e-commerce website. *IEEE Access : Practical Innovations, Open Solutions*, 11, 40488–40510. DOI: 10.1109/ACCESS.2023.3247003

Kumar, M. (2022). Post-quantum cryptography Algorithm's standardization and performance analysis. *Array (New York, N.Y.)*, 15, 100242. DOI: 10.1016/j.array.2022.100242

Kumar, V. S., Shaheen, , Rajani, D., & Medikondu, N. R. (2023). Secure Deep Learning Framework for Cloud to Protect the Virtual Machine from Malicious Events. *Wireless Personal Communications*, 131(3), 1859–1879. DOI: 10.1007/s11277-023-10524-y

Kumar, Y. V., Poornachandra, S., & Kumar, C. S. (2021). Deep Learning for Intrusion Detection: A Survey. *Artificial Intelligence Review*, 34(1), 1–33. PMID: 32836651

Kushwaha, N., & Pant, M. (2018). Link based BPSO for feature selection in big data text clustering. *Future Generation Computer Systems*, 82, 190–199. DOI: 10.1016/j.future.2017.12.005

Lad, S. (2024). Harnessing Machine Learning for Advanced Threat Detection in Cybersecurity. *Innovative Computer Sciences Journal, 10*(1).

Laila, D. A., Al-Na'amneh, Q., Aljaidi, M., Nasayreh, A. N., Gharaibeh, H., Al Mamlook, R., & Alshammari, M. (2024). Enhancing 2D Logistic Chaotic Map for Gray Image Encryption. In R. Assessment & C. for Cybersecurit (Eds.), *IGI Global* (pp. 170–188). .

Laila, D. A., Al-Na'amneh, Q., Aljaidi, M., Nasayreh, A. N., Gharaibeh, H., Al Mamlook, R., & Alshammari, M. (2024). Enhancing 2D Logistic Chaotic Map for Gray Image Encryption. In Risk Assessment and Countermeasures for Cybersecurity (pp. 170-188). (n.d.).

Laila, D. A.-N. ((2024).). Enhancing 2D Logistic Chaotic Map for Gray Image Encryption. In Risk Assessment and Countermeasures for Cybersecurity (pp. 170-188).

Laila, D. A.-N. ((2024).). Simulation of Routing Protocols for Jamming Attacks in Mobile Ad-Hoc Network. In Risk Assessment and Countermeasures for Cybersecurit.

Lakumarapu, S., Nithyanandhan, R., Bhargavi, V. S., Anish, T. P., & Nalini, M. (2024, August). Machine Learning Approaches for Liver Disease Prediction: A Comparative Analysis. In 2024 5th International Conference on Electronics and Sustainable Communication Systems (ICESC) (pp. 159-164). IEEE.

LeCun, Y., Bengio, Y., & Hinton, G. (2015). Deep Learning. *Nature*, 521(7553), 436–444. DOI: 10.1038/nature14539 PMID: 26017442

LeCun, Y., Bottou, L., Bengio, Y., & Haffner, P. (1998). Gradient-Based Learning Applied to Document Recognition. *Proceedings of the IEEE*, 86(11), 2278–2324. DOI: 10.1109/5.726791

Le, D. C., & Zincir-Heywood, N. (2021). Exploring anomalous behaviour detection and classification for insider threat identification. *International Journal of Network Management*, 31(4), e2109. DOI: 10.1002/nem.2109

Lee, H. W., Kim, N. R., & Lee, J. H. (2017). Deep neural network self-training based on unsupervised learning and dropout. *Int J Fuzzy Logic Intell Syst*, 17(1), 1–9. DOI: 10.5391/IJFIS.2017.17.1.1

Legg, P. A., Buckley, O., Goldsmith, M., & Creese, S. (2015). Automated insider threat detection system using user and role-based profile assessment. *IEEE Systems Journal*, 11(2), 503–512. DOI: 10.1109/JSYST.2015.2438442

Le-Khac, N.-A., Jacobs, D., Nijhoff, J., Bertens, K., & Choo, K.-K. R. (2020). Smart vehicle forensics: Challenges and case study. *Future Generation Computer Systems*, 109, 500–510. DOI: 10.1016/j.future.2018.05.081

Li, H. W. (2024). Driving Intelligent IoT Monitoring and Control through Cloud Computing and Machine Learning. arXiv preprint arXiv:2403.18100.

Li, X., Li, X., Jia, J., Li, L., Yuan, J., Gao, Y., & Yu, S. (2023). A high accuracy and adaptive anomaly detection model with dual-domain graph convolutional network for insider threat detection. *IEEE Transactions on Information Forensics and Security, 18, .* , 1638–1652.

Li, B., Wu, Y., Song, J., Lu, R., Li, T., & Zhao, L. (2020). DeepFed: Federated deep learning for intrusion detection in industrial cyber–physical systems. *IEEE Transactions on Industrial Informatics*, 17(8), 5615–5624. DOI: 10.1109/TII.2020.3023430

Lin, H., Sun, B., Wu, J., & Xiong, H. (2016, June). Topic detection from short text: A term-based consensus clustering method. In 2016 13th International Conference on Service Systems and Service Management (ICSSSM) (pp. 1-6). IEEE.

Lin, P. (2016). Why ethics matters for autonomous cars. *Autonomous Driving: Technical, Legal and Social Aspects*, 69–85.

Lin, G. B., Bie, Y., Lei, M., & Zheng, K. (2014). a behavior trust model in cloud computing environment. [ACO-BTM.]. *Int. J. Comput. Intell. Syst.*, 7(4), 785–795. DOI: 10.1080/18756891.2013.864479

Lin, J. W., Chen, C. H., & Chang, J. M. (2013). QoS-aware data replication for data-intensive applications in cloud computing systems. *IEEE Transactions on Cloud Computing*, 1(1), 101–115. DOI: 10.1109/TCC.2013.1

Li, S., Chen, Y., Chen, L., Liao, J., Kuang, C., Li, K., Liang, W., & Xiong, N. (2023). Post-quantum security: Opportunities and challenges. *Sensors (Basel)*, 23(21), 8744. DOI: 10.3390/s23218744 PMID: 37960442

Liu, C., Yang, J., & Wu, J. (2020). Web intrusion detection system combined with feature analysis and SVM optimization. *EURASIP Journal on Wireless Communications and Networking*, 33(1), 2020. DOI: 10.1186/s13638-019-1591-1

Liu, H., Zhang, S., Zhang, P., Zhou, X., Shao, X., Pu, G., & Zhang, Y. (2021). Blockchain and federated learning for collaborative intrusion detection in vehicular edge computing. *IEEE Transactions on Vehicular Technology*, 70(6), 6073–6084. DOI: 10.1109/TVT.2021.3076780

Liu, Q., Li, P., Zhao, W., Cai, W., Yu, S., & Leung, V. C. (2018). A survey on security threats and defensive techniques of machine learning: A data driven view. *IEEE Access : Practical Innovations, Open Solutions*, 6, 12103–12117. DOI: 10.1109/ACCESS.2018.2805680

Li, Y., Han, S., & Ren, Y. (2018). Network Anomaly Detection with Long Short-Term Memory Networks. *IEEE Access : Practical Innovations, Open Solutions*, 6, 14137–14147.

Li, Y., Huang, G. Q., Wang, C. Z., & Li, Y. C. (2019). Analysis framework of network security situational awareness and comparison of implementation methods. *EURASIP Journal on Wireless Communications and Networking*, 2019(1), 1–32. DOI: 10.1186/s13638-019-1506-1

Lowe, J., & Kuru, K. (2024). Development of Machine Intelligence for Self-Driving Vehicles Through Video Capturing. *MESA 2024 - 20th International Conference on Mechatronic, Embedded Systems and Applications, Proceedings*. DOI: 10.1109/MESA61532.2024.10704876

Maddireddy, B. R., & Maddireddy, B. R. (2021). Evolutionary Algorithms in AI-Driven Cybersecurity Solutions for Adaptive Threat Mitigation. *International Journal of Advanced Engineering Technologies and Innovations*, 1(2), 17–43.

Madhu, G., Govardhan, D. A., & Rajinikanth, D. T. (2011). Intelligent semantic web search engines: a brief survey. arXiv preprint arXiv:1102.0831.

Mahajan, S., Khurana, M., & Estrela, V. V. (Eds.). (2024). *Applying Artificial Intelligence in Cybersecurity Analytics and Cyber Threat Detection*. John Wiley & Sons. DOI: 10.1002/9781394196470

Mahbooba, B. *Enhancing Trust in Detecting Security Threats Using Machine Learning Approaches and its relevance in the Internet of Things Scenarios* (Doctoral dissertation, The Insight Centre for Data Analytics).

Mahesh, B. (2020). Machine learning algorithms-a review. *International Journal of Science and Research (IJSR).Internet.*, 9(1), 381–386.

Maheshwaran, T., Muthumarilakshmi, S., Vinoth, N. A. S., Suganya, K., Maheswari, B., & Girija, P. (2024). Securing E-Commerce Strategies With Cloud, Blockchain, AI, and ML. In *Strategies for E-Commerce Data Security: Cloud, Blockchain, AI, and Machine Learning* (pp. 470–500). IGI Global. DOI: 10.4018/979-8-3693-6557-1.ch019

Maithili, K., Ponmalar, A., Yamini, B., Karthikeyan, M., Anish, T. P., Maheswari, B., & Siva Subramanian, R. (2024). Advances in AI and Machine Learning for Healthcare Informatics. In *Machine Learning and Generative AI in Smart Healthcare* (pp. 1–22). IGI Global. DOI: 10.4018/979-8-3693-3719-6.ch001

Manikandakumar, M., & Karthikeyan, P. (2019). *A Comprehensive Study on Internet of Things Security: Challenges and Recommendations, Handbook of Advancing Consumer-Centric Fog Computing Architectures.* IGI Global.

Manikandakumar, M., & Karthikeyan, P. (2023). Weed classification using particle swarm optimization and deep learning models. *Computer Systems Science and Engineering*, 44(1), 913–927. DOI: 10.32604/csse.2023.025434

Manikandakumar, M., Sharmi, K. M., & Devi, S. S. (2015). Analyzing spam messages and detecting the zombies using spam count and percentage-based detection algorithm. *International Journal of Applied Engineering Research: IJAER*, 10(55), 1284–1289.

Mansouri, N. (2016). Adaptive data replication strategy in cloud computing for performance improvement. *Frontiers of Computer Science*, 10(5), 925–935. DOI: 10.1007/s11704-016-5182-6

Mansouri, N., Javidi, M. M., & Zade, B. M. H. (2021). Hierarchical data replication strategy to improve performance in cloud computing. *Frontiers of Computer Science*, 15(2), 1–17. DOI: 10.1007/s11704-019-9099-8

Ma, Q., Sun, C., Cui, B., & Jin, X. (2021). A novel model for anomaly detection in network traffic based on kernel support vector machine. *Computers & Security*, 104, 102215.

Marchant, G. E., & Lindor, R. A. (2012). The coming collision between AVs and the liability system. *Santa Clara Law Review*, 52, 1321.

Ma, X., & Wang, Z. (2024). Computer security technology in E-commerce platform business model construction. *Heliyon*, 10(7), e28571. DOI: 10.1016/j.heliyon.2024.e28571 PMID: 38586367

McLaren, P., Russell, G., & Buchanan, B. (2017, July). *Mining malware command and control traces. In 2017 Computing conference*. IEEE.

Mealha, D., Preguiça, N., Gomes, M. C., & Leitão, J. (2019, March). Data replication on the cloud/edge. In *Proceedings of the 6th Workshop on Principles and Practice of Consistency for Distributed Data* (pp. 1-7).

Meghanathan, N. (2013). Review of access control models for cloud computing. *Computer Science & Information Science*, 3(1), 77–85. DOI: 10.5121/csit.2013.3508

Mehdi, R. (2023). Implementing and evaluating a new Silent Rank Attack in RPL-Contiki based IoT networks. *Journal of Electrical Engineering*, 74(6), 454–462. DOI: 10.2478/jee-2023-0053

Mehraj, S. &. (2020). *International Conference on Computer Communication and Informatics (ICCCI)* (pp. 1-6). IEEE.

Mihalcea, R., Liu, H., & Lieberman, H. (2006). NLP (natural language processing) for NLP (natural language programming). In *Computational Linguistics and Intelligent Text Processing: 7th International Conference, CICLing 2006, Mexico City, Mexico, February 19-25, 2006.* [Springer Berlin Heidelberg.]. *Proceedings*, 7, 319–330.

Miloudi, I. E., Yagoubi, B., & Bellounar, F. Z. (2021, October). A Survey of Dynamic Replication Strategies in Cloud Computing Systems. In *2021 International Conference on Networking and Advanced Systems (ICNAS)* (pp. 1-6). IEEE. DOI: 10.1109/ICNAS53565.2021.9628963

Mishra, A. K., Puthal, D., & Tripathy, A. K. (2023, May). A secure rpl rank computation and distribution mechanism for preventing sinkhole attack in iot-based systems. In IEEE INFOCOM 2023-IEEE Conference on Computer Communications Workshops (INFOCOM WKSHPS) (pp. 1-6). IEEE.

Mohammed, A., Alqarni., Sajjad, Hussain, Chauhdary. (2023). A Security Scheme for Statistical Anomaly Detection and the Mitigation of Rank Attacks in RPL Networks (IoT Environment). DOI: 10.48084/etasr.6433

Mohammed, A. A. A. (2024). Fortifying Digital Frontiers: A Survey on Enterprise Ransomware Resistance. *Nanotechnology Perceptions*, •••, 111–127.

Mohammed, Y. B., Badara, M. S., & Dan'azumi, H. (2024). An Intelligence-Based Cybersecurity Approach: A Review. *Journal of International Communication*, 4(1), 32–43.

Mohd, N., Bhatla, S., & Upadhyay, D. (2021). Using machine learning for cyber security enhancement. *Webology*, 18(4), 2381–2386.

Moor, J. (2004). *The Ethics of Artificial Intelligence*. Cambridge University Press.

Mudgal, A. (2025). Leveraging AI and ML for Proactive Threat Detection for E-Commerce. In *Strategic Innovations of AI and ML for E-Commerce Data Security* (pp. 281–322). IGI Global.

Musa, O. (2024, January). Na, Fei, Zhu., Fawaz, Mahiuob, Mohammed, Mokbal. (2024). An ensemble learning framework for the detection of RPL attacks in IoT networks based on the genetic feature selection approach. *Ad Hoc Networks*, 152, 103331. Advance online publication. DOI: 10.1016/j.adhoc.2023.103331

Mutemi, A., & Bacao, F. (2024). E-Commerce Fraud Detection Based on Machine Learning Techniques: Systematic Literature Review. *Big Data Mining and Analytics*, 7(2), 419–444. DOI: 10.26599/BDMA.2023.9020023

Nadella, G. S., & Gonaygunta, H. (2024). Enhancing Cybersecurity with Artificial Intelligence: Predictive Techniques and Challenges in the Age of IoT. *International Journal of Science and Engineering Applications*, 13(04), 30–33.

Nadkarni, P. M., Ohno-Machado, L., & Chapman, W. W. (2011). Natural language processing: An introduction. *Journal of the American Medical Informatics Association : JAMIA*, 18(5), 544–551. DOI: 10.1136/amiajnl-2011-000464 PMID: 21846786

Narang, N., & Kar, S. (2021). A hybrid trust management framework for a multi-service social IoT network. *Computer Communications*, 171, 61–79. DOI: 10.1016/j.comcom.2021.02.015

Narayanan, G., & Kannan, S. (2024). Enhancing security in cloud-based VM migration: A trust-centric hybrid optimization approach. *The International Arab Journal of Information Technology*, 21(1), 166–177. DOI: 10.34028/iajit/21/1/15

Nasir, R., Afzal, M., Latif, R., & Iqbal, W. (2021). Behavioral based Telecommunication Systems, using deep learning. *IEEE Access : Practical Innovations, Open Solutions*, 9, 143266–143274. DOI: 10.1109/ACCESS.2021.3118297

Nasr, R. (2022). Customised Intrusion Detection for an Industrial IoT Heterogeneous Network Based on Machine Learning Algorithms Called FTL-CID. *Sensors (Basel)*, 23(1), 321–321. DOI: 10.3390/s23010321 PMID: 36616920

National Institute of Standards and Technology (NIST). (2024). Announcing Issuance of Federal Information Processing Standards (FIPS) FIPS 203, Module-Lattice-Based Key-Encapsulation Mechanism Standard, FIPS 204, Module-Lattice-Based Digital Signature Standard, and FIPS 205, Stateless Hash-Based Digital Signature Standard. https://www.govinfo.gov/content/pkg/FR-2024-08-14/pdf/2024-17956.pdf

Nawaz, F. A., Khan, A. R., & Boillat, T. (2022). AI-enhanced solutions during COVID-19: Current trends and future innovations. *Annals of Medicine and Surgery (London)*, 80, 80. DOI: 10.1016/j.amsu.2022.104158 PMID: 35855874

Neupane, S., Mitra, S., Fernandez, I. A., Saha, S., Mittal, S., Chen, J., Pillai, N., & Rahimi, S. (2024). Security Considerations in AI-Robotics: A Survey of Current Methods, Challenges, and Opportunities. *IEEE Access : Practical Innovations, Open Solutions*, 12, 22072–22097. DOI: 10.1109/ACCESS.2024.3363657

Nikravan, M., Movaghar, A., & Hosseinzadeh, M. (2018). A Lightweight Defense Approach to Mitigate Version Number and Rank Attacks in Low-Power and Lossy Networks. *Wireless Personal Communications*, 99(2), 1035–1059. DOI: 10.1007/s11277-017-5165-4

NIST. (2013). *Cloud Computing Standards Roadmap*. National Institue of Standards and Tecnology Special Publication.

Nivethitha, S. G., Gauthama Raman, M. R., Gireesha, O., Kannan, K., & Shankar Sriram, V. S. (2019). An improved rough set approach for optimal trust measure parameter selection in cloud environments. *Soft Computing*, 23(22), 11979–11999. DOI: 10.1007/s00500-018-03753-y

Niyaz, Q., Sun, W., & Javaid, A. Y. 2016 A deep learning based ddos detection system in software-defined networking (SDN). *CoRR. vol. abs/*1611.07400.

Nyholm, S., & Smids, J. (2016). The ethics of accident-algorithms for self-driving cars: An applied trolley problem? *Ethical Theory and Moral Practice*, 19(5), 1275–1289. DOI: 10.1007/s10677-016-9745-2

Ojo, B., Ogborigbo, J. C., & Okafor, M. O. (2024). Innovative solutions for critical infrastructure resilience against cyber-physical attacks. *World Journal of Advanced Research and Reviews*, 22(03), 1651–1674. DOI: 10.30574/wjarr.2024.22.3.1921

Olaniyi, O. O., & Omubo, D. S. (2023). The importance of COSO framework compliance in information technology auditing and enterprise resource management. *International Journal of Innovative Research and Development*, 12(4).

Omrany, H. A.-O.-D., Al-Obaidi, K. M., Hossain, M., Alduais, N. A. M., Al-Duais, H. S., & Ghaffarianhoseini, A. (2024). IoT-enabled smart cities: A hybrid systematic analysis of key research areas, challenges, and recommendations for future direction. *Discover Cities*, 1(1), C. DOI: 10.1007/s44327-024-00002-w

Osita, G. C., Chisom, C. D., Okoronkwo, M. C., Esther, U. N., & Vanessa, N. C. (2022). Application of Emerging Technologies in Mitigation of e-Commerce Security Challenges. *CCU J. Sci*, 2, 2734–3766.

Osman, M., He, J., Mahiuob, F., Mokbal, M., & Zhu, N. (2021). Artificial Neural Network Model for Decreased Rank Attack Detection in RPL Based on IoT Networks. *International Journal of Network Security*, 23, 496–503.

Padiet, P., Islam, R., & Khan, M. A. (2024). Users' Scenario-Base for Analysing Insider Threat Detection Based on User's Downloads Activity Logs. *Future of Information and Communication Conference*, 457–472.

Paintal, S. (2021). Ecommerce and online security. [IJM]. *International Journal of Management*, 12(1).

Pallathadka, H., Ramirez-Asis, E. H., Loli-Poma, T. P., Kaliyaperumal, K., Ventayen, R. J. M., & Naved, M. (2023). Applications of artificial intelligence in business management, e-commerce and finance. *Materials Today: Proceedings*, 80, 2610–2613. DOI: 10.1016/j.matpr.2021.06.419

Pal, P., Chattopadhyay, P., & Swarnkar, M. (2023). Temporal feature aggregation with attention for insider threat detection from activity logs. *Expert Systems with Applications*, 224, 119925. DOI: 10.1016/j.eswa.2023.119925

Patel, N. (2024). SECURE ACCESS SERVICE EDGE (SASE): EVALUATING THE IMPACT OF CONVEREGED NETWORK SECURITY ARCHITECTURES IN CLOUD COMPUTING. *Journal of Emerging Technologies and Innovative Research*, 11(3), 12.

Pathan, A.-S. M., & Mohammed, M. M. Z. E. (2015). Building Customer trust in cloud computing with an ICT-enabled global regulatory body. *Wireless Personal Communications*, 85(1), 77–99. DOI: 10.1007/s11277-015-2729-z

Patro, S. P., Padhy, N., & Panigrahi, R. (2016). Security issues over E-commerce and their solutions. *International Journal of Advanced Research in Computer and Communication Engineering*, 5(12), 81–85. DOI: 10.17148/IJARCCE.2016.51216

Perez, A. J., Labrador, M. A., & Barbeau, S. J. (2010). G-sense: A scalable architecture for global sensing and monitoring. *IEEE Network*, 24(4), 57–64. DOI: 10.1109/MNET.2010.5510920

Pete O'Doherty, C. V.-P. (2023). *"Protecting From Within" A review commissioned by the Police Service of Northern Ireland (PSNI) and the Northern Ireland Policing Board (NIPB), into the PSNI data breach.*

Petit, J., & Shladover, S. E. (2014). Potential cyberattacks on automated vehicles. *IEEE Transactions on Intelligent Transportation Systems*, 16(2), 546–556.

Petit, J., Stottelaar, B., Feiri, M., & Kargl, F. (2015). Remote attacks on automated vehicles sensors: Experiments on camera and lidar. *Black Hat Europe*, 11, 995.

Pfisterer, D., Romer, K., Bimschas, D., Kleine, O., Mietz, R., Truong, C., Hasemann, H., Kröller, A., Pagel, M., Hauswirth, M., Karnstedt, M., Leggieri, M., Passant, A., & Richardson, R. (2011). SPITFIRE: Toward a semantic web of things. *IEEE Communications Magazine*, 49(11), 40–48. DOI: 10.1109/MCOM.2011.6069708

Potluri, S., & Diedrich, C. (2016). Accelerated deep neural networks for enhanced intrusion detection system. In: *Proceedings of the IEEE 21st international conference on emerging technologies and factory automation (ETFA).* IEEE; p. 1–8. vol. DOI: 10.1109/ETFA.2016.7733515

Poudyal, S., & Dasgupta, D. (2020, December). AI-powered ransomware detection framework. In *2020 IEEE Symposium Series on Computational Intelligence (SSCI)* (pp. 1154-1161). IEEE. DOI: 10.1109/SSCI47803.2020.9308387

Pourhabibi, T., Ong, K. L., Kam, B. H., & Boo, Y. L. (2020). Fraud detection: A systematic literature review of graph-based anomaly detection approaches. *Decision Support Systems*, 133, 113303.

Prakash, S., Venkatasubbu, S., & Konidena, B. K. (2022). Streamlining regulatory reporting in US banking: A deep dive into AI/ML solutions. *Journal of Knowledge Learning and Science Technology ISSN: 2959-6386 (online), 1*(1), 148-166.

Prakash, N., Vignesh, J., Ashwin, M., Ramadass, S., Veeranjaneyulu, N., Athawale, S. V., Ravuri, A., & Subramanian, B. (2024). Enabling secure and efficient industry 4.0 transformation through trust-authorized anomaly detection in cloud environments with a hybrid AI approach. *Optical and Quantum Electronics*, 56(2), 251. DOI: 10.1007/s11082-023-05781-x

Prinzel, L. J., Krois, P., Ellis, K. K., Vincent, M., Stephens, C., Oza, N., . . . Matthews, B. L. (2024). The Adaptable and Resilient Safety System: The Human Factor in Future In-Time Aviation Safety Management Systems. In AIAA SCITECH 2024 Forum (p. 1603).

Pschorr, J., Henson, C. A., Patni, H. K., & Sheth, A. P. (2010). Sensor discovery on linked data.

QNX. B. (2020). WP.29 Cybersecurity Vehicle Regulation Compliance: Ultimate guides: Blackberry QNX. In *Ultimate Guides | BlackBerry QNX.* Blackberry. https://blackberry.qnx.com/en/ultimate-guides/wp-29-vehicle-cybersecurity

Qureshi, K., Rana, S., Ahmed, A., & Jeon, G. A. (2020). novel and secure attacks detection framework for smart cities industrial internet of things. *Sustainable Cities and Society*, 61, 102343. DOI: 10.1016/j.scs.2020.102343

Raghavendra, T., Anand, M., Selvi, M., Thangaramya, K., Kumar, S. S., & Kannan, A. (2022). An intelligent RPL attack detection using machine learning-based intrusion detection system for Internet of Things. *Procedia Computer Science*, 215, 61–70. DOI: 10.1016/j.procs.2022.12.007

Rahaman, M., Bakkireddygari, S. S., Chattopadhyay, S., Gomez, A. L., Arya, V., & Bansal, S. (2024). Infrastructure and Network Security. In *Metaverse Security Paradigms* (pp. 108–144). IGI Global. DOI: 10.4018/979-8-3693-3824-7.ch005

Rahman, F. H., Au, T.-W., Newaz, S. H. S., Suhaili, W. S., & Lee, G. M. (2020). Find my trustworthy fogs: A fuzzy-based trust evaluation framework. *Future Generation Computer Systems*, 109, 562–572. DOI: 10.1016/j.future.2018.05.061

Rahmani, M. K. (2022). *Blockchain-Based Trust Management Framework for Cloud Computing-Based Internet of Medical Things (IoMT): A Systematic Review*. Computatio. [Retracted] DOI: 10.1155/2022/9766844

Raimundo, R., & Rosário, A. (2021). The impact of artificial intelligence on data system security: A literature review. *Sensors (Basel)*, 21(21), 7029. DOI: 10.3390/s21217029 PMID: 34770336

Rajendran, V. S. (2015). Hybrid model for dynamic evaluation of trust in cloud services. *Wireless Networks*, ●●●, 1–12.

Rajesh, M. V., & Chintalapudi, S. R. (2021). A Review on Applications of Machine Learning In E-Commerce. *Advances and Applications in Mathematical Sciences*, 20(11), 2831–2841.

Rana Hassam Ahmed, M. H. H. A. S. Z. M. H. T. (2024). ENHANCING AUTONOMOUS VEHICLE SECURITY THROUGH ADVANCED ARTIFICIAL INTELLIGENCE TECHNIQUES. *Journal of Computer Science and Electrical Engineering*, 6(4). Advance online publication. DOI: 10.61784/jcsee3017

Ranathunga, T. M. (2020). A DLT-based trust framework for IoT ecosystems. In. *International Conference on Cyber Security and Protection of Digital Services (Cyber Security) (pp. 1-8). IEEE.*

Randive, K., Mohan, R., & Sivakrishna, A. M. (2023). An efficient pattern-based approach for insider threat classification using the image-based feature representation. *Journal of Information Security and Applications*, 73, 103434. DOI: 10.1016/j.jisa.2023.103434

Rangaraju, S. (2023). Secure by Intelligence: Enhancing Products with AI-Driven Security Measures. *EPH-International Journal of Science And Engineering*, 9(3), 36–41. DOI: 10.53555/ephijse.v9i3.212

Rao, S. D. P. (2024). *HARNESSING AI FOR EVOLVING THREATS: FROM DETECTION TO AUTOMATED RESPONSE*. Journal of Science Technology and Research (JSTAR).

Rawindaran, N., Jayal, A., & Prakash, E. (2021). Machine learning cybersecurity adoption in small and medium enterprises in developed countries. *Computers*, 10(11), 150. DOI: 10.3390/computers10110150

Ring, M., Wunderlich, S., Scheuring, D., Landes, D., & Hotho, A. (2019). A survey of network-based intrusion detection data sets. *Computers & Security*, 86, 147–167.

Rizvi, S. M., Mitchell, J., Razaque, A., Rizvi, M. R., & Williams, I. (2020). A fuzzy inference system (FIS) to evaluate the security readiness of cloud service providers. *Journal of Cloud Computing (Heidelberg, Germany)*, 9(1), 1–17. DOI: 10.1186/s13677-020-00192-9

Rjoub, G., Islam, S., Bentahar, J., Almaiah, M. A., & Alrawashdeh, R. (2024). Enhancing IoT Intelligence: A Transformer-based Reinforcement Learning Methodology. *arXiv preprint arXiv:2404.04205*. DOI: 10.1109/IWCMC61514.2024.10592607

Roshanaei, M., Khan, M. R., & Sylvester, N. N. (2024). Enhancing Cybersecurity through AI and ML: Strategies, Challenges, and Future Directions. *Journal of Information Security*, 15(3), 320–339. DOI: 10.4236/jis.2024.153019

Rouissat, M., Belkheir, M., Alsukayti, I. S., & Mokaddem, A. (2023). A Lightweight Mitigation Approach against a New Inundation Attack in RPL-Based IoT Networks. *Applied Sciences (Basel, Switzerland)*, 13(18), 10366. DOI: 10.3390/app131810366

Roy, S., Majumdar, A. K., & Ghosh, S. K. (2019). AI for Cybersecurity: A Survey. *IEEE Access : Practical Innovations, Open Solutions*, 7, 56986–57017.

Russell, S., Norvig, P., & Tegmark, M. (2018). AI, Ethics, and the Future of Humanity. *Science*, 361(6407), 890–891.

Ruta, M., Scioscia, F., & Di Sciascio, E. (2012, September). Enabling the Semantic Web of Things: framework and architecture. In *2012 IEEE Sixth International Conference on Semantic Computing* (pp. 345-347). IEEE.

Saba, T., Rehman, A., Sadad, T., Kolivand, H., & Bahaj, S. A. (2022). Anomaly-based intrusion detection system for IoT networks through deep learning model. *Computers & Electrical Engineering*, 99, 107810. DOI: 10.1016/j.compeleceng.2022.107810

Saeed, S. (2023). A customer-centric view of E-commerce security and privacy. *Applied Sciences (Basel, Switzerland)*, 13(2), 1020. DOI: 10.3390/app13021020

Sahay, R., Geethakumari, G., & Mitra, B. J. (2020). A holistic framework for prediction of routing attacks in IoT-LLNs "Mehdi, Rouissat., Mohammed, Belkehir., Allel, Mokaddem., Merahi, Bouziani., Ibrahim, S., Alsukayti. (2024). Exploring and mitigating hybrid rank attack in RPL-based IoT networks. *Journal of Electrical Engineering*, 75(3), 204–213. DOI: 10.2478/jee-2024-0025

Sahay, R., Geethakumari, G., Mitra, B., & Sahoo, I. (2020). Efficient Framework for Detection of Version Number Attack in Internet of Things. In *Advances in Intelligent Systems and Computing*. Springer International Publishing.

Sailaja, M., Ahad, A., Sivaramakrishna, K., & Hussain, A. (2021, November). Machine Learning Medical Resource Allocation. [). IOP Publishing.]. *Journal of Physics: Conference Series*, 2089(1), 012082.

Salem, A. H., Azzam, S. M., Emam, O. E., & Abohany, A. A. (2024). Advancing cybersecurity: A comprehensive review of AI-driven detection techniques. *Journal of Big Data*, 11(1), 105. DOI: 10.1186/s40537-024-00957-y

Salunkhe, S. D., & Patil, D. (2016, August). Division and replication for data with public auditing scheme for cloud storage. In *2016 International Conference on Computing Communication Control and automation (ICCUBEA)* (pp. 1-5). IEEE.

Sarao, P. (2019). Machine learning and deep learning techniques on wireless networks. *International Journal of Engineering Research & Technology (Ahmedabad)*, 12(3), 311–320.

Sarker, I. H. (2021). Machine learning: Algorithms, real-world applications and research directions. *SN Computer Science*, 2(3), 160. DOI: 10.1007/s42979-021-00592-x PMID: 33778771

Schlenoff, C. I., Kootbally, Z., Rachakonda, P., Lightman, S., Vassilev, A., Wollman, D. A., & Griffor, E. (2024). Standards and Performance Metrics for On-Road Automated Vehicles.

Shachi, M., Shourav, N. S., Ahmed, A. S., Brishty, A. A., & Sakib, N. (2021). A survey on detection and prevention of SQL and NoSQL injection attack on server-side applications. *International Journal of Computer Applications*, 183(10), 1–7. DOI: 10.5120/ijca2021921396

Shafee, A. (2020, October). Botnets and their detection techniques. In *2020 International Symposium on Networks, Computers and Communications (ISNCC)* (pp. 1-6). IEEE.

Shakya, A. K., Pillai, G., & Chakrabarty, S. (2023). Reinforcement learning algorithms: A brief survey. *Expert Systems with Applications*, 231, 120495. DOI: 10.1016/j.eswa.2023.120495

Shaller, A., Zamir, L., & Nojoumian, M. (2023). Roadmap of post-quantum cryptography standardization: Side-channel attacks and countermeasures. *Information and Computation, 295. Information and Computation*, 105112, 105112. Advance online publication. DOI: 10.1016/j.ic.2023.105112

Shankar, S. P., Agrawal, H., & Naresh, E. (2022). A Survey on Different Approaches to Automating the Design Phase in the Software Development Life Cycle. In Research Anthology on Agile Software, Software Development, and Testing (pp. 542-564). IGI Global. DOI: 10.4018/978-1-6684-3702-5.ch027

Shankar, S. P., Supriya, M. S., Varadam, D., Kumar, M., Gupta, H., & Saha, R. (2023). A Comprehensive Study on Algorithms and Applications of Artificial Intelligence in Diagnosis and Prognosis: AI for Healthcare. In Digital Twins and Healthcare: Trends, Techniques, and Challenges (pp. 35-54). IGI Global.

Shankar, S. P., Varadam, D., Bharadwaj, A., Saxena, T., Mohta, R., & Shankar, A. (2023). Artificial Intelligence for Defence: A Comprehensive Study on Applying AI for the Airforce, Navy, and Army. In Emerging Trends, Techniques, and Applications in Geospatial Data Science (pp. 244-262). IGI Global.

Shankar, S. P., & Chaudhari, S. S. (2023). Framework for the Automation of SDLC Phases using Artificial Intelligence and Machine Learning Techniques. *International Journal on Recent and Innovation Trends in Computing and Communication*, 11(6s), 379–390. DOI: 10.17762/ijritcc.v11i6s.6944

Shankar, S. P., & Chaudhari, S. S. (2024). Analysis of Bio Inspired Based Hybrid Learning Model for Software Defect Prediction. *SN Computer Science*, 5(7), 825. DOI: 10.1007/s42979-024-03171-y

Shankar, S. P., Naresh, E., & Agrawal, H. (2022). Optimization of association rules using hybrid data mining technique. *Innovations in Systems and Software Engineering*, 18(2), 251–261. DOI: 10.1007/s11334-021-00387-6

Shankar, S. P., Pushp, D., Makadia, N., Dubey, R., Nayak, A., & Chaudhari, S. S. (2023, September). Software Defect Predictor and Classifier Tool Using Machine Learning Techniques. In *2023 International Conference on Network, Multimedia and Information Technology (NMITCON)* (pp. 1-6). IEEE. DOI: 10.1109/NMITCON58196.2023.10275871

Shanmugam, L., Katari, M., & Thirunavukkarasu, K. (2024). Blockchain and Machine Learning Integration for Data Privacy and Security. *European Journal of Technology*, 8(3), 1–11. DOI: 10.47672/ejt.2006

Sharafaldin, S., Lazarevic, A. L., & Borodovsky, L. A. (2018). Intrusion Detection Using Recurrent Neural Networks. *Computers & Security*, 76, 100–116.

Sharma, G., Grover, J., & Verma, A. (2023). Performance evaluation of mobile RPL-based IoT networks under version number attack. *Computer Communications*, 197, 12–22. DOI: 10.1016/j.comcom.2022.10.014

Sharma, G., Malley, D. J., Parle, D., Akowua, K., & Padgaonkar, N. (2024, March). Analysis and Study of Intelligent Testbed for Safeguarding Nuclear and Defense Industry from AI-Enabled Cyberattacks. In *2024 IEEE International Conference on Interdisciplinary Approaches in Technology and Management for Social Innovation (IATMSI)* (Vol. 2, pp. 1-6). IEEE. DOI: 10.1109/IATMSI60426.2024.10502505

Sharma, R. K. (2018). Artificial Intelligence and Machine Learning in Cybersecurity. *International Journal of Engineering and Advanced Technology*, 8(2), 142–146.

Shirgaonkar, M., Shinde, A., Sankpal, P., & Gutte, V. (2022, March). Cloud Computing Security using Cryptographic Algorithms. In *2022 6th International Conference on Computing Methodologies and Communication (ICCMC)* (pp. 31-37). IEEE. DOI: 10.1109/ICCMC53470.2022.9753711

Shukla, P. K., Raghuvanshi, C. S., & Sharan, H. O. (2024). Building an Intrusion Detection System on Ecommerce Data using Regression Analysis. *International Journal of Intelligent Systems and Applications in Engineering*, 12(4s), 731–743.

Silva, G. H. G., Holanda, M., & Araujo, A. (2016, June). Data replication policy in a cloud computing environment. In *2016 11th Iberian conference on information systems and technologies (CISTI)* (pp. 1-6). IEEE.

Singh, A., Rakhra, M., Singh, D., Kaur, B., & Kaur, H. (2024). Improving Insider Threat Detection with User and Role-Based Behavior. *2024 11th International Conference on Reliability, Infocom Technologies and Optimization (Trends and Future Directions)(ICRITO)*, 1–6.

Singh, M., Mehtre, B. M., & Sangeetha, S. (2019). User behavior profiling using ensemble approach for insider threat detection. *2019 IEEE 5th International Conference on Identity, Security, and Behavior Analysis (ISBA)*, 1–8.

Singh, A., & Chatterjee, K. (2024). Trust management in online computing environment: A complete review. *Journal of Ambient Intelligence and Humanized Computing*, 15(1), 491–545. DOI: 10.1007/s12652-023-04676-9

Singh, J., Wazid, M., Das, A. K., Chamola, V., & Guizani, M. (2022). Machine learning security attacks and defense approaches for emerging cyber physical applications: A comprehensive survey. *Computer Communications*, 192, 316–331. DOI: 10.1016/j.comcom.2022.06.012

Singh, K., Booma, P. M., & Eaganathan, U. (2020, December). E-commerce system for sale prediction using machine learning technique. []. IOP Publishing.]. *Journal of Physics: Conference Series*, 1712(1), 012042. DOI: 10.1088/1742-6596/1712/1/012042

Singh, M., Mehtre, B. M., & Sangeetha, S. (2020). Insider threat detection based on user behaviour analysis. *Machine Learning, Image Processing, Network Security and Data Sciences: Second International Conference, MIND 2020, Silchar, India, July 30-31, 2020. Proceedings*, 2(Part II), 559–574.

Somu, N. K., Kirthivasan, K., & Shankar Sriram, V. S. (2017). A rough set-based hypergraph trust measure parameter selection technique for cloud service selection. *The Journal of Supercomputing*, 73(10), 4535–4559. DOI: 10.1007/s11227-017-2032-8

Song, G., Jang, K., Eum, S., Sim, M., & Seo, H. (2023). NTT and inverse NTT Quantum circuits in CRYSTALS-Kyber for post-quantum security evaluation. *Applied Sciences (Basel, Switzerland)*, 13(18), 10373. DOI: 10.3390/app131810373

Song, S., Gao, N., Zhang, Y., & Ma, C. (2024). BRITD: Behavior rhythm insider threat detection with time awareness and user adaptation. *Cybersecurity*, 7(1), 2. DOI: 10.1186/s42400-023-00190-9

Sood, S. K. (2012). A combined approach to ensure data security in cloud computing. *Journal of Network and Computer Applications*, 35(6), 1831–1838. DOI: 10.1016/j.jnca.2012.07.007

Soyjaudah, K. M. S., Catherine, P. C., & Coonjah, I. (2016, April). Evaluation of UDP tunnel for data replication in data centers and cloud environment. In 2016 international conference on computing, communication and automation (ICCCA) (pp. 1217-1221). IEEE.

Srivastava, A. (2021). The Application & Impact of Artificial Intelligence (AI) on E-Commerce. *Contemporary Issues in Commerce & Management*, 1(1), 165–175.

Srivastava, P., & Khan, R. (2018). A review paper on cloud computing. *International Journal of Advanced Research in Computer Science and Software Engineering*, 8(6), 17–20. DOI: 10.23956/ijarcsse.v8i6.711

Staff, F. (2024). A Beginner's Guide to the ISO/SAE 21434 Cybersecurity Standard for Road Vehicles. In *Beyond Security*. https://www.beyondsecurity.com/blog/iso-sae-21434-standard-road-vehicles

Steingartner, W., Galinec, D., & Kozina, A. (2021). Threat defense: Cyber deception approach and education for resilience in hybrid threats model. *Symmetry*, 13(4), 597. DOI: 10.3390/sym13040597

Stoian, N. A. (2020). Machine learning for anomaly detection in iot networks: Malware analysis on the iot-23 data set (Bachelor's thesis, University of Twente).

Stottelaar, B. G. B. (2015). *Practical cyber-attacks on AVs*. University of Twente.

Suarez-Tangil, G., Tapiador, J. E., Peris-Lopez, P., & Blasco, J. (2014). Dendroid: A text mining approach to analyzing and classifying code structures in android malware families. *Expert Systems with Applications*, 41(4), 1104–1117. DOI: 10.1016/j.eswa.2013.07.106

Subha, S., Balakrishnan, C., & Anish, T. P. (2024, August). Optimizing Machine Learning Algorithms for Heart Disease Prediction in Healthcare: A Comparative Study. In 2024 5th International Conference on Electronics and Sustainable Communication Systems (ICESC) (pp. 866-872). IEEE.

Sudha, K., Nithyanandhan, R., Anish, T. P., Girija, P., & Nalini, M. (2024, July). Enhancing Healthcare Data Security in the Cloud: Integrating ML-Based Intrusion Detection Systems. In 2024 2nd World Conference on Communication & Computing (WCONF) (pp. 1-7). IEEE.

Sun, D., Liu, M., Li, M., Shi, Z., Liu, P., & Wang, X. (2021). DeepMIT: a novel malicious insider threat detection framework based on recurrent neural network. *2021 IEEE 24th International Conference on Computer Supported Cooperative Work in Design (CSCWD)*, 335–341.

Sun, D. W., Chang, G. R., Gao, S., Jin, L. Z., & Wang, X. W. (2012). Modeling a dynamic data replication strategy to increase system availability in cloud computing environments. *Journal of Computer Science and Technology*, 27(2), 256–272. DOI: 10.1007/s11390-012-1221-4

Syed, F. M., & ES, F. K. (2024). AI-Powered Security for Internet of Medical Things (IoMT) Devices. *Revista de Inteligencia Artificial en Medicina*, 15(1), 556–582.

Tahar, G. E. (2024). Lightweight Mitigation Against DIO Suppression Attack In RPL-Based IoT Networks. *In 2024 6th International Conference on Pattern Analysis and Intelligent Systems (PAIS)*, (pp. (pp. 1-6). IEEE.).

Tahirkheli, A. I., Shiraz, M., Hayat, B., Idrees, M., Sajid, A., Ullah, R., Ayub, N., & Kim, K. I. (2021). A survey on modern cloud computing security over smart city networks: Threats, vulnerabilities, consequences, countermeasures, and challenges. *Electronics (Basel)*, 10(15), 1811. DOI: 10.3390/electronics10151811

Tamimi, A. A., Dawood, R., & Sadaqa, L. (2019, April). Disaster recovery techniques in cloud computing. In *2019 IEEE Jordan International Joint Conference on Electrical Engineering and Information Technology (JEEIT)* (pp. 845-850). IEEE. DOI: 10.1109/JEEIT.2019.8717450

Tang, M., Dai, X., Liu, J., & Chen, J. (2017, September). D. X. ((2016)). Towards a trust evaluation middleware for cloud service selection. *Future Generation Computer Systems*, 74, 302–312. Advance online publication. DOI: 10.1016/j.future.2016.01.009

Tang, T. A., Mhamdi, L., McLernon, D., Zaidi, S. A. R., & Ghogho, M. (2016). Deep learning approach for network intrusion detection in software defined networking. In: *Proceedings of the international conference onwireless networks and mobile communications (WINCOM)*. IEEE; p. 258–63. DOI: 10.1109/WINCOM.2016.7777224

Tan, S. (2024). Bridging the Gap: Machine Learning and Vision Neural Networks in AVs for the Aging Population. *International Journal of Advanced Computer Science and Applications*, 15(10). Advance online publication. DOI: 10.14569/IJACSA.2024.0151030

Tao, X., Lu, S., Zhao, F., Lan, R., Chen, L., Fu, L., & Jia, R. (2024). User Behavior Threat Detection Based on Adaptive Sliding Window GAN. *IEEE Transactions on Network and Service Management*, 21(2), 2493–2503. DOI: 10.1109/TNSM.2024.3355698

Tassorelli, C., Onishchenko, K., Halker Singh, R. B., Duan, M., Dupont-Benjamin, L., Hemstock, M., Voller, C., McAllister, P., Nahas, S. J., Gandhi, P., & Ailani, J. (2024). Comparative efficacy, quality of life, safety, and tolerability of atogepant and rimegepant in migraine prevention: A matching-adjusted indirect comparison analysis. *Cephalalgia*, 44(2), 03331024241235156. Advance online publication. DOI: 10.1177/03331024241235156 PMID: 38410850

Tavallaee, M., Bagheri, E., Lu, W., & Ghorbani, A. A. (2009). A Survey of Machine Learning for Network Security. *Computer Networks*, 54(3), 491–510.

Thakran, Y., & Toshniwal, D. (2014). A novel agglomerative hierarchical approach for clustering in medical databases. In Recent Advances in Intelligent Informatics: Proceedings of the Second International Symposium on Intelligent Informatics (ISI'13), August 23-24 2013, Mysore, India (pp. 245-252). Cham: Springer International Publishing.

Thakur, M. (2024). Cyber security threats and countermeasures in digital age. [JASE]. *Journal of Applied Science and Education*, 4(1), 1–20. DOI: 10.54060/a2zjournals.jase.42

Thakur, M. R., Khilnani, D. R., Gupta, K., Jain, S., Agarwal, V., Sane, S., Sanyal, S., & Dhekne, P. S. (2012). Detection and prevention of botnets and malware in an enterprise network. *International Journal of Wireless and Mobile Computing*, 5(2), 144–153. DOI: 10.1504/IJWMC.2012.046776

Thanalakshmi, P., Rishikhesh, A., Marion Marceline, J., Joshi, G. P., & Cho, W. (2023). A quantum-resistant blockchain system: A comparative analysis. *Mathematics*, 11(18), 3947. DOI: 10.3390/math11183947

Theodoropoulos, T., Rosa, L., Benzaid, C., Gray, P., Marin, E., Makris, A., Cordeiro, L., Diego, F., Sorokin, P., Girolamo, M. D., Barone, P., Taleb, T., & Tserpes, K. (2023). Security in Cloud-Native Services: A Survey. *Journal of Cybersecurity and Privacy*, 3(4), 758–793. DOI: 10.3390/jcp3040034

Thiyagu, T., & Krishnaveni, S. (2022, December). RPL Attacks Detection and Prevention in IOT Networks with Advanced GRU Deep Learning Algorithm. In 2022 Smart Technologies, Communication and Robotics (STCR) (pp. 1-5). IEEE.

Thiyagu, T., & Krishnaveni, S. (2022). RPL Attacks Detection and Prevention in IOT Networks with Advanced GRU Deep Learning Algorithm. *2022 Smart Technologies* [STCR]. *Communication and Robotics*, 1–5, 1–5. Advance online publication. DOI: 10.1109/STCR55312.2022.10009350

Tirulo, A., Chauhan, S., & Dutta, K. (2024). Machine learning and deep learning techniques for detecting and mitigating cyber threats in IoT-enabled smart grids: A comprehensive review. *International Journal of Information and Computer Security*, 24(3-4), 284–321. DOI: 10.1504/IJICS.2024.141601

Toulas, B. (2023). *Verizon Insider Data Breach hits over 63,000 employees.*

Tyagi, H., & Kumar, R. (2021). Attack and anomaly detection in IoT networks using supervised machine learning approaches. *Revue d'Intelligence Artificielle*, 35(1), 11–21. DOI: 10.18280/ria.350102

Usman, A., Schadek, R., & Theel, O. (2017, January). A Novel Highly Available Data Replication Strategy exploiting Data Semantics, Coding Techniques and Prior At-Hand Knowledge. In 2017 IEEE 22nd Pacific Rim International Symposium on Dependable Computing (PRDC) (pp. 301-310). IEEE.

Vangoor, V. K. R., Yellepeddi, S. M., Ravi, C. S., Venkata, A. K. P., & Katari, P. (2024). Zero Trust Architecture: Implementing Microsegmentation in Enterprise Networks. *Journal of Artificial Intelligence Research and Applications*, 4(1), 512–538.

Velasco, L., Ahmadian, M., Ortiz, L., Brito, J. P., Pastor, A., Rivas, J. M., Barzegar, S., Comellas, J., Martin, V., & Ruiz, M. (2024). Scenarios for optical encryption using quantum keys. *Sensors (Basel)*, 24(20), 6631. DOI: 10.3390/s24206631 PMID: 39460111

Velmurugan, S., Prakash, M., Neelakandan, S., & Radhakrishnan, A. (2024). Provably secure data selective sharing scheme with cloud-based decentralized trust management systems. *Journal of Cloud Computing (Heidelberg, Germany)*, 13(1), 86. DOI: 10.1186/s13677-024-00634-8

Venketbabu, T., Aswathy, M. P., Sangeetha, J., Anish, T. P., Nalini, M., & Subramanian, R. S. (2024, October). Revolutionizing Image Processing: Innovations Impacts and Future Trends. In 2024 2nd International Conference on Self Sustainable Artificial Intelligence Systems (ICSSAS) (pp. 901-907). IEEE.

Verma, A., Verma, S. K., Pandey, A. C., Grover, J., & Sharma, G. (2024). Li-MSD: A lightweight mitigation solution for DAO insider attack in RPL-based IoT. *Future Generation Computer Systems*, 159, 327–339. DOI: 10.1016/j.future.2024.05.032

Wang, Y., Qiu, X., Zhang, C., Mi, W., Li, L., & Ji, Y. (2009, September). Effective data replication in heterogeneous structured P2P networks. In 2009 5th International Conference on Wireless Communications, Networking and Mobile Computing (pp. 1-4). IEEE.

Wang, Z., Liu, Y., He, D., & Chan, S. (2021). Intrusion detection methods based on integrated deep learning model. computers & security, 103, 102177.

Wang, B. W., Wang, P., & Tu, Y. (2021). Customer satisfaction service match and service quality-based blockchain cloud manufacturing. *International Journal of Production Economics*, 240, 108220. DOI: 10.1016/j.ijpe.2021.108220

Wang, G., Hao, J., Ma, J., & Huang, L. (2010). A new approach to intrusion detection using artificial neural networks and fuzzy clustering. *Expert Systems with Applications*, 37(9), 6225–6232. DOI: 10.1016/j.eswa.2010.02.102

Wang, S., Chen, Z., Xiao, Y., & Lin, C. (2021). Consumer Privacy Protection With the Growth of AI-Empowered Online Shopping Based on the Evolutionary Game Model. *Frontiers in Public Health*, 9, 9. DOI: 10.3389/fpubh.2021.705777 PMID: 34307290

Wang, Y., Cai, W. D., & Wei, P. C. (2016). A deep learning approach for detecting malicious JavaScript code. *Security and Communication Networks*, 9(11), 1520–1534. DOI: 10.1002/sec.1441

Wang, Y., Li, L., Zhou, Y., & Zhang, H. (2024). A comprehensive review of MI-HFE and IPHFE cryptosystems: Advances in internal perturbations for post-quantum security. *Axioms*, 13(11), 741. DOI: 10.3390/axioms13110741

Wang, Z., Ren, X., Li, S., Wang, B., Zhang, J., & Yang, T. (2021). A malicious URL detection model based on convolutional neural network. *Security and Communication Networks*, 2021(1), 5518528.

Warmer, M. (2011). *Detection of web based command & control channels* (Master's thesis, University of Twente).

Warrendale, P. (2021). SAE and ISO Publish Joint Automotive Cybersecurity Standard. In *SAE International*. https://www.sae.org/news/press-room/2021/09/sae-and-iso-publish-joint-automotive-cybersecurity-standard

Wazid, M., Das, A. K., Chamola, V., & Park, Y. (2022). Uniting cyber security and machine learning: Advantages, challenges and future research. *ICT Express*, 8(3), 313–321. DOI: 10.1016/j.icte.2022.04.007

Wei, Y., Chow, K. P., & Yiu, S. M. (2020). Insider threat detection using multi-autoencoder filtering and unsupervised learning. *Advances in Digital Forensics XVI: 16th IFIP WG 11.9 International Conference, New Delhi, India, January 6–8, 2020, Revised Selected Papers 16. Springer International Publishing.*, 273–290.

Xu, C., & Li, J. (2024). Design of Intelligent Software Security System Based on Spark Big Data Computing. *Wireless Personal Communications*, •••, 1–21. DOI: 10.1007/s11277-024-11015-4

Xu, G., Cao, Y., Ren, Y., Li, X., & Feng, Z. (2017). Network security situation awareness based on semantic ontology and user-defined rules for Internet of Things. *IEEE Access : Practical Innovations, Open Solutions*, 5, 21046–21056. DOI: 10.1109/ACCESS.2017.2734681

Yalamuri, G., Honnavalli, P., & Eswaran, S. (2022). A review of the present cryptographic arsenal to deal with post-quantum threats. *Procedia Computer Science*, 215, 834–845. DOI: 10.1016/j.procs.2022.12.086

Yang, L. X., & Yang, X. (2012). Propagation behavior of virus codes in the situation that infected computers are connected to the Internet with positive probability. *Discrete Dynamics in Nature and Society*, 2012(1), 693695. DOI: 10.1155/2012/693695

Yaseen, A. (2023). AI-driven threat detection and response: A paradigm shift in cybersecurity. *International Journal of Information and Cybersecurity*, 7(12), 25–43.

Yilmaz, E., & Can, O. (2024). *Unveiling Shadows: Harnessing Artificial Intelligence for Insider Threat Detection. Engineering, Technology & Applied Science Research, 14(2), 13341-13346* (Vol. 14). ngineering, Technology & Applied Science Research.

Younis, Y. A., Kifayat, K., & Merabti, M. (2014). An access control model for cloud computing. *Journal of Information Security and Applications*, 19(1), 45–60. DOI: 10.1016/j.jisa.2014.04.003

Youssef, H. A. H., & Hossam, A. T. A. (2023). Privacy issues in AI and cloud computing in e-commerce setting: A review. *International Journal of Responsible Artificial Intelligence*, 13(7), 37–46.

Yuan, S., & Wu, X. (2021). Deep learning for insider threat detection: Review, challenges and opportunities. *Computers & Security*, 104, 102221. DOI: 10.1016/j.cose.2021.102221

Yuan, S., Zheng, P., Wu, X., & Tong, H. (2020). Few-shot insider threat detection. *Proceedings of the 29th ACM International Conference on Information & Knowledge Management*, 2289–2292.

Yu, S., Wang, C., Ren, K., & Lou, W. (2010, March). *Achieving secure, scalable, and fine-grained data access control in cloud computing. In 2010 Proceedings IEEE INFOCOM*. Ieee.

Zahra, F., Jhanjhi, N. Z., Brohi, S. N., Khan, N. A., Masud, M., & AlZain, M. A. (2022). Rank and wormhole attack detection model for RPL-based internet of things using machine learning. *Sensors (Basel)*, 22(18), 6765. DOI: 10.3390/s22186765 PMID: 36146111

Zarsky, T. (2016). The trouble with algorithmic decisions: An analytic road map to examine efficiency and fairness in automated and opaque decision making. *Science, Technology & Human Values*, 41(1), 118–132. DOI: 10.1177/0162243915605575

Zeadally, S., Adi, E., Baig, Z., & Khan, I. A. (2020). Harnessing artificial intelligence capabilities to improve cybersecurity. *IEEE Access : Practical Innovations, Open Solutions*, 8, 23817–23837. DOI: 10.1109/ACCESS.2020.2968045

Zhang, Z., Al Hamadi, H., Damiani, E., Yeun, C. Y., & Taher, F. (2022). Explainable artificial intelligence applications in cyber security: State-of-the-art in research. *IEEE Access : Practical Innovations, Open Solutions*, 10, 93104–93139. DOI: 10.1109/ACCESS.2022.3204051

Zhou, Y., De, S., Wang, W., & Moessner, K. (2016). Search techniques for the web of things: A taxonomy and survey. *Sensors (Basel)*, 16(5), 600. DOI: 10.3390/s16050600 PMID: 27128918

Zhu, F., Patumcharoenpol, P., Zhang, C., Yang, Y., Chan, J., Meechai, A., Vongsangnak, W., & Shen, B. (2013). Biomedical text mining and its applications in cancer research. *Journal of Biomedical Informatics*, 46(2), 200–211. DOI: 10.1016/j.jbi.2012.10.007 PMID: 23159498

About the Contributors

Mohammed Amin Almaiah is an Associate Professor in the Department of Computer Science at University of Jordan. Almaiah is among the top 2% scientists in the world from 2020 up to now. He is working as Editor in Chief for the International Journal of Cybersecurity and Risk Assessment. He has published over 115 research papers in highly reputed journals such as the Engineering and Science Technology, an International Journal, Education and Information Technologies, IEEE Access and others. Most of his publications were indexed under the ISI Web of Science and Scopus. His current research interests include Cybersecurity, Cybersecurity-Risk Assessment and Blockchain .

***

Mahmoud Mohammad Aljawarneh. Received the B.S., M.S. and PhD degree in Information Technology from University of Sindh, Jamshoro, Pakistan, in 2011, 2014, and 2019 respectively. From 2012 to 2014 and 2016 to 2018, he was a Research Assistant with the Institute of Information and Communication Technology, University of Sindh, Jamshoro, Pakistan. And From January 2020 to March 2022: he was an Assistant Professor, Computer Science Department, Szabist University, Hyd Campus, Pakistan. And From October 2022 to Current: he is working as an Assistant Professor, Faculty of Information Technology, Applied Sciences Private University, Amman, Jordan. His research interest includes Pervasive Computing, Context-awareness, Internet of Things (IoT), Cybersecurity, Machine Learning (ML).

Sridevi B. has more than 20 years of experience in teaching and research. Her areas of expertise are Networks and Image processing.

Lakshmi D is presently designated as a Senior Associate Professor in the School of Computing Science and Engineering (SCSE) & Assistant Director, at the Centre for Innovation in Teaching & Learning (CITL) at VIT Bhopal. She has 17 international conference presentations, and 21 international journal papers inclusive of SCOPUS & SCI (cumulative impact factor 31). 3 SCOPUS indexed book chapters. A total of 24 patents are in various states and 18 patents have been granted at both national and international levels. One Edited book with Taylor & Francis (SCOPUS Indexed). She has won two Best Paper awards at international conferences, one at the IEEE conference and another one at EAMMIS 2021. She received two awards in the year 2022. She received two awards in the year 2022. She has addressed innumerable guest lectures, acted as a session chair, and was invited as a keynote speaker at several international conferences. She has conducted FDPs that cover approximately ~80,000 plus faculty members including JNTU, TEQIP, SERB, SWAYAM, DST, AICTE, MHRD, ATAL, ISTE, Madhya Pradesh Government-sponsored, and self-financed workshops across India on various titles.

Pradeep Kumar G. has more than 15 years of experience in teaching and research. His areas of expertise are Networks and Image processing.

Rahaf Hazaymih received her B.Sc. in Computer Engineering from Jordan University of Science and Technology in 2020. She is currently pursuing a Master's degree in Data Science. Rahaf is working as an AI Engineer, with research interests in Natural Language Processing (NLP), Artificial Intelligence (AI), Machine Learning (ML), Data Science, Cybersecurity, and the Internet of Things (IoT).

Jayashankari J Assistant Professor at AMET University, Chennai, India. Hold master degree in Computers Science and Engineering from Annamalai University, Chidambaram .Currently doing research in Annamalai University, Chidambaram, India. She has a teaching and research experience of around 16 years.

Karthikeyan B. has more than 15 years of experience in teaching and research. His areas of expertise are VLSI and Image processing.

Christian Kaunert is Professor of International Security at Dublin City University, Ireland. He is also Professor of Policing and Security, as well as Director of the International Centre for Policing and Security at the University of South Wales. In addition, he is Jean Monnet Chair, Director of the Jean Monnet Centre of Excellence and Director of the Jean Monnet Network on EU Counter-Terrorism.

Kavitha K. has more than 20 years of experience in teaching and research. Her areas of expertise are Networks and signal processing.

Karthikeyan P. has more than 20 years of experience in teaching and research. His areas of expertise are VLSI and Image processing.

Suveetha P. has more than 20 years of experience in teaching and research. Her areas of expertise are VLSI and Image processing.

Sahana P. Shankar completed her B.E in Information Science and Engineering and MTech in Software Engineering from Ramaiah Institute of Technology, Bangalore. She is a third rank holder in B.E and a first rank holder with gold medal in MTech. She has worked with Unisys as an Associate Engineer for three years. She holds a US Patent in the field so software testing. She has worked with RIT as a Teaching Assistant for 6 months under the TEQIP-II scholarship program. She has published papers in various international journals and conferences. She has also authored several book chapters. She is an ISTQB certified software tester. She is pursuing her PhD from VTU, Belgaum. She is currently working with Ramaiah University of Applied Sciences, Bangalore as an Assistant Professor in the Department of Computer Science and Engineering since 2018.

Bhupinder Singh working as Professor at Sharda University, India. Also, Honorary Professor in University of South Wales UK and Santo Tomas University Tunja, Colombia. His areas of publications as Smart Healthcare, Medicines, fuzzy logics, artificial intelligence, robotics, machine learning, deep learning, federated learning, IoT, PV Glasses, metaverse and many more. He has 3 books, 139 paper publications, 163 paper presentations in international/national conferences and seminars, participated in more than 40 workshops/FDP's/QIP's, 25 courses from international universities of repute, organized more than 59 events with international and national academicians and industry people's, editor-in-chief and co-editor in journals, developed new courses. He has given talks at international universities, resource person in international conferences such as in Nanyang Technological University Singapore, Tashkent State University of Law Uzbekistan; KIMEP University Kazakhstan, All'ah meh Tabatabi University Iran, the Iranian Association of International Criminal law, Iran and Hague Center for International Law and Investment, The Netherlands, Northumbria University Newcastle UK,

Saja Smadi I am an artificial intelligence specialist. I studied a bachelor's degree in mathematics and now I am about to finish my master's degree in artificial intelligence.

Deepak Varadam holds a Masters Degree in Microsystems Engineering from Heriot-Watt University, Edinburgh (Scotland), U.K. and P.G.Diploma in ECE from Napier University, U.K. He worked as a Postgraduate Masters Research Scientist under Biomedical Microengineering Group (BMG) at Heriot-Watt University. He is currently working as an Assistant Professor in Faculty of Engineering and Technology, Computer Science and Engineering Department at Ramaiah University of Applied Sciences (RUAS) since 2010. He has been actively participating in delivering corporate trainings, seminars and have publications in national, international journals and conferences. His research interests is in MEMS, Embedded Systems, Software Engineering, Computer Graphics, AI, Blockchain, and IoT. He is currently an ExeCom Member of the IEEE RUAS Student Chapter.

Index

A

Adware 24, 29
Anomalies 1, 9, 10, 12, 13, 28, 35, 36, 44, 45, 47, 48, 50, 51, 52, 53, 60, 61, 64, 71, 81, 82, 83, 84, 85, 86, 87, 89, 90, 93, 101, 102, 188, 190, 282, 284, 285, 286, 288, 289, 290, 291, 292, 296, 298, 299, 300
Anomaly detection 7, 10, 11, 12, 25, 33, 34, 44, 48, 49, 51, 54, 57, 59, 63, 64, 66, 70, 79, 81, 82, 83, 84, 85, 86, 87, 89, 94, 95, 101, 102, 112, 113, 119, 130, 253, 256, 276, 287, 288, 289, 290, 294, 295, 299
Artificial Intelligence 1, 3, 5, 7, 10, 12, 13, 14, 15, 16, 18, 19, 20, 23, 40, 41, 43, 44, 48, 51, 57, 58, 82, 112, 114, 129, 147, 171, 189, 193, 194, 251, 252, 253, 277, 281, 282, 291, 293, 294, 300, 301, 302, 303
Autoencoders 59, 61, 65, 66, 80
Autonomous Vehicles 37, 173

B

Blockchain 6, 18, 36, 118, 170, 194, 202, 206, 208, 214, 215, 251, 252, 276, 277, 279, 284, 285, 288, 298, 300, 303

C

Cloud Computing 4, 6, 26, 32, 40, 46, 98, 138, 217, 218, 220, 221, 222, 223, 224, 226, 229, 230, 231, 233, 234, 235, 237, 238, 239, 251, 252, 253, 254, 256, 259, 260, 261, 262, 276, 277, 278, 279, 291, 303
Cloud markets 256, 257, 259, 277
Concrete pooling 156
Consistency 160, 219, 230, 237
COOJA 118, 120, 133, 137, 140
Cyber 2, 3, 4, 5, 6, 7, 8, 9, 10, 13, 14, 15, 16, 18, 19, 20, 21, 23, 24, 27, 30, 34, 36, 38, 39, 41, 43, 44, 45, 46, 55, 57, 59, 60, 61, 85, 94, 100, 110, 113, 114, 130, 148, 173, 174, 175, 176, 177, 179, 181, 182, 185, 188, 192, 195, 209, 214, 251, 252, 253, 261, 276, 279, 283, 284, 285, 286, 287, 288, 289, 290, 291, 293, 294, 295, 298, 299, 300, 301, 303
Cyber-attacks 6, 24, 38, 61, 110, 175, 176, 181, 185, 188, 195, 285, 286, 287, 293, 294, 295, 298
Cyber security 3, 5, 14, 16, 18, 19, 20, 21, 30, 36, 39, 41, 44, 46, 55, 57, 94, 209, 279, 283, 286, 287, 289, 300, 301, 303

D

Data Replication 217, 218, 219, 220, 222, 224, 225, 230, 231
Data Science 155, 302
Decreased rank 115, 118, 121, 128, 130, 140, 148
Deep Learning 2, 4, 7, 8, 9, 10, 11, 12, 18, 21, 23, 24, 26, 34, 39, 43, 48, 51, 52, 55, 57, 60, 61, 63, 64, 71, 79, 80, 82, 83, 86, 90, 94, 101, 102, 113, 119, 120, 127, 128, 129, 130, 131, 137, 139, 140, 148, 149, 194, 253, 254, 278, 282, 288, 291, 294, 295, 297, 300
Digital World 1, 19, 294, 295

E

E-commerce 20, 170, 235, 238, 249, 257, 258, 259, 260, 281, 282, 285, 286, 287, 288, 289, 290, 291, 292, 293, 294, 295, 296, 297, 298, 299, 300, 301, 302, 303
Ensemble models 24, 72, 76, 77
Ethics 16, 57, 173, 176, 178, 181, 185, 193, 194, 226

F

Fuzzy inference 247, 248, 261, 279, 286, 300

G

Gradient Boosting 31, 115, 117, 120, 122, 123, 124, 128

H

Hello Flooding 115, 121, 125, 126, 127, 128

I

Incident Response 18, 34, 43, 50, 52, 53, 56, 181, 183, 185, 186, 188, 189, 190
Indirect Attacks 136
Insider Threat Detection 97, 100, 101, 102, 103, 112, 113, 114, 251, 252, 253, 254
Intrusion Detection Systems 16, 24, 34, 45, 49, 51, 54, 61, 62, 63, 71, 97, 119, 120, 170, 181, 183
IoT 2, 3, 4, 5, 6, 12, 13, 20, 21, 31, 37, 38, 40, 60, 61, 64, 79, 85, 95, 115, 116, 117, 118, 119, 120, 127, 128, 129, 130, 131, 133, 134, 137, 138, 139, 140, 147, 148, 149, 151, 152, 153, 168, 169, 202, 204, 207, 214, 252, 253, 259, 276, 277, 278, 279, 295

L

Luminol 81, 82, 83, 84, 87, 89, 90, 93

M

Machine learning 1, 2, 4, 5, 7, 8, 9, 10, 11, 12, 13, 14, 16, 18, 21, 23, 25, 28, 31, 37, 39, 40, 43, 44, 47, 51, 53, 55, 57, 58, 59, 60, 61, 64, 65, 66, 70, 71, 79, 81, 82, 84, 85, 87, 88, 94, 95, 101, 103, 112, 113, 115, 116, 117, 120, 122, 124, 127, 128, 129, 130, 131, 147, 148, 152, 155, 160, 163, 164, 170, 174, 184, 189, 191, 192, 195, 251, 252, 253, 256, 257, 259, 276, 277, 278, 281, 282, 283, 284, 285, 286, 291, 293, 294, 297, 300, 301, 302, 303
Malicious Insider Psychological 97
Malicious Traffic 9, 48, 52, 84, 85
Malware 1, 2, 3, 4, 6, 7, 8, 10, 11, 12, 13, 16, 23, 24, 27, 28, 29, 32, 34, 35, 38, 39, 40, 41, 44, 47, 48, 49, 52, 54, 57, 60, 81, 83, 86, 95, 112, 129, 147, 188, 251, 276
Mobile Security 1, 2, 4, 10, 11, 12

N

Natural Language Processing 12, 23, 24, 26, 27, 35, 40, 43, 50, 57, 161, 294
Network Monitoring 43, 44, 48, 50
Network Security 8, 9, 16, 20, 30, 31, 35, 39, 41, 43, 44, 46, 47, 50, 51, 54, 55, 56, 57, 58, 79, 86, 87, 88, 119, 130, 138, 139, 140, 253, 256, 260, 290

P

P2P model 157, 162, 167
Pattern recognition 8, 26, 27, 63, 64, 283, 288, 289, 295
PQC 197, 198, 202, 203, 204, 205, 207, 208, 209, 210, 212, 213
Prophet 81, 82, 83, 84, 87, 89, 90, 93

Q

Quantum Computers 24, 197, 198, 200, 201, 202, 203, 204, 205, 206, 211, 212
Quantum cryptography 197, 198, 200, 202, 203, 204, 205, 206, 209, 211, 212, 214
Quantum threats 215

R

Random Forest 59, 62, 71, 72, 73, 75, 76, 77, 78, 85, 112, 115, 117, 118, 120, 122, 123, 128, 129, 147, 251, 276, 282, 286
Ransomware Attacks 11, 23, 28, 35, 36
Recurrent Neural Networks 8, 9, 10, 48, 58, 60, 82, 83, 87, 90
Role-Based Profile 97, 113
RPL Attacks 120, 122, 128, 130, 131, 134, 139, 148, 149

S

Safety 2, 3, 6, 34, 149, 173, 174, 175, 176, 177, 178, 179, 180, 181, 182, 183, 184, 185, 186, 187, 189, 191, 192, 193, 194, 201, 261, 285, 288, 289, 291, 293, 294
Search Engine 151, 152, 168, 283
Security 1, 2, 3, 4, 5, 6, 7, 8, 9, 10, 11, 12, 13, 14, 15, 16, 17, 18, 19, 20, 21, 23, 24, 26, 28, 30, 31, 32, 33, 34, 35, 36, 38, 39, 40, 41, 43, 44, 45, 46, 47, 48, 49, 50, 51, 52, 53, 54, 55, 56, 57, 58, 60, 63, 64, 79, 80, 83, 86, 87, 88, 93, 94, 95, 98, 100, 102, 112, 113, 114, 116, 117, 118, 119, 128, 130, 133, 134, 135, 137, 138, 139, 140, 145, 146, 147, 154, 170, 173, 174, 175, 176, 177, 179, 180, 181, 182, 183, 184, 185, 186, 188, 189, 190, 192, 193, 194, 195, 197, 198, 199, 200, 201, 202, 203, 204, 205, 206, 207, 208, 209, 210, 211, 212, 214, 215, 217, 218, 219, 220, 221, 222, 223, 224, 226, 227, 228, 229, 231, 233, 234, 235, 237, 238, 251, 252, 253, 254, 255, 256, 257, 258, 259, 260, 261, 262, 263, 264, 274, 276, 277, 279, 281, 282, 283, 284, 285, 286, 287, 288, 289, 290, 291, 292, 293, 294, 295, 296, 297, 298, 299, 300, 301, 302, 303
Security Mechanism 289, 295, 298
Semantic Search 151, 152, 153, 156, 168
Store 197, 198, 202, 208, 217, 219, 221, 222, 236, 237, 238, 239, 292

T

Threat Detection 1, 2, 4, 7, 8, 9, 10, 13, 16, 20, 24, 34, 39, 43, 44, 47, 48, 50, 52, 54, 55, 61, 97, 100, 101, 102, 103, 111, 112, 113, 114, 191, 192, 251, 252, 253, 254, 259, 284, 285, 287, 289, 291, 294, 295
Tokenization 151, 157
Trust 6, 16, 43, 53, 54, 55, 56, 79, 98, 99, 129, 136, 180, 193, 211, 233, 234, 235, 236, 237, 238, 239, 240, 241, 242, 244, 246, 247, 248, 249, 251, 252, 253, 254, 255, 257, 259, 260, 261, 262, 263, 264,

265, 266, 267, 268, 269, 272, 273, 274, 276, 277, 278, 279, 284, 285, 286, 287, 288, 289, 290, 292, 293, 294, 295, 299, 301
Trust Framework 233, 244, 255, 259, 279
Trust Model 235, 240, 241, 242, 244, 246, 247, 251, 259, 260, 261, 265, 267, 268, 269, 272, 273, 276, 278

V

version number 115, 118, 119, 121, 125, 126, 127, 128, 130, 133, 134, 135, 136, 137, 138, 140, 141, 142, 143, 144, 145, 146, 147, 148, 149
Version Number Modification 133, 134, 136

www.ingramcontent.com/pod-product-compliance
Lightning Source LLC
LaVergne TN
LVHW062137300926
849161LV00010B/2559
* 9 7 9 8 3 6 9 3 9 9 1 9 4 *